D1518174

LIVING ABROAD IN
GUATEMALA

AL ARGUETA

PRIME LIVING LOCATIONS IN GUATEMALA

M E X I C O

El Naranjo

Río San Pedro

Río Usumacinta

Sierra del Lacandón

Cooperativa Bethel

El Subín

Sayaxché

Comitán

Presa de la Angostura

Playa Grande (Cantabal)

HUEHUE-
TENANGO

Sierra de los Cuchumatanes

QUICHÉ

Sierra de Chamea

ALTA
VERAPAZ

Ciudad Cuauhtémoc

La Mesilla

Todos Santos Cuchumatán

**THE WESTERN
HIGHLANDS**

Huehuetenango

Nebaj

Sacapulas

Río Negro (Río Chixoy)

Cobán

Purulhá

SAN
MARCOS

Volcán Tacaná
4,093m

Volcán
Tajumulco
4,220m

TOTO-
NICAPÁN

Santa Cruz
Del Quiché

Sierra de Chuacús

Salamá

BAJA
VERAPAZ

San Marcos

Tapachula

El Carmen

Quetzaltenango

Chichicastenango

Joyabaj

Río Suchiate

Totonicapán

Volcán
Santa María

SOLOLÁ

Sololá

CHIMAL-
TENANGO

**GUATEMALA
CITY**

Ciudad Hidalgo

Ciudad
Tecún Umán

QUEZAL-
TENANGO

Volcán Atitlán

SACATE-
PÉQUEZ

GUATEMAL

Volcán de Agua

Cuilap

Tilapa

Retalhuleu

RETALHULEU

**THE PACIFIC
COAST**

**LA ANTIGUA
GUATEMALA**

Amatitlán

SANTA
ROSA

Champerico

SUCHITEPÉQUEZ

Río Madre Vieja

Escuintla

ESCUINTLA

Chiquimulilla

P A C I F I C

O C E A N

Sipacate

Puerto
San José

Iztapa

Monterrico

Las Lisas

© AVALON TRAVEL

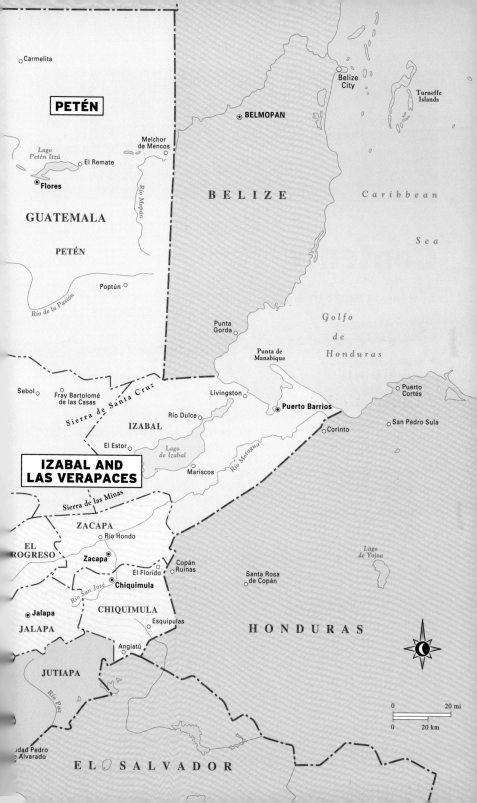

Contents

At Home in Guatemala 6

WELCOME TO GUATEMALA 9

▶ **Introduction** 10
    The Lay of the Land. 12
    Flora and Fauna. 18
    Social Climate 26

▶ **History, Government, and Economy** 31
    History. 32
    Government. 64
    Economy 68

▶ **People and Culture.** 72
    Ethnicity and Class 74
    Customs and Etiquette 77
    Gender Issues 81
    Religion 83
    The Arts. 86
    Sports and Recreation 90

▶ **Planning Your Fact-Finding Trip.** 97
    Preparing for Your Trip 98
    Arriving in Guatemala 101
    Sample Itineraries. 104
    Practicalities 109

DAILY LIFE 147

▶ **Making the Move.** 148
    Immigration and Visas. 149
    Moving with Children. 156
    Moving with Pets 157
    What to Take 161

▶ **Housing Considerations** 165
    Renting 169
    Buying Property 173
    Building Your Own Home. 183
    Household Expenses. 186

▶ **Language and Education** . . . 187
    Learning Spanish. 188
    Education. 191

▶ **Health and Safety** 195
    Preventive Measures. 196
    Medical Services 198
    Health Hazards 200
    Environmental Factors 206
    Safety 208

▶ **Employment** 216
    Self-Employment. 217
    The Job Hunt. 223
    Working for a Nonprofit 225

▶ **Finances** 227
    Cost of Living. 228
    Banking 232
    Taxes 234
    Investing 236

▶ **Communications.** 238
    Telephone Service. 240
    Email and the Internet. 242

Postal Mail and Shipping 243
Media 245

▶ **Travel and Transportation** . . 249
Map 248
Getting to Guatemala 250
Getting Around 260
Driving 265

PRIME LIVING
LOCATIONS **273**

▶ **Overview** 275
Map 274

▶ **Guatemala City** 281
Map 282
The Lay of the Land 283
Daily Living 286
Housing 288
Where to Live 289
Getting Around 297

▶ **La Antigua Guatemala** 303
Map 302
The Lay of the Land 305
Daily Living 307
Housing 311
Where to Live 314
Getting Around 317

▶ **The Western Highlands** 319
Map 318
Quetzaltenango (Xela) 322
Lake Atitlán 327

▶ **The Pacific Coast** 340
Map 342

Puerto San José and Vicinity . . . 344
Monterrico and Vicinity 347
Retalhuleu and Vicinity 352

▶ **Izabal and Las Verapaces** . . 355
Map 356
Izabal 358
Las Verapaces 365

▶ **Petén** 369
Map 370
Flores and Santa Elena 376
Lake Petén Itzá 377
Poptún 380

RESOURCES **385**
Consulates and Embassies 386
Government Organizations 387
Environmental Organizations . . . 389
Planning Your Fact-Finding Trip . . 390
Making the Move 391
Housing Considerations 392
Language and Education 393
Health 396
Employment and Volunteering . . 398
Finance 398
Communications 399
Travel and Transportation 401
Prime Living Locations 403
Glossary 405
Spanish Phrasebook 409
Suggested Reading 416
National Holidays 419

INDEX **420**

At Home in Guatemala

My dad likes to tell an anecdote from a recent trip to Guatemala. As the story goes, he met a visiting Costa Rican who remarked, "It's a good thing Americans don't know Guatemala exists or none of them would live in Costa Rica." Indeed, literature on living abroad in Mexico and Costa Rica abounds, but the absence of such information on Guatemala is remarkable given its striking beauty and increasing popularity with foreign visitors. For me, the vacuum of information on Guatemala as an expat locale finds its source in the country's virtual non-presence in the North American collective consciousness.

As my dad's Costa Rican acquaintance soon discovered, Guatemala has everything the rest of Central America offers, and then some. Packed into a country the size of Tennessee are soaring volcanoes, rugged mountains, raging rivers, mountain lakes, Caribbean and Pacific coasts, and the region's most cosmopolitan city. Besides the gorgeous surroundings, Guatemala enjoys a near-perfect climate thanks to its tropical latitude and mountain topography. It also has adequate infrastructure, with the region's most modern international airport, good roads, and modern communications.

Guatemala offers the opportunity to return to a simpler state of being surrounded by nature and lively Latin/Mayan culture. You can live on significantly less than it would cost in the United States, but you don't have to give up life's comforts or "slum it" in order to live here. For better or worse, the economic elites that have dominated the country's culture and politics for centuries have ensured its relatively high level of sophistication. On any given day, you can sip locally grown morning coffee on a

balcony overlooking three sentinel volcanoes, walk the cobblestone streets of a Spanish colonial town in the afternoon, and enjoy dinner that same evening in a cosmopolitan city at one of Latin America's finest restaurants.

Maybe you've already been to Guatemala and have experienced firsthand all it has to offer. You may find yourself haunted by memories of its landscape or the sound of galloping marimba music and gurgling colonial fountains. You may be wondering if you can jump the chasm from Guatemala as a splendid transient experience to Guatemala as your new home.

As you decide to embark on this transition, you'll encounter Guatemala in its many facets. There is a dark side to the beauty, and you will probably find yourself trying to come to grips with Guatemala's strange contrasts and juxtapositions. Like most of its neighbors, Guatemala is no stranger to huge wealth disparities, a history of violence, and rising crime statistics. Much of this is a legacy of the country's 36-year civil war.

It can be said without hesitation that Guatemala's governments have historically been in power mainly to serve the interests of the elite. While the latter are quick to emulate North American consumption patterns, the American ideals of freedom and equality have yet to fully take hold. In many cases, Guatemala's challenges (and opportunities) are precisely what bring foreigners here. They want to make a difference and see things change.

In the end, you'll find that no country is perfect, but you may just find that Guatemala is perfect for you.

▶ WHAT I LOVE ABOUT GUATEMALA

- The air smells like an earthy mix of flowers, dirt, rain, and coffee beans.
- There's color everywhere, from pastel-colored homes to the vibrant wardrobes of its indigenous inhabitants.
- I can spend the day in what feels like Los Angeles or 17th-century Spain, depending on my whims.
- It's really hard to beat the weather in Antigua, Guatemala City, or Lake Atitlán.
- There are rainforests, with Mayan ruins as an added bonus.
- Good, strong coffee is locally grown.
- You can find state-of-the-art dental care at affordable prices.
- There are black-sand beaches and 33 volcanoes.
- It's still kind of exotic because few people know Guatemala exists, or they just have no idea how beautiful it is.

WELCOME TO GUATEMALA

© AL ARGUETA

INTRODUCTION

It seems many people these days have a similar dream. It involves selling all or most of their worldly belongings and trading in their lives in North America or Europe for a simpler state of being in a developing country. The allure of this lifestyle often comes from previous travel to parts of the developing world and fond memories of cobblestone streets, colonial architecture, warm, sunny weather and friendly local culture. Some would-be expats are tired of living in a society where they seem to live only to work, rather than work as a part of daily living. For younger travelers, the desire to relocate to a developing nation is often the product of a sense of adventure and the desire to embrace alternatives to the daily grind that causes so many of their older counterparts to drop out of the race. In other cases, expats have worked for many long years, and are seeking a peaceful place to retire for much less than it would cost to do so in the United States. Still others left their native countries many years ago and are now seeking to return to the land they've been missing all these years.

Guatemala, it seems, attracts all of the above. You'll find no shortage of foreign expats or Guatemalans returned from living life abroad. But whatever your reason for coming to Guatemala, you will soon find that it will most likely not be at all what you expected. For starters, there's the language, which you'll really need to learn in order to get everything out of the experience that living here entails. There's also the culture, which you'll need to learn to navigate in order to live and work here. And that's just the beginning.

Those who have been to Guatemala and have lived here for any amount of time are familiar with the rewards and challenges of living in this unique country. It's certainly not for everyone and those seeking an extension of Costa Rica or even Mexico will most likely be disappointed. While Guatemalans share many Latin American cultural traits with their neighbors, their country's history and social dynamics are also quite different. The national pride of Mexicans or the *pura vida* mentality of Costa Ricans are mostly absent in Guatemala, replaced by a somewhat reserved demeanor and innate distrust of outsiders. Thirty-six years of civil war and, in the war's aftermath, skyrocketing crime levels, persisting wealth disparities, social inequality and the presence of an almost failed state make life in Guatemala particularly challenging. Many Guatemalans you meet on the street seem almost resigned to their country's fate. It's all part of the Guatemalan mentality that sees it all as quite tragic or quite humorous, depending on who you ask. Guatemalans are notorious for making light of situations that anywhere else might elicit national outrage or mourning. Here, the latest political scandal, natural disaster, or crime wave just makes more fodder for jokes told on a Sunday afternoon after lunch with the family. Truth be told, most Americans would be appalled by the opinions expressed in confidence by well-to-do Guatemalans who spend $10 on a box of Kleenex while the vast majority of their countrymen live on $2 a day.

I realize I'm not painting a pretty picture here, but like anything that is beautiful there is often an ugliness just below the surface. So now that I've told the worst, let me also tell you about the Guatemala that I love, for there is also this lovely country that is woven into the tapestry of my soul, much like the technicolor weavings produced by my country's Mayan inhabitants. For all its faults, Guatemala still has an almost gravitational pull, and those who have felt it know what I speak of. There seems to be a magic in the air here. You can feel it from the moment you look out the window from your landing airplane as you fly over majestic mountain ranges, volcanoes, and a sprawled capital city that spills over into neighboring ravines and plateaus. You'll sense it as you walk off the aircraft into a new airport terminal replacing its once-wonky predecessor and then look over the modern skyline out in the distance.

What is it? Were I to call it by name, I'd say it's a mixture of hope and change. The closer you look into the Guatemalan tapestry, the more you'll find that there is real potential for a better Guatemala, and you can sense that it's starting to happen. It's on the horizon, much like the thick anvil-head clouds that loom in the southern skies during the rainy season, just waiting to bring their abundant showers upon the land. To provide another analogy, it's like a beautiful spring flower emerging from cold, rocky soil and the icy chill of winter's grip.

I've lived elsewhere in Central America, and I can honestly say that the natural beauty of its neighbors pales in comparison to that of Guatemala. The same goes for the quality of basic infrastructure. Culturally, and I know I'm biased here, the homogenized cultures of peoples and neighboring countries that haven't suffered collectively seem to me at once innocent and jejune. For me, Guatemala as a nation can be likened to the grapes that go into making a fine wine. Viticulture enthusiasts will tell you that grapes receiving too much rain or fertilizer, that are strangers to the hardships thrust forth by the elements, make for lackluster wine. I think the same can be said for nations and their people.

And so it's up to you to decide to invest in this emerging country; to do business here, to play here, to share your knowledge with others, to help make it a better place. In the end, you'll have to decide what to do with Guatemala's constant juxtapositions, but you just might find that the challenges of living here are vastly outweighed by the rewards. This book will show you how to navigate the balance beam separating the chasm between the two.

The Lay of the Land

COUNTRY DIVISIONS

Guatemala is the third-largest country in Central America. It occupies 108,888 square kilometers (42,042 square miles), making it about the size of Tennessee. The country shares borders with Mexico, Belize, Honduras, and El Salvador. Politically, Guatemala is divided into 22 *departamentos* (departments).

The country divides rather neatly into various geographical zones. The volcanic highlands run through the country's center, going west to east from Mexico to El Salvador. Elevation tends to get lower closer to the Salvadoran border. The eastern areas of Alta and Baja Verapaz are largely mountainous but also largely composed of limestone. A curious feature of this area, found in its northern limits, is the presence of small, forested limestone hills much like those found in parts of China. Going east from Guatemala City toward Honduras, the terrain is largely dominated by semi-arid flatlands covered by cacti.

Moving closer to the Caribbean coast in the department of Izabal, the terrain once again becomes lush and largely filled with banana plantations. A small sliver of Caribbean coastline runs between the Honduran border and Belize but features white-sand beaches, swamplands, and some impressive tropical rainforests. Small mountains are interspersed throughout parts of the Caribbean coastal region.

Running roughly parallel to the highlands, to the south, are the Pacific coast flatlands. This is a rich agricultural area once covered in tropical forest but now home to vast sugarcane and coffee plantations, the latter being on the slopes of the highland zones as they ascend from the coastal plain. The Pacific coast is also home to wetlands, mangrove swamps, and beaches of curiously dark color because of their proximity to the country's volcanic chain.

The northern third of Guatemala is a vast Ohio-sized limestone flatland known as Petén. Once covered entirely in tropical forests, it has increasingly become deforested in its southern parts, with only the northern third retaining large unbroken swathes of forest.

GEOGRAPHY

Within Guatemala's relatively small area are 14 distinct ecosystems found at elevations ranging from sea level to over 4,000 meters (13,000 feet). Many people think of Guatemala as a sweltering tropical country, which is only partially true. While it does feature warm tropical coastal environments and hot lowland jungles, a rugged spine of mountains and volcanoes runs through the country's center. In the tropics, elevation mostly determines climate, and this is certainly the case in Guatemala. Temperatures drop dramatically the higher you go in elevation, and precipitation varies greatly depending on what side of a mountain chain you're on. All of this translates into a dizzying array of landscapes, making Guatemala a delight to explore.

Mountains

The highest of Guatemala's mountains are actually volcanic peaks. There are 33 total with a handful currently active. Volcán Tajumulco, at 4,220 meters (13,845 feet), is the highest point in all of Central America, followed closely by nearby Volcán Tacaná, at 4,110 meters (13,484 feet). The most frequently climbed volcanoes include the active Pacaya, near Guatemala City; the three volcanoes on the shores of Lake Atitlán; and Agua and Acatenango

Guatemala is home to Central America's highest volcanic peaks.

near Antigua. Some volcanoes, like Chicabal and Ipala, feature turquoise lagoons, which fill their craters. Other active volcanoes include Fuego and Santiaguito.

Among the non-volcanic mountains, the Sierra de los Cuchumatanes, near the border with Mexico, is Guatemala's, and Central America's, highest mountain chain. It stands 3,837 meters (12,588 feet) at its highest point. Its smooth, rounded peaks attest to years of erosion from being glaciated thousands of years ago. Other noteworthy mountain chains include the Sierra de las Minas, in the eastern part of the country. Protected as a private forest reserve, it still contains large stands of virgin cloud forest. Farther east near the Caribbean coast are the Cerro San Gil and Montañas del Mico, which are still covered in dense tropical rainforest. Petén has relatively few mountains, but the foothills of the Maya mountains of neighboring Belize run into the department's southeastern corner with an elevation of over 1,000 meters (3,300 feet) at Petén's highest point. Petén's other noteworthy mountain range is the remote and mostly forested Sierra del Lacandón, at the far western edge of the department bordering Mexico and exceeding 600 meters (2,000 feet) at its highest point.

Guatemala's mountain scenery comes largely as a product of its geographic location at the intersection of the North American, Cocos, and Caribbean plates, making it one of the most seismically and volcanically active places in the world. Indeed, Guatemala is no stranger to earthquakes. Among the many fault lines running through the country are the parallel Chixoy-Polochic and Motagua faults. The latter is responsible for the most recent major earthquake to rock Guatemala, a magnitude-7.5 whopper in February 1976 that killed thousands and wiped entire villages off the face of the map. A series of massive earthquakes in 1776 resulted in the relocation of the Guatemalan capital from the Panchoy Valley (Antigua Guatemala) to the Valley of the Hermitage, where it remains today, better known as Guatemala City.

Rivers

Guatemala has several rivers worthy of mention. The greatest of these is the Usumacinta, which is formed by the confluence of the Chixoy and Pasión Rivers, making it Central America's most voluminous river. Guatemalan author Virgilio Rodríguez Macal, in his novel *Guayacán,* calls it the "father and lord of the Central American rivers." The Usumacinta forms much of Guatemala's border with Mexico and continues its northwesterly flow all the way to the Gulf of Mexico. On the Guatemalan side, the Usumacinta borders the relatively untouched Sierra del Lacandón National Park, which harbors dense tropical rainforests. Rafting trips once made their way down the Usumacinta, visiting Yaxchilán (Mexico) and the Guatemalan site of Piedras Negras, but sadly an increase of violent armed robberies has meant their indefinite suspension. The Usumacinta is indeed a wild frontier and is an active waterway for drug smuggling, contraband logging, and boats carrying illegal immigrants on their journey north. An on-again, off-again Mexican dam project has been vehemently opposed by environmentalists, and until 1996, Guatemalan rebels camped out in the jungle. The project would reportedly flood Piedras Negras, Yaxchilán, and several smaller sites along the Usumacinta. The project appears to have been called off, for the time being.

The Pasión, an Usumacinta tributary, meanders through southern Petén. Much like the larger Usumacinta, its watershed was extremely important in Mayan times. Several Mayan sites lie near the river. In the arid southeastern part of the country, the Río Motagua connects the highlands to the Caribbean Sea and forms a dry river valley of agricultural importance since Mayan times. Other notable rivers include the Río San Pedro, also in Petén; the Verapaces-area Río Cahabón, which has excellent white-water year-round; and the Río Dulce, a lazy tropical river connecting Lake Izabal to the Caribbean.

Lakes and Lagoons

Guatemala has several lakes noteworthy for their size, recreational opportunities, and sheer natural beauty. Foremost among these is highland Lake Atitlán, called "the most beautiful lake in the world" by author Aldous Huxley during his travels through the region. The lake's spectacular mountain scenery is punctuated by the sentinel presence of three towering volcanoes along its southern shores. Near Guatemala City, Lake Amatitlán has been a weekend getaway for city-dwellers since time immemorial, but industrial pollution has spoiled the once-clear waters. Still, Guatemalans have taken on the ominous task of rescuing its waters with foreign help, and the lake may soon be safe again for swimming. An aerial tram operating on surrounding hillsides has recently re-opened the area to visitors, making a side trip to this tranquil spot increasingly alluring for wonderful views of the rugged mountain terrain. The largest of Guatemala's lakes, Lake Izabal, is a tropical lake connected to the Caribbean by the aforementioned Río Dulce. The Río Polochic Delta, on Izabal's southwestern shore, is becoming increasingly popular as a bird-watcher's paradise. Petén's Lake Petén Itzá is also a tropical flatland lake, with the added bonus of tropical forests, crystal-clear waters, and a variety of accommodations from which to enjoy all of these. Because much of Petén is limestone, the lake's waters have a distinct turquoise color near the lakeshore and from the air look very much like those of the Mexican Caribbean. Farther east toward Belize is Yaxhá lagoon, near the ruins of the same name. The lagoon and its aggressive crocodiles were made famous by the *Survivor Guatemala* television series filmed here in the summer of 2005.

There are many beautiful lagoons in the Guatemalan highlands. Some, atop volcanoes like Ipala and Chicabal, are believed by the Maya to harbor mystical powers and are the site of rituals. Laguna Lachuá is a beautiful, almost perfectly round lagoon in the jungle Ixcán region just north of the highlands. The surrounding rainforest has been preserved, but unfortunately it is an ecological island—a green square in a surrounding ocean of deforestation.

The Coasts

Guatemala has a significant amount of coastline along the Pacific Ocean and it remains largely undeveloped. Among the Pacific coast's attractions are a few places with surf-worthy waves, excellent sail fishing, and beaches that have an exotic feel because of their dark sands. Among the best places to hit the beach are Monterrico and Las Lisas. On the Caribbean side, there are a few pleasant white-sand beaches on the remote peninsula of Punta de Manabique as well as closer to the towns of Puerto Barrios and Lívingston. There is excellent scuba diving in the outlying Belize cayes and around Punta de Manabique.

CLIMATE

Guatemala has a tropical climate, though temperatures vary greatly between regions because of differences in altitude. The coastal plains and lowlands have an average yearly temperature of about 27°C (80°F), with little seasonal change. Mountain valleys 1,200–1,800 meters (4,000–6,000 feet) high are usually comfortably mild. Major cities such as Guatemala City, Antigua, and Quetzaltenango all lie at these altitudes, meaning they have mostly pleasant year-round spring-like temperatures of 16–21°C (60–70°F). Higher mountain peaks and valleys sometimes have frost, and average 4°C (40°F). Keep in mind that these are averages, and certain times of year are markedly warmer than others. The North American winter solstice often brings the arrival of cold fronts that make temperatures in the highlands dip below freezing not only on mountain summits, but also in highland cities such as Quetzaltenango. If you're traveling to Guatemala between the months of November through February, bring a warm sweater or two for the chilly highlands and a heavy jacket if you plan to climb some volcanoes. At the other extreme, March–April, coinciding with the spring equinox, is the warmest time of year. Temperatures in the Petén lowlands, Izabal, and Pacific coast plain routinely hover around 38°C (100°F) during these months. Guatemala City and Antigua hover at around 29°C (85°F).

There are distinct dry and rainy seasons in Guatemala. The dry season runs from November to the beginning of May. During March and April, haze from dust and agricultural burning tends to obliterate any views of surrounding scenery. The volcanoes around Antigua and Lake Atitlán become extremely difficult to spot during this time of year, and the whole country tends to look like Los Angeles.

The rainy season generally lasts from May to November, with daily showers during most of this period, usually in the afternoon. Mornings are usually sunny and clear, with a gradual buildup of giant rain clouds throughout the day, culminating in a torrential downpour. The latter months tend to be the rainiest, with deluges sometimes lasting entire days. The rainy season is sometimes referred to as *invierno,* meaning winter, though it is officially summer in the northern hemisphere, where Guatemala lies. *Verano,* or summer, refers to the tail end of the dry season.

The Pacific coastal plain and western highlands receive 76–150 centimeters (30–60 inches) of rain a year, and the eastern highlands average 51–76 centimeters (20–30 inches). Again, these figures vary greatly from place to place depending on factors such as altitude and what side of the mountain chain you're on. An example of this is the presence of ample rainfall and lush cloud forests on the forested slopes of the Sierra de las Minas in contrast to semi-arid plains in the mountain's rainshadow along the neighboring Motagua Valley. Petén receives 200–381 centimeters (80–150 inches) of rain annually, falling throughout most of the year. The rainiest place in Guatemala is said to be the

Cerro San Gil rainforest, on the Caribbean coast, where warm, moist air rises up from the ocean and dumps precipitation on this small mountain chain. There is really no dry season to speak of in this area.

There are sometimes breaks in the rainfall, known as *canícula*, for a week or two in July and/or August. Rainfall can vary substantially from year to year due to factors such as the presence of El Niño or La Niña. El Niño often means a prolonged dry season, which can lead to intense wildfires in forested areas such as Petén.

Hurricanes and tropical storms sometimes hit Guatemala during the latter months of the rainy season, causing widespread damage. Much of this is due to soil saturation on deforested and waterlogged hillsides giving way to devastating mudslides, as occurred in parts of the Lake Atitlán basin following Hurricane Stan in 2005. Hurricane Mitch also left a trail of devastation along the Caribbean coast in 1998, obliterating much of the banana harvest and destroying thousands of homes.

Flora and Fauna

Guatemala harbors an astounding degree of biodiversity, due greatly to the variety of ecosystems found within its borders. Its location in the Central American land bridge between North and South America means it is the southernmost range for certain North American species as well as the northernmost range for certain southern hemisphere species. Fourteen of the 38 Holdridge Life Zones are represented in Guatemala.

FLORA

The cornucopia of plant life encompasses 8,000 varieties of plants, including more than 600 types of orchids. Of these, nearly 200 are unique to Guatemala. The rugged cloud forests of Sierra de las Minas, meanwhile, boast the presence of 17 distinct species of pine trees found nowhere else on earth. Endemic orchid species include Guatemala's national flower, the rare monja blanca, or "white nun." It is found in the cloud forests of the Verapaces region.

Guatemala means "land of the trees" in ancient Mayan-Toltec language. According to 2005 figures, 37 percent of Guatemala remained covered in forest in 2005, down from 40 percent in 2001. Among the different types of forest present in Guatemala's varied climate zones are tropical rainforest, tropical dry forests, evergreen forests, and cloud forests. In some cold, mountainous parts of Guatemala there are temperate forests whose broadleaf trees' leaves briefly change color before falling to the ground, though not at all to the extent of the displays of fall foliage present in parts of North America.

The forests of Petén are officially classified mostly as tropical moist and tropical wet forests. Guatemala's only true rainforests, strictly speaking, are found in the Cerro San Gil along the Caribbean coast.

Most of Guatemala's remaining forest cover is found in Petén, especially the northern third of the department in a huge park known as the Maya Biosphere Reserve. The Verapaces, Izabal, Quiché, and Huehuetenango also have significant amounts of forest cover remaining. Many of these forests are on remote mountains that have remained inaccessible and have therefore escaped the ravages of the advance of the agricultural frontier. Significant wetlands, including four of international importance, are found in Petén, Izabal, and the western portion of the Pacific coast plains near the Mexican border. Mangrove forests are found on the Pacific and Caribbean coasts.

Among the plants you'll find in Guatemala's tropical forests is the towering ceiba (*Ceiba pentandra*), which is Guatemala's national tree and was considered sacred by the Maya. It has a wide trunk and buttressed roots with branches found only at the very top. They can reach heights of 60 meters. You will often find them in cleared fields being one of only a few trees left standing amidst grazing cattle. The most famous example is along the footpath at the entrance to Tikal National Park, where visitors are often photographed standing next to the tree's colossal trunk.

Another common tropical forest tree is the *chicozapote,* from which chicle is extracted for use in the manufacture of chewing gum. *Chicleros* cut V-shaped notches in the tree's trunk, allowing the sap to drip down the tree to a receptacle placed there for its collection. These days chicle goes to Japan, which still favors the traditional base for making gum. During the early 20th century, most of Guatemala's chicle went to the Wrigley Company.

The *ramón,* or breadnut tree, is found throughout the tropical flatlands and was widely used during Mayan times for making tortillas and drinks, among other things. Archaeologists have linked the increasing consumption of *ramón* seeds to decreasing food production cycles during Mayan times, speculating that it served as a replacement to more traditional staples during periods of drought.

One of the most curious plants found in the tropical forests is the strangler fig, or *mata palo* (*Ficus obtusifolia*), which wraps itself around its host, eventually killing it. It has thick roots and looks much like a wooden rope wrapped around a tree. It's easy to spot and you'll recognize it when you see it.

Guatemala's forests contain excellent hardwoods, the most prominent of these being cedar (*Cedrela angustifolia*) and mahogany (*Swientenia alicastrum*). Much of the Petén forest has been logged, legally and illegally. Peasant forestry cooperatives operate in the multiple-use zone of the Maya Biosphere Reserve sustainably harvesting eco-certified hardwoods. Guatemalan mahogany is highly prized in the making of furniture. The cabinets of the Four Seasons resort on Costa Rica's Pacific coast, for example, are made from Guatemalan mahogany. Also important as a forest product is xate palm (*Chamaedorea spp*), which is harvested in the forests using sustainable methods, though overcutting is entirely possible. The bright green palm leaves are used in floral arrangements throughout the United States and Europe.

FAUNA
Birds

Guatemala's abundant birdlife includes over 700 different species. Although not nearly as popular a bird-watching destination as Belize or Costa Rica, Guatemala has become increasingly well known among birders now that pristine areas conducive to the activity are no longer the site of skirmishes between army and guerrilla forces, as was the case during the civil war. This has opened up new areas to bird-watching, and Guatemalans are quickly taking steps to gain some ground in catering to this very lucrative tourism market.

The forests of Petén still harbor a healthy harpy eagle population.

Among the highlights of a visit to Guatemala is the opportunity to spot its rare, endangered national emblem, the resplendent quetzal (*Pharomacrus mocino*). The quetzal gives its name to the national currency and was revered by the Maya for its long green tail feathers used in ceremonial headdresses. Quetzals have become increasingly rare due to the loss of their cloud forest habitat, but still survive on the slopes of the Lake Atitlán volcanoes, parts of the Sierra de los Cuchumatanes, and particularly in the Sierra de las Minas. A forest preserve in Baja Verapaz, known as the Quetzal Biotope, has been set aside specifically to protect the quetzal. It can

SAVING GUATEMALA'S SCARLET MACAWS

Among the Petén region's most beautiful creatures are the brightly colored scarlet macaws, which once roamed freely throughout Petén. You'll probably run into these large parrots throughout your travels in Guatemala, as they are popular pets in hotel courtyards on account of their colorful red, blue, and yellow plumage, including two beautiful red tail feathers, in addition to their boisterous squawking and ability to mimic human speech. Unfortunately, their populations have been decimated thanks to wildlife poaching for the international pet trade and to habitat loss. Still, there remain pockets where macaws continue to nest, and local scientists have taken it upon themselves to help protect what's left of Guatemala's dwindling numbers of these exotic birds.

In the dense forests that still surround the site of Waka'-Perú, biologists from several agencies working in Petén, including ProPetén and Wildlife Conservation Society, have established protected nesting grounds. There are 21 nests in hollow forest trees, and additional artificial nests are being created. The latter involve creating hollowed-out tree trunks, which are then placed high in the treetops. Biologists report success with this new method. Like most parrots, scarlet macaws lay 2-4 white eggs in a tree cavity, with their young hatching after about 25 days. They fly about 105 days later and leave their parents as late as one year after birth.

The nests at Waka'-Perú enjoy year-round protection by a newly created joint military-police force charged with safeguarding Guatemala's natural resources.

Volunteers are welcome at the site, giving visitors an exciting opportunity to help out in the conservation of Guatemala's exotic creatures while helping to fund the biological station's efforts.

often be seen on the grounds of one of the area lodges feeding on aguacatillo trees. The larger nearby Sierra de las Minas Biosphere Reserve is also a safe bet. Some grass-roots organizations like Proyecto Eco-Quetzal are working with local communities in Alta Verapaz to promote sustainable tourism in the hopes they will see the economic value of preserving the forest instead of destroying it for slash-and-burn agriculture.

Among endemic species is the flightless Atitlán grebe (*Podilymbus gigas*), commonly known as poc, which was officially declared extinct in 1989. The introduction of nonnative large- and smallmouth bass into the lake seems to have precipitated its drastic decline in numbers from about 200 in 1960 to only 32 in 1983. The bass ate the young grebes as well as the crabs and fish species on which poc fed.

Endemic to the northern Petén region is the Petén ocellated turkey (*Meleagris ocellata*), readily seen strutting around Tikal. It is smaller but much more colorful than its northern relatives, somewhat resembling a peacock. Other interesting birds found in Guatemala's tropical forests include the

BALAM: GUATEMALA'S JAGUARS

Among the most beautiful and highly revered rainforest animals both in ancient and modern times is the jaguar (*Panthera onca*), which inhabits Mexico, Central America, and parts of South America. It is one of the big cats, along with the leopard, lion, and tiger, and is the third largest of these. Jaguars are similar to leopards, though their spots present different arrangements (they are spots within spots, or rosettes, and are larger). Jaguars are also stockier in build. They inhabit mostly forested lands but will also range across grasslands and open terrain. Also notable is their love of water and ability to swim. These gorgeous jungle cats are largely solitary and known for their hunting skills. They will attack cattle in areas fringing jungle zones and have been known to attack jungle camps in order to stalk human prey, usually children. Their powerful jaws are capable of puncturing tortoise shells.

Perhaps for these reasons, the Maya had great respect and reverence for the jaguar, which they called *balam*. Jaguars were a symbol of power and strength and were believed to act as mediums for communication between the living and the dead. Kings were often given names incorporating the word *balam*, which they viewed as their companions in the spiritual world and protectors of the royal household. Rulers wearing jaguar pelts and man-jaguar figures frequently appear in pre-Columbian art. The jaguar was the patron deity of Tikal and is featured in a royal burial scene depicted on a human bone fragment found in the burial tomb of Hasaw Chan K'awil (Heavenly Standard Bearer) in which the ruler travels to the underworld in a canoe rowed by mythical animal figures.

Ranges for female jaguars are in the vicinity of 25-40 square kilometers, with the range of males being roughly twice as much and encompassing that of two or three females. Male jaguars' ranges do not overlap. For this reason, attempts to conserve existing numbers of jaguars require large expanses of territory such as that found in Guatemala's Maya Biosphere Reserve. The reserve adjoins parks in neighboring Mexico and Belize as part of

keel-billed toucan (*Ramphastos sulfuratus*), a perennial jungle favorite because of its large, colorful, banana-like beak. Many of these can be seen at Tikal around sunrise and sunset flying among the temples peeking out from the forest canopy. A large variety of parrots also inhabit the Petén forests. The most impressive of these is the scarlet macaw (*Ara macao*), which once inhabited large parts of Petén as well as the Pacific coastal plain. It now inhabits only very remote parts of the Petén forests. Conservationists are fighting to save the birds from local extinction, and protected nesting sites have been established in the Maya Biosphere Reserve, specifically in Laguna del Tigre National Park. Rounding out the list of noteworthy birds is the harpy eagle (*Harpia harpyja*), a large, powerful raptor that also enjoys healthy populations at Tikal National Park.

a vast biological corridor. An estimated 550-650 jaguars remain in the Maya Biosphere Reserve.

Scientists have been studying jaguars in the Maya Biosphere Reserve and are trying to get a more accurate estimate of their remaining numbers in addition to a better understanding of their behavioral patterns. Within the Laguna del Tigre National Park, biologists have been using radio collars to track five jaguars and a puma in the area surrounding the site of Waka'-Perú in an effort to determine migration patterns along an important biological corridor connecting this area with Mirador-Río Azul National Park. It is not uncommon to see jaguar prints on the muddy trails in the vicinity of Waka'-Perú. Ironically, in 2006, a camera crew visiting the park to film a program on scarlet macaws for Guatemalan TV channel Guatevisión was unable to find any macaws but did manage to get a jaguar sighting on tape. Recent video monitoring along 15 stations in the central core of Tikal National Park detected seven jaguars during a two-month period. The Sierra del Lacandón National Park is also believed to harbor large numbers of these jungle cats.

Luckily, you don't need to go traipsing through the jungle with a saucer of milk if you want to see a jaguar, though chances are it will see you first. Guatemala City's excellent zoo has jaguars, as does Petén's ARCAS wildlife rescue center. A jaguar cub was born in Guatemala City's zoo as recently as 2003. Several zoos in the United States have partnered with facilities in Central America to breed jaguars in captivity. Sacramento's zoo welcomed the arrival of Tina, a Guatemalan jaguar, and Mulac, a male jaguar from Belize, in 2002.

As part of a larger regional initiative with Mexico and Belize, known as Selva Maya, local conservation groups Defensores de la Naturaleza and Fundación Monte Carlo Verde launched the SalvaBalam campaign in 2006, aimed at increasing public awareness of the jaguar's plight and raising funds for continued study of these fascinating creatures. For more information, visit www.defensores.org.gt.

Land Mammals

Guatemala's list of native land mammals is impressive, with a large variety of exotic cats, primates, and other furry creatures. The largest of Guatemala's cats is the jaguar (*Felis onca*), found in lowland parts of Petén, Izabal, and the Verapaces. Referred to as *tigre* by locals, it is known to sometimes wander into *chiclero* camps as well as to kill livestock in remote cattle ranches that have encroached on remote areas. Sightings of this beautiful spotted cat are rare, so consider yourself lucky if you are able spot one in the wild. Its tracks are more likely to be seen on travels to the remote forests of the Maya Biosphere Reserve, which can be exciting enough. Other cats include the jaguarundi (*Herpailurus yaguarondi*), puma (*Puma concolor*), and their smaller relatives the margay (*Leopardus wiedii*) and ocelot (*Leopardus pardalis*).

Among the most widely seen mammals are monkeys. You are likely to hear the roar of howler monkeys (*Alouatta pigra*) during the early morning hours if camping overnight in Petén. Less aggressive, smaller, and more playful are spider monkeys (*Ateles geoffroyi*). The gray fox (*Urocyon cinereoargenteus*) can often be seen in the early morning and evening among Tikal's temples. More exotic forest dwellers include the pig-like collared peccary (*Tayassu tajacu*) and white-lipped peccary (*Tayasu pecari*) as well as the hefty Baird's tapir (*Tapirus bairdii*) and the tamandua anteater (*Tamandua mexicana*).

Also easy to spot are some of the smaller mammals, particularly in parks such as Tikal and Yaxhá. Among these are the raccoon-like white-nosed coati (*Nasua narica*), which practically walk up to you at Tikal; mouse-like agoutis (*Dasyprocta punctata*); and kinkajous (*Potos flavus*).

If you happen to like bats, Guatemala harbors over 100 species of the flying critters. Many of these are found in the limestone caves of Petén and the Verapaces. Most of these are harmless to humans, feeding on fruits and insects. There are blood-sucking vampire bats (*Desmodus rotundus*) flying about, though these feed mostly on cattle.

Sea Life

Five species of sea turtles can be seen on Guatemala's Atlantic and Pacific coasts, where they also come ashore to lay their eggs. These are olive ridley, hawksbill, leatherback, green, and loggerhead. Of these, olive ridley, leatherback, and hawksbill turtles nest on the Pacific shores and can be seen at the Monterrico-Hawaii Biotope. Between September and January, visitors to this park have the rare opportunity to hold baby sea turtles in their hands before releasing them to begin their mad dash across the sand and a lifetime at sea. If they survive to adulthood, the females will return to very same beach to lay their eggs and begin a new life-cycle. All of these turtle species are endangered due to the harvesting of their eggs by poor coastal dwellers in search of food and a means to supplement their incomes.

Guatemala's Pacific sailfish have become the object of widespread praise in the angling circuit, with blue marlin, Pacific sailfish, and yellowfin tuna just waiting to be caught. Humpback whales can also be seen breaching in the Pacific waters. As for the Caribbean coast, Guatemala just missed out on the Belize barrier reef, as it ends right at the doorstep of the Punta de Manabique peninsula. The barrier reef is easily accessible, however, along with the wonders of its corals and exotic fish. Although lacking the barrier reef per se, the waters off Guatemala's Atlantic coast are certainly not devoid of exotic sea life. Bottle-nosed dolphins readily follow motorboats as they make their way along the Caribbean coast. The endangered manatee (*Trichechus manatus*), or sea cow, has become increasingly rare as the large, slow, sea-grass-eating mammal has fallen prey to hunting, motorboats, and drowning in fishing nets. A small reserve in Izabal's El Golfete is attempting to protect the few that remain in Guatemalan waters.

Amphibians

There are 112 species of amphibians represented in Guatemala. Unfortunately, Guatemala is out of range for some of the more interesting and colorful miniature frogs, such as poison arrow frogs, found farther south in Costa Rica and Panama. That being said, there are still some interesting frogs to be found in Guatemala's tropical forests; among these are the red-eyed tree frog (*Agalychnis callidryas*) and the similar Morelet's tree frog (*Agalychnis moreletti*). Fleischmann's glass frog (*Hyalinobatrachium fleischmanni*) is translucent and lime green with small yellow spots and yellowish hands. Its organs and bones are visible through the abdominal skin. All three of these prefer vegetation near rivers and streams.

Reptiles

With 214 species of reptiles, there is no shortage of snakes in Guatemala. Among the ones to watch out for is the fer-de-lance (*Bothrops asper*), known locally as *barba amarilla*. The aggressive pit viper is found in abundant quantities in the tropical forests of Petén, Izabal, and the Verapaces, though you are not likely to see one. Baby fer-de-lance can be especially dangerous as they are yet unable to control the amount of poison they inject into a bite.

Other snakes include tropical rattlesnakes (*Crotalus durissus*), several species of colorful coral snakes, and nonvenomous boa constrictors.

If you watched the *Survivor* TV series, you probably noticed there are crocodiles in Guatemala, particularly in and around Lake Yaxhá. The crocodiles seen on *Survivor* are Morelet's crocodiles (*Crocodylus moreleti*). The larger American crocodile (*Crocodylus acutus*) can be found in coastal areas, swamps, and larger rivers in Petén and Izabal. Many species of river turtles inhabit the tropical lowlands. Basilisk lizards and at least two species of iguana round out the highlighted list of Guatemala's reptiles.

Insects and Small Creatures

This heading might give some readers "the itchies," but in addition to the myriad species of arachnids such as tarantulas and scorpions or plentiful amounts of mosquitoes in some places, Guatemalan lands are host to many other, more beautiful creatures. Among these are thousands of species of butterflies, including the beautiful blue morpho, which you might see flitting about the forest in an iridescent flash of blue. While hiking Guatemala's forests, keep an eye out for the industrious leaf-cutter ants, which cut pathways through the forest and carry small pieces of bright green leaves to their nest, where they are used as compost for underground fungus farms. Butterflies and leaf-cutters are virtually guaranteed favorites among younger travelers to these parts.

Social Climate

Guatemala is a land of contrasts, and this extends to the country's social landscape. It's hard to pin down a definition or convenient summary of the country in social terms because of its ethnic diversity, which translates into correspondingly vast socioeconomic disparities. While many of its neighbors are very homogenized in terms of racial makeup and socioeconomic status, Guatemala is a pluri-cultural and multiethnic country where flashy displays of wealth and abject poverty exist side-by-side.

© AL ARGUETA

American brands like Coca-Cola are advertised on the streets of Guatemala.

STANDARD OF LIVING

Guatemala's social indicators provide a picture of one of the poorest countries in the hemisphere, where infant mortality, illiteracy, and malnutrition are still not completely addressed. At the same time, it doesn't take long after arriving in Guatemala to realize that many people live quite well here.

In rural towns and villages populated by the country's Mayan descendants, conditions can be quite basic and it will feel like you've stepped into a time warp. On the other hand, you can spend time in one of many Guatemala City shopping malls, office buildings, or high-rise condominiums and feel like you're still in the United States. Long story short, Guatemalans run the gamut from desperately poor to filthy rich, even by North American standards. For the person looking to move to Guatemala, this translates into the opportunity to live a pared-down lifestyle with an appreciation for the simple things in life or the chance to live quite comfortably for significantly less than it would cost in the United States.

POLITICAL AND ECONOMIC STABILITY

Guatemala has enjoyed democratically elected governments since 1985, at which time a new constitution also took effect. Aside from a brief period in the early 1990s lasting less than a week, these governments have been free of the coups-d'etat that marked the country's turbulent civil war. The Guatemalan civil war, incidentally, ended in 1996 thanks to a U.N.-brokered peace treaty. Although Guatemalans may not always be happy with their elected governments, political stability has at least reached a point where removing a government via military force is no longer an acceptable option. Guatemala's integration into the world economic marketplace and the presence of foreign investment dictate the need for the continued preservation of democratic institutions. That being said, the power of the military establishment has not been completely curtailed. Despite peace accord provisions dictating the reduction of its size and budget, Guatemalan military forces continue to grow in numbers and government funding.

The biggest threat to Guatemala's continued stability comes from drug trafficking and the presence of organized crime. Drug traffickers now control remote areas of the country being used as a corridor between Colombia and the United States. Recently, Mexican cartels have become embroiled in an all-out war in an attempt to remove local cartels from the picture and establish hegemony over drug trafficking in Guatemala and throughout Central America. Other forms of organized crime, such as robbery and kidnapping, are on the rise, and day-to-day living in Guatemala does indeed require a heightened sense of vigilance. This is especially the case in Guatemala City. Areas of the country that have fallen under control of narco-mafias include parts of Petén, parts of the western highlands, and the remote reaches of Izabal and Las Verapaces.

State security forces are generally not well trained and under-funded. As in most of Latin America, corruption is a big issue. The current Guatemalan government, it should be noted, appears particularly inept or unwilling to take concrete actions to curb the power of drug cartels, which spawn a number of other problems, including land invasions in national parks and illegal logging. For these reasons, poor Guatemalans living in remote areas absent state

INTERNATIONAL COMMISSION AGAINST IMPUNITY IN GUATEMALA

In an attempt to fight so-called "parallel powers" and the infiltration of organized crime into the Guatemalan state, the country recently enlisted the help of a United Nations-created entity known as the International Commission Against Impunity in Guatemala (CICIG). CICIG is an independent entity and provides a glimmer of hope in addressing the evils undermining the country's political stability. Its official mandate is the investigation and prosecution of the illegal security organizations supposedly involved in corruption, drug trafficking, organized crime, and political violence and responsible for attacks against human rights workers. According to Human Rights First, CICIG has the potential to:

• Uncover the full extent of the illegal security organizations and dismantle their underlying structure.

• Investigate and promote the prosecutions of members of illegal security organizations responsible for crimes and attacks against human rights defenders.

• Prevent future attacks on human rights defenders by putting an end to the culture of impunity that encourages such attacks.

• Recommend public policies for eradicating illegal security groups and preventing their re-emergence.

• Support, strengthen, and assist Guatemalan institutions to uphold the rule of law.

It remains to be seen whether CICIG can contribute to dismantling Guatemala's parallel powers and take concrete actions toward the overall improvement of the country's deteriorating security conditions.

presence often take matters into their own hands. Public lynching of alleged kidnappers, murderers, and other criminals is not at all uncommon.

Conditions in Guatemala appear much more promising on the economic plane. For better or worse, Guatemala has always been a country where capitalism functions in its most dramatic forms. In addition to a history of continued macroeconomic stability, Guatemala offers a favorable investment climate bolstered by numerous incentive laws and adherence to regional free trade initiatives such as DR-CAFTA (U.S.–Dominican Republic–Central American Free Trade Agreement). As this book was being completed, nearby Costa Rica was still scrambling to enact legislation aimed at approving DR-CAFTA, which has been partially blocked by large state participation in the economy, specifically the state monopoly on telecommunications. Guatemala's telecommunications, it should be noted, were deregulated in the early 1990s.

Infrastructure in Guatemala in many ways exceeds that of its neighbors, with good ports, roads, and the region's most modern international airport. Economic growth in 2008 was a robust 6 percent.

Whereas the tourism potential of many of Guatemala's neighbors has been heavily tapped by the international investment community, the country's phenomenal natural resources and tourism potential are quite probably its greatest source of untapped potential. Investors looking to cash in on Guatemala's myriad possibilities for tourism investment can still get in on the game relatively early.

GUATEMALANS AND FOREIGNERS

Many Guatemalans have a natural fascination with foreigners. Whether you're visiting a remote coffee farm in the highlands or hanging out at a bar in Antigua, foreigners are, with rare exceptions, very welcome visitors. Guatemalans are aware of the country's often obscure (as in nonexistent) or negative international image, so they are enthusiastic to glean from you impressions of a visit to their country. Despite its problems, Guatemalans love their country and are aware of its tremendous natural beauty, amazing ethnic diversity, and untapped potential. You, as a foreigner, in many ways validate the good things Guatemala has to offer.

In certain echelons of society, your simply being American can grant almost instant access to places few locals might see, such as the homes of the country's wealthy elite. Wealthy Guatemalans are more apt to trust and be able to relate to you as a foreigner than many of their less affluent countrymen.

Many Guatemalans across socioeconomic strata have family members living in the United States, both legally and illegally, or have plans to perhaps migrate to the United States someday in search of the American dream. They will, unsurprisingly, have many questions for you about life in the United States.

Unlike in neighboring countries, there seems to be a markedly reduced tendency to see locals mingling with foreigners for the sheer purpose of romantic conquest. It's not to say that it doesn't exist here; it's just not as common as in, say, Honduras or Costa Rica.

WHY PEOPLE COME TO GUATEMALA

Guatemala attracts a very different breed of expat. Whether it's the neo-hippies seeking an epiphany of sorts on the shores of Lake Atitlán or the ex-New Yorker trying her hand at running a bed-and-breakfast in Antigua while enjoying a much slower pace of life, you'll find the Guatemalan expat community a diverse bunch. Guatemala has begun attracting retirees in greater numbers, drawn to the country for its perfect climate and greatly reduced cost of living. As the country has traditionally been a cultural tourism destination, you'll find few expats come here for life on the beach, though that too is starting to change.

I've met a number of folks who've migrated to Guatemala's Pacific beaches from Costa Rica, where they've started successful sailfishing operations.

Many of those who come to Guatemala fall in love with its highland scenery, certainly the most dramatic in all of Central America, and its Mayan culture. Whereas the rest of Central America offers little in the way of cultural diversity, Guatemala's deep Mayan roots are the source of fascination for many a foreign traveler and resident. In many cases, these expats are involved with NGOs working to improve living conditions for the country's rural poor. You may be drawn to Guatemala as a place where you can hope to make a difference. As anyone who's witnessed the country's dramatic juxtapositions of physical beauty and human suffering can tell you, there's just something about this place that grabs hold of you and won't let go.

In short, Guatemala is not for everyone, but those who live here and love it will tell you there's no place they'd rather be. Despite its problems, the rewards of living here are numerous.

HISTORY, GOVERNMENT, AND ECONOMY

Guatemala's history is complicated and fascinating, though it often reads like a tragic novel. An understanding of this history is crucial for those trying to decide if Guatemala is right for them. You can't live in Guatemala without escaping the reality of its turbulent past, as what you see before you is an outpicturing of the failures of successive governments and a legacy of violence and gross inequality.

Guatemala has unfortunately not been blessed with good government. The country shows a marked history of colonialism and the establishment of a power arrangement in which the wealthy have ruled with the support of the armed forces. Its judiciary and legislative branches are grossly inefficient and corrupt, making the addressing of grievances highly challenging. Justice, it seems, is never quite served in Guatemala. Still, there is hope on the horizon.

WELCOME TO GUATEMALA

History

PREHISTORY

It is generally accepted that the first inhabitants of the American continent came in waves by way of a land bridge across the Bering Strait connecting Siberia to Alaska, some 25,000 years ago. The migrants continued to make their way southward, possibly using boats to assist them, and eventually came to populate, albeit thinly, large portions of the Americas occupying a diverse range of climates. It is believed passage via the Bering Strait was intermittently open until about 10,000 years ago when the last ice age ended, submerging the land bridge with rising sea levels.

MAYAN CIVILIZATION

The peoples that settled the New World eventually grew in population and transitioned from hunter-gatherers to nascent agricultural societies. The developing civilizations then made a clear transition from hillside swidden agriculture to more intensive forms of cultivation, including terrace farming, the construction of drainage ditches, and the development of fertilizers, which in turn produced large food surpluses. With greater food security, the population was gradually able to become more specialized in

© AL ARGUETA
Tikal flourished during the Mayan civilization.

its individual occupations, paving the way for advances in writing, art, architecture, mathematics, and astronomy that would later come to full fruition. A common language and universal belief system are thought to have existed throughout the Mayan region, providing the needed social cohesion that served as a catalyst for the development of a larger civilization.

Today, the remains of this civilization can be seen throughout northern Guatemala's Petén region at sites such as Tikal, Uaxactún, Yaxhá, Piedras Negras, and El Mirador, to name a few. The inhabitants of the Mayan cities now lying in ruins spent their time trading,

© AL ARGUETA

Modern high-rises contrast with Kaminaljuyú temple mounds in Guatemala City.

stargazing, and fighting wars before abandoning their cities, to be later reclaimed by the surrounding jungle.

Our knowledge of the Maya comes largely from the edification of large carved monuments, or stelae, which documented the lives of the individual city-states' rulers and historical events associated with their reign, such as battles, marriage alliances, successions, etc. The Maya constructed the temples and palaces we see today atop previous constructions so that what we see now is literally the pinnacle of their progress.

Of particular note is what is sometimes referred to as the Classic Maya collapse, giving the impression that the civilization collapsed and vanished into thin air. This is certainly not the case. The Mayan civilization proper indeed came crashing down for reasons that are becoming increasingly evident, and the Maya simply dispersed into other parts of present-day Mexico, Guatemala, Belize, and Honduras while falling prey to increasing cultural and military dominance from invading central Mexican Toltecs.

The site of modern-day Guatemala City was originally occupied by Kaminaljuyú, whose commercial dominance was established largely on the strength of its strategic location for the trading of obsidian and jade.

THE PRECONQUEST PICTURE

Toltec-Maya Yucatán cities, such as Chichén Itzá and Uxmal, finally gave out sometime in the late 13th century and were abruptly abandoned. At about the same time, the Guatemalan highlands were invaded by groups of Toltec-Maya, though it is uncertain whether they are the product of a mass exodus from the Yucatán cities or a new group from the Toltec heartland in the Gulf of Mexico. In any case, their arrival in the Guatemalan highlands signaled a transition from the existence of relatively peaceful, religious village societies to ones increasingly secular and warlike.

Quickly establishing themselves as a ruling elite, the Toltec invaders founded a series of competing empires including the K'iche', Kaqchikel, Tzutujíl, Mam, Ixil, Achi', and Q'eqchi', among others. Interestingly, these and other tribes encompassing the highland indigenous groups continue to form the basis for today's cultural landscape, with differentiation based on their individual dialects.

Among these tribes, the K'iche' and Kaqchikel emerged as dominant forces, a rivalry the conquering Spanish would later use to their advantage. Prior to the arrival of the Spanish, the highland region was engulfed in a widespread power struggle between rival groups for cultivable land to feed an increasing population.

THE SPANISH CONQUEST

After the Spanish conquered the Aztec empire and captured its capital at Tenochtitlán in 1521, the K'iche' sent ambassadors north to Mexico informing Hernán Cortés of their desire to be vassals of the newly established power structure. In 1523 Cortés dispatched Pedro de Alvarado to Guatemala on a fact-finding mission meant to verify the veracity of the tribe's claim. If indeed Cortés's intentions were limited to fact-finding, he could have done better than to choose Alvarado for the job. Alvarado is described as handsome, athletic, distinguished, eloquent, and graceful, among other things, from Spanish accounts of the conquest. He was also extremely cruel.

Alvarado arrived in Guatemala along the Pacific coast flatlands accompanied by 120 horsemen, 173 horses, 300 soldiers, and 200 Mexican warriors from the allied Tlaxcalan armies. He made his way up to the highlands, where he met the K'iche' in battle near present-day Quetzaltenango, also known as Xelajú. An estimated 30,000 K'iche' were unable to forge alliances with neighboring tribes to repel the Spanish invasion and faced the Spanish alone. Legend has it Alvarado met Tecún Umán, grandson of the K'iche' ruler, in hand-to-hand combat, cutting him down.

Following these events, the K'iche' invited the Spanish to their capital at Utatlán for the signing of a formal surrender but secretly planned to ambush them from the safety of their mountain fortress. Alvarado knew an ambush when he saw one and so he withdrew to the city's outskirts, followed by the K'iche' rulers, whom he seized and later had burned at the stake. Eight days of fighting followed, with the Spanish enlisting the help of the rival Kaqchikels to finally gain the upper hand against the K'iche'. Utatlán was then burnt to the ground.

The Kaqchikel alliance with the Spanish stuck for a time, with the Spanish establishing the first capital of Guatemala alongside the Kaqchikel capital of Iximché, from which they launched raids to conquer Guatemala's remaining highland tribal groups. The campaign would last several years and was made increasingly difficult when the Kaqchikel severed their alliance with the Spanish in 1526 in response to demands for tribute. They abandoned their capital at Iximché and took refuge in the mountains, launching a guerrilla war. The Spanish then moved the Guatemalan capital, establishing the city of Santiago de Los Caballeros on November 22, 1527. Now known as Ciudad Vieja, it lies near present-day Antigua.

Indigenous uprisings and resistance would continue throughout Guatemala's history into the present-day as the various groups have responded to repressive policies imposed by those in power. The recently ended civil war has been likened by scholars, human rights activists, and journalists to a kind of "second conquest" aimed at eliminating the indigenous population through genocidal extermination attempts.

A final aspect of the conquest that bears mentioning is the work of European diseases and their hand in greatly reducing the population of the indigenous peoples who had no resistance to smallpox, plague, typhus, and measles. These diseases were responsible for the loss of more than three-quarters of Guatemala's two million inhabitants in the first 30 years following contact with the Spanish. It is thought that a third of the population died before Alvarado's invading army even set foot in the indigenous peoples' Guatemalan homeland.

COLONIAL GUATEMALA

The Guatemalan capital required 10 years from its founding to complete and included a cathedral, town hall, and Alvarado's palace. Alvarado died in 1541 while in Mexico attempting to subdue an uprising. The city was destroyed shortly thereafter by a mudslide that rolled down Agua volcano after an earthquake and heavy rains combined to unleash the contents of the flooded crater.

Guatemala's capital was then moved a few miles away to present-day Antigua. It would serve as the administrative headquarters of the newly established Audiencia de Guatemala, which included the provinces of San Salvador, Nicaragua, Honduras, Costa Rica, Chiapas, and Guatemala. The city of Santiago de los Caballeros, as it was officially known, would grow to become the third-largest city in Spanish colonial America, surpassed only by Mexico City and Lima. In 1776, a series of devastating earthquakes destroyed most of the city's buildings and churches, leading to a final move of the Guatemalan capital to Valle de la Ermita (Valley of the Hermitage), just over a mountain to the east, where it has resided ever since.

The colonial period is significant in that it completely transformed Guatemala's physical and cultural landscape, establishing new cities and institutionalizing new economic and religious systems that would come to form the basis for a racist hierarchy persisting largely unaltered to this day. Guatemala's history displays a striking symmetry throughout the years. The key to understanding many of the more recent tragedies to befall its people lies in understanding the significance of earlier events dating back to just before the conquest.

At the center of Guatemala's new power structure was the Catholic church, which arrived with the conquistadors and included various sects such as Franciscans, Mercedarians, Dominicans, and Jesuits. These were granted large concessions of land and indigenous peoples allowing them to amass huge fortunes from the cultivation of cash crops including sugar, indigo, and wheat. This power structure was held in place by institutions established by the Spanish crown, namely the *encomienda* and *repartimiento*.

The *encomienda* was a grant of Indian labor and tribute, though not necessarily of land, over a geographical area. The *encomenderos* holding such a grant were allowed to tax the indigenous peoples under their care and to conscript them for labor in exchange for their promise to maintain order and educate the indigenous populace in the Spanish language and Catholicism.

The *repartimiento,* which is essentially indistinguishable from its predecessor, is a reformed version of the encomienda system, at least on paper. It put control of the distribution of workers into the hands of local magistrates and called for the donation of a percentage of laborers from populations close to Spanish settlements, between 2 and 4 percent of the indigenous population.

Further adding to the transformation of community organization in the conquered territories was the establishment of *reducciones,* part of the larger process of *congregación,* consisting of towns founded in the Spanish vein with the purpose of congregating indigenous populations into manageable settlements and assimilating them into the dominant culture and religion. They would also serve as a handy nearby source from which to pool labor.

INDEPENDENCE

Guatemalan, and indeed Central American, independence came more as a result of pressures from without than from a genuine internal uprising demanding freedom from Spanish rule. This is not to say that all was well with Spanish colonial rule, as there were policies and social stratifications in place contributing to unrest among the lower strata of society. Spanish policies kept wealth and power in the hands of Spanish-born elites, or *chapetones*. *Criollos,* or those born in the New World of Spanish descent, were the next rung down the ladder, with the lowest standings reserved for mixed-blood *mestizos* and full-blooded Indians.

Napoleon's invasion of Spain in 1808 led to the imposition of a liberal constitution on Spain in 1812. When Mexican general Agustín Iturbide declared his own country's independence from Spain, Guatemala followed suit. The reigning Captain General Gabino Gaínza bowed to demands for independence but hoped to maintain the existent power structure with the support of the church and landowning elites. The declaration of independence essentially maintained the old power structure under new management. Mexico quickly dispatched troops to annex Guatemala, and all of Central America, to Iturbide's new empire.

Iturbide was dethroned in 1823, and Central America, minus the state of Chiapas, declared its independence from Mexico. This second declaration joined the remaining states in a loose federation and adopted many U.S.-modeled liberal reforms, such as the abolition of slavery. A protracted power struggle between liberals advocating a secular, more egalitarian state and conservatives wanting to maintain the church-dominated political and economic structures marked the early years of independence. The Central American Federation was weakened not only by inner power struggles within individual member states, but also by a struggle to determine regional leadership over neighboring states.

JUSTO RUFINO BARRIOS AND THE LIBERAL REFORMS

The liberals would finally succeed in 1871 under the leadership of General Justo Rufino Barrios, who, along with Miguel García Granados, set out from Mexico with a force of just 45 men, gaining numbers as their approach to the capital grew closer. The capital was taken on June 30, 1871, and Granados was installed as the leader of the new liberal government. Granados made only limited reforms, and by 1872 a frustrated Barrios marched to the capital with his troops and demanded elections, which he won overwhelmingly.

Among the reforms quickly instituted by Barrios, who would go down in Guatemalan history as "The Reformer," were educational reform and separation of church and state. Barrios was the first of the *caudillos,* military strongmen who ruled the country with an iron fist and sense of absolute omnipotence, mostly uninterrupted, until the revolution of 1944. He masterfully strengthened his power over the entire country with links to local strongmen in rural areas wielding power on his behalf but unable to challenge his hold because of the restricted development of secondary market centers and the overwhelming economic dominance of Guatemala City.

To further exercise his dominion, Barrios professionalized the military, creating a new military academy, the Escuela Politecnica, still in existence today. The addition of rural militia further strengthened national control over the rural hinterlands. Barrios was decidedly pro-western and sought to impose a European worldview to suppress what he saw as a vastly inferior Indian culture. Liberal economic policies ensured minimal protection of village lands, Indian culture, or the welfare of peasant villages.

During this time, coffee came to dominate the Guatemalan economy and Barrios's economic policies ensured the availability of a peasant workforce to supply the labor-intensive coffee harvest with its share of needed workers. Furthermore, the increasingly racist attitudes of Guatemala's coffee elites toward the Indians served to justify the coercive means used to secure this labor force. The Indians were seen as lazy, making forced labor and the submission of the indigenous masses both necessary and morally justified. In this regard, the *mandamiento,* which came to replace the *repartimiento,* was increasingly enforced in the last two decades of the 19th century, requiring villages to supply a specified number of laborers per year.

Increasingly, however, elites found more coercive ways to exact labor from the Indians by way of debt peonage. Rural workers were required to carry a *libreto,* a record containing an individual's labor and debt figures. *Habilitadores,* or labor contractors, were charged with advancing money to peasants in exchange for labor contracts. The contractors often used alcohol as an added incentive and took advantage of widespread peasant illiteracy to ensure many of them contracted debts they would never be able to repay. In this way, depressed rural wages from debt peonage and low-cost labor increased the wealth of agricultural elites while making the rural peasantry even poorer.

MANUEL ESTRADA CABRERA

Justo Rufino Barrios died in battle in 1885 while fighting to create a re-unified Central America under Guatemalan leadership. He was succeeded by a string of short-lived *caudillo* presidents. The next to hold power for any significant time period was Manuel Estrada Cabrera, whose legacy included undivided support for big business and crackdowns on labor organization. He ruled from 1898 until his overthrow in 1920, having been declared mentally insane. Among Cabrera's many peculiarities was the construction of several temples to honor Minerva, the Roman goddess of wisdom. Cabrera's legacy includes gross corruption, a beefed-up military, and a neglected educational system.

Export agriculture continued its unprecedented growth under Cabrera, thus paving the way for the dominance of two foreign groups that would come to control much of Guatemala's economy in later years. The first of these were German coffee planters who settled in the region of Las Verapaces. By 1913 this German enclave owned 170 of the country's coffee plantations, with about half of them in the vicinity of Cobán. The other significant foreign presence in Guatemala during this time was the U.S.-owned United Fruit Company (UFCo), aptly nicknamed "El Pulpo" (The Octopus), and its tentacles consisting of International Railways of Central America (IRCA) and the UFCo Steamship Lines. Its vast control of land, rail, and steamship transportation, in addition to Guatemala's sole Caribbean port, Puerto Barrios, made it a political and economic powerhouse. Its political clout would be seen in the mid-20th century, when, together with the CIA, it would be directly responsible for ousting Guatemala's president, Jacobo Arbenz Guzmán, from power when land reform policies interfered with the company's vast land holdings.

JORGE UBICO

After the overthrow of Estrada Cabrera in 1920 the country entered a period of instability and power struggles culminating in the rise to power of Jorge Ubico. Continuing in the now well-established pattern of megalomaniacal, heavy-handed leadership that would come to characterize many of Guatemala's presidents, Ubico continued the unconditional support for U.S. agribusiness and the local oligarchy. By 1940, 90 percent of Guatemala's exports were sold to the United States. Ubico caved in to U.S demands for the expulsion of the German coffee planters from Guatemala during World War II, evidencing the increasing U.S. hold on Guatemalan domestic policy.

Within Guatemala, Ubico embarked on various reforms, including ambitious road-building projects, as well as improvements in health care and social welfare. Debt peonage was also outlawed but was replaced by a vagrancy law enforcing compulsory labor contributions of 150 days upon landless peasants in either rural plantations or in the government road-building programs. Ubico's reforms always had in mind the modernization of the state economy. Far from an attempt to free the indigenous peoples from coercive labor practices, the vagrancy law asserted centralized control over the national labor force while keeping the political power of the oligarchy firmly in check.

Ubico was also obsessed with internal security. He saw himself as a reincarnated Napoleon and became increasingly paranoid, creating a network of spies and informers used to repress opposition to his increasingly tyrannical rule. Much of this opposition came from the indigenous peasant population, whom Ubico ignored and regarded as retrograde and inferior. This led to numerous revolts in the late 1930s and early 1940s. The discovery of an assassination plot in 1934 led to the execution of 300 suspected conspirators within 48 hours.

THE OCTOBER REVOLUTION OF 1944

Opposition finally reached a head in June 1944 when widespread discontent erupted in violent street protests by large portions of the urban middle class demanding democratic opportunities and new economic policies. Ubico was forced to resign after 14 years in office. When his interim replacement signaled to be more of the same, young students, professionals, and forward-thinking military officers orchestrated a widespread social movement culminating in his overthrow in what has been dubbed "The October Revolution." Elections were called for December of that same year. In a radio address, then front-running presidential candidate Juan José Arévalo, an exiled professor living in Argentina, described the transcendental nature of the recent events: "What has occurred in Guatemala is not a *golpe de estado* (coup d'etat); it is something more profound and beneficial; it is a revolution... It is a revolution that will go to the roots of the political system... In a word: It is a revolution called to wash, to purify our political life, to quiet everyone, and to honor Guatemala."

Arévalo would go on to win the election with an overwhelming majority and take office on March 1, 1945.

A DECADE OF "SPIRITUAL SOCIALISM"

Guatemala made much progress under Arévalo, who quickly set out on the road of badly needed structural reform. Prominence was given to education and health care with the construction of new schools and hospitals, immunization programs, and literacy campaigns. A new national budget allowed for a third of government spending to go into these programs, which were further facilitated by a new constitution drafted prior to Arévalo's taking office. Ubico's hated vagrancy laws were abolished, and in their place a labor code was instituted establishing union representation and granting workers the right to strike. Many of the farms expropriated from German planters during World War II, now in state hands, were transformed into peasant cooperatives. Government policies provided technical assistance and credit for peasant farmers and protected their lands from usurpation by agricultural elites and foreign agribusiness.

The gains in social justice ruffled the feathers of many of Guatemala's traditional power elites, including the church, urban business elites, the landed aristocracy, and the politicians who defended their interests. They increasingly opposed much of the reformist legislation passed by Arévalo in congress. A divided military also became the source of much opposition, with Arévalo surviving 25 coup attempts originating from conservative sectors of the armed forces. Meanwhile, U.S. business interests became increasingly unsettled by the reforms. At the top of this list was the United Fruit Company. As opposition stiffened, Arévalo was unable to fully implement the social transformation of the country he had intended and passed on to his successor an increasingly polarized political landscape.

His successor, Jacobo Arbenz Guzmán, continued along the path of reform, concentrating on fomenting economic development and independence from foreign intervention in politics and the economy. At the core of his economic development program was the Agrarian Reform Law of 1952, intended to redistribute land ownership by breaking up large plantations and promoting high productivity on smaller, individually owned farms. The urgent need for land reform was historically evident in the nature and function of institutions that, over time, placed Guatemalan land in the hands of a wealthy few, to the detriment of indigenous peasants. It is estimated that 2 percent of the country's population controlled 72 percent of all arable land in 1945, but only 12 percent of it was being utilized.

Central to the law were stipulations limiting expropriation to lands lying fallow. Arbenz himself was not immune from land expropriation, giving up 1,700 acres of his own land in the process. Also among the lands to be expropriated were extensive holdings by United Fruit ceded to the company under Estrada Cabrera and Ubico, which had made United Fruit Guatemala's largest landowner. Fully 85 percent of its holdings remained uncultivated. The Agrarian Reform Law allowed for the compensation of expropriated lands based on values declared for tax purposes, which United Fruit had, of course, grossly underreported.

Unfortunately for Arbenz and his reformist policies, UFCo had strong ties to the U.S. government and, more specifically, the CIA. Among United Fruit's shareholders were U.S. Secretary of State John Foster Dulles and his brother, CIA director Allen Dulles.

On the home front, it was clear that Arbenz had incurred the wrath of the oligarchy and conservative military sectors. He faced increasing political fragmentation despite attempts to forge a functional revolutionary coalition of political parties to further his goals, and he looked to several dedicated, competent individuals for support in implementing the agrarian reform and labor organization. Many inside and outside of Guatemala conveniently labeled Arbenz and his supporters Communist, though how much influence the Communists actually had in Guatemala is still hotly debated. In 1952 Guatemala's official Communist party, the Partido Guatemalteco de los Trabajadores (PGT, Guatemalan Labor Party), was legalized. Communists subsequently gained considerable minority influence over important peasant organizations and labor unions, but not over the governing political body, winning only 4 of 58 seats.

In any case, the country became increasingly unstable. This instability, combined with Arbenz's tolerance of the PGT and other Communist and labor influences, caused Washington to grow increasingly alarmed. The CIA finally orchestrated the overthrow of Arbenz in 1954 in the form of a military invasion from Honduras dubbed "Operation Success," led by two exiled Guatemalan military officers. The invading forces established Colonel Carlos Castillo Armas, who had previously led a failed coup against Arbenz, as chief of state. A series of military governments supported by the nascent military oligarchy partnership and conservative elements of Guatemalan society followed. Thus began one of the most tragic chapters in Guatemala's already turbulent history.

THE CIVIL WAR (1960-1996)

With the professionalization of Guatemala's army now in place thanks to the policies of Barrios and Ubico, the military was now poised to become the country's dominating political force and would do so for the next 30 years. Further paving the way for military dominance over Guatemalan politics was the Cold War climate and the fight against Communism. U.S. policy and military aid would assist the dictators' rise to power and facilitate their increasingly repressive nature, all in the name of defeating Communist insurrection.

Among the new regime's first moves was the revocation of the 1945 constitution, with the consequent reversal of the reforms of the previous years. The rule of the oligarchy was firmly reestablished, and a wave of repression against peasants, labor unions, and agrarian reformers was unleashed.

Castillo Armas would only be in power until 1957, when he was shot by one of his own palace guards. Political turmoil ensued, followed by the rise to power of Miguel Ydígoras Fuentes, an army officer from the Ubico years now representing the National Democratic Renovation Party. His five years in office were characterized by incompetence, corruption, nepotism, patronage, and economic decline. Opposition to Ydígoras grew, with young army officers led by Marco Yon Sosa and Turcios Lima attempting an unsuccessful coup in 1960. Ydígoras was finally ousted by a military coup in 1963 with approval from Washington after Arévalo threatened to return to Guatemala to run in the next election, firmly putting the establishment in both Guatemala and Washington on edge.

During the subsequent military government of Alfredo Enrique Peralta Azurdia, Turcios Lima and Yon Sosa launched a guerrilla offensive from the eastern highlands, marking the beginning of a protracted armed conflict between leftist rebels and the Guatemalan government. Ironically, both had received U.S. military training while serving in the Guatemalan forces and now used their skills to attack local army garrisons. The battle was soon joined by another armed rebel group, the Fuerzas Armadas Rebeldes (FAR, Rebel Armed Forces). The PGT, meanwhile, formed an alliance with the rebels while advocating the return of Arévalo.

A self-proclaimed "third government of the revolution" came to power in 1966 under Julio Cesar Montenegro of the center-left Partido Revolucionario, who tried to continue in the vein of Arévalo and Arbenz. It was clear, however, that his hands were tied and power was in the hands of the military. Political violence escalated during his administration, with death squads killing hundreds of students, unionists, academics, and peasant leaders.

By the end of the decade the guerrilla movement had been virtually

© AL ARGUETA

The United States and Guatemalan military have a long history of cooperation.

eliminated from the eastern highlands. FAR shifted its focus to Guatemala City, where it kidnapped and murdered the U.S. ambassador in 1968.

Electoral fraud and political violence, accompanied by economic decline, would mark much of Guatemala's history between 1970 and 1990. A reign of terror became firmly entrenched, with successive governments each going to greater lengths to contain the guerrilla threat and repress an increasingly unsatisfied populace from which the movement drew its support. At the heart of the matter was a system of government that ensured the continued prosperity of a wealthy minority to the detriment of a poor, landless, illiterate peasant class forced to work the elites' land. The demands of a growing urban middle class, meanwhile, were repressed with the help of the armed forces and right-wing death squads.

The United States, meanwhile, continued to pour money and logistical support into the increasingly bloody repression. Three years after the election of Carlos Arana Osorio in 1970, who was nicknamed "the butcher of Zacapa," 15,000 Guatemalans had been killed or disappeared. The United States did its share by training 32,000 Guatemalan policemen through the Agency for International Development (AID) via its public safety program. Guatemala's Policía Nacional was notoriously linked to the paramilitary death squads operating with impunity in the cities and countryside. Many off-duty policemen filled the ranks of these right-wing extremist groups, working parallel to, but with unofficial sanction from, the more traditional forms of counterinsurgency.

In 1971, another guerrilla unit, the Organización Revolucionario del Pueblo en Armas (ORPA, Revolutionary Organization of the People in Arms), was formed. The unit was led by Rodrigo Asturias, the son of Nobel Prize novelist Miguel Angel Asturias. It operated in the vicinity of Lake Atitlán, Quetzaltenango, San Marcos, and Suchitepéquez, setting up operations in a strategically important corridor between the highlands and the agriculturally rich coastal lowlands. ORPA spent eight years recruiting local combatants, then training and indoctrinating them into its ranks. Believed to be the most disciplined of the rebel organizations, it launched its first offensive in 1979 with the occupation of a coffee farm near Quetzaltenango.

Yet another guerrilla organization, the Ejército Guerrillero de los Pobres (EGP, Guerrilla Army of the Poor), exploded onto the scene in 1975 with the much-publicized execution of a notoriously ruthless Ixcán landlord. It had spent three years developing political consciousness among the peasantry in the remote Ixcán jungle, where it operated prior to launching its first assault. The Guatemalan military began increasingly violent reprisals against the peasantry living in remote jungle outposts, some of whom kept the guerrillas fed and supplied. In Ixcán, as well as throughout Guatemala, peasants would become increasingly caught in the cross-fire between the military and the rebel groups often serving as a scapegoat for the army's wrath.

On February 4, 1976, a massive earthquake struck the Guatemalan highlands, leaving 23,000 dead, 77,000 injured, and about a million homeless. The reconstruction efforts saw a renewed push to reform the inherent injustices of Guatemalan society with increased activity on behalf of the trade unions. In 1977, President Jimmy Carter, citing increasingly gross human rights violations, cut off military aid to Guatemala.

The 1978 elections were rigged to the benefit of Romeo Lucas García, who unleashed a fresh wave of repression against the usual victims but now also added academics, journalists, and trade unionists to the mix. The guerrilla war grew increasingly strong in rural Guatemala at this time, with the number of total combatants estimated at 6,000 distributed among the four guerrilla groups, along with some 250,000 collaborators. The guerrillas actively recruited from a historically disenfranchised peasant base, particularly in the Ixil and Ixcán regions, which only strengthened the army's resolve to do away with the insurgency and intensified punitive measures against real and perceived collaborators. Peasants, priests, politicians, and anyone perceived to have ties to the guerrillas were massacred in the thousands. It is estimated that 25,000 Guatemalans were killed during the four-year Lucas regime.

Many atrocities were committed by the Lucas regime in a spiral of violence—making the Spanish conquest look increasingly benign by comparison—including an army massacre in the village of Panzós, Alta Verapaz, and the firebombing of the Spanish embassy in Guatemala City during a peaceful occupation by peasant leaders. In Panzós, at least 35 peasants, including some children, lay murdered in the town square with dozens more injured or killed as they tried to make their escape. The occupation of Guatemala City's Spanish Embassy was carried out by Ixil peasants on January 31, 1980. Without regard for embassy staff or the Spanish ambassador, Policía Nacional forces stormed the embassy and firebombed it. The sole survivor was the Spanish ambassador. The victims included the father of Nobel Peace Prize winner Rigoberta Menchú, who recounts this and other atrocities in her book, *I, Rigoberta Menchú*. Spain severed diplomatic relations with Guatemala in the aftermath of the massacre, not restoring them until several years later.

In addition to the ambassador's survival, it should be noted that one of the peasant activists also survived the tragedy, only to be murdered a few days later by a paramilitary death squad while recovering in a local hospital.

In 1982, Guatemala's armed rebel groups—FAR, EGP, ORPA, and

PGT-FA—consolidated to form the Unidad Revolucionaria Nacional Guatemalteca (URNG, Guatemalan National Revolutionary Unity), which would go on to fight for its ideals as a political force, while continuing armed resistance, and negotiate a peace treaty with the government in 1996.

Efraín Ríos Montt

The 1982 elections were again manipulated by the extreme right, this time to the benefit of Aníbal Guevara, but a coup on March 23 orchestrated by young military officers installed General Efraín Ríos Montt as the head of a three-member junta. The coup leaders cited the rigging of elections three times in eight years as justification for their actions, which were supported by most of the opposition parties. It was hoped Guatemala could be somehow steered once again on the path of peace, law, and order and that the terror would stop.

Ríos Montt was an evangelical Christian with ties to Iglesia del Verbo, one of several U.S.-based churches gaining ground in Guatemala after the 1976 earthquake. Among his many eccentricities was the delivery of weekly Sunday night sermons in which he expressed his desire to restore law and order, eliminate corruption, and defeat the guerrilla insurgency, allowing for the establishment of a true democracy.

On the surface things did seem to get better, particularly in the cities, thanks to an odd mix of heavy-handed discipline and strict moral guidelines governing all facets of government operations. Montt, for example, made a regular show of executions of alleged criminals before firing squads. He also offered amnesty to the guerrillas during the month of June 1982, but only a handful of these accepted. Some later accounts of the Guatemalan civil war attribute this to communities being either held hostage by guerrilla occupation and unable to make the trip down from the mountains or simply too frightened and distrustful of the military.

Whatever the reason, the cool response to Montt's amnesty offer unleashed a new wave of counterinsurgency terror against the guerrillas and the indigenous peoples believed to be aiding and abetting them. Under a scorched earth campaign, entire villages were destroyed, with survivors being resettled into a series of so-called "model villages," allowing the army to keep a close watch on the peasantry while indoctrinating them with anti-Communist rhetoric. The repression was made worse by a new system of conscripted labor in the form of civil defense patrols (PACs) composed of rural peasants controlled by the army. PACs were forced to make routine night patrols and report any suspicious activities. Failure to do so would result in their own suspicion in the army's eyes, meaning further reprisals on their villages. In this way, two modern-day variants of important colonial structures survived well into Guatemala's recent history, the *congregación* and the *encomienda*.

An estimated 100,000 of Guatemala's indigenous Mayan descendants fled the violence, flooding refugee camps in neighboring Mexico or migrating farther north to the United States during the reign of Lucas García and Ríos Montt.

Cerezo and the Democratic Opening

Ríos Montt was eventually overthrown in August 1983 after just over a year in power by a military coup with U.S. backing. The underlying ideal was to get Guatemala firmly on the road back to democracy. Elections were called to take place in 1985, and General Mejía Víctores was installed as an interim chief-of-state. Repression in the countryside continued to escalate under the military's tireless scorched earth campaign. The Ixil Triangle alone saw the displacement of 72 percent of its population and the destruction of 49 villages. Totals for Guatemala at this time included the destruction of 440 villages and over 100,000 dead. In this context, the first free election in over three decades took place. A new constitution was also drawn up at this time.

Vinicio Cerezo Arévalo, a Christian Democrat, won the election with an overwhelming majority of the vote and widespread hope for change in Guatemala with the country firmly on the road to democracy. It was clear that the military still held the cards, however, and kept Cerezo under a tight leash via the Estado Mayor Presidencial, a notorious military security force officially charged with presidential protection but in reality designed to keep presidential power in check. Cerezo candidly admitted that the military still held 75 percent of the power.

Cerezo sought to give the democratic opening a chance, knowing that the military's power could not be broken in the five years his term in office would last, by taking a nonconfrontational approach to the demands of Guatemala's various societal sectors. He kept a happy courtship with the powerful business interests, landowners, and generals. Among the latter was his defense minister, General Héctor Alejandro Gramajo, who curtailed much of the violence in the countryside and allowed Cerezo to survive numerous coup attempts.

In September of 1987 the Central American heads of state convened in the eastern highland town of Esquipulas, where they signed a treaty aimed at bringing the pacification and democratization of the region. Costa Rica's Oscar Arias Sánchez would later win the Nobel Peace Prize for his role in bringing the peace plan to fruition. Esquipulas II, as it was called, would open the doors for peace negotiations between the Guatemalan government and the URNG.

Although the levels of repression and violence dropped, they by no means disappeared. The armed struggle continued in remote corners of the highlands and Petén, while death squads continued their reign of terror.

Formal labor organization was once again given the official go-ahead, and widespread protests marked much of Cerezo's later years as the average Guatemalan saw little economic improvement.

Jorge Serrano Elías

Barred from running for a second term under the 1985 constitution, Cerezo yielded power to his successor, Jorge Serrano Elías, in 1991. Also barred from running under the new constitution was Efraín Ríos Montt, though there was much speculation as to his role behind the scenes because Serrano had served in his government. The new constitution specifically prohibited anyone rising to power as the result of a military coup from running for president, a decision Montt has repeatedly tried unsuccessfully to have rescinded.

Indigenous rights advocates, already enjoying greater freedom since the democratic opening, received a huge bolster from the awarding of the Nobel Peace Prize in 1992 to activist Rigoberta Menchú Tum for her efforts in bringing worldwide attention to the genocidal civil war still raging on in the countryside. The Guatemalan military issued an official protest to what it saw as disgraceful approval for an advocate of Communist insurrection but removed its opposition on the wave of worldwide fanfare for the awarding of the prize to Menchú.

Guatemala's historical problems continued to plague the nation, and Serrano's incompetence at the helm soon became evident. The peace process stalled with the Catholic church's mediator accusing both sides of intransigence. Popular protests against Serrano's government, bolstered by corruption charges involving his suspected links with Colombian drug cartels, forced him to declare an auto-coup in May 1993. He assumed dictatorial powers, citing the country's purported spiral into anarchy, and also dissolved the congress, citing the gross corruption of the legislative body while calling for the election of a new one.

Widespread protests and the withdrawal of U.S. support for Serrano's government resulted in his removal from office just two days later. Congress met and voted on the appointment of Ramiro de León Carpio, the country's human rights ombudsman, to succeed Serrano and finish out his term.

De León quickly set about rearranging the military high command in an attempt to purge some of the more radical elements and achieve a measure of political stability, though it was clear his powers over the military were limited. The URNG declared a cease-fire as a measure of goodwill toward the new administration. The guerrillas made some progress with the new administration, eventually signing an accord on Indigenous Rights and Identity as well as a Human Rights Accord establishing the creation of U.N.-mandated MINUGUA to oversee the implementation of the peace accords once the final agreement was reached. Although optimistic at first, Guatemalans soon lost hope in the De León administration when they saw he was incapable of addressing crime, constitutional reform, and land and tax issues.

Alvaro Arzú Irigoyen

Former Guatemala City mayor Alvaro Arzú won the 1996 presidential elections thanks to a strong showing in the capital despite widespread electoral abstention elsewhere. Arzú, a businessman, represented the Partido de Avanzada Nacional (PAN, National Advancement Party), with deep roots in the oligarchy and a commitment to economic growth fostered by the development of the private sector under a free market. He quickly appointed new defense, foreign, and economic ministers and set out to sign a final peace accord with the URNG.

The agreement for a "Firm and Lasting Peace" was signed on December 29, 1996, in the Palacio Nacional de la Cultura, which once served as the presidential palace. After years of bloodshed, the final death toll stood at 200,000 with about 50,000 being cases of forced disappearance. A subsequent U.N. report by the Historical Clarification Commission (CEH) squarely placed blame for most of the violence in the hands of the military and the civil defense patrols, with 80 percent of the victims said to be of Mayan origin. "The majority of human rights violations occurred with the knowledge or by order of the highest authorities of the state," the report declared. It further stated that, "State terror was applied to make it clear that those who attempted to assert their rights, and even their relatives, ran the risk of death by the most hideous means. The objective was to intimidate and silence society as a whole, in order to destroy the will for transformation, both in the short and long term."

The ambitious peace accords marked the culmination of years of negotiations between the government and guerrillas; if properly implemented, they would serve as the basis for the construction of a completely different Guatemala. Unfortunately, the provisions set forth in the accord have yet to be fully adopted. One example of this disappointing trend was the failure to amend the constitution via a May 1999 referendum to officially redefine the country as "multiethnic, pluricultural, and multilingual," as stipulated in the Accord on Indigenous Rights and Identity. Voters stayed away from the polls in droves and the few who did vote decided against the reforms.

THE 1996 PEACE ACCORDS

In addition to officially marking the end of hostilities between leftist insurgents and the Guatemalan government, the U.N.-brokered 1996 peace accords established a starting point from which to address the historical grievances leading to the conflict and to begin the construction of a more equitable society. From the start, the agreements established a fact-finding mission known as the Historical Clarification Commission (CEH) to investigate culpability for wartime atrocities committed largely against the country's Mayan population. The CEH and an independent wartime inquiries body created by Guatemala's Catholic church, the Recuperation of the Historical Memory Project (REMHI), blamed the vast majority of atrocities on the army, with some violations also committed on the part of the guerrillas. Since the findings, many family members of victims of the civil war have sought to bring to justice those responsible for crimes against humanity, including genocide, torture, and illegal arrest. Because of the inadequacies of the Guatemalan judiciary, many have been forced to seek recourse in international courts, as in the case of the suit filed in a Spanish court under universal jurisdiction by the Rigoberta Menchú Foundation against eight government officials accused of crimes against humanity.

The accords also created an ambitious framework for reestablishing the rule of law as the country returned to peacetime, while seeking to address the war's underlying causes. In this regard, agreements were reached in the following areas: human rights, socio-economic and agrarian issues, the strengthening of civil society and the role of the

© AL ARGUETA

Guatemala's Policía Nacional Civil was created by the 1996 Peace Accords.

army in a democratic society, and the rights and identity of indigenous peoples. Interestingly, these were negotiated by the establishment of a consensus among various sectors of society working with the Guatemalan government to have their interests and demands addressed at the negotiating table.

The first accord in the long process of negotiations dating back to 1991 was the Human Rights Accord, signed in March 1994. While human rights were already guaranteed on paper in the 1986 constitution, the accord was significant in that it created a new mechanism for ending their systematic violation via a U.N. verification mission known as MINUGUA.

The Accord on Socio-Economic and Agrarian Issues officially recognizes poverty as a problem and hints at government responsibility to ensure the well-being of the general populace. It committed the government to increasing the tax base as a percentage of GDP from 8 percent (the lowest in the hemisphere) to 12 percent within the next four years. A glaring omission was the ubiquitous issue of land reform. The government's conservative economic policies and the need to get Guatemala's wealthy elite to support the peace process were undoubtedly behind the relative weakness of this accord's reach.

In contrast, a relatively far-reaching accord, if fully implemented, is the Accord on Strengthening of Civilian Power and the Role of the Army in a Democratic Society, signed in September 1996. It covers the demilitarization of Guatemalan society, in which the military has long had its tentacles, requiring far-reaching constitutional reforms in order to be fully implemented. The accord limits the role of the military to the defense of Guatemala's territorial integrity. It eliminated the much-hated Civil Defense Patrols and counterinsurgency security units while reducing the size and budget of the military by a third. It also created a new civilian police force to replace the notoriously corrupt Policía Nacional, with a mandate to guarantee citizen safety. Lastly, it mandates necessary reforms of the judicial system, to eliminate pervasive impunity. The importance of this last point cannot be understated, as the state of the judiciary serves as a type of barometer in the progress report for Guatemala's democratization. As the CEH described in its final report: "The justice system, nonexistent in large areas of the country before the armed confrontation, was further weakened when the judicial branch submitted to the require-

ments of the dominant national security model...by tolerating or participating directly in impunity, which concealed the most fundamental violations of human rights; the judiciary became functionally inoperative with respect to its role of protecting the individual from the state and lost all credibility as guarantor of an effective legal system. This allowed impunity to become one of the most important mechanisms for generating and maintaining a climate of terror."

The 1995 Accord on Identity and Rights of Indigenous Peoples issues a ground-breaking call to amend the 1985 constitution to redefine Guatemala as, "multiethnic, multilingual, and pluricultural." Its full implementation requires deep reforms in the country's educational, judicial, and political systems, laying the foundation for a new entitlement of Guatemala's indigenous majority to make claims upon the state and creating a new context for social interactions. It thus goes beyond mere antidiscrimination protections for Guatemala's indigenous majority.

The far-reaching accords offer hope for the construction of a brand-new Guatemala along more equitable lines. The implementation of the reforms called for in the accords, however, has been a daunting task. A major blow to the implementation of the peace accords came in 1999 after a constitutional referendum defeated 50 proposed reforms. Although the peace accords only called for 12 such changes, it is believed that many Guatemalans voted against the package of 50 reforms because they simply felt uninformed about what they were voting to approve. The government did little to explain the nature of the numerous complex reforms or

(CONTINUED ON NEXT PAGE)

THE 1996 PEACE ACCORDS (continued)

to promote their approval. Voter apathy was widespread, with just 18 percent of eligible voters participating in the referendum. In areas where voters were mostly in favor of the reforms, mainly the rural areas most affected by the civil war, voter turnout was generally less than in the capital, which voted overwhelmingly against them.

Whatever the reasons, failure to implement the key changes to Guatemala's legal framework to allow full implementation of the accords meant change would have to come via the legislature. In Guatemala, this is easier said than done. The Portillo administration, in office from 2001 to 2004, was particularly reluctant to implement the main elements of the accords or to use them as a basis for the elaboration of government policy. Observers pointed out that the peace process stalled, and in many cases receded, under Portillo. Among the most critical areas requiring immediate attention were human rights, justice, and security.

The peace accords were officially taken up again by the Berger administration, as government policy with concrete plans for new legislation to address many of the pending elements of the agreements. Many laws associated with the accords had trouble making their way through congress, however, in a legislative assembly that was notorious for its inability to reach consensus

on many issues. On a positive note, the reduction of the military by one-third was completed, as stipulated in the accords, and a plan for its modernization is currently in the works. Its official mandate now includes protecting the country's borders and combating drug traffic, environmental depredation, and smuggling of illegal immigrants.

In the end it can be said that the peace accords have brought some degree of benefit to Guatemalan society. Some of the agreements have been fully complied with, state repression has ended, and some opportunity for political participation has opened up in recent years. There are still, however, many lingering issues, including lack of security, poverty, socioeconomic exclusion, and a high degree of confrontation between varying sectors of society. Structural problems also persist, a case in point being the glaring deficiencies in the judiciary, leaving it open to manipulation and corruption while preventing it from being truly at the service of the country's citizenry. In essence, what we are seeing is a reflection of the peace accords' intimate connection to the process of Guatemala's continued democratization. Ironically, it is this very process of democratization that opened the door for the ending of the civil war via negotiations in the first place, and which will ensure that the spirit and the letter of the accords are eventually fulfilled.

The Catholic church issued its own report on the violence during the country's civil war, which also placed the blame for the majority of the atrocities in the hands of the military. Two days after issuing his report, Bishop Juan Gerardi Conedera was murdered in his garage, much to the outrage of the general populace. By this time, most political killings had all but ceased, and the murder sent shockwaves of indignation throughout Guatemalan society, which was clamoring for justice against Gerardi's killers. It soon became clear the act was a reprisal from military factions intent on demonstrating their continued hold on the country's power structure.

Subsequent investigations and attempts to bring the guilty parties to justice ended in frustration as key witnesses, prosecutors, and judges fled the country in the face of death threats. While political kidnappings and disappearances became mostly a thing of the past, the country's security situation drastically worsened in the aftermath of the civil war. Bank robberies, murders, extortionary kidnappings, and armed robbery were at an all-time high. Using many of the same methods as in the "disappearance" of thousands of Guatemalans, kidnappers unleashed a wave of terror in which 1,000 people were abducted in 1997 alone. The country, at the time, had the fourth-highest kidnapping rate in the world.

U.S. President Bill Clinton visited Guatemala in March 1999 for a summit meeting with the Central American presidents. In a surprising declaration, he expressed regret on behalf of the United States government for its role in the atrocities committed during the country's civil war, saying that U.S. support for military forces that "engaged in violent and widespread repression" in Guatemala "was wrong."

The crime spree was largely blamed on a power vacuum created during the departure of Guatemala's Policía Nacional and its subsequent replacement by the new Policía Nacional Civil, in accordance with the peace accords. The new police force was trained by experts from Spain, Chile, and the United States. It was hoped that a more professional police force would help bring greater security once fully established, but it quickly became evident that this was not the case. Meanwhile, political murders such as the Gerardi and Myrna Mack murders remained unresolved, shedding light on the lackluster state of Guatemala's judicial system, a situation exacerbated by widespread lynching of supposed criminals in remote areas where the rule of law was merely a vague concept.

Security issues aside, Arzú was a gifted administrator and government corruption remained at low levels, for Guatemala. Arzú's strengths as Guatemala City's mayor had always been infrastructure and public works. His time as president was no different in this regard, with various infrastructure projects being completed during his term in office. Guatemalans widely recognize his hard work backed by a concrete list of accomplishments, and he is still popular in opinion polls. If Guatemala were to ever allow former presidents to run in elections, it is speculated that Arzú might give opponents a run for their money.

Arzú also privatized many state entities, including the notoriously ineffi-cient telephone company, as part of a neoliberal economic approach to state participation in the economy. Guatemala's telecommunications laws have sub-sequently been heralded for their contributions to vast improvements in ser-vice coverage, increased competition, and lowered prices. At the end of Arzú's presidency, however, many critics pointed to a perceived affinity for serving the interests of Guatemala's wealthy elite, a criticism his successor would play largely to his advantage at the polls in the 1999 election campaign.

POST-WAR GUATEMALA
Alfonso Portillo and the "Corporate Mafia State"

During the 1999 elections, Alfonso Portillo ran on a populist ticket, hoping to lure the lower classes away from his main opponent, who was fashioned after Arzú. He promised to cut poverty by ending corruption and tax evasion. His party, the Frente Republicano Guatemalteco (FRG, Guatemalan Republican Front), was actually the brainchild of Ríos Montt, the mastermind behind some of the worst atrocities against Guatemala's indigenous peoples during the army's scorched earth campaign of the early 1980s. He was forbidden, once again, from running in the election. It never stopped him from trying.

Another important campaign issue, and one Portillo played masterfully to his advantage, was citizen safety in the face of skyrocketing crime rates. A long-past incident in Mexico whereby Portillo killed two men in self-defense before fleeing the country was dug up during the campaign but actually worked in his favor in machismo-dominated Guatemalan society. Portillo played off the incident as evidence that he was willing and able to take a hard stance on crime.

History has not been kind in its assessment of the Portillo administration. It can be confidently stated without fear of exaggeration that the Portillo admin-istration was one of the worst, if not *the* worst, of Guatemala's governments to date. Among the elements of his atrocious legacy was the solidifying of what analysts have called the "Corporate Mafia State," defined in a February 2002 Amnesty International report as, "The 'unholy alliance' between traditional sectors of the oligarchy, some 'new entrepreneurs,' elements of the police and military, and common criminals."

Among the few achievements under the Portillo administration was the 2001 conviction of three persons involved in the Gerardi murder. Although two military officers and a priest were tried and convicted of the murder, the general consensus was that the intellectual authors of the crime were still at large. Progress was also made in the case of the long-running saga of the murder of anthropologist Myrna Mack. The material author of the crime, Noel de Jesús Beteta, is currently serving a 25-year prison sentence. The intellectual author, Colonel Juan Valencia Osorio, was sentenced to 30 years in prison in 2002, but an appeals court granted his release the following year. Shortly after an order for his re-arrest and return to prison, Valencia escaped while under military custody, under dubious circumstances.

Meanwhile, Efraín Ríos Montt, the dictator who presided over some of the worst atrocities during the army's scorched earth campaign of the early 1980s, got himself elected president of congress. From his position, he and the military interests were said to run the show via the creation of a parallel power structure, while Portillo remained a convenient government front man. Corruption, always a problem plaguing Guatemala's governments, ballooned to unparalleled proportions. Scandals involved embezzlement by the Interior Minister as well as a highly publicized cover-up involving Ríos Montt himself.

In an event subsequently labeled "Guategate" by the local press, Ríos Montt and 19 other FRG congressmen were accused of secretly altering a liquor tax law, which had already been passed by congress, at the behest of powerful liquor interests. The altered rate lowered the tariffs by as much as 50 percent. When opposition parties denounced the illegal changes to the law, congressional records from the meeting disappeared, while other documents were falsified. Although a popular outcry arose to have Montt and the other congressmen stripped of their diplomatic immunity to stand trial for their actions, the crime remained in impunity, as is so often the case in Guatemala.

In May 2003, the FRG nominated Ríos Montt as its presidential candidate in the elections to be held in November of that year. Once again, his candidacy was rejected by the electoral authorities and by two lower courts, in accordance with the constitutional ban on coup participants running for presidential office. In July 2003 the Constitutional Court, with several judges appointed by the FRG, approved his candidacy for president, ignoring the constitutional ban that had prevented him from running in previous elections. Adding insult to injury, Ríos Montt had publicly (and correctly) predicted the margin by which he would win the decision prior to its announcement. Days later, the Supreme Court suspended his campaign for the presidency and agreed to hear a complaint presented by two opposition parties.

Ríos Montt denounced the ruling as tampering with the judicial hierarchy and issued veiled threats concerning possible agitation by supporters of his candidacy. Days later, on July 24, a day known as Black Thursday, thousands of ski-masked and hooded FRG supporters invaded the Guatemala City streets armed with machetes, guns, and clubs. They had been bused in from the interior by the FRG and were led in organized fashion by well-known FRG militants, including several congressmen, who were photographed by the press while coordinating the actions.

The demonstrators quickly targeted the offices of outspoken media opposing Ríos Montt's candidacy, holding an entire building hostage for several hours after trying to occupy it. They also marched on the courts and opposition party headquarters, shooting out windows and burning tires in city streets. Journalists were attacked, including a TV cameraman who died of a heart attack while running away from an angry mob. The rioters finally disbanded after the second day of riots when Ríos Montt publicly called on them to return to their homes.

Following the unrest, the Constitutional Court, laden with allies of Ríos Montt and Portillo, overturned the Supreme Court decision and cleared the way for Ríos Montt to run for president. A majority of Guatemalans were disgusted with his actions and the corrupt legacy of his party. They expressed their discontent at the polls, where Ríos Montt finished a distant third in the presidential race.

Óscar Berger Perdomo

The winner after a second, run-off election between the top two candidates was Óscar Berger Perdomo of GANA (Gran Alianza Nacional, or Grand National Alliance), a former Guatemala City mayor who represented the interests of the economic elite but surrounded himself with a diverse cabinet. Among them was Rigoberta Menchú, who was named the governmental goodwill ambassador for the peace accords, which the government promised to take up again.

The new government's first priority quickly became cleaning up the mess left behind by the FRG. The national treasury had been ransacked of more than US$1 billion, with corruption on an unprecedented scale involving theft, money laundering, monetary transfers to the army, and creation of secret bank accounts in Panama, Mexico, and the United States by members of Portillo's staff. Berger promised to bring corrupt officials from the FRG government to justice. Remarkably, he was able to make good on his promises, and many corrupt officials are now behind bars awaiting trial, although some have managed to escape prosecution due to the inefficiency and corruption still rampant in the country's judicial system. Portillo, meanwhile, quietly fled the country by slipping into El Salvador in the early morning hours of February 18, 2004, before flying from there to Mexico, where he still resides. Guatemalan authorities are still seeking his extradition on several charges.

Crime and lack of security continued to be problems affecting a wide spectrum of the population. Gang violence plagued Guatemala City and numerous other cities and towns. The police force increasingly came under fire for corruption, initiating a long process of cleansing out its corrupt elements in the hopes of making it more effective. In the face of the police force's inability to abate the continuing upswing in violent crime, which included 16 daily homicides, Berger was forced to integrate joint police-military patrols. These came under fire as evidence of increasing militarization, contrary to the 1996 peace accords.

The economic picture was severely disrupted when thousands of rural peasant farmers had their crops annihilated and their villages destroyed by Hurricane Stan in October 2005. Government reconstruction efforts in the storm's aftermath were slow in making it to affected communities.

Despite some public opposition, Berger was able to implement many of his neoliberal economic policies, including laws governing the concession of government services and construction projects to private entities, securing mining rights for multinational mining conglomerates, and the ratification of DR-CAFTA, the Central American Free Trade Agreement.

The judicial and legislative branches continued to come under fire for gross inefficiency and corruption charges. The existence of clandestine groups, a legacy of the corporate mafia state with links to state agents and organized crime, continued to plague the government. Meanwhile, the creation of a U.N.-sponsored Commission for the Investigation of Illegal Groups and Clandestine Security Organizations (CICIACS) was blocked by Constitutional Court rulings. A second, reworked version of the proposal, known as the International Commission Against Impunity in Guatemala (CICIG), was the product of an agreement signed between the United Nations and Guatemalan government in December 2006, though it would need congressional approval. The United States and other foreign governments offered financial support for the program, which was to be composed of expert international detectives providing material support to the Public Ministry in its investigations of parallel power structures.

In February 2007, the urgent need to get CICIG up and running was demonstrated by a heinous crime perpetrated against three visiting Salvadoran diplomats and their chauffeur, who were found dead shot execution-style and burned in their car on the outskirts of Guatemala City. Following an unprecedented investigation fueled by outrage from Salvadoran authorities, the perpetrators turned out to be high-ranking police officers from the Department of Criminal Investigations operating as contract killers. Things really came to a head when the captured policemen were executed by a death squad while awaiting questioning in a high-security prison just days later. Initial government statements and doublespeak had pinned the blame for the executions on fellow prison inmates, including gang members. The incident opened a can of worms in which high-ranking government officials have been implicated in the continued operation of death squads and ties to organized crime. The reconstruction of the Policía Nacional Civil, already a matter of national concern, came to the forefront following these incidents.

As Berger's presidency drew to a close, the general consensus was that his time as president was marked by mostly good intentions but also some modest gains, particularly in terms of a redress of Guatemala's historical ills. Among the glaring omissions was a long-term, inclusive strategy to develop rural areas, where the majority of Guatemala's indigenous peoples live. Delays in the reconstruction process after Hurricane Stan were continually cited as symptoms of weak leadership and an inability to coordinate efforts to reach a common goal.

Among the positive aspects of his presidency were infrastructural projects, or *megaproyectos,* including new roads and airports to make Guatemala more attractive to investors. The creation of so-called *gabinetes móviles* (mobile cabinets) was also a welcome aspect of Berger's administration, allowing those in rural areas the opportunity to have their demands personally addressed by the president and his cabinet members during visits to their towns and cities. Continued economic growth and a more favorable investment climate were duly recognized by international financial organizations. The full effect of DR-CAFTA, which officially took effect on July 1, 2006, remains to be seen.

The 2007 Elections

The 2007 elections featured an interesting mix of presidential hopefuls, including Rigoberta Menchú and well-known evangelical pastor and radio personality Harold Caballeros. The front-runners were Álvaro Colom, a self-proclaimed social democrat of the UNE party (Unidad Nacional de la Esperanza, or National Unity for Hope), and Otto Pérez Molina of the Partido Patriota (Patriot Party), an ex-military hardliner whose main campaign promise was to combat Guatemala's rapidly deteriorating security situation with a "strong hand." To no one's surprise, Pérez Molina and Colom would eventually face each other in a November run-off election when none of the dozen or so presidential candidates received a majority vote in the September polls.

CICIG became a hot campaign issue in July 2007 after two rogue UNE party congressmen inexplicably voted against its creation during a congressional assembly, despite assurances by Colom that he and his party were pro-

CICIG. This also raised questions about whether or not Colom truly held the reins of power over UNE, questions that came to the forefront when one of these congressmen, party Adjunct Secretary General César Fajardo, was accused of master-minding a plot against Colom's campaign manager, José Carlos Marroquín. The attempt on Marroquín's life was supposedly in retaliation for the firing of ex-military personnel (formerly members of ex-president Portillo's security team) from Colom's security detail. CICIG was eventually approved by Guatemala's congress on August 1, 2007.

The weeks leading to the November run-off were a thrill ride, with both candidates vehemently accusing each other of corruption. Newspapers readily dished out the dirt on both of the candidates' supposed past follies and present hypocrisy. Voters, meanwhile, feared Pérez Molina's "strong hand" policies would return Guatemala to the dark ages of the civil war, but they were also suspicious of Colom's appeals to social democracy, which smacked of demagogy and were vaguely reminiscent of the Portillo campaign. It should be noted Pérez Molina, a retired army general, was part of the reformist wing of the Guatemalan military and was a signer of the 1996 peace accords, so it's not clear just how militarized his policies may have become once in power. Persistent rumors of ties to organized crime continued to haunt the UNE party during the campaign, but in the end Colom's appeals to Guatemala's mostly poor indigenous majority won him the victory in the countryside, though he was decidedly the loser among Guatemala City voters. As is usually the case for Guatemalan voters, their choice for president came down to what (or who) they perceived to be the lesser of two evils.

Álvaro Colom

Shortly before taking office, Vice President Rafael Espada, a well-known former Houston heart surgeon, told MSNBC that, "Guatemala is sick, very sick, in intensive care." Colom chose Espada as a running mate in part because of his credibility with Guatemalan elites, though some had doubts regarding his limited political experience. The foreign press was generally kind in its assessment of Colom and was happy to back a social democrat with the U.S. government seal of approval. He told the Associated Press he was confident his government could make Guatemala more conciliatory and that he and Espada knew the country's problems inside and out.

As usual, however, campaign promises led to few tangible results during the early days of the administration, despite a much-touted "100 Day Plan" to combat nagging grievances such as spiraling crime rates and a generally somber economic outlook. It became clear early on that the oft-quoted

U.S. bumper sticker reading: "If you're not completely appalled, you haven't been paying attention," might also be applied to Guatemala's new government. These early days were marked by a palpable sense of a lack of direction on the part of the Colom government, as it reacted (or failed to react) to one issue after another.

Colom and Espada frequently made contradictory statements to the press, especially concerning government officials who were to be removed from office. Colom was apparently bent on cleaning house and quickly requested the resignation of many government officials, some of whom had good service records, replacing them with some

Wildlife poaching is fueled by land grabs in Guatemala's national parks.

very questionable appointments. The removal of Civil Aviation Director José Manuel Moreno Botrán, in favor of a coffee farmer whose only connection to civil aviation was a private pilot's license, is a particular case in point. The official reason for the removal was supposedly financial malfeasance in the construction of Guatemala City's new airport, though evidence to back these claims was never found. It should be noted that the International Civil Aviation Organization (ICAO) oversaw the funding and execution of the project in its entirety.

On at least two occasions, Colom completely butchered the names of his new appointees, as if he had no idea who he was talking about. Making matters worse, and a matter of national disdain, is Colom's marked speech impediment.

At about the same time, the press started reporting on a surprising element of power behind the scenes, First Lady Sandra Torres de Colom. It became a matter of public scrutiny that she was also in fact presiding over cabinet meetings. Torres de Colom was placed at the helm of the newly created Council for Social Cohesion, which oversees the health and education ministries, among others. The legal framework creating the mechanism granted her tremendous powers and complete control over a US$282 million budget free from any third party oversight. Torres de Colom, according to several analysts, in fact became Guatemala's co-president, usurping powers that would normally fall under the jurisdiction of government ministers and the vice president.

Colom faced a number of crises just weeks after taking office. Land grabs involving huge areas of Guatemala's national parks by peasants working on behalf of powerful drug traffickers were widely publicized, but the government seemed powerless to do anything to stop them. One of these peasant groups in the Izabal *departamento* went so far as to kidnap four Belgian tourists, demanding their release in exchange for that of their organization's leader, imprisoned weeks before. The prisoners were released days later by security forces, following a nebulous operation in which one peasant was shot to death.

Other government scandals included donations of private aircraft by members of the Guatemalan elite for personal use by Colom during official state visits abroad. Although Colom initially made declarations to the effect that the government was paying for these services, subsequent investigations found this not to be the case. The greatest scandal in Colom's first three months in office involved the firing of security consultant Víctor Rivera, a naturalized Venezuelan who presided over investigations involving drug trafficking, kidnapping, bank robberies, and other important cases, including the murder of three Salvadoran diplomats in February 2007. He had worked with three successive governments, but his contract was abruptly terminated by Colom in April 2008. Days later, just minutes after granting a candid interview to

© NASA

An aerial view of the acres of Guatemalan tropical forests that go up in flames yearly.

THE GUATEMALA-BELIZE BORDER DISPUTE

During your travels in Guatemala, you might be surprised to find the neighboring country of Belize included as part of Guatemala on many maps produced in-country. It would seem that Belize is just another Guatemalan *departamento* despite its status as an independent nation since 1981. Guatemala did not in fact recognize its neighbor's independence until 10 years later in a highly criticized and unconstitutional move by President Jorge Serrano Elías. Guatemala's constitution clearly states that any decision regarding the independence or territorial integrity of Belize must be submitted to a public referendum. And so, the debate continues over the "Belize question." It seems to be one of those issues that just won't go away, with succeeding governments always promising a final solution to this centuries-old problem.

Several governments have used the issue as a diversionary tactic during times of civil unrest, particularly during the military regimes of the 1970s. Matters came to a head in 1977 when Great Britain sent 6,000 troops to the border in anticipation of an invasion by Guatemalan troops during the presidency of military strongman Romeo Lucas García. Today, there are occasional reports of incidents along the northern Petén region's eastern border with Belize when Guatemalan peasants are forcefully evicted from the no-man's land along the border in clashes with Belizean security forces. The border is often referred to as a *zona de adyacencia,* or imaginary border area. Guatemalan newspapers love to publicize these incidents of supposed injustice against unarmed peasants, calling for a final solution to the long-standing problem.

The dispute dates back to colonial times, when Spain officially claimed all of the Central American coast but was unable in practice to enforce its claim. English privateers and traders established a beachhead along the southern coast of Belize and extracted valuable timber products, including mahogany. The English presence was officially recognized by Spain in 1763, granting the British the right to extract forest products but

the daily newspaper *Prensa Libre,* Rivera and his secretary were intercepted in a drive-by shooting that left Rivera dead, his secretary injured, and 18 bullet holes in his white Toyota Starlet. The government remained silent for two days after the murder, adding to suspicions that they were probably behind it, though only human rights champion Helen Mack would dare go on record saying so.

Other scandals during the first year in office included the uncovering of wiretaps and unauthorized surveillance in the Palacio Nacional and presidential offices by unknown sources. In October 2008, ex-president Alfonso Portillo returned to Guatemala from his Mexican exile after his visa expired. Although he should have faced numerous charges on counts of well-documented financial malfeasance during his administration, he was released on bail the same refusing them the right of permanent settlement. The first permanent settlements came soon after Central American independence from Spain, the British clearly taking advantage of the power vacuum created in the aftermath of Spanish rule. The weakness of Guatemala's early governments was evident in an 1859 treaty that officially recognized the British presence and "lent" the Belize territory to them for further resource extraction in exchange for a payment of £50,000 and the construction of a road from Belize to Guatemala City. Great Britain never held up its end of the bargain on either point, and so the treaty was rendered null and void. British occupation of the lands continued, however, and the land eventually became known as the colony of British Honduras, which was granted its independence from England in 1981.

In recent years, Guatemala has limited its claims to the southern half of Belize, from the Río Sibún to the Río Sarstún, arguing that historical documents support its claims and include this territory as part of the region of Las Verapaces. Some Guatemalan analysts believe there might be a case here, though the reasons for Guatemala's insistence in this matter remain a mystery. Belize has repeatedly stated that it will not cede "a single inch of its territory," but in December 2008 both countries agreed to take the issue to the International Court in The Hague after Organization of American States-mediated negotiations reached a stalemate. In early 2009, both Belize and Guatemala were preparing referendums to officially obtain their electorates' consent to submit the dispute to international arbitration.

It's doubtful Guatemala will ever be able to recover its full claim, though the possibility for co-management of the Sapodilla Cayes Marine Park (also claimed by Honduras) as a tri-national park might be the most realistic outcome of any internationally mediated settlement on this matter. It would give Guatemala the one thing its geography and tourist offerings lack: white-sand Caribbean beaches with clear, turquoise waters.

day. Many saw this as evidence that Colom and Portillo were in cahoots, an accusation Colom vehemently denied during TV broadcasts in which he addressed the nation after returning from yet another trip abroad.

As Colom's first year in office came to a close, many were already looking forward to the 2011 elections. They cited the country's worsening security situation as their biggest complaint against Colom. Meanwhile, the president denounced a supposed plot intended to destabilize the government, ending with the ultimate goal of his assassination. Analysts widely accused him of crying wolf and attempting to gain sympathy. They also cited his claims as being the product of alienation from prominent societal sectors most Guatemalan presidents succumb to as they find themselves unable to further their intended policies for lack of political negotiating power.

On May 10, 2009, prominent Guatemala City lawyer Rodrigo Rosenberg was assassinated while bicycling in Zona 14. The next day, a video surfaced in which he plainly accused the government of orchestrating his death. In the video, recorded just days before his death, Rosenberg states, "If you are hearing this message, it means that I, Rodrigo Rosenberg Marzano, was murdered by the president's private secretary, Gustavo Alejos, and his associate Gregorio Valdez, with the approval of Mr. Alvaro Colom and Sandra de Colom." The alleged reason for the murder given by Rosenberg was his representation of Mr. Khalil Musa and his daughter Marjorie Musa, who were murdered in April 2009. The circumstances surrounding the Musas' murder were still being investigated, but Rosenberg claimed it was a government plot to silence opposition to government corruption in Guatemala's Banrural, including claims of money laundering and using it as a front to fund campaign funds for a future run for office by Sandra Torres de Colom. Mr. Musa had been appointed to Banrural's board of directors, but his appointment was withheld by the government over a period of three months prior to his murder.

Rosenberg fought valiantly for the solving of the Musas' murder and had received death threats in the days leading up to his murder. In light of these allegations, an outraged Guatemalan populace took to the streets demanding Colom's resignation. Colom, meanwhile, denied any wrongdoing and ordered a full investigation. He also orchestrated counter-demonstrations with UNE party affiliates, bussing in supporters to the capital from the provinces. At this writing, the murders were still being investigated by CICIG, though many of the assertions made by Rosenberg in his video were corroborated through other sources, most importantly evidence of Musa's pending appointment to Banrural. An eyewitness also stepped forward with information regarding the identities of three of the six material authors of Rosenberg's murder, which were provided to CICIG and the FBI, who were aiding in the investigation.

Government

ORGANIZATION

Guatemala is a constitutional democracy. The president is the chief of state, assisted by a vice president, both of whom are elected to office for a single four-year term. The president is constitutionally barred from a second term, but the vice president may run for office after a four-year hiatus from office. The Congreso de la República is the national (unicameral) legislative body, currently consisting of 158 members. Congressmen serve four-year terms running concurrently with the presidential term. Guatemala has 22 administrative subdivisions (departments) headed by governors appointed by the president. Popularly elected mayors or councils govern Guatemala City and 331 other municipalities.

JUDICIAL SYSTEM

The judicial branch is independent of the executive branch and the legislature and consists of a Constitutional Court and a Supreme Court of Justice. The Constitutional Court is the highest court in the land and consists of five judges elected for five-year terms, with each judge serving one year as president of the court. Congress, the Supreme Court of Justice, the Superior Council of the Universidad de San Carlos de Guatemala, and the bar association (Colegio de Abogados) each elect one judge, and the president appoints the fifth. The Supreme Court of Justice consists of 13 magistrates who serve five-year terms and elect a president of the court each year from among their members. The judiciary suffers from a poor public image because of suspicions that it has become porous to influence from drug traffickers as well as being corrupt and inefficient.

ELECTIONS

The current power balance is a product of the 1985 constitution formulated before the country's official return to democracy in 1986. A series of reforms in 1993 shortened terms of office for president, vice president, and congressmen from five years to four; for Supreme Court justices from six years to five; and increased terms for mayors and city councils from two and a half years to four.

Between 1954 and 1986, Guatemala was ruled primarily by a military-oligarchy alliance that installed presidents periodically via widely fraudulent elections or military coups. In the few elections considered free and fair during this time period, the military quickly stepped in to assert its dominant role while ensuring that the president remained a figurehead. All of the elections from 1985 onwards have been considered free and fair, though the military still holds much power in Guatemala, probably more so than in any other Latin American country. Much of Guatemala's democratic process has consisted of a gradual strengthening of the state while trying to limit the power of the military. Other general characteristics of the democratic process have been the growth of citizen participation from all sectors of society in an atmosphere of greater freedom concurrent with the gradual strengthening of institutions having extremely limited experience with governance under a democratic system.

POLITICAL PARTIES

Guatemala's political parties constitute a veritable alphabet soup and change from year to year depending on the capricious nature of alliances between different factions. Parties are unstable, to say the least, and no party has won a presidential election on more than one occasion. As an election approaches, a fresh batch of newly formed parties begins to make the rounds. The ruling party following the 2007 elections was the Unidad Nacional de la Esperanza, or UNE (National Unity of Hope). Some of the other parties, in order of their percentage of congressional seats, are the Gran Alianza Nacional (GANA), Partido Patriota (PP), Frente Republicano Guatemalteco (FRG), Encuentro por Guatemala (EG), and Partido Unionista (PU). The Unidad Revolucionaria Nacional Guatemalteca (Guatemalan National Revolutionary Unity, also URNG-MAIZ) is the political party formed by the former guerrilla movement, which fought against the government during the country's 36-year civil war. It holds two congressional seats.

BUREAUCRACY

There is still a long way to go in the consolidation of a genuine functioning democracy in Guatemala. The judiciary and legislative branches are badly in need of reform and have lost virtually all credibility with their constituents. The current situation is still very much like that described in 2000 by the Asociación de Investigación y Estudios Sociales (ASIES) (Guatemalan Institute of Political, Economic, and Social Studies), a nongovernmental organization:

> In our society, agents or former agents of the state have woven a secret, behind-the-scenes network dedicated to obstructing justice. They have created a virtual alternative government that functions clandestinely with its own standardized and consistent modus operandi. In such a context, crimes are not clarified, and those responsible are not identified. Society finally forgets the cases and becomes resigned.
>
> If the actual material authors left evidence at the scene of their crimes, they then decide who to implicate as scapegoats. If there are actually any inquiries and if these eventually lead to any arrests, these are always of low-ranking members of the army, or at best, an official not in active service.
>
> When they can't pin the crime on some scapegoat, the scene of the crime is contaminated and legal proceedings are obstructed and

proceed at a snail's pace. If, nonetheless, investigations still continue, these powerful forces hidden behind the scenes destroy the evidence. And of course it cannot be forgotten that pressure, threats, attacks, and corruption are all part of the efforts to undermine and demoralize the judiciary, who, knowing they are not able to count on a security apparatus that will guarantee that the law is enforced, feel obliged to cede in the face of this parallel power.

The powerlessness of the Guatemalan judiciary has forced some people to seek remedies for their grievances in international courts under universal jurisdiction established by the United Nations concerning crimes against humanity. One example is the suit filed before the Spanish National Court in 1999 by the Rigoberta Menchú Foundation against eight former Guatemalan officials, including General Efraín Ríos Montt, for murder, genocide, torture, terrorism, and illegal arrest. The case seeks to try those responsible for wartime abuses and centers around the 1980 attack on the Spanish Embassy in Guatemala City that claimed the lives of 37 peasant activists, among them Menchú's father, and embassy staff. The Spanish court has heard other cases involving genocide and established a precedent for universal jurisdiction in the 1998 arrest of Chile's General Augusto Pinochet in the United Kingdom. He remained in custody for 14 months until British authorities ruled Pinochet was unfit for trial and let him return to Chile.

In July 2006, a Spanish judge ordered the detention of all eight accused after an unfruitful visit to Guatemala with the intention of gathering testimonies from plaintiffs and questioning the accused. Ríos Montt and General Mejía Víctores effectively paralyzed the process with a series of appeals upheld by the Constitutional Court. Menchú admitted the difficulty of getting Guatemalan officials to execute the arrest orders, calling it, "A test of the Guatemalan justice system."

As for the legislature, there is currently talk of reducing the number of congressmen, elected partly by proportional representation. The Guatemalan congress has suffered in recent years from a gradual erosion of confidence on the part of its constituents because of gross inefficiency, corruption, and growing suspicion of widespread links to drug trafficking. In essence, a majority of Guatemalans view their congressional body as practically useless and expensive to maintain.

Political parties, likewise, have suffered a gradual decline in credibility. The general pattern since 1986 has been one of great expectation for change prior to elections and the installation of a new government, followed by disappointment with the new government's failure to deliver on its promises, ending in frustration and renewed hope for change with the next round of elections. The government of Álvaro Colom appeared to be no exception to this pattern after its first year in power. Opinion polls point to a growing desire to see the emergence of better leadership and an authentic political class, something Guatemala still lacks.

Economy

Guatemala's gross domestic product in 2005 was US$27.5 billion, an increase of 3 percent over the previous year, with a per capita GDP of about US$2,000. Inflation was about 9 percent for the same year. Although it is the largest economy in Central America, large sectors of the population remain only marginally active in the economy. Guatemala is also the region's most populous country. The economy has been growing steadily since the 1996 peace accords and has demonstrated macroeconomic stability.

AGRICULTURE, TRADE, AND INDUSTRY

Agriculture accounts for 23 percent of GDP, with agricultural exports of coffee, sugar, bananas, cardamom, vegetables, flowers and plants, timber, rice, and rubber being the chief products. Guatemala exported US$3.8 billion worth of goods in 2005, with 75 percent of these being agricultural products. Light industry contributes to 19 percent of the GDP and manufactures include prepared food, clothing and textiles, construction materials, tires, and pharmaceuticals. The service sector accounts for 58 percent of Guatemala's GDP. The United States is Guatemala's biggest trading partner, accounting for over half of the country's exports and a third of its imports. Other important trading partners include the neighboring Central American countries, Mexico, South Korea, China, and Japan.

In terms of employment, agriculture is the largest employer, with half of the population employed by this sector. Services, bolstered by tourism, employ 35 percent of the population, and industry employs the remaining 15 percent. Unemployment in 2003 was 7.5 percent.

After the signing of the 1996 peace accords, Guatemala appeared poised for rapid economic growth, but a financial crisis in 1998 disrupted the expected pace. Despite gains in industry, the country's economy still showed much of its historical susceptibility to world commodity prices, specifically coffee. A collapse in coffee prices severely impacted rural incomes and brought

© AL ARGUETA

Coffee is big business in Guatemala.

the industry into a serious recession, though exports of this commodity have bounced back since then.

Foreign investment has remained weak, with Guatemala unable to capitalize on foreign investment to the same degree as its neighbors. A notable exception to this is the privatization of utilities. Potential investors cite corruption, crime and security issues, and a climate of confrontation between the government and private sector as the principal barriers to new business.

Guatemala's economy is dominated by the private sector, which generates about 85 percent of the GDP. The government's involvement is small, with its business activities limited to public utilities, many of which have been privatized under a neoliberal economic model, and the operation of ports and airports and several development-oriented financial institutions. The Berger administration passed legislation allowing for more private sector concessions of services in 2006.

The U.S.–Dominican Republic–Central America Free Trade Agreement (DR-CAFTA), was ratified by Guatemala on March 10, 2005. Priorities within DR-CAFTA include the elimination of customs tariffs on as many categories of goods as possible, opening services sectors, and creating clear and easily enforceable rules in areas such as investment, customs procedures, government procurement, electronic commerce, intellectual property protection, the use of sanitary measures for the protection of public health, and resolution of business disputes. Import tariffs were lowered as part of Guatemala's membership in the Central American Common Market, with most now below 15 percent.

Other priorities include increasing transparency and accountability in Guatemala's public finances, broadening the tax base as part of the peace accords, and completing implementation of reforms of the finance sector. The implementation of these changes involved reforming Guatemalan laws and a long, involved process in the national legislature. The process finally ended in June 2006, with DR-CAFTA officially taking effect on July 1, 2006, after the U.S. Department of Commerce officially certified the country in compliance with the trade agreement.

The ratification of DR-CAFTA was met with protests in Guatemala City. Its detractors feared the loss of jobs, increased dependence on food imports, and a broadening of the deep gap between Guatemala's rich and poor. Peasant organizations and at least one NGO calculated the loss of up to 100,000 jobs in the agricultural sector. The government offered to counteract perceived imbalances through a series of credits supporting small and medium-sized businesses, which employ more than 70 percent of the population and are the engine of the rural economy. Nontraditional export sectors were quick to point out the treaty will create an estimated 50,000 new jobs in nontraditional agriculture in the first two years of its implementation. Whatever the result, the implementation of DR-CAFTA will certainly involve major adjustments requiring the strengthening of agro-industry, and small farms in particular, via expansion to new markets and the application of new technologies, among other things.

Another major contributor to Guatemala's economy is the money sent home by 1.5 million expatriate Guatemalans living and working in the United States. In 2008, this amounted to US$4.3 billion, which Guatemalans on the receiving end used to supplement their incomes, start businesses, and put into savings. This phenomenon has helped to widely ameliorate the country's endemic poverty and accounts for almost 12 percent of the GDP. Although dollar amounts for money sent from abroad showed continued growth in 2008, Guatemalans feared an increase in deportations of Guatemalan nationals from the United States would negatively impact the local economy.

DISTRIBUTION OF WEALTH

It remains to be seen whether DR-CAFTA will aggravate or alleviate Guatemala's skewed wealth and land distribution patterns, which are already some of the most unequal in the world. The wealthiest 10 percent of the people receive almost half of all income, and the top 20 percent receive two-thirds. About 80 percent of the population lives in poverty, with two-thirds of that number living in extreme poverty and surviving on less than US$2 a day. Belying these patterns of wealth and income distribution are Guatemala's social development indicators, such as infant mortality and illiteracy, which are among the worst in the hemisphere. Chronic malnutrition among the rural poor worsened with the onset of the late-1990s coffee crisis and devastation wrought by Hurricane Stan in 2005.

TOURISM

On a much more positive note, tourism has greatly impacted the economy in recent years, particularly since the end of the civil war in 1996. In 2004, Guatemala received one million visitors for the first time and increased visitor numbers have continued in the years since. In 2007, Guatemala registered 1.6 million foreign arrivals with a tourism expenditure totaling US$1.2 billion. According to the World Tourism Organization, between 2003 and 2004 Guatemala had the largest increase of international arrivals of any country in the Americas, with a growth of 34.3 percent. Guatemala's tourist arrivals doubled between 2003 and 2007. In Central America, only Costa Rica receives more visitors.

About 30 percent of Guatemala's visitor arrivals come from North America, with another 34 percent coming from Central America, particularly El Salvador. U.S. visitors may be closing the gap, however, as statistics from the peak Easter travel season of 2006 show more Americans arriving in Guatemala than Salvadorans. Approximately 18 percent of Guatemala's tourists come from Europe, and another 18 percent come from various other countries.

Much of the money generated by tourism stays in local hands, as many communities have been able to capitalize on their proximity to area attractions by catering to the demands of an increasing number of visitors. Foreign tourism investment is limited mostly to main tourist areas, and local entrepreneurs have done an excellent job of filling in the void created by the lack of foreign investment.

The government, meanwhile, is actively promoting tourism abroad via ad campaigns sponsored by the state tourism agency, INGUAT (Instituto Guatemalteco de Turismo), and investing in much-needed infrastructural improvements to the country's airports. The industry also got a boost from the filming of the CBS television series *Survivor* in the rainforests of Petén, which aired in 2005.

The main obstacle to the continued growth of Guatemala's tourism industry is security, and the Guatemalan government is actively working to make travel safer for visitors to Guatemala. Among the improvements in visitor security is the establishment of tourism police (Politur) in the main tourist destinations. In many places, their presence has resulted in fewer occurrences of robbery and assault.

PEOPLE AND CULTURE

Guatemalans are a complex breed. First, there are the city-dwellers, who are as cosmopolitan as the residents of any North American city of comparable size. Social stratification, racism, and classicism also figure prominently into the makeup of many middle- and upper-class Guatemalans, in particular those living in urban areas. You may even find urban Guatemalans downright rude, though they are careful to put on their best appearances for foreigners.

Then there are Guatemala's rural poor and middle class. You'll find most of them warm and friendly; you may even be the object of their gracious hospitality. If you're a real "salt of the earth" kind of person, you'll fit right in. If you decide to stay in Guatemala, you may have to get past some cultural isolationism, as rural Guatemalans are naturally suspicious of outsiders once you set out to get past the informal, superficial relationships of a passing traveler. This is not surprising given the country's penchant for violent social upheaval, class struggle, and an unfortunate more recent phenomenon, rising crime statistics.

© AL ARGUETA

Let's face it; the country has its fair share of social problems, and you will have to learn to live with these while attempting to make a go of things down here. Perhaps the greatest challenges for expat residents living in Guatemala are the constant contradictions between wealth and poverty. There's really no way around this, and after a while you'll start to see it everywhere. It colors your daily life in seemingly innocuous ways like traveling on a Guatemala City highway over a bridge overlooking slums built into a ravine on your way to lunch at a fancy Zona 10 restaurant in your friend's late-model BMW. It also colors your day-to-day interactions with people and you'll see it in the myriad ways Guatemalans treat each other.

It's no secret that the country has a legacy of violence from which it is still trying to recover. Its governments and leaders, with few exceptions, have mostly stayed in power long enough to rape the country of its resources and contribute to the wealth of fellow cronies while turning a blind eye to crime, social inequality, and widespread violence. The general populace seems resigned to live in a country where things simply happen, where governments make promises and then fail to deliver, where the rich will continue living their privileged lives and the poor will continue to somehow survive. Perhaps this is all the legacy of Spanish colonial government and the clashing of two very distinct cultures from opposite ends of the earth. Maybe it's the legacy of 36 years of civil war. What is certain is that Guatemala's cultural and sociopolitical makeup is a subject of much academic speculation, and you will certainly come to form your own opinions after some time living here.

I realize I haven't painted a very pretty picture of my fellow Guatemalans here. It's just sometimes difficult to live in such a beautiful country with so many sad contradictions. Part of living in Guatemala will involve you finding a way to live with the contradictions and keep your sanity. It may even involve you fighting to bring about change against seemingly overwhelming odds, as many upstanding Guatemalans and foreigners do. You may find allies in the strangest of places as you embark on your quest to make Guatemala a better place and live by example. It's all part of the experience.

This section will help you take the pulse of Guatemala's unique heartbeat and prepare you for the culture shock that is living in Guatemala. It's good to know what you're getting into.

Ethnicity and Class

DEMOGRAPHICS

Guatemala's population is one of the fastest-growing in Latin America, with 2004 census figures placing the population at just over 14 million. The annual growth rate was 2.61 percent, and 43 percent of the population is under the age of 15. The country's population density is 116 people per square kilometer, with an urban-to-rural ratio of 38.7 percent to 61.3 percent. Population density is much less in the northern Petén department, comprising a third of Guatemala's total land area but harboring only about 5 percent of the population. Urbanization is greatest in the western highlands region centered around Guatemala City and Quetzaltenango.

ETHNIC DIVERSITY

Guatemala has an incredible wealth of ethnic diversity, as attested to by the as-of-yet-unfulfilled push to amend the national constitution to officially describe the country as "pluricultural, multilingual, and multiethnic." The country is divided about evenly between descendants of indigenous Maya (comprising 21 different linguistic groups) and *ladinos,* who are of Mayan descent but have adopted European culture and dress in addition to the Spanish language. A sizable percentage of the population is a mixture of Mayan and European, also known as *mestizo.* A much smaller percentage of the population is of purely European descent, primarily from Spanish and German families, and they control a disproportionate fraction of the country's wealth. Many of these are direct descendants of the *criollo* (New World Spanish-born elite) families dominating the country's economy since colonial times. Indigenous Maya descendants are found in greatest numbers in the western highlands, with Guatemala City, the Pacific, Caribbean, and Petén lowlands being largely *ladino.*

Roughly half of Guatemalans are of Mayan descent.

Additionally, there are two non-Mayan ethnicities thrown into the mix, Xinca and Garífuna. Only about 100–250 Xinca-speakers remain, confined to a small area near the Salvadoran border. The Garinagu (plural of Garífuna), a mixture of Amerindian and African peoples, arrived from St. Vincent via Roatán, Honduras, in the early 1800s and settled in the Guatemalan Caribbean coastal town of Lívingston. Their culture is more similar to that of the Western Caribbean, with whom they identify more readily, than the rest of Guatemala.

Mayan Groups

Ethnicity and language are intertwined when it comes to Guatemala's principal Mayan groups, which include K'iche', Kaqchikel, Tz'utujil, Mam, Ixil, Q'eqchi', Poqomchi', Poqomam, and Q'anjob'al. By far the most numerous group is K'iche,' with nearly one million speakers. Just over 400,000 people speak Kaqchikel, and there are about 686,000 Mam speakers.

ECONOMIC CLASS STRUCTURES
The Oligarchy

The direct result of Guatemala's Spanish colonial legacy granting privileges to Spanish-born elites is the modern-day oligarchy. In many cases, families can trace their roots to these colonial-era *criollo* families. As in neighboring El Salvador, where there is frequent reference to "The Fourteen Families," the Guatemalan oligarchy has a strong history of intermingling to the exclusion of outer echelons of society. For the purpose of this discussion, the oligarchy will also encompass the "new rich" and the subsequent generations of landowning business elites who remain firmly in control of Guatemala's politics and economy.

Much has been written about the Guatemalan elite's support for right-wing governments and military policies aimed at eliminating the threat of Communist subversion during the country's civil war (1960–1996). Although the war had genocidal aspects, it was also very much related to the distribution of wealth and the 1950s-era reforms that threatened economic elites' hegemony. In essence, the oligarchy allied with the military in an attempt to maintain the status quo.

The oligarchy also found a willing ally in the Unites States, which was happy to support Guatemalan elites in their emulation of U.S. consumption patterns and the expansion of private enterprise. Stephen Connely Benz, in his book *Guatemalan Journey,* provides some interesting insights on Guatemala's oligarchy and the way in which U.S. government aid via the U.S. Agency for International Development (USAID) may have unknowingly exacerbated

Guatemala's inequitable social structures. He argues that capitalism, prior to the arrival of USAID, already functioned in its most brutal form in Guatemala, and he points to the history of "the conservative oligarchy and the essentially feudalistic economic system that remained the principal obstacle to a more equitable distribution of wealth." He goes on to say that, "This oligarchy did not care for democracy, modernization, or even economic liberalism; what it cared for was the perpetuation of an extremely lucrative arrangement... It was, in short, a segment of society that had long gotten its way and was principally interested in maintaining its privileges—reform was the furthest thing from its interests, unless by economic reform one meant lower export taxes, privatization of services, and the liberalization of price controls." In essence, Benz argues, U.S. aid money given to support agro-industry and free enterprise went directly to the oligarchy and thus helped perpetuate the continuance of a "wildly unjust, cash-crop-driven economy that necessitated U.S. aid for the impoverished masses in the first place."

More recently, the Guatemalan elites' uncontested hold on the reins of power can be seen in the stalling of the 1996 peace accords. Although the accords contain many provisions that would contribute to make Guatemala a more just society, the vast majority of these reforms have fallen by the wayside. Ironically, the major economic reforms taking place since the signing of the peace accords largely involve the lower export taxes and privatization of services Benz speculated about.

On a practical level, you can see the Guatemalan elite at fancy restaurants, shopping malls, and hotel lobbies in Guatemala City. You'll recognize them by their entourage of bodyguards, nannies to mind the children, and chauffeur-driven late model luxury cars. They'll greet each other in courteous fashion and it will seem like everyone in the restaurant knows each other and is part of the same tight-knit clan. On a positive note, absent large quantities of U.S. foreign investment in Guatemalan real estate and tourism infrastructure, the oligarchy's presence has given Guatemala the condos, office buildings, and five-star hotels it would otherwise lack.

The Upper and Middle Classes

Guatemala's upper class has close ties to the oligarchy, and there is a bit of a gray area where the two intersect. Social class in Guatemala is very much about putting on appearances in an attempt to gain favor with the upper echelons of society. Statistically, Guatemala has the third-highest per capita private aircraft ownership in the Americas, which gives you some idea of the purchasing power of wealthy Guatemalans. The country's wealth can also be seen in the fact that many homes that would be considered high-end in neighboring Central American countries such as Nicaragua and Honduras would be quite middle class in Guatemala. To give you an idea of how this is possible, keep in mind that the wealthiest 10 percent of the population receives almost one-half of all income and the top 20 percent receives two-thirds.

Some might argue that Guatemala has no true middle class, but I would disagree. Middle class in Guatemala most certainly looks different than it does in the United States and even compared to neighboring Central American countries. It's also proportionally smaller, but not altogether nonexistent. You'll find most of the country's middle class living in urban areas such as Guatemala City and Quetzaltenango.

Lower Classes

It's no surprise that, in a country where race and social standing go hand in hand, the vast majority of the country's poor are of Mayan descent. This applies to those living in poverty in highland villages and urban slums or trying to eke out a living in the Petén lowlands. About 80 percent of Guatemala's population lives in poverty, with about two-thirds of that number living in extreme poverty on less than US$2 a day. Guatemala's social indicators, such as infant mortality and illiteracy, are among the worst in the hemisphere.

Customs and Etiquette

You'll find most Guatemalans are warm and friendly. In many instances, they will be very curious about you as a foreigner, particularly in areas that are still getting accustomed to a growing presence of foreign travelers and residents. Urban and rural settings have varying degrees of formality, though politeness and good manners are appreciated by Guatemalans from all walks of life and will get you far.

DRESS AND APPEARANCE

Guatemala is in many ways a rather formal and conservative country, probably owing to its legacy of colonialism and its status as the main base of regional power for the Spanish colonial aristocracy. It's a very class-conscious society, with good grooming, neat dress, and cleanliness coming to be expected. In many instances, the way you look is the way you'll be treated. You'll notice this the first time you go to a Guatemala City shopping mall (especially on weekends) and see well-dressed urbanites going for a cup of coffee or heading out to see a movie. Sneakers and shorts are considered much too casual for many events foreigners would find them perfectly acceptable for. This is starting to change, however, and you'll also see younger Guatemalans wearing shorts, T-shirts, and flip-flops typical of the Abercrombie & Fitch look that is also wildly popular with Guatemalan youth from wealthy families. If you plan on going out to dance clubs, be sure to bring a good pair of shoes, as you won't make it past the front door wearing sneakers. Dress is much more relaxed at the beach or in the countryside.

For business travelers, suits are still very much the norm for men. Professional women tend to wear conservative dresses or two-piece suits. The less affluent will pay careful attention to dress as neatly as possible, especially for trips to the capital or other urban centers.

Backpackers, known as *mochileros,* often get a bum rap as an unkempt group who contribute very little to the economy and only cause trouble for hotel owners and tourist service operators. This is generally manifested as a form of marked distrust, though this is usually not the case in places that cater to these types of travelers as their main clientele, such as budget hostels.

ETIQUETTE

The formality of Guatemalan culture also extends to etiquette. Guatemalans take titles seriously (including *doctor* or *doctora* for doctors, *profesor(a)* for a professor or teacher, and *licenciado(a)* for an attorney or holder of a bachelor's degree). Whenever possible, they should be used when addressing the individual in person or via correspondence. Women usually greet men and each other with air kisses. Men will greet friends with a handshake different from the standard business handshake. Grips tend to be firm. When meeting someone for the first time, it's customary to say, *"mucho gusto"* (a shortened version of "nice to meet you"). Simply saying *"hola"* is considered too casual. Other greetings include *"buenos días"* (good morning), *"buenas tardes"* (good afternoon), and *"buenas noches"* (good evening). Particularly in rural areas, people will greet each other with one of these as they pass each other along the trail, road, or street. In urban settings, you'll often hear one of these greetings when someone walks into a place of business, like a doctor's office, for example. Another formality is the use of *"buen provecho"* (bon appetit) when walking into a restaurant where people are eating and *"muchas gracias"* upon getting up from the table after a meal.

Photographing People

It's never a good idea to photograph Mayan people without their permission, as they consider it highly offensive and it intrudes upon their spiritual beliefs. The old photographers' rule contending that it's easier to apologize (for taking a candid photo) than to ask permission doesn't really apply in Guatemala. This is especially true concerning photographs of children, and you should be careful not to show them undue interest and attention, as persistent rumors of foreigners involved in child-snatching of Guatemalan children for organ transplant abroad have led to mob incidents on at least two occasions, with two people killed and one seriously injured. (The last incident was seven years ago in the village of Todos Santos.) In both cases, the foreigners were trying to photograph a child. This scenario is most plausible in the highlands, though not exclusively so.

It can be understandably difficult at times to refrain from taking photographs, because Mayan children (and Mayan people in general) are especially beautiful and can provide some wonderful opportunities for portraiture or candid shots. On the up side, the situation forces you to interact with the locals and get to know them. You'll soon find that many are willing to let you photograph them (often for the promise of sending them a photo), and your photographs will be better because of the rapport you've established with the subject.

GUATEMALAN BEHAVIOR
Confianza and Saving Face

One of the main traits of Guatemalan behavior is what is known as being *en confianza*. Attaining this level in your interpersonal relationships means having a high level of openness, trust, and comfort with those you are *en confianza* (in confidence) with. Once you have reached this level in your relationship with someone else, you will most likely be visiting their home and sharing a few meals. *Confianza* is just as important for making friends as it is for doing business and overall success in Guatemalan society. You can erode your *confianza* by displaying character flaws such as losing your temper in public or dressing inappropriately, but Guatemalans will never confront you directly. Instead they will do what is known as "saving face." There may be a perceptible chill in their demeanor toward you.

Another player in the Guatemalan social lingo is the concept of *pena,* directly linked to the concept of saving face. To have *pena* is to feel badly, as in the case of imposing on your host or needing to say something unpleasant or accusatory. North Americans are very direct and to the point, which is not at all how Guatemalans are. They will go to great lengths to avoid the *pena* of having to tell you something or ask something of you they are not comfortable with.

North Americans (or those who have spent extended periods of time there) often find this idiosyncrasy quite frustrating. Vice President Rafael Espada, who spent several years as a prominent surgeon in Houston prior to being elected to office, highlighted this characteristic during an interview with *Prensa Libre* following his first year back in Guatemala. He said this face-saving mechanism whereby people will tell you what they think you want to hear was one of his biggest frustrations. Espada said it was hard to get things done when people have given you assurances that the wheels are set in motion when oftentimes they haven't even started on what you asked them to do in the first place.

Conversation

Guatemalans tend to use the *vos* form of *tú* (you), a derivative of the archaic *vosotros* now used only in Spain. This is particularly the case with two men of the same age or similar social standing. It shouldn't be used to address a person of perceived lesser social stature, as it's somewhat demeaning when used in this way, though upper-class Guatemalans tend to do it anyhow. Stick to the formal *usted* unless the person switches to the informal *tú* or *vos*.

Related to the above concept of *pena* is that you need to keep in mind what people are saying in between the lines. Guatemalans tend to beat around the bush, so to speak, and you must use a keen sensitivity to the subject at hand (and the speaker) to decipher what is being implied.

Personal Space and Privacy

Guatemalans might be a bit "touchy feely" by North American standards. It's not uncommon to see two heterosexual male friends walking with their arms around each other. This is more common with school-aged children, however. Guatemalans generally greet each other with hugs and kisses (or air kisses if it's a stranger of the opposite gender). They will also grab your arm when trying to emphasize a point. I have a beloved uncle who does this quite frequently.

North Americans' love for privacy might at times seem strange to Guatemalans. This is something to keep in mind if you are living with a host family. What might seem like a normal degree of privacy to you may seem like seclusion and isolation, on your part, to them. Most host families who have had a number of North American visitors have grown accustomed to this.

Gender Issues

Guatemala is a Latin country and is certainly no exception to the cultural prevalence of machismo. Among its characteristics are cat-calling attractive women as they walk by while simultaneously holding a mother's or sister's virtue and personal safety in high esteem (and defending it with utmost vigor). Most Guatemalan women simply ignore unwanted advances and cat-calling. Following the long-established traditions of machismo, it is not at all uncommon for men to have a mistress, though the aforementioned Guatemalan characteristic making openly displayed vice unacceptable means you won't find men bragging about their exploits or flaunting them quite as much as in some neighboring Central American cultures.

However, violence toward women is one of Guatemala's societal ills. Hardly a day goes by without some headline related to an assault or murder against a woman.

WOMEN TRAVELING ALONE

Solo female travelers and residents might find themselves the object of unwanted attention. Guatemalan women are accustomed to fairly constant harassment by men on the street, including cat-calls, whistling, and horn-honking, which they tend to ignore. This is usually the best tactic, though it's somewhat difficult to put into practice. Take a deep breath and count to 10. Your best bet as a preventive measure in this regard is to dress demurely, particularly in urban areas. Although much less likely, there's also the possibility of being groped by a passing stranger. It usually happens in an instant, with nary a second glance from the perpetrator. If it should come to a case of a lingering pervert, some Guatemalan women will scream at the perpetrator something along the lines of *"cerdo"* (pig), which usually scares him off. The last thing he wants is to be confronted in public, and he certainly wouldn't expect it. Foreign women tend to be common targets for men who just can't keep their hands to themselves. Women should never walk alone in Guatemala after dark.

LOVE, MARRIAGE, AND FAMILY

Guatemalans are extremely family-oriented. Marriage is still wildly popular as an institution, though Guatemalans are no strangers to loveless marriages, divorce, or single-parent homes. Divorce and single-parent homes are more prevalent in the "modern" society of Guatemala City, though there are many orphans and one-parent homes in highland areas affected by the violence of the civil war. Machismo also dictates the prevalence of extramarital affairs and the occasional fathering of illegitimate children.

Most Guatemalans are married by their mid-20s, but as in the United States those going for graduate degrees tend to wait a little longer. Two-income homes are becoming increasingly popular, so parents often hire nannies to look after their children. Wealthy Guatemalan women, whether or not employed, tend to favor nannies to assist in the child-rearing process.

It seems that many visiting foreign females in Antigua have a local boyfriend. Perhaps it's the allure of the exotic or an appreciation for the rugged masculinity displayed by some Guatemalan men that makes them attractive to *gringas*. You'll no doubt encounter many a Guatemalan-American couple during your time in Guatemala. On the flip side, Guatemalan men appreciate the confidence and independence exhibited by some North American women. North American men tend to like the generally submissive and respectful attitude many Guatemalan women show toward their husbands.

Family bonds are very strong, and it's not uncommon for mothers-in-law to live with married couples if there's no one else for her to live with. Social time is spent largely with family members, and it can be difficult to break into people's social circles as an outsider because of these strong family bonds.

GAY AND LESBIAN CULTURE

The prevalence of machismo can make things difficult, if not downright dangerous, for gay and lesbian couples choosing to express mutual affection publicly. Gay and lesbian travelers and residents will want to keep a low profile while in public areas in Guatemala so as not to attract unwanted attention. Homosexuality is still not widely accepted in Guatemala, and many commonly used slurs and epithets apply directly to gays. Still, things may be starting to change, as Guatemalans are quick to emulate the cultural standards they see on international TV, specifically the greater acceptance of gay men and lesbians portrayed in the U.S. media. Acceptance of homosexuality, in this way, appears directly linked to socioeconomic status or at least access to cable television. Some openly gay Guatemalans live with their partners and are open about their relationships with friends and family, though financial and social independence figure prominently into this decision.

As is the case anywhere in the world, religious beliefs and prejudices vary and affect how gay men and lesbian women are treated in any society. It all depends on the individual. I've witnessed innkeepers issue disparaging remarks about gay and lesbian guests behind their backs, but I've also run into uncommon acceptance of homosexuality.

As in any other international city, there's a growing gay and lesbian movement in Guatemala City, where there are a number of gay bars and nightclubs, mostly in Zona 1. As with most venues, things are constantly changing, so log on to www.gayguatemala.com for the latest.

Religion

Religion in Guatemala is fairly complex, with traditional Mayan spirituality still very much a presence, particularly in the highlands, along with Catholicism and the more recent incursions of evangelical Christianity. In much smaller numbers, Guatemala's Jewish population is centered in Guatemala City. There is also a small Muslim population with at least one mosque in Guatemala City.

MAYAN SPIRITUALITY

Mayan spirituality has its origins in pre-Columbian religious practices and a cosmology that venerated natural phenomena, including rivers, mountains, and caves. The soaring temples of the Maya and other Mesoamerican civilizations were built to mimic mountains and were usually built in alignment with the cardinal directions. The solstices were very important in this regard, and many of the temple pyramids and observatories were built in precise fashion so as to mark these events. Caves were also sacred to the Maya and believed to be passages to the underworld, a belief that persists to this day. Archaeologists speculate that at least one powerful economic center, Cancuén, lacked buildings of strictly religious significance due to its proximity to the massive Candelaria cave network nearby.

The Mayan calendar is still in use in parts of Guatemala today, particularly the western highlands, and is pegged closely to the agricultural cycle. Maize is a sacred crop and is believed to have been the basis for the modern formation of man by the gods, as told in the K'iche' book of myths and legends, the *Popol Vuh,* discovered by a Spanish priest in Chichicastenango in the 18th century. Although the vast majority of the Maya's sacred writings were burned by Bishop Diego de Landa in a 16th-century Yucatán bonfire, three Mayan texts, known as codices, survive in European museums. The *Chilam Balam* is another sacred book based on partially salvaged Yucatecan documents from the 17th and 18th centuries.

Modern-day Mayan religious practices, also known as *costumbre,* often take place in caves, at archaeological sites, and on volcanic summits. They often include offerings of candles, flowers, and liquor with the sacrifice of a chicken or other small animal also thrown in for good measure.

Another curiosity of the western highlands is the veneration of a folk saint known as Maximón or San Simón with a particularly persistent following in Santiago Atitlán and Zunil. The cigar-smoking, liquor-drinking idol is a thorn in the side of many Catholic and evangelical groups whose followers sometimes profess conversion to Christianity but often still hold allegiance to Maximón, who is thought to represent Judas and/or Pedro de Alvarado. Syncretism, combining Mayan religious beliefs and Catholicism, is a major player in highland Maya spirituality.

The cult following of folk saints is also tied to the presence of *cofradías,* a form of Mayan community leadership with roots in Catholic lay brotherhoods wielding religious and political influences. The *cofradías* are responsible for organizing religious festivities in relation to particular folk saints, and a different member of the *cofradía* harbors the Maximón idol in his home every year.

THE CATHOLIC CHURCH

Catholicism has played an important role in Guatemala ever since colonial times, though the state increasingly took measures to limit its power starting in the late 19th century, when liberal reformers confiscated church property and secularized education. More recently, the church wrestled with its official mandate of saving souls and its moral obligation to alleviate the misery and injustice experienced by many of its subjects, particularly the Maya. Many parish priests, faced with the atrocities and injustices of the civil war, adopted the tenets of liberation theology, seeking a more just life in the here and now and officially opposing the military's scorched earth campaign throughout the highlands. Many clergy paid for their beliefs with their lives or were forced into exile. Even after the civil war ended, Bishop Juan Gerardi was murdered in the days following his issuance of a scathing report on civil war atrocities perpetrated mostly by the military. The church remains a watchdog and defender of the poor, which is evident in the ongoing work of the Archbishop's Human Rights Office.

Although there are many churches throughout the country, the Catholic church often has trouble finding priests to fill them, a factor that has contributed to the explosive growth of evangelical Christianity. Pope John Paul II visited Guatemala three times during his term at the helm of the Vatican; the last visit was for the purpose of canonizing Antigua's beloved Hermano Pedro de San José Betancur.

Catholicism can still draw a big crowd, though; most noticeably during Holy

Week, with its elaborate processions reenacting Christ's crucifixion, and the annual pilgrimage to Esquipulas on January 16 to pay homage to the Black Christ residing in the town's basilica.

EVANGELICAL CHRISTIANITY

According to some estimates, a third of Guatemala now claims adherence to Protestantism and, more specifically, evangelical Christianity. The growth of this sect will become obvious as you travel around the country and hear the sounds of loud evening worship services, known as *cultos,* emanating from numerous churches, particularly in the highlands. The trend toward evangelical Christianity dates to the aftermath of the 1975 earthquake, which destroyed several villages throughout the highlands. International aid agencies, several of them overtly Christian, rushed into Guatemala at a time of great need and gained many grateful converts in the process. During the worst of the civil war violence of the 1980s, many Guatemalans sought comfort in the belief of a better life despite the hardships of the present. Other factors making evangelical Christianity attractive to Guatemalans include the tendency toward vibrant expressions of faith, spontaneity, and the lack of a hierarchy, making spiritual leaders more accessible to common people.

A notorious legacy of Guatemala's trend toward Protestantism was the dictatorship of Efraín Ríos Montt, a prominent member of Guatemala City's Iglesia El Verbo (Church of the Word), who sermonized Guatemalans on subjects including morality, Christian virtues, and the evils of Communism via weekly TV broadcasts. Meanwhile, a scorched earth campaign aimed at exterminating the guerrilla presence raged on in the highlands, though violence in the cities was widely curtailed and order somewhat restored. He faces charges of genocide in a Spanish court, though it's doubtful he will ever be brought to justice. Also disturbing was the brief presidency of Jorge Serrano Elías, another self-proclaimed evangelical currently exiled in Panama after he dissolved congress in a failed auto-coup ending in his ouster a few days later. His government faced widespread corruption charges.

On a more promising note, it is a well-documented fact that some Guatemalan villages have converted to evangelical Christianity almost in their entirety, with astounding results. The town of Almolonga, near Quetzaltenango, is a particular case in point. Alcoholism, which once ran rampant (as in other parts of the highlands), is now virtually unheard of, and the city jail has been closed for years. It is hailed as a "miracle city" by evangelical leaders, who like to point out that it was once a hotbed of cult worship for the folk idol Maximón.

The town exports its fantastic fruits and vegetables to El Salvador, including carrots the size of a human arm, making it very prosperous.

Evangelicals these days, while still adhering to the belief in a better afterlife, are also very much focused on making things better in the here and now. There is a growing movement toward producing a generation of morally grounded political leaders with a vision to develop the country along inclusive lines that address Guatemala's substantial needs and challenges, though it remains to be seen if they can overcome the unfortunate legacy handed to them by the substandard Christian leadership experienced by Guatemalans thus far.

The Arts

LITERATURE

Guatemala's first literary figure was Jesuit priest and poet Rafael Landívar (1731–1793). A native of Antigua, his most well-known work is *Rusticatio Mexicano,* a poem describing rural customs of the times. Landívar was forced to leave Guatemala in 1767 when his order was expelled from the Americas by the Spanish crown. The country's best-known writer is Miguel Ángel Asturias (1899–1974), winner of the 1967 Nobel Prize in Literature. His most famous works include *El Señor Presidente* (1946), about the maniacal dictator Manuel Estrada Cabrera, and *Hombres de Maíz* (1949, translated as *Men of Maize*) about the Mayan peasantry. One of the characters in the latter is a guerrilla warrior by the name of Gaspar Ilom, a name that Asturias's son Rodrigo, influenced by his father's writings, would appropriate as a pseudonym while leading one of the guerrilla factions of the Unidad Revolucionaria Nacional Guatemalteca. Other of his well-known works include *El Papa Verde* (1954, *The Green Pope,* about the United Fruit Company) and *Weekend en Guatemala* (1968, about the 1954 coup that ousted Jacobo Arbenz Guzmán).

Modern Guatemalan authors of note include Francisco Goldman, author of several novels, including *The Long Night of White Chickens,* which takes place mostly in Guatemala; *The Ordinary Seaman* (1997), and *The Divine Husband* (2004). Arturo Arias is another modern-day author known for having written the screenplay for the movie *El Norte* and the book *After the Bombs,* chronicling the Arbenz period and the aftermath of his overthrow. Víctor Perera has written several excellent books on Guatemalan culture and history, including *Unfinished Conquest* (1993) and *Rites: A Guatemalan Boyhood* (1986).

VISUAL ARTS

Guatemala's rich history in the visual arts dates to pre-Columbian times, with the painting of exquisite murals and the carving of stelae by the Maya. The colonial period also left a substantial artistic legacy, mostly by anonymous artists. An exception is the work of Thomas de Merlo (1694–1739), whose paintings can still be seen in Antigua's Museo de Arte Colonial. Sculptor Quirio Cataño carved the Black Christ of Esquipulas in 1595, now an object of much veneration attracting pilgrims from all over Central America.

More recently, Kaqchikel painter Andrés Curruchich (1891–1969) pioneered the primitivist style of painting from his hometown in Comalapa, Chimaltenango.

The currents of *indigenismo* ran strongly throughout the 20th century and were marked by an often-romanticized portrayal of indigenous culture, as evidenced by the murals found in Guatemala City's Palacio Nacional de la Cultura, which are the work of Alfredo Gálvez Suárez (1899–1946). Also in this vein was sculptor Ricardo Galeotti Torres (1912–1988), whose works include the giant marimba sculpture found in Quetzaltenango and the Tecún Umán statue in the plaza of Santa Cruz del Quiché.

Perhaps Guatemala's best-known visual artist, Carlos Mérida (1891–1984) was a contemporary of Pablo Picasso, whom he met while studying painting in Paris between 1908 and 1914. His *indigenista* art pre-dates the work of Mexican muralists the likes of Diego Rivera by about seven years and sought to unify European modernism with themes more specific to the Americas. Mérida's work exhibits three major stylistic shifts throughout the years: a figurative period from 1907 to 1926, a surrealist phase from the late 1920s to the mid-1940s, and a geometric period from 1950 until his death in 1984. Many of his works can be seen in Guatemala City's Museo de Arte Moderno, which bears his name. Mérida's murals also grace the walls of several Guatemala City public buildings.

© AL ARGUETA

Sculptures by Efraín Recinos adorn the exterior of Guatemala City's airport.

Another artist whose work adorns Guatemala City architecture is sculptor and engineer Efraín Recinos, designer of the city's Centro Cultural Miguel Ángel Asturias. A large Recinos mural composed of blue and green tiles was formerly housed inside La Aurora International Airport but was recently demolished as part of the airport renovation project. The large, white sculptures lining the airport's exterior facade were also created by Recinos and have been restored and incorporated into the terminal's new design.

In March 2007, Guatemala City hosted a sculpture festival with the participation of 12 internationally acclaimed artists working over a two-week period to create unique art pieces from blocks of marble. It was the first event of its kind held in Central America.

ARCHITECTURE

In addition to the well-documented architectural legacy of the Maya, Guatemala is also known for its baroque architecture, found mostly in Antigua and Guatemala City cathedrals and government buildings. This style of architecture is a Spanish adaptation to local conditions marked by the prevalence of earthquakes, with squat, thick-walled structures designed to weather numerous tremors throughout the years. Architecture in rural towns and villages tends to be rather functional with a recent trend toward grotesque multistory concrete buildings replacing more traditional construction. Classic forms of rural architecture consist (or consisted) largely of whitewashed adobe houses with red tile roofs.

Guatemala City has its fair share of assembly line high-rise condominiums, though it also has some noteworthy modern architecture. If you have an interest in this topic, a recommended book is *Six Architects* (Ange Bourda, 2002), filled with wonderful color photographs chronicling the work of six Guatemala City architects who merged into a single firm and are responsible for several of the city's nicest buildings.

In April 2007 the Parisian Grande Arche de la Défense played host to a fascinating 48-image exhibit by photographer Ange Bourda chronicling the rich history of Guatemalan architecture from pre-Columbian times to the present.

MUSIC

Guatemala's national instrument is the *marimba,* a huge wooden xylophone with probable African origins. You'll often hear marimba in popular tourist regions such as Antigua, where its cheerful notes can be heard emanating from garden courtyards housed in the city's larger hotels. Pre-Columbian musical instruments consisted largely of drums, wooden flutes, whistles, and bone rasps. An excellent place to check out the history and origins of Guatemala's highland Maya musical traditions is Casa K'ojom, just outside Antigua in Jocotenango.

It's also not uncommon to hear music with Mexican influence in Guatemala, with the occasional mariachi band contracted to liven up a birthday party. *Tejano* and *ranchera* music can often be heard. You'll also hear American rock bands here and there, sometimes on bus rides, though the sounds favored by bus drivers seem to have gotten stuck somewhere around 1984.

On the Caribbean coast, the Garífuna population tends to favor the mesmerizing beats of *punta* and reggae, with variations including *punta rock* and *reggaeton,* English-Spanish rap laid over slowed-down Caribbean-style techno and reggae beats.

Grammy Award–winning rock musician Ricardo Arjona is Guatemala's best-known international recording artist. He resides in Mexico City. Spanish-language pop and rock are, of course, also widely heard throughout Guatemala.

CRAFTS

Guatemala is world-famous for the artistic quality and variety of its crafts, with weaving at the top of the list. Each village has its own unique style, and you can recognize villagers from a particular location based solely on their traditional attire. Among the most fascinating hand-woven pieces are *huipiles,* embroidered blouses worn by highland Maya women featuring colorful motifs that often include plants, animals, and lightning bolts in a dizzying array of colors. While you are certainly welcome to purchase village attire, it's never a good idea to wear it around while in Guatemala, as indigenous peoples find this highly offensive (or downright hilarious, at best). Many people buy *huipiles* to frame and hang as home decor,

© AL ARGUETA

Weaving is a way of life in Guatemala.

laying the blouse flat with the large head opening at its center or hanging it from a wooden rod. You can see examples where this has been tastefully done in numerous Antigua boutique hotels.

Jade jewelry mined from local quarries is a popular item in upscale shops in Antigua. Primitivist paintings are popular in the villages of San Pedro and Santiago, on the shores of Lake Atitlán. For wool blankets, check out Momostenango, though you can also find them in markets throughout the country. The best wood carvings are found in the village of El Remate, in the northern Petén department, though traditional wooden ceremonial masks are still an item found exclusively in the western highlands.

Sports and Recreation

HIKING
Guatemala's terrain, featuring mountains, volcanoes, and vast forested flatlands, is a hiker's dream. Adding to the allure of hiking in Guatemala is the opportunity to interact with locals along the way. Many hiking circuits in Guatemala, particularly in the Verapaz cloud forests and the plateaus of the western highlands region, are operated via local community tourism initiatives. In addition to providing the opportunity to see the environment and culture through the eyes of local inhabitants, hiring the services of community guides also provides locals with a much-needed source of income and instills a sense of pride in their home. It also speaks loudly to the value (both economic and moral) of conserving precious ecosystems when tourists come from faraway lands to enjoy them.

Among the most popular hikes are the summits of several of Guatemala's 33 volcanoes (some active), including Agua, Acatenango, Pacaya, San Pedro, Santa María, and Tajumulco.

Many tourism circuits operated by local community tourism initiatives include adequate visitors centers, and there are often campsites. The same is true for the government-run system of parks and protected areas.

PARKS AND PROTECTED AREAS
Guatemala has over 90 protected areas encompassing about 28 percent of the country's total land area. Among the different types of protected areas are biosphere reserves, national parks, biotopes, natural monuments, wildlife refuges, and private nature reserves. Several of these are encompassed within larger areas, as is the case with the national parks and biotopes making up the larger

Maya Biosphere Reserve. Most of Guatemala's protected areas, including the biosphere reserves, have been created since 1990. All of Guatemala's volcanoes are protected areas. There are also laws in effect to protect endangered wildlife species; among these are Guatemala's big cats and parrots.

The Comisión Nacional de Áreas Protegidas (CONAP, National Protected Areas Council) is the entity charged with administering Guatemala's protected areas. It was created in 1990, along with the Comisión Nacional del Medio Ambiente, which oversaw broader environmental matters and was replaced in 2000 by the Ministerio de Ambiente Y Recursos Naturales (MARN, Ministry of the Environment and Natural Resources). CONAP has been historically underfunded and undermanned, leaving few resources with which to protect vast areas of land from invasion. Private conservation groups have stepped in to assist CONAP in its mandate, and there are now several parks co-administered or primarily administered by private organizations. A specially trained police force began operating in Guatemala's protected areas in 2005, particularly in the Maya Biosphere Reserve, aided by M-16s and AK-47s to combat well-armed timber and wildlife poachers. All the parks have at least rudimentary ranger stations. In an ongoing effort to attract more park visitation, many have excellent facilities for guest accommodations and well-marked trails.

BIKING

Road biking is a fairly popular sport in Guatemala, particularly in the highlands, where mountain roads offer unique challenges of strength and endurance. The country even has its own version of the Tour de France, known as La Vuelta Ciclística a Guatemala (The Biking Circuit of Guatemala). The event takes place yearly sometime in August.

More popular with visitors, mountain biking is increasingly popular in the hills around Antigua and Lake Atitlán thanks in part to a number of excellent local outfitters.

ROCK CLIMBING

Rock climbing is a relatively new phenomenon in Guatemala, though there are now at least two outfitters specializing in this activity. The rock faces fronting Lake Amatitlán, near Guatemala City, and an area known as La Muela (The Molar, also known as Cerro Quemado), near Quetzaltenango, are the prime climbing spots. Difficulty ratings of the various routes range from 5.8 to 5.13. It's also possible to rappel inside a waterfall, also known as canyoning, in Jalapa and other areas.

BEACHES

While Guatemala is not as well known for its beaches as some of its Central American neighbors, it nonetheless boasts some nice stretches on both the Pacific and Caribbean coasts. On the Pacific, the wild black-sand beaches found along the coast near the Manchón Guamuchal wetlands are one of the region's best-kept secrets. If you're escaping the chilly highlands from Quetzaltenango for some sand and surf, other good bets include Tilapa, Tilapita, and Playa El Tulate. The closest beach to Guatemala City is Puerto San José, reached in about 90 minutes by a four-lane highway, though it's certainly not the most pleasant of the country's beaches. Just west of San José is Chulamar, with at least one recommended resort hotel.

Farther east, there are some lovely stretches between Iztapa and Monterrico. The 25-kilometer road connecting both towns is experiencing a modest construction boom of stylish resort hotels, with land speculators quickly snapping up the remaining parcels of oceanfront property. East of Monterrico, Hawaii also has pretty stretches of nearly deserted beaches, though there are increasing numbers of Guatemala's elite building vacation homes here. The end of the line is Las Lisas, another attractive, though very remote, beach close to the Salvadoran border.

On the Caribbean coast, Guatemala has some fairly decent white-sand beaches on the Punta de Manabique promontory. Along the coastline between Lívingston and the Belize border, the nicest beaches are at palm-fringed Playa Blanca. For talcum-powder white-sand beaches lapped by turquoise waters, head off the coast to the Belize barrier reef, where you'll find the Zapotillo Cayes.

FISHING
Sailfishing

The Pacific Ocean waters off the port of Iztapa are hailed as the "Sailfish Capital of the World," with world records for single-day catch-and-release firmly supporting these claims. Apparently, a unique swirl of ocean currents between Mexico and El Salvador creates an eddy unusually rich in pelagic fish, such as herring and mackerel, right on Guatemala's doorstep. Sailfish and marlin gather to feed on this bait, along with large concentrations of dorado, yellowfin tuna, and wahoo. The result is some of the world's best sailfishing.

Numerous outfitters have set up shop in Iztapa offering sailfishing year-round, though the most active season is between November and May because of the colder weather prevalent in the North American region from which most fishers hail from. The Presidential Challenge, a yearly sportfishing event that has been held for the past 10 years, usually takes place here in January.

Lake Fishing

Thanks to grand plans for recreational options to be offered on behalf of now-absconded Pan American Airways, Lake Atitlán saw the introduction of largemouth bass in the late 1950s. The lake's extreme depths make catching the larger fish said to inhabit the deeper waters quite a challenge, which only adds to the allure of fishing these waters. Your best bet for catching "the big one" is during the annual spring spawning season, between March and May.

WATER SPORTS
White-Water Rafting and Kayaking

Guatemala has a number of white-water rivers with rapids ranging class II–VI (class VI being unrunnable waterfalls). The most popular river for rafting and kayaking is the Río Cahabón, found in the region of Las Verapaces. It features some of Central America's finest stretches of white water complemented by jungles, caves, hot springs, and waterfalls. Also in the Verapaces region, the Río Candelaria winds its way through its namesake cave system and is a great place for river tubing and kayaking, allowing the chance to explore these fascinating caves to their full extent. Another worthy white-water excursion is Petén's Río Chiquibul, at the eastern end of the department near the Belize border. Although the rapids are not quite as exhilarating as those on the Cahabón, it's highly attractive for its jungle-lined riverbanks and proximity to Mayan sites such as Tikal and Yaxhá.

For more sedate kayaking on ocean kayaks, Lakes Petén Itzá and Atitlán are good bets.

Scuba Diving and Snorkeling

It's possible to scuba dive off the Caribbean coast near Punta de Manabique, though you're probably better off heading just a bit farther north to the exquisite Zapotillo Cayes, part of the Belize barrier reef. Several outfitters arrange trips from Lívingston. Scuba diving is also a popular activity in Lake Atitlán, where you might even be able to feel the heat emanating from underwater lava flows in this still-active volcanic region. Another peculiarity of diving here is that the lake is at a rather high altitude just over 5,000 feet, adding another variable to the mix.

Surfing

An emerging surfing scene is centered around the Pacific coast village of Sipacate, which enjoys excellent breaks. Iztapa also reportedly has good breaks,

THE RAGING RAPIDS OF THE RÍO CAHABÓN

Guatemala's best white-water river is the class III-IV Río Cahabón. In addition to the exhilarating rapids, the traverse downstream on its emerald waters is interspersed with more tranquil stretches affording opportunities to view several species of birds and explore caves, waterfalls, and hot springs along its forested banks.

The Cahabón is the same river that flows into a cave under the limestone pools of Semuc Champey, re-emerging several hundred meters downstream. Most river trips begin at a put-in point near Lanquín. There are some rather menacing rapids along this stretch of the Upper Cahabón, including Rock and Roll, Entonces, and Las Tres Hermanas, making for an adrenaline-filled ride. The Middle Gorge has some nice jungle scenery and continuous class III rapids. There are a few more challenging rapids after passing the bridge at a place called Oxec before reaching an obligatory take-out point at Takinkó to portage the class VI (not runnable) Chulac Falls. A dam was once planned here, but dam builders seem to have gone cold on the idea after discovering a fault line running right beneath the proposed dam site. The two-day trip camps here.

The Lower Gorge is a boatload of fun, with titillating rapids like Saca Corchos (Corkscrew) and Saca Caca. There are stops along the way to explore caves and enjoy lunch at El Pequeño Paraíso, a small side stream with delightful waterfalls and hot springs flowing into the Cahabón. The next rapid is appropriately named Lose Your Lunch, shortly after which the river widens and you are treated to a serene stretch of river with mountainous jungle-clad banks. The take-out is at Cahaboncito, where the intrepid can take a plunge into the river from a 30-foot bridge.

Rafting the Cahabón affords the opportunity to see some remote natural attractions and come in contact with the local people inhabiting the area. As is often the case in Guatemala, the beauty coexists with a sobering reality. In addition to still-forested areas you will see some steep, badly deforested slopes given over to corn cultivation, shedding light on the desperate plight of peasants willing to live and grow their crops anywhere they can.

as does Monterrico. A useful website for checking out Guatemala's surf scene is www.surfinguatemala.com.

Boating

Boaters will find marinas on both Guatemalan coasts. On the Pacific, a new marina was being planned with partial backing from Dutch interests near the aging port facilities of Champerico. Farther east, the Marina Pez Vela caters to sportfishing boats and is adjacent to the Puerto Quetzal Cruise Ship Terminal. It has restaurants and good tourism infrastructure. On the Caribbean coast, you'll find many boats traveling up the Río Dulce from the Caribbean coast and docking at any of a number of marinas in the river's namesake town.

© AL ARGUETA

Golf is gaining popularity in Guatemala and there are several good courses.

GOLF

Guatemala has some excellent golf courses, all in or around Guatemala City and La Antigua, housed in private clubs open to foreign visitors. Some Guatemala City courses afford excellent views of the city from spectacular locations in the mountains flanking the urban area. New golf courses were in the planning stages on the Pacific coast adjacent to IRTRA's theme parks at Xocomil and Xetulul, near Retalhuleu, and along the coastal corridor between Iztapa and Monterrico. Guatemala's newest golf course, La Reunión Antigua Golf Resort, is on the outskirts of La Antigua, along the road to the Pacific coast. It enjoys a prime location with spectacular views of four surrounding volcanoes.

SPECTATOR SPORTS
Fútbol

Guatemalans love their soccer, known as *fútbol*. It is by far the most widely played sport in the country, with every town or village having at least something that resembles a soccer field. Almost everywhere you go, you'll find games being played on Sunday afternoons. As for professional soccer-playing, the two most popular teams in the country's four-team national soccer league, denoted by the colors of their jerseys, are the Rojos (Municipales) and Cremas (Comunicaciones). The two usually end up going head-to-head at the end of the season for the championship title.

Games can be seen at Guatemala City's Estadio Mateo Flores, but be advised it can get quite rowdy. In 1996, things got so out of hand that a stampede ensued when stands collapsed, killing 100 people. The soccer stadium was remodeled in the aftermath. If you've always wanted to see a Latin American soccer match, you might want to check it out. Guatemala also has a few star players in U.S. Major League Soccer and on some European teams.

International games played by the national squad are a big event, as Guatemala has never been to a World Cup. Guatemala is part of CONCACAF, the Caribbean, North, and Central American Confederation. CONCACAF gets three slots for the World Cup, which usually end up going to the United States, Mexico, and Costa Rica. In 2004–2005, the national squad (also known as *la bicolor*) got closer than it's ever been, advancing into the final round of the World Cup qualifiers tied in points with Costa Rica after beating Honduras 1-0. Post-game celebrations spilled into the streets and lasted into the wee hours of the morning. Unfortunately, their high hopes ended in bitter disappointment. Things got off to a great start with a 5-1 routing of Trinidad and Tobago, but Guatemala then lost 2-0 to the United States and never fully recovered.

Baseball

Known locally as *béisbol,* games can be seen at Parque Minerva's ballpark. The game has become increasingly popular in recent years and you'll often see league games going on at area ballparks, usually on Saturday mornings.

PLANNING YOUR FACT-FINDING TRIP

There really is no substitute for going somewhere and seeing it with your own eyes as you try to determine whether or not it's the right place for you. You'll be able to determine exactly what you like about Guatemala and also what you're not so crazy about. You may find you absolutely love Guatemala but dislike the people, or you may find yourself, like so many others, utterly captivated by both. A well-planned reconnaissance trip to Guatemala will reveal many things in unexpected ways and is the first part of your new adventure abroad.

WHEN TO GO

Guatemala has two seasons, rainy and dry. A visit during each has its own distinct advantages. The rainy season usually begins at the end of May, with the summer months marking the early part of the rainy season characterized by short afternoon or early evening showers that usually clear up by nighttime. By September or October, however, the weather is often socked in for

© AL ARGUETA

days with rain and clouds. If you don't mind the rains, it makes a great time to visit, as foreign visitors are noticeably fewer during these two months and many hotels offer discounts in hopes of filling their rooms. Some parts of the country, most prominently the Caribbean coast, are rainy throughout most of the year.

The dry season runs from November to early May. December through February are the coldest months, with cold fronts from the north often making their way down to this neck of the woods, bringing temperatures into the mid-60s for daytime highs in mountain areas like Antigua, Quetzaltenango, and Guatemala City. Things tend to warm up dramatically in March and April before the arrival of the first rains in mid-May. During this time, thick haze from heat, dust, and agricultural burning clouds the views of Guatemala's stunning mountain scenery, easily viewable during other months of the year.

The high tourist season in Guatemala runs from December to Holy Week (usually in April), with a second high season between mid-June and early September. Europeans on holiday are very much in evidence during this time, as are Salvadorans, for whom Guatemala is a favorite destination during their annual August vacations. Language schools in Quetzaltenango and Antigua are usually full with college students during the summer months, and rates go up accordingly. School lets out in Guatemala during the middle of October, with the local equivalent of summer vacation taking place until January. Families with children tend to take over many of the destinations popular with Guatemalan travelers, and flights to Guatemala City are often full with the well-to-do (and their families) returning from a stateside shopping spree. Personally, my favorite time for a visit is between mid-May and mid-June, when the rains have usually arrived, greening up the scenery, and just before the summer high season.

Preparing for Your Trip

READ UP

It's a good idea to read up on Guatemala prior to your trip there. Much has been written about its recent history, as well as its rich cultural history. Guidebooks and travel articles in magazines and newspapers will get you excited about your trip and keep you informed. Online forums are also great places to check out. Recommended are moon.com and Lonely Planet's Thorn Tree forum (http://thorntree .lonelyplanet.com). Of course, you should also check out *Moon Guatemala*. I've offered additional suggestions for in-depth reading at the end of this book.

YOU CAN BE COMFORTABLE *AND* LOOK GOOD

As a writer/photographer and frequent traveler to Guatemala, I often find the need to be comfortable while traveling and yet be ready to hit the ground running upon arrival. Sometimes I'm headed from the airport straight to a meeting or I'm being whisked off to Lake Atitlán shortly after landing in Guatemala City. At other times, I'm only in town for a few days and need to pack items requiring little care but that still look good and are easily paired. That's how I discovered Nau.

Nau (www.nau.com) offers phenomenal clothing colored mostly in earth tones and using a variety of synthetic and natural fibers. The gorgeous fabrics offer the softest of hands and combine with elegant design and expert tailoring to create pieces that feel right at home in a Guatemala City board room or in your volcano-view Antigua hotel room. Nau's clothes are great for layering and include a number of outerwear products for those chilly Guatemalan mountains. Among the fabrics used are recycled polyester, merino wool, and organic cotton/spandex blends.

Nau donates 2 percent of your purchase to social/environmental organizations, and you can even choose where to send your donation from among their Partners for Change. You can look good, be comfortable, and feel good about supporting a company that works to make a difference.

STUDY MAPS

Familiarize yourself with Guatemala's unique geography before your trip. Be able to quickly find Guatemala City on a map and locate where it is in relation to the main expat hangouts. Look at the country's topography. Notice it's not *all* mountainous? Check out roads and locate off-the-beaten-path villages. If you're really into geography, check out Google Earth and download the program to your computer. You'll be able to view satellite images of Guatemala City and the country's forests, lakes, and volcanoes in incredible detail. It's a great resource for studying the country's geography and getting a glimpse of what you'll see once you're in-country.

WHAT TO TAKE

Everyone packs differently. As a photographer, I often wish I could pack light, but I find this is usually not the case, as I invariably wind up kicking myself for not having packed some gizmo needed somewhere along the way. Those of you able to pack light, I salute you. Incidentally, if you're like me, make sure you bring all your photography supplies to Guatemala, as it's extremely difficult to locate necessary items. Professional slide film is only available in one place that I can think of in Guatemala City, though for digital shooters the city's shopping malls can probably supply most of your needs. Depending on your personal taste, you may or may not want to carry everything in a large backpack. Luggage with wheels is another good option if you just don't see yourself hauling around a backpack. In either case, bring a separate, smaller backpack for day trips and everyday use.

Getting back to the basics, keep in mind that Guatemala's huge variety of ecosystems also means you might find yourself changing clothes more often than a Milan runway model. It's a good idea to dress in layers. Pack a good assortment of short-sleeved T-shirts, sweaters and/or fleece, shorts and pants. Shorts are perfectly acceptable in resort and beach towns, but not so much in Guatemala City or large urban areas, where people tend to dress up and the climate isn't really all that warm. I'm a big fan of synthetic fabrics that are quick-drying and can wick away moisture during strenuous hikes in the backcountry. Lightweight travel pants might be your new best friend, especially for trips to jungle areas where mosquitoes are usually a concern. For shirts, where mosquitoes are rampant, try sticking to lighter colors, and bring lightweight shirts with long sleeves you can roll up. This will also keep you cooler under the rays of the hot tropical sun. Guatemala's mountainous areas can get downright cold, especially after it rains, and the damp chill seems to permeate your very bones. Pack a light rain jacket and at least a sweater or two. Also pack plenty of sunscreen and bug spray, and don't forget a wide-brimmed hat or at least a ball cap.

If you plan on doing some adventure hiking, bring everything you need, as rental equipment or that provided by local outfitters is usually not the greatest. These items include tents, sleeping pads, hammocks with mosquito netting, and sleeping bags. If you have one, it's always a good idea to bring along a water filter for those backcountry adventures.

Footwear is an extremely important consideration. For serious jungle hiking, bring high, military-style boots that you can wear in the mud and that will also protect you against snakebites. If you plan on white-water rafting or cave exploration, bring amphibious sandals with a good tread that you can wear on the boat or on slippery cave surfaces. On a totally different plane, if you plan on checking out the nightlife scene in Guatemala City, bring a good pair of dress shoes, as sneakers are verboten in the city's trendy nightclubs.

Finally, for visits to remote highland villages with large numbers of poor children, bring pencils, crayons, and other gifts to donate to local schools. You'll be surprised how something as simple as a writing instrument can bless a child. Packing photos of family and loved ones back home is also a great way to cross cultural barriers with friendly Guatemalans you'll meet along the way.

Currency

Your main source for cash these days will most likely be ATM and credit cards. ATMs are found almost everywhere throughout the country. For more remote areas, a stash of cash (in various places on your body) is the best way to go. Travelers checks make a fine backup when traveling in more touristy areas. Be sure to have your ATM card and credit card PIN so you can access your cash from a machine.

Arriving in Guatemala

Most foreign visitors arrive in Guatemala City's La Aurora International Airport, the country's main aviation hub. Recently remodeled and expanded, La Aurora is modern, manageable, pleasant, and quite functional. Many of the better hotels in nearby Zona Viva offer complimentary shuttles to and from the airport. There are also reasonably priced shuttle vans to Antigua and onward to Lake Atitlán. Official airport taxis are also available and can be booked from a kiosk inside the airport terminal.

CUSTOMS AND IMMIGRATION

U.S. and Canadian citizens need valid passports for travel to Guatemala. The passport must have validity for at least six months beyond the arrival date. Although you may or may not be asked for this documentation, children

Guatemala City's La Aurora International Airport

traveling with one parent must have a notarized letter providing official permission from the other parent.

Immigration and customs processes at La Aurora airport are very straightforward. Customs (known as SAT) will look at your declaration paperwork (to be filled out on the airplane prior to arrival) and will either put you in a line where your bags will be searched and applicable duties (if any) collected or simply wave you on. Most foreign travelers are waived on, as what they're mostly looking for are arriving Guatemalans with loot from stateside shopping sprees. A disproportionate number of bags per traveler are usually a sure tip-off.

Most U.S. carriers flying to Guatemala don't collect fees for second bags checked in on international flights, so it's a good idea to bring as much with you one bit at a time if you're taking frequent trips. You're limited to 50 pounds per bag (unless you have frequent flier elite status), but it's still cheaper to pay the airline for an extra 20-pound allotment than to ship items.

TRANSPORTATION

Taxis are easily booked from a kiosk inside the airport terminal, as are rental cars. If you're arriving on a later flight and have never driven Guatemala City's chaotic streets before, it might make more sense to take advantage of free airport shuttles to Zona 10 hotels and have the rental car company drop off the vehicle at your hotel the next morning. You could also just as easily take a cab or shuttle from your hotel to the airport the next morning and pick up the car then. Avis, Budget, Hertz, and National have kiosks inside the airport terminal. Their lots are across the road fronting the airport's three-level parking garage.

If most of your travel involves the Guatemala City and Antigua area, my advice is to forgo car rental in favor of taxis and shuttle buses. You can also hire a driver to take you around for about US$75–100 a day. Local hotel concierges can usually recommend someone for you. Doing so will allow you to get a feel for the city without the stress of having to drive on its unfamiliar streets. It will also allow you to witness first-hand the particular style of Guatemalan urban driving you'll need to adopt if you end up living here.

If you're altogether bypassing Guatemala City, you'll find shuttle vans to Antigua are easily booked upon arrival at the airport. There is also a very helpful INGUAT (Instituto Guatemalteco de Turismo) information desk just after passing customs. It's staffed by English-speaking agents who can help you get your bearings.

Under no circumstances should you take a Guatemala City public bus. The recently unveiled Transmetro is perfectly safe and efficient, but its coverage area is limited. It will not get you to or from the airport.

Rural buses can also be dangerous thanks to careless drivers, winding roads, and inadequate mechanical upkeep. Robberies are also common. In some very remote areas, they may be your only public transportation option. For most places frequented by foreign travelers, shuttle vans are the way to go and are reasonably priced.

Domestic air transport is still in its infancy, although there are ongoing improvements to local airports aimed at getting a network of domestic air service up and running. The only scheduled domestic passenger air service is between Guatemala City and Flores. Only two or three carriers fly the route, and fares hover in the vicinity of US$200 roundtrip. Cities with new local airports that may see air service soon include Quetzaltenango, Huehuetenango, Puerto San José, Puerto Barrios, and Retalhuleu.

TIPPING AND TAXES

A 10 percent service charge is included on most restaurant tabs, so most Guatemalans don't tip. If the service is exceptional, you might want to leave an extra 5–10 percent. Sales tax, at a rate of 12 percent and known as IVA, is also added to the bill. IVA applies to all goods and services. Taxes on hotel rooms include the 12 percent IVA plus another 10 percent that goes to INGUAT, the state tourism agency, adding 22 percent to the cost of your stay. Many smaller hotels include the tax in quoted prices, but when booking larger properties online you may not see the total price reflected until the final step in the booking process.

Taxi drivers aren't normally tipped, though they'll often keep the change if it's very little. Bellhops, maids, and tour guides are tipped. Surprisingly, food delivery personnel (such as pizza delivery people) are not tipped by Guatemalans, but I'll often throw in a few quetzales and a heartfelt thank you. I personally feel that anyone riding around in the rain on a motorcycle and dropping off food to your doorstep deserves a little something for the effort, not to mention the convenience to you.

SAFETY PRECAUTIONS

It's no secret that Guatemala has a reputation for crime. If you're reading this book, you're probably aware of this and have factored it into your decision to travel there. Guatemala City can be particularly dodgy, as is to be expected from a city of its size and socioeconomic discrepancies. The best thing is to stay alert and be proactive so as not to be an easy target for petty theft. Always keep a close watch on your baggage and carry money in concealed pockets or tucked into a money belt.

It's a good idea to make photocopies of important documents such as passports and plane tickets, while keeping the originals in a separate and secure place. Some travelers make scans or take digital photographs of these documents and email them to themselves in order to access them while on the road, if necessary. It's also a good idea to bring important phone numbers (such as credit card numbers to report a lost or stolen card) with you on your trip. These numbers are found on the back of your card. Most card companies allow you to call collect from outside the United States to report the loss or theft of a card.

Sample Itineraries

Unless you're moving to Guatemala for business and have little prior notice, you will most likely at least have visited the country before. Having traveled around parts of the country, you will have some familiarity with its different offerings. Despite its small size, Guatemala packs in a number of different environments, and part of your fact-finding trip will involve deciding what sort of environment you'd like to live in. Do you want to live near cosmopolitan Guatemala City in the hills overlooking the city? If so, you can live a lifestyle very similar to that of Southern California, though the beach will be a slightly longer distance away. Others might prefer the solitude and sweltering jungle of the Petén plains or the Izabal coast, hoping to start a small ecolodge or similar venture. Still others might prefer the cool highlands and splendid volcanic scenery of Lake Atitlán, Quetzaltenango, or La Antigua Guatemala. The following suggested travel strategies can help you narrow down your options. If you have a whole month to explore, you can try to see and experience as much as possible in that time or focus on one area to get a better feel for the day-to-day routine of life in your selected locale.

TEN DAYS: SAMPLING GUATEMALA'S EXPAT HOTSPOTS

This itinerary allows you to sample Guatemala's main expat locales, including La Antigua, Guatemala City, Lake Atitlán, and Quetzaltenango. All of these are easily reached via shuttle buses, so there's no need to rent a car and negotiate Guatemala's twisting mountain roads on your own, unless you really want to.

Days 1 and 2: Guatemala City and Vicinity

Try to catch one of the numerous flights getting in to Guatemala City around midday. Check in to one of the nearby Zona 10 hotels and spend the afternoon at leisure, strolling the Zona Viva and grabbing a bite to eat in one of the plentiful cafés or restaurants. If there's time, check out one of the local museums as well as the newly opened Oakland Mall, to get a feel for prices on imported luxury items.

For your second day, hire a driver and to take you to the Carretera a El Salvador suburbs. Get familiar with the area and stop at Pradera Concepción shopping mall to get a feel for local prices and see what's available in local stores. Eat lunch at El Portal del Angel, overlooking the city.

Make your way back down to the valley. Make prior arrangements to meet with a realtor after lunch and see some of the city's residential areas, including Zonas 14, 15, and 16. Look at high-rise condos or homes, depending on your preference. You can also see properties in Carretera a El Salvador, in which case you should substitute the morning taxi driver for the realtor.

Treat yourself to dinner at Jake's or Tamarindos before turning in for the night.

Days 3 and 4: La Antigua Guatemala

Get up early and take a shuttle (they pick up at major hotels) or taxi to La Antigua Guatemala. The ride out from the city will give you a glimpse of the working-class areas of the city and the view from the hills bordering the western side of the valley. The road then meanders through pine forests and down steep slopes into the Antigua valley. Check in to your hotel and take the rest of the morning to explore the city and its cultural attractions. After lunch, continue to explore Antigua's cobblestone streets. Stop in to one of the local expat hangouts and chat up the locals about life in Antigua. Be sure to pick up a copy of *Revue* magazine for the low-down on local hotspots, jobs, and the real estate market.

For your second day in Antigua, stop by a realty office and get information on local properties to get a feel for price ranges and how people live. With prior arrangements, you can explore some of the neighboring towns and villages with the help of a realtor. If golf is your thing, be sure to check out the new golf resort in neighboring Alotenango. Alternatively, hire a taxi and do some exploring on your own or visit one of the local coffee *fincas*.

Days 5-7: Lake Atitlán

Take an early shuttle van from Antigua to Panajachel, on the shores of Lake Atitlán. Check out the town and talk to expats at local hangouts. Take the afternoon to take in the gorgeous lake scenery from the public beach, then head to neighboring Santa Catarina Palopó for dinner at Casa Palopó hotel's phenomenal restaurant in time for sunset drinks. Alternatively, head straight to the hotel from Antigua and take a day to relax and enjoy.

On your second day, you can get information on the area from local realtors or take a boat to one of the neighboring villages. Pick your favorite two villages based on the descriptions provided in the *Prime Living Locations* chapters and spend one night at each.

Days 8 and 9: Quetzaltenango

Take an early morning boat ride back to Panajachel in time to catch a shuttle bus to Quetzaltenango, known locally as Xela. Explore Parque Centroamérica and the surrounding city streets. On your second day, consider a day trip to one of the neighboring villages, Santa María volcano, or Chicabal lagoon.

Day 10: Back to Guatemala City or Antigua

For the final day, take an early shuttle bus from Quetzaltenango back to Guatemala City or La Antigua and explore anything that might still be on your list. La Aurora airport is easily accessible from either city for your flight out the next day.

TWO WEEKS

If you have two weeks to check out Guatemala as a feasible living option, consider the above itinerary with a few modifications. Two weeks will allow you some extra time to further explore the areas that interest you most or tack on a trip to one of the more undiscovered regions of the country. This itinerary picks up where the last one left off and includes one of three options.

Option One: Pacific Coast Add-On

On day 10 of the 10-day itinerary, head back to Guatemala City and rent a car. From there, drive the fast toll road to the Pacific coast. Spend the next four days exploring the Pacific coast at your leisure, with plenty of time to spend the night at each of three beach towns. Start at Marina del Sur, near Puerto San José. Spend two nights there (with prior arrangement). Your arrival may already be on the late side because of the Guatemala City stopover, so you'll want that extra night. From there, head over to Iztapa and Monterrico, spending a night at each or somewhere along the Iztapa–Monterrico corridor. The exotic black-sand beaches, palm trees, and warm breezes may have you soon looking for cheap beachfront property. On your last day, head back from the coast. Divert to the town of Escuintla along the way and take the road from there to La Antigua in order to take in some different scenery. You'll pass neighboring Alotenango along the way. If there's time, stop in for lunch at its new golf resort, La Reunión, about 17 kilometers from Antigua.

Option Two: Cobán and Vicinity

After renting a four-wheel-drive vehicle in Guatemala City, spend the evening there. Early the next morning (day 11), head east and then north to the Verapaces. Stop at the Quetzal Biotope, right beside the road about an hour from Cobán, and try your luck at spotting the country's national bird in this protected cloud forest. Spend the afternoon in Cobán exploring its quiet streets. You can also explore nearby towns and take in the wonderful countryside. Eat at least one meal at El Bistro and talk to its expat owners. The next morning, head up to Semuc Champey and explore its gorgeous limestone pools. You can overnight there. On day 13, continue north to the Candelaria caves and the ruins of Cancuén. Overnight at Candelaria Lodge. On the last day, make the long drive from the caves all the way back to Guatemala City. If you wish to see more of Cobán and check out housing options, forgo the Candelaria caves/Cancuén portion of the trip.

Option Three: Tikal and Petén

If you're a hardy soul and think you might want to make a go of it in Guatemala's hot, humid Petén rainforests, this might be the option for you. Take an evening flight from Guatemala City to Flores on day 10, staying overnight in the island town. Explore Flores the following morning, including CINCAP's information center. Gain an appreciation for the rainforest ecosystem with a trip to nearby Ixpanpajul jungle park or take a boat to the lakeside villages of San Andrés and San José to see if their laid-back atmosphere suits you. Overnight in Flores.

For day 12, get an early start and take a bus to Tikal National Park. Take all day to explore the ruins and surrounding jungle. Marvel at this ancient wonder as you watch the sunset from atop Temple IV. Overnight in the park. The next day, head to the lakeside town of El Remate, midway between Tikal and Flores. Enjoy the lake's warm, turquoise waters and the placid jungle setting. On the final day, take the 30-minute bus ride to the airport and a flight back to Guatemala City.

ONE MONTH

If you have a whole month to spend in Guatemala, consider spending it all in one place (assuming you have your heart set on a particular region) and getting a feel for the pace of life there. This gives you plenty of time to get to know some locals and expats, assess the cost of living, and see where you'd fit in. Alternatively, you could pack everything into a whirlwind tour of Guatemala. This itinerary combines all of the other routings, which conveniently begin and end in Guatemala City. You'll quickly see why it's the country's main transportation hub.

Days 1-10: Main Expat Locales
The 10-day itinerary allows you to make the most of this time in Guatemala and provides a glimpse of the main expat locales.

Days 11-14: The Pacific Coast
Dig deeper and explore the Pacific coast. This itinerary follows option one under the two-week itinerary and allows you to see the seaside communities of Marina del Sur (Puerto San José), Iztapa, and Monterrico.

Days 15-23: Verapaces and Petén
You can explore Alta Verapaz based on the *Cobán and Vicinity* option and then continue north to Petén with your rental car. Be sure to allow a full day for the long drive from Flores all the way back to Guatemala City.

Days 23-30: Various Options
Return the rental car in Guatemala City and then spend some down time getting a better feel for any of the locales that have sparked your interest. This could be a week in Antigua, Lake Atitlán, or even Guatemala City to answer many of the questions that undoubtedly have arisen during your travels.

Or, if you still feel like traveling, keep the rental car and stop about midway between Flores and Guatemala City in Río Dulce (Izabal department). Take in the relaxed Caribbean atmosphere and visit some of the local sights. You may even have time to take a sailing trip down the river and out to the Belize cayes. You can also split your time and spend just two or three days here before returning for some more time in La Antigua or Guatemala City. On the Flores–Río Dulce leg of the trip, you also have the option of staying at the fabled Finca Ixobel lodge, owned by an American expat. There is plenty to see and do in the surrounding pine-tree-studded landscape.

Practicalities

The hotels, restaurants, and attractions covered in this section will keep you busy, housed, and well fed. I've tried to include my top picks for each area. For a more exhaustive treatment of local restaurants, accommodations, and attractions, as well as places off the beaten path, check out my travel guidebook, *Moon Guatemala*. As always, things change in the dynamic Guatemalan tourism market. New places open and others close. Nearly all of the places below have been in business for quite some time.

GUATEMALA CITY
Accommodations

Many of the capital's budget accommodations can be found in the downtown sector of Zona 1. Among the best budget options is **Posada Belén** (13 Calle A 10-30, Zona 1, tel. 2253-4530, www.posadabelen.com, US$45 d), located on a quiet side street. The *posada* is an 1873 home converted into a lovely 10-room museum inn tastefully decorated with Guatemalan bedspreads, paintings and weavings. Its gracious hosts, René and Francesca, speak English and can help you plan your onward journeys into Guatemala's rugged interior. Amenities include telephone and Internet access. All rooms have private baths, and rates include breakfast.

Although Zona 10 is home to many of Guatemala City's high-end accommodations, it also boasts a great budget hostel. **Xamanek Student Inn** (13

© AL ARGUETA

Bustling Guatemala City is Central America's largest metropolis.

Calle 3-57, Zona 10, tel. 2360-8345, www.mayaworld.net/xamanek, US$14 pp in dorms, US$35 private doubles) is a friendly sort of place with clean dormitories sharing spotless bathrooms with hot showers and two rooms with private baths. Services include laundry, airport pickup, Internet, bag storage, and free use of the kitchen. Room rates include pancakes and coffee. There are two gardens and a living room for chilling out.

Among the city's most stylish digs is **Otelito** (12 Calle 4-51, Zona 10, tel. 2339-1811, www.otelito.com, US$120–160 d), with 12 rooms (all named after local produce) housed in a modern home-turned-upscale hotel. The decor is minimalist with a different color scheme in evidence during each of the year's four seasons. There's chill-out music playing on the speakers throughout the property, wireless Internet throughout, a business center, and a book exchange. Movies are shown nightly. A hip, frosted-glass lounge and restaurant mean you don't even have to leave your hotel to enjoy some of Zona Viva's best food in a delightful atmosphere.

Another top contender is the fabulous, 239-room **Real InterContinental Guatemala** (14 Calle 2-51, Zona 10, tel. 2379-4548, U.S. toll-free tel. 888/424-6835, www.intercontinental.com, US$125–485 d), with a wonderful lobby featuring Guatemalan paintings and sculpture, a new sushi restaurant, a French café, and a boulangerie/patisserie. The comfortable, stylish rooms feature in-room Internet access, down pillows, Egyptian cotton sheets, and flat-screen cable TV. Bathrooms have rain showerheads, and the safety deposit boxes are large enough to accommodate a laptop. Guests have use of an in-room iPod. There are free airport shuttles and a pleasant swimming pool on a deck overlooking the city. President George W. Bush and wife Laura spent the night here during their 24-hour visit to Guatemala in March 2007.

Outside the city in the surrounding hillsides along Carretera a El Salvador is the wonderful **Vista Real Guatemala** (Km 8.5 Carretera a El Salvador, tel. 2420-7720, www.quintareal.com.gt, US$100–899 d). It scores big points for great city views and its neocolonial architecture featuring Mexican artistic touches. Its 129 rooms are all comfortable and well-furnished with some truly splendid features, including vaulted wooden ceilings and neocolonial archways in some rooms. The Suite Gran Clase rooms are a good value and substantially nicer than the Master Suites, which are only slightly less expensive.

Food

Guatemala City has a number of excellent restaurants frequently garnering top spots in travel magazine surveys of Latin American eating establishments. The city also has a plethora of the usual fast-food franchises and U.S. casual dining chains.

A long-time local favorite, **Altuna** (5a Avenida 12-31, Zona 1, tel. 2251-7185, and 10a Calle 0-45, Zona 10, tel. 2332-6576, www.restaurantealtuna .com, noon–10 P.M. Tues.–Sat., noon–5 P.M. Sun., US$7–22) is also one of the city's fanciest offerings, with impeccable service and an elegant atmosphere. Specialties include fish and seafood dishes including paella and lobster, but they also serve land-based fare including *jamón serrano* and *chorizo.*

For absolutely astounding views of the city from a perch along Carretera a El Salvador, you can't top **El Portal del Angel** (Km 11.2 Carretera a El Salvador, tel. 2369-6007, noon–9 P.M. Mon.–Thurs., noon–10 P.M. Fri.–Sun., US$8–35). The food is just as good as the views, and the tasteful decor, with walls in vivid hues adorned with cool paintings of Catholic saints, makes this place truly heavenly. There's another location in Zona 11 at Paseo Miraflores, minus the city views.

For gourmet Guatemalan cuisine served in a classy atmosphere accented by a high-roofed thatch ceiling, head to **Kacao** (2a Avenida between 13 and 14 Calles, Zona 10, tel. 2337-4188 or 2337-4189, lunch and dinner daily, US$15–20). You can try a variety of traditional Guatemalan dishes including spicy beef and chicken dishes in *pepián* and *jocón* sauces as well as corn-based delicacies like *chuchitos* and *tamales.*

Pecorino (11 Calle 3-36, Zona 10, tel. 2360-3035, www.ristorantepecorino .com, noon–1 A.M. Mon.–Sat., US$15–20) is an excellent choice for its authentic Italian food, including brick oven pizza, seafood dishes, steak, pasta, salads, and panini served in an attractive Old World atmosphere. There's also a huge wine selection.

Guatemala City also boasts some excellent options for enthusiasts of fusion cuisine. **Jake's** (17 Calle 10-40, Zona 10, tel. 2368-0351, noon–3 P.M. and 7–10:30 P.M. Mon.–Sat., noon–4 P.M. Sun., US$10–25), started by New York City artist-turned-chef Jake Denburg, is considered among the top 10 restaurants in Latin America. Several features combine to make a visit to Jake's something truly special, including its wonderful atmosphere in

© AL ARGUETA

Tamarindos is one of Guatemala City's finest restaurants.

POLLO CAMPERO AND THE CULT OF FRIED CHICKEN

If, like most people traveling to the United States from Guatemala, you fly out on a commercial airline flight, don't be surprised by the distinct smell of fried chicken onboard your aircraft. One look at the overhead bins will quickly reveal them crammed tight with boxes of fried chicken. Meet Pollo Campero, which along with coffee and bananas may be one of Guatemala's main exports.

Guatemalans have always had an affinity for the stuff. It's actually quite good, though I've never taken it along as a carry-on. Many travelers take a box home for homesick relatives craving a taste of the land they left behind. Although Pollo Campero has opened up shop in recent years in several U.S. cities, expatriate Guatemalans still make a point of stopping at the location in La Aurora airport to pick up a box. To illustrate the utter hold it has on the Guatemalan masses, the closed-for-remodeling airport location operated out of a street-side trailer during the airport's recent renovation, at a time when all other businesses were simply closed.

You may be asked by U.S. customs if you're carrying food, and this question might specifically address your smuggling of Pollo Campero. Rest assured, customs officials are happy to let the cooked chicken cross the American threshold after applying the requisite X-rays. Some Newark Airport Customs officers even claim to have the uncanny ability to distinguish chicken from a Guatemalan Pollo Campero versus a San Salvador outlet, though I've never taken them up on offers to verify their claims.

Pollo Campero is becoming more than just a Guatemalan phenomenon, however. An aggressive company expansion includes the opening of numerous new locations throughout North America, Europe, and even Asia in the coming years. In 2007, Campero opened outlets in Jakarta, Indonesia, and Shanghai, China, with ambitious goals to open 500 more restaurants in China within the next five years. Campero already operates 220 restaurants in 10 countries, including 38 locations in the United States. It employs more than 7,000 and is the largest fast-food chain in Latin America. With such aggressive expansion plans, Pollo Campero may be headed for a location near you, and I don't mean seat 25F.

a converted house with tile floors and wooden ceilings, eclectic decor including some interesting black-and-white photographs, tables covered in butcher paper (crayons supplied), and most of all, the food. Highlights include lobster tortellini and the signature dish, the Vaquero Chino (Chinese Cowboy), a tenderloin steak prepared in a base sauce of sweet soy, espresso, and anise. The wine list is also impressive, and rounding out your meal with one of the delectable homemade cheesecakes is a must.

Also among Latin America's top restaurants is **Tamarindos** (11 Calle 2-19A, Zona 10, tel. 2360-2815, reservaciones@tamarindos.com.gt, 12:30–3 P.M. and 7:30 P.M.–1 A.M. Mon.–Sat., US$10–20) which makes some fine sushi and does an excellent job of combining Thai, Italian, and Guatemalan flavors into some irresistible dishes. There is pleasant indoor and outdoor garden patio seating, and the hip ambiance is set by postmodern decor and electronica music on the stereo. Try the vegetarian pad thai or the four-cheese gnocchi.

Sights

Boston's Fenway Park has its Green Monster and so does Guatemala City. Now known as **Palacio Nacional de la Cultura** (6a Calle between 6a and 7a Avenidas, Zona 1, 9 A.M.–noon and 2–5:30 P.M. daily, adults US$5 including guided tour), the former presidential palace, built between 1939 and 1943 during the time of maniacal dictator Jorge Ubico, is a large, green stone structure with elements of colonial and neoclassical architecture. With most of Guatemala's presidents preferring to reside in other parts of the city, it has not housed a president during a term in office for at least 10 years.

The palace is one of Guatemala City's most interesting attractions, as it affords the visitor a glimpse into Guatemala's colonial and dictatorial legacy. After all, Guatemala City was once the capital of the entire Central American isthmus, and nowhere else in the region were colonial institutions so imbedded in the national fiber. Similarly, Guatemala's *caudillos* (military strongmen) needed a residence befitting their status as rulers of a quasi-feudal kingdom, to which end the palace served them quite well. The 1996 peace accords were signed here, and it was subsequently converted into a museum (tel. 2253-0748, 8 A.M.–3 P.M. daily, free). Today it is also used to host visiting dignitaries and movie stars, notably President George W. Bush and Mel Gibson.

Among the city's excellent museums is **Museo Miraflores** (7a Calle 21-55, Zona 11, Paseo Miraflores, tel. 2470-3415, 9 A.M.–7 P.M. Tues.–Sun., US$2 adults, US$1 children/students), detailing the history of the Mayan site of Kaminaljuyú, which once occupied part of the valley that is home to modern-day Guatemala City. Just outside the museum's main entrance is a replica of an irrigation canal similar to those found throughout the Mayan city as early as 600 B.C. Inside, the large window panels provide fantastic views of the stark contrast between old and new, with the green temple mound of structure B-V-3 flanked by modern glass buildings in the background. Also at the entrance is a scale model of what the city probably looked like in its heyday, built into the museum floor under a glass case. In the main exhibit area, you'll find a comprehensive history of Kaminaljuyú in English and Spanish, as well as a burial display, pottery, jade jewelry, stone sculptures, and obsidian blades. There are also old photographs of the site's excavation and maps showing the large area once occupied by the ancient city. You are free to explore the temple mounds outside (there are steps built into them). A few more temple mounds can be found in the vicinity of the museum, having been completely closed in by one of the city's larger shopping complexes.

Detailing Guatemala's modern-day cultural legacy is the not-to-be-missed **Museo Ixchel** (6a Calle Final, Zona 10, tel. 2331-3739, 9 a.m.–5 p.m. Mon.–Fri., 9 a.m.–1 p.m. Sat., www.museoixchel.org, US$3.50 adults, US$2 students). On the grounds of the Francisco Marroquín University, this museum is dedicated to Mayan culture with an emphasis on weaving and traditional costumes. Anyone with even a casual interest in Mayan weaving will find the museum enthralling, as it manages to condense the country's rich weaving heritage spanning a fairly vast geographical range into a single place with excellent displays and an attractive setting. The museum is housed in a beautiful brick building built to resemble a Mayan *huipil,* or hand-woven embroidered blouse. On display are pre-Hispanic objects, photographs, hand-woven fabrics, ceremonial costumes, weaving tools, and folk paintings by Guatemalan artist Andrés Curruchich. There are interactive multimedia displays, a café, bookstore, and *huipiles* for sale in the excellent gift shop. Displays are in English and Spanish.

While you're busy getting your bearings and establishing what life in Guatemala City might be like, be sure to check out the city's **Zona Viva.** Within Zona 10, east of Avenida La Reforma all the way to 6a Avenida and running north–south from 10a Calle to 16 Calle, the Zona Viva is among Guatemala City's most pleasant commercial districts with a variety of hip cafés, trendy boutiques, lively bars and nightclubs, excellent restaurants, and expensive hotels. It's Guatemala City at its best, and after long periods of time in the country's hinterlands, it can be downright refreshing.

Unlike in downtown Guatemala City, you'll find plenty of trees sheltering the streets from the harsh tropical sun in addition to wide, pedestrian-friendly sidewalks. Zona Viva's many high-rise buildings harbor banks, office buildings, the bulk of Guatemala City's international hotel chain properties, and condominiums. None of these buildings is more than 20 stories high, as the airport's proximity limits vertical expansion of the adjacent areas, giving the neighborhood a cosmopolitan feel without the claustrophobic concrete jungle look found in larger international cities. Interspersed between office buildings are the area's many dining and entertainment options, and tucked away into the side streets are some of Guatemala's nicest residences sheltered behind walls, barbed wire, and bougainvillea.

During the day, Zona Viva's streets are mostly the haunt of businesspeople due to the area's prominence as the city's main financial district. By night, especially on weekends, it becomes the enclave of young folks heading to the area's bars and nightclubs or to dinner at a fancy restaurant.

LA ANTIGUA GUATEMALA
Accommodations

Antigua has a wide variety of accommodations ranging from budget backpacker hostels to some of the region's fanciest boutique hotels and even a golf resort. The excellent value **Casa Cristina** (Callejón Camposeco #3A, between 6a and 7a Avenida, tel. 7832-0623, www.casa-cristina.com, US$22–37 d) has beautifully decorated, colorful rooms with wrought-iron accents, Guatemalan bedspreads, tile floors, and private hot water bathrooms. Pricier "standard plus" rooms have cable TV, while deluxe rooms also have gorgeous volcano views and mini-fridges. Room rates include unlimited use of wireless Internet, purified drinking water, coffee, and tea.

Hotel Posada San Pedro (3a Avenida Sur #15, tel. 7832-3594, www.posada sanpedro.net, US$35 d) is also stylish and comfortable, featuring 10 spotless rooms with firm beds, tile floors, wooden furnishings, attractive tile bathrooms, and cable TV. Guests also enjoy use of a living room and full kitchen. There's a second location at 7a Avenida Norte #29 (tel. 7832-0718), with the same rates but slightly smaller, less attractive rooms.

A perennial favorite for its classic charm and colonial ambiance is **Posada de Don Rodrigo** (5a Avenida Norte #17, tel. 7832-0291, US$68 d). It's well located near the Arco de Santa Catalina. Housed in a very old colonial mansion, the inviting rooms have been updated with all the comforts of a modern hotel. The staff wear traditional costumes, and marimba can often be heard in the main courtyard.

Top pick among the chain hotels is **Porta Hotel Antigua** (8a Calle Poniente #1, tel. 7832-2801, www.porta hotels.com, US$150–225). There are

a room with a view at Posada de Don Rodrigo

© AL ARGUETA

© AL ARGUETA

The Posada de los Leones is one of Antigua's finest hotels.

77 sumptuous rooms with chimneys, colorful walls with faux finishes, Guatemalan decor, and charming stained hardwood floors in its standard and deluxe rooms and suites. There's a restaurant serving excellent Guatemalan and international dishes overlooking the swimming pool set amidst tropical gardens, as well as a fully stocked quaint wooden bar. Candles provide atmosphere at night, and a colonial fountain graces the entrance to the hotel. The service is excellent, as is the courteous and friendly staff. An excellent boutique property.

Posada de los Leones (Las Gravileas #1, tel. 7832-7371, www.lionsinnantigua.com, US$165–250 d) is set amidst coffee trees and tropical gardens. Its six spacious, absolutely gorgeous rooms feature high ceilings, hardwood floors, and a delightful array of classy European and Guatemalan decorative touches. On the house's second floor is Antigua's loveliest terrace overlooking tropical gardens, the surrounding coffee plantation, and the volcanoes off in the distance. You can enjoy drinks on the terrace in addition to a lap pool, a comfortable living room, and a library. There is wireless Internet throughout the house.

Guatemalan investors recently unveiled Antigua's very own golf resort, much to the delight of local elites and foreign golf enthusiasts. **La Reunión Antigua Golf Resort** (tel. 6637-4089, www.antiguagolfresort.com, US$278–330 d) lies 17 kilometers from Antigua in neighboring Alotenango on the road to the Pacific coast. Each of the resort's 26 suites is stylishly decorated with Guatemalan furnishings and includes a private plunge pool and outdoor shower on a lovely patio. Choose from a master suite or the more spacious Suite Gran Clase with volcano views and Jacuzzi. The resort's restaurant, Argentilia, is an Argentine-style steak house which also offers tasty pasta dishes and a good wine selection.

Food

Despite its small size, Antigua holds a tremendous concentration of great eateries. **Doña Luisa Xicotencatl** (4a Calle Oriente #12, tel. 7832-2578,

7 A.M.–9:30 P.M. daily, US$5–10) serves delicious breakfasts, snacks, pastries, and light meals in a delightful garden courtyard. There are freshly baked breads and cakes available all day from the bakery at the front of the building.

Café Condesa (Portal del Comercio #4, tel. 7832-0038, 7 A.M.–8 P.M. Sun.–Thurs., until 9 P.M. Fri.–Sat., US$5–12) is a great place to get some pep in your step with an early breakfast and coffee or to refuel later in the day. There are excellent cakes, pastries, sandwiches, and salads served in a pleasing garden atmosphere or you can enjoy their all-day breakfasts. A Sunday brunch is served from 10 A.M. until 2 P.M. and includes scrambled eggs, home-fried potatoes, silver dollar pancakes, quiche, homemade bread and muffins, just to name a few items. If you're on the go, grab a cup of their excellent coffee at the Condesa Express next door.

Café Sky (corner of 6a Calle Oriente and 1a Avenida Sur, tel. 7832-7300, 8 A.M.–11 P.M. daily, US$5–12) serves up a variety of tasty menu items, including sandwiches, lasagnas, and quesadillas. There are wonderful volcano views from the restaurant's rooftop terrace location.

Another good choice is **Restaurante Las Palmas** (6a Avenida Norte #14, tel. 7832-9734, www.laspalmasantigua.com, 9 A.M.–10 P.M. daily, US$7–12). Among the varied menu items are fish in cilantro sauce, spinach lasagna, shrimp in alfredo pasta, and filet mignon. There are whirring ceiling fans, a fully stocked bar, and vibrant tropical Latin decor.

One of Antigua's legendary restaurants is **La Fonda de la Calle Real** (3a Calle Poniente #7, tel. 7832-0507, noon–10 P.M. daily; 5a Avenida Norte #5,

© AL ARGUETA

Antigua has a number of bars popular with expats and travelers.

tel. 7832-2629, noon–10 P.M. daily; 5a Avenida Norte #12, tel. 7832-3749, 8 A.M.–10 P.M. daily, US$5–15), with three branches, the nicest of which is the one on 3a Calle Poniente. There is a varied menu of Guatemalan favorites including chiles rellenos as well as tasty grilled meats. If you can't decide, do like Bill Clinton did and order the filling sampler menu.

For fine dining, **Mesón Panza Verde** (5a Avenida Sur #19, tel. 7832-2925, www.panzaverde.com, lunch and dinner Tues.–Sat., brunch and lunch Sun., US$15–25) is easily one of Guatemala's best options thanks to the culinary prowess of its Swiss-born, French-trained chef, Cristophe Pache, and its sophisticated European ambiance. The mostly French cuisine is heavy on meat and fish dishes. The wine list is impressive, as are the desserts. A Sunday brunch is served 10 A.M.–1 P.M. You can enjoy your meal in the main dining room surrounded by fine art under a vaulted ceiling or alfresco in La Cueva, a covered patio beneath baroque arches beside a gurgling fountain.

Sights

Antigua packs a lot of history into a small area, and you might feel overwhelmed by all the stunning ruined architecture. You can explore on your own or hire the services of a local guide to show you around. Recommended guides include **Martha Hettich** (1a Avenida Sur #4A, tel. 7832-2134 or 5792-2459, www.marthahettich.com). She does recommended guided historical and shopping tours of Antigua and the highlands, by appointment only. Martha can also tell you stories garnered from years spent in Guatemala and is a wealth of historical information.

Practically an Antigua institution, **Antigua Tours** (3a Calle Oriente #22, tel. 7832-5821, www.antiguatours.net) offers excursions guided by Elizabeth Bell (author of *Antigua Guatemala: The City and Its Heritage*) Tuesday, Wednesday, Friday, and Saturday at 9:30 A.M. Tours on Monday and Thursday at 2 P.M. are guided by Roberto Spillari. All tours meet at the fountain in Antigua's central park and cost US$20. There is also a guided tour of nearby villages, including San Antonio Aguas Calientes, San Pedro Las Huertas, and San Juan del Obispo, going out Monday–Friday at 2 P.M. and lasting three hours. It costs US$35 per person with a two-person minimum.

Antigua's **Parque Central,** or central park, is easily the most beautiful in the country and is the hub of activity for shoe-shiners, strolling lovers, tour groups, ice cream vendors, and foreign visitors. Gracing the central part of the square is a lovely fountain dating to 1936, a re-creation of an earlier version from 1738 destroyed by earthquakes. The park is bordered by the lovely Catedral de

Santiago, the Palacio de los Capitanes Generales, Palacio del Ayuntamiento, and a commercial arcade known as the Portal del Comercio.

Three blocks north of the park along 5a Avenida Norte (also known as Calle del Arco) is one of Antigua's most recognizable landmarks, the **Arco de Santa Catalina.** It is all that remains of a convent dating to 1613. As the convent grew, it expanded to include a structure across the street. The arch, then, was built to allow the nuns to cross over to the other side while avoiding contact with the general populace in accordance with strict rules governing seclusion. Its current version with a clock tower is a reconstruction dating to the 19th century, as the original was destroyed in the 1773 earthquakes. The clock is a French model, which needed to be wound every three days. It stopped working after the 1976 earthquake but was repaired in 1991. Looking south through the archway, you'll find some nice framing for an unobstructed view of Agua volcano. The archway is practically an Antigua icon and is beautifully painted in a rich yellow hue with white accents that have become delightfully aged.

In the hills north of the city stands the giant stone cross that gives the hill its name, **Cerro de la Cruz.** From this lookout point, there are sweeping views south over the city with Agua volcano in the background. Robberies were once frequent here until the creation of the tourism police, who began escorting visitors to the site and pretty much put an end to these crimes. It's still a good idea to go along with a police escort and to visit during daylight hours. Escorts are available free from the Politur (tourism police) station near the central plaza. Bring along your camera and some water. It's about a 30-minute walk from the plaza. From the top of the hill, you can see the entire Antigua valley, and the cross makes for a nice foreground element.

No tour of Antigua would be complete with a visit to at least one of its ruined convents. **Iglesia y Convento de las Capuchinas** (2a Avenida Norte and 2a Calle Oriente, 9 A.M.–5 P.M. daily, US$4) was abandoned after being destroyed in the earthquake of 1773. Restoration began in 1943 and is still being carried out today. The convent's foundation dates to 1726, making it the city's fourth, and is the work of renowned Antigua architect Diego de Porres. There are beautiful fountains and courtyards flanked by sturdy stone pillars with stately arches and flowering bougainvillea. It is certainly the most elegant of Antigua's convents and well worth a look for those with even a casual interest in colonial Latin American architecture. The convent was the haunt of the Capuchin nuns from Madrid, a rather strict order limiting its numbers to 28 and requiring the nuns to sleep on wooden beds with straw pillows and to sever all ties to the outside world.

The church consists of a single nave lacking side aisles. There are two choir areas, one adjacent to the altar on the ground floor and another on the second floor at the end of the nave.

Following the 1773 earthquakes and the subsequent transfer of the Guatemalan capital to its new location, many of the convent's historical artifacts were likewise transferred to their new home in the San Miguel de Capuchinas convent in modern-day Guatemala City.

The city's not-to-be-missed museum is **Centro Cultural Casa Santo Domingo,** housed inside the Casa Santo Domingo hotel (3a Calle Oriente #28, tel. 7832-0140, 9 A.M.–6 P.M. Mon.–Sat., 11:15 A.M.–6 P.M. Sun., US$5). The site was once the city's largest and wealthiest monastery, with a church completed in 1666 but damaged and eventually destroyed by the 18th-century earthquakes. Several museums are housed within the same complex, including the colonial museum harboring Catholic relics, among them an old Roman coin found during the excavations for the hotel's construction. Other highlights of this wonderful historical complex include a gorgeous monastery church, cleared of rubble and restored in the early 1990s. It is now frequently used for weddings. Below this area are two crypts. The first of these, the Cripta del Calvario, has a well-preserved crucifixion mural. The other crypt harbors two graves with human bones.

There is also a small archaeological museum, but the highlight here is the **Museo Vigua de Arte Precolombino y Vidrio Moderno,** a fantastic, well-presented juxtaposition of colonial and pre-Columbian artifacts mixed with glass art. Rounding out the impressive list of attractions is the Casa de la Cera, an elaborate candle shop.

THE WESTERN HIGHLANDS
Lake Atitlán Accommodations

As the largest lakeside town, **Panajachel** has the greatest variety of accommodations. In the budget category, a great choice is **Hotel Sueño Real** (tel. 7762-0608, US$24–33 d), featuring comfortable rooms beautifully decorated with Guatemalan accents, private hot water bathroom, fan, and TV. There's a lovely second floor terrace, and Internet access is available on the first floor. The nicest room is on the second floor, just off the patio.

Slightly pricier, **Rancho Grande Inn** (Calle Rancho Grande, tel. 7762-2255, www.ranchograndeinn.com, US$55–77 d) dates to the 1940s and has 12 attractive rooms, suites, and cabins housed in faux-thatch-roof villas fronting a well-manicured lawn and tropical gardens. There's a nice kidney-shaped swimming pool with a partial wooden deck. Rates include a deliciously filling breakfast

including pancakes, eggs, beans, and good, strong coffee to put some pep in your morning step.

Panajachel's classiest accommodations are at **Hotel Atitlán** (tel. 7762-1441, www.hotelatitlan.com, US$120–190 d), just outside of town on a lovely and quiet lakeside plot. The lodge does a wonderful job of combining old school charm with modern amenities in its well-furnished, tastefully decorated rooms featuring tile floors, antiques, and colorful textiles. All rooms have balconies with gorgeous lake views. There are extensive tropical gardens, an attractive swimming pool, and boat docks. The hotel's restaurant is a favorite with well-to-do Guatemalans.

Enjoy a delicious meal at Casa Palopó's phenomenal restaurant.

In neighboring **Santa Catarina Palopó** is Lake Atitlán's finest hotel. **Casa Palopó** (Km 6.8 Carretera a San Antonio Palopó, tel. 7762-2270, www.casapalopo.com, US$125–276 d) is a colonial villa-turned-boutique hotel. Its comfortable rooms feature floor-to-ceiling windows with magnificent lake views and come loaded with antiques, brightly painted walls, exquisite furnishings, and wonderful extras like Italian cotton sheets and Aveda bathroom products. The small swimming pool is surrounded by lush gardens and overlooks the lake. Also on the property, farther up the hill is the even more alluring Villa Palopó, decorated with a tasteful mix of African tribal relics and Indonesian hardwood furnishings. There are hardwood floors and ceilings and fantastic lake views from each of the two suites (US$199.50-235 d). You can rent the whole villa for US$683 to US$998, depending on the season. The villa has its own lap pool, also overlooking the lake, and butler service.

Also in Santa Catarina, along the road heading back toward Panajachel, is lovely **Terraza Choi** (www.terrazachoi.com, US$70 d). More a private house than a hotel, it makes a great place to stay for folks seeking an insider's perspective on living in Guatemala. Expat owner James Gregory is happy to share his experiences living and working in Guatemala, and the villa makes a very comfortable base from which to explore Lake Atitlán. There are phenomenal lake views from the top floor terrace and a staircase that leads to the house's private lakeside dock. The house is beautifully decorated with original paintings made by the owner's mother.

Elsewhere around the lake, **Santa Cruza La Laguna** boasts several good hotels of its own. **El Arca de Noé** (tel. 5515-3712, www.atitlan.com/arca.htm, US$12–35 d) is run by friendly Wolfgang and Anna Kallab, an Austrian and German couple who arrived on the scene over 20 years ago. The delightful lodge has 10 rooms, half of them with private bathrooms. Three of the rooms are lovely stone-and-wood cottages. All of the rooms are rustic but nicely decorated with Guatemalan fabrics. Delicious breakfasts and lunches are served à la carte. Anna loves to cook and treats her guests to a delicious six-course dinner consisting of Guatemalan and European specialties for around US$10, served family-style. The lodge is solar-powered.

American-owned **Villa Sumaya** (tel. 5510-0229, www.villasumaya.com, US$45–85 d) has 14 beautiful rooms, all named after jungle animals. Some are housed in a thatch-roofed complex, others are farther up the hill in separate cabins. All of the spacious rooms have private hot water bathrooms, warm Guatemalan wool blankets, and patios with furniture and lovely hammocks. The rooms up the hill have mosquito netting and larger bathrooms with tubs, one of which is impressively built into the side of the mountain with lava rock adorning the semi-outdoor shower. There's an impressive hardwood-floor and thatch-roof yoga center, which is often booked months in advance by groups from the United States. Other amenities include a massage parlor, library, and two hot tubs. The restaurant here is correspondingly excellent, consisting of vegetarian selections as well as fish, meat, and chicken dishes prepared by two talented chefs. Delicious baked goods are also produced daily. Breakfast and lunch are à la carte. Dinner is a set menu served family-style. The outdoor café is housed in a pretty wooden patio overlooking the lake.

In neighboring **Jaibalito** is the wildly popular **La Casa del Mundo** (tel. 5218-5332 or 5204-5558, www.lacasadelmundo.com, US$27–60 d), a charming inn built into the side of a rocky cliff. There are rooms with shared or private bathrooms, all housed in wonderful stone cottages with outrageous lake views and decorated with tasteful Guatemalan accents. There's excellent swimming in a rocky cove where the water is an exquisite shade of emerald. There are kayaks for rent (US$4–7), and mountain biking can be arranged via Antigua-based Old Town Outfitters with at least two days' notice. The trail to Santa Cruz or San Marcos passes right outside the lodge's back door. Meals are served at set times in a small dining room on the ground floor of the main house. Dinner is served family style and costs US$10. The service here is excellent, and the Guatemalan-American owners are very friendly.

In **San Marcos La Laguna,** check out **Posada Schumann** (tel. 5202-2216, www.posadaschumann.com, US$15–50 d). It's the first place you'll come across if, like most people, you arrive into town at their dock. Most of the comfortable, well-furnished, and tastefully decorated rooms are housed in quaint stone-and-mortar cottages. An excellent value, room 12 is a deluxe second-floor wooden bungalow (US$25–36 d, depending on season) with its own deck. Rooms 8 and 10 have awesome volcano and lake views. The restaurant overlooking the well-tended gardens serves sandwiches, smoothies, and Guatemalan fare for breakfast and lunch, though the service can be slow.

In **San Pedro La Laguna,** the hippest budget place in town is the friendly, Israeli-owned **Zoola** (tel. 5534-3111, agmon2003@yahoo.com, US$3 in dorms to US$10 d), found along a trail east of the dock where boats come in from Panajachel. It has eight rooms, half of them with private bathrooms, and dorm beds. There's a movie lounge, book exchange, purified water from their own well, and a massage room, but the crowning achievement is the beautiful thatch-roof hammock lounge with comfortable pillows on wooden floors.

If you're on a bigger budget, your best bet is the brand-new **Mikaso Hotel** (tel. 5973-3129, www.mikasohotel.com, US$8 pp in dorm or US$25–45 d), with 11 rooms and a dormitory housed in an attractive Spanish neocolonial style building fronting the lakeshore. Rooms have tile bathrooms, ceiling fans, tile floors, and tasteful decor. The rooftop restaurant here is also quite smart, serving Mediterranean Spanish food including delicious *bocadillos* (sandwiches) and open from 7 A.M. to 10 P.M. Movies are shown three times a week on Wednesday, Friday, and Sunday nights.

Quetzaltenango Accommodations

Hotel Modelo (14 Avenida A 2-31, Zona 1, tel. 7761-2529, US$40 d) is a well-located, excellent-value hotel in an old colonial home run by a friendly Guatemalan family. The nicest rooms are in a section fronting the street and opening to a pleasant garden courtyard. All have private bathrooms, tile floors, cable TV, charming antique furniture, and warm wool blankets. The restaurant serves excellent breakfasts. When the main building fills up, guests are sent down the street to the equally pleasant **Anexo Hotel Modelo** (tel. 7765-1271, US$30 d). The rooms facing the street here are brighter and tend to feel airier, as they get sun and breezes all afternoon, which is more comfortable for those of us with rainy season mold allergies. Readers have complained about noise from a next-door dance hall.

The haunt of Guatemala's oligarchy on visits to Xela, **Pensión Bonifaz** (4a Calle 10-50, Zona 1, tel. 7765-1111, US$65–100 d) is a beautiful hotel, though it tends to feel stuffy thanks to the pretentious front desk staff, who put on airs to deal with their clientele. It has spacious, well-decorated rooms with private bathrooms, desks, and cable TV. Amenities include a restaurant, small gift shop, and a heated swimming pool in a pretty garden courtyard under an opaque ceiling letting in just enough sunlight. There's wireless Internet on the first floor, and the rooms just above it (123–130) get a signal. More modern rooms are housed in a newer section, but those in the original building harbor all the charm.

A gorgeous flower garden and rock waterfall set the mood as you enter Xela's most wonderfully atmospheric hotel, **Casa Mañen B&B** (9a Avenida 4-11, Zona 1, tel. 7765-0786, www.comeseeit.com, US$50–100 d), with nine tastefully decorated rooms featuring exquisite furnishings, wool blankets and throw rugs, terra cotta floors, cable TV, and private bathrooms. There's a rooftop terrace bar with wonderful city views. The delicious breakfast is served in a pleasant dining room looking out to the peaceful garden courtyard.

Lake Atitlán Food

The following food recommendations are in the area of Panajachel and Santa Catarina Palopó.

In a pleasant garden patio decorated with Asian-style spherical paper lamps, **Deli Jasmín** (Calle Santander, close to the lakeshore, tel. 7762-2585, 7 A.M.– 6 P.M. Wed.–Mon., US$5–10) serves delicious all-day breakfasts including bagels and English muffins in addition to healthy fare such as tofu and vegetarian dishes. The deli sells teas, jams, whole wheat bread, and cookies for you to take away. Farther up Calle Santander and under the same management is **Deli Llama de Fuego** (tel. 7762-2586, 7 A.M.–10 P.M. Thurs.–Tues., US$5–10), with much the same menu and surroundings.

For scrumptious Pan-Asian cuisine, check out **Las Chinitas** (Calle Santander, tel. 7762-2612, 8 A.M.–10 P.M. daily, US$5–12), where you can savor Malaysian curries and Thai dishes, among other dishes, at moderate prices. **Maktub'ar Café Jardín** (Calle Santander, tel. 7762-2151, 10 A.M.–1 A.M. Tues.– Fri., 8 A.M.–1 A.M. Sat.–Sun.) has a nice garden atmosphere and serves excellent fruit smoothies and delicious breakfasts.

Duck, escargot, lamb chops, and wiener schnitzel are on the menu at **Chez Alex** (halfway down Calle Santander, tel. 7762-0172, noon–3 P.M. and 6–10 P.M. daily, US$10–12), served in a tasteful atmosphere.

Casablanca (intersection of Calle Principal and Calle Santander, tel.

7762-1015, noon–11 P.M. daily, US$10–25) serves delicious pastas, chicken, meat, and seafood dishes accompanied by Chilean wines in a sophisticated atmosphere.

In Santa Catarina Palopó and on par with the fancy digs at Casa Palopó hotel is **6.8 Palopó.** The hotel's restaurant is a bit on the expensive side (US$15–25 for typical meal), but the food is certainly some of the best you'll find on the shores of Lake Atitlán. Among the culinary highlights are black lake bass in a sublime Thai chili and teriyaki sauce, a delightful roast duck in a dark chocolate and fig sauce, and a scrumptious steak bérnaise. Take in the spectacular lake views and sunsets from an airy terrace where you can enjoy a drink or romantic candle-lit dinner.

Quetzaltenango Food

Café El Árabe (4a Calle 12-22, Zona 1, tel. 7761-7889, noon–midnight daily, US$5–15) serves delicious Middle Eastern fare including fresh hummus and tasty falafel. It's conveniently located just off the plaza and can also be a lively place at night.

Café Baviera (5a Calle 13-14, tel. 7761-5018, 7 A.M.–8:30 P.M. daily, US$5–12) has a decidedly German atmosphere chock-full of antiques where you can enjoy scrumptious pastries, sandwiches, crepes, and shakes in addition to some of the best coffee in town.

Casa Babylon (5a Calle and 13 Avenida, tel. 7761-2320, 11:30 A.M.–11 P.M. daily, US$5–12) has a ground floor kitchen where you can watch your food being prepared. On offer are a variety of cocktails, a good Italian and French wine list, and nonalcoholic beverages including fresh fruit smoothies. Menu items include falafel, salads, tacos, quesadillas, pita pizzas, pastas, and vegetarian dishes. There are two more floors including a nice third-floor lounge.

Xela now boasts an excellent Tex-Mex restaurant with the recent addition of **Dos Tejanos** (4a Calle 12-33, Pasaje Enríquez, 7 A.M.–11 P.M. daily), where you can dig into authentic Texas barbecue ribs, chicken, and brisket.

Royal Paris (14 Avenida A 3-06, Zona 1, tel. 7761-1942, noon–11 P.M. Tues.–Sun., 6–11 P.M. Mon., US$10–25) is a very popular, highly authentic French restaurant with dishes that include crepes, baked Camembert, and onion soup as well as meat and chicken, which you can enjoy accompanied by excellent wines. There's live music on Friday and Saturday nights, and French or Italian movies are shown on Tuesday at 8 P.M.

Lake Atitlán Sights

In addition to the gorgeous lake, the Atitlán basin boasts numerous natural and cultural attractions. Just outside of Panajachel, 200 meters past Hotel Atitlán, **Reserva Natural Atitlán** (tel. 7762-2565, www.atitlan.com/resnat .htm, 8 A.M. to 5 P.M. daily, US$5 adults, US$2 students/children) is a wonderful nature preserve on the grounds of a former coffee farm. The reserve offers myriad attractions, including a visitors center, a zipline between trees in the forest canopy, a butterfly farm, a lakeside beach, and well-designed nature trails with hanging bridges leading to waterfalls, where you can spot monkeys and coatis (*pizotes*) along the way. Recently added to the reserve are spacious and attractive accommodations for up to six people; decks overlook the surrounding forests. Rates are US$55 s/d during the week and US$65 s/d on weekends. You are also welcome to camp here for US$14. Tent rentals cost US$4.50 per person.

If you're interested in the lake's geology and anthropological history, check out the **Museo Lacustre Atitlán** (Hotel Posada de Don Rodrigo, Calle Santander, tel. 7832-3594, 8 A.M.–6 P.M. Sun.–Fri., 8 A.M.–7 P.M. Sat., US$5 admission for nonguests). It features well-displayed exhibits on the geological history of Lake Atitlán and its creation, along with subaquatic Mayan archaeology, including ceremonial urns and incense burners, mostly from late pre-Classic and Classic times.

If you're not content with simply gazing at Atitlán's volcanoes, try climbing one of them. The most popular volcano climb (though certainly not an easy trek, by any means) is **Volcán San Pedro.** The volcano became a national park in 2006, so it is hoped that, as was the case with Pacaya volcano,

© AL ARGUETA

Volcán San Pedro is a popular climb.

its newly protected status will result in greater police presence and an end to the robberies that frequently happen near the summit. For now, check with locals before heading up the volcano. Under no circumstances should you attempt this hike alone, as it seems the easiest way to get robbed. Always go with a local guide. There is a visitors center at the trailhead, which is just off the road to Santiago. The hike is fairly strenuous, as the trail runs straight up the mountain with very little in the way of switchbacks. It takes 4–5 hours to reach the summit, which is still densely covered in thick cloud forest. There's a small gap in the trees at the top from which there are views of Santiago and the lake. Start your hike early in the day to avoid the midday heat and the clouds that typically gather at the summit of the lake's volcanoes in the afternoon.

Quetzaltenango Sights

Like the rest of Guatemala's important urban centers, Xela is built around a central park. The city's sprawling **Parque Centroamérica** is lined with government offices, museums, and a shopping arcade, among other buildings, and is itself splendidly shaded by trees and adorned by neoclassical monuments and flower beds. It gives the city a decidedly European feel, enhanced by the presence of several Greek columns, and is a fine place for people-watching or enjoying the warm afternoon sun amidst the surrounding buzz of activity. An artisans' market is held here the first Sunday of every month.

The legacy of maniacal dictator Manuel Estrada Cabrera's quest to emulate all things European, the neoclassical **Templo Minerva** is a monument to the Greek goddess of wisdom. It stands at the corner of Calle Minerva and Calle Rodolfo Robles. The temple looks over the city's bus terminal and busy market.

For the active traveler there's hiking up **Volcán Santa María,** which affords excellent views from its summit all the way to Lake Atitlán and over its active, much smaller neighbor, **Volcán Santiaguito.** Several local companies offer guided trips. It is very easy to get lost on these peaks, so a guide is strongly recommended. Hikers have gotten lost on the slopes of Volcán Santa María in the past.

THE PACIFIC COAST

Things are heating up along Guatemala's Pacific coast, which once lacked adequate accommodations to justify staying overnight on the beach. Cruise ships regularly dock at Puerto San José, and a number of area attractions have opened up to cater to visiting day-trippers.

Accommodations

Iztapa is undoubtedly Guatemala's sailfishing capital, and many area lodges are geared directly toward that clientele. Across the Canal de Chuiquimulilla and right on the beach, Iztapa's nicest accommodations are at the **Sailfish Bay Lodge** (U.S. toll-free tel. 800/638-7405, direct tel. 2426-3909, www .sailfishbay.com, US$125 d), run by American expatriate Robert Fallon. Accommodations here are usually sold as part of a sailfishing package, but you are more than welcome to stay on your own. The Guatemalan Pacific coast's best-kept secret is a modern, well-designed lodge featuring a thatch-roof seaside bar and swimming pool with Jacuzzi, comfortable ocean-view rooms with all the usual amenities, and an excellent restaurant fronting the canal. You can enjoy gorgeous views of three volcanoes rising above the surrounding mangroves as you dine. There are surfboards for guests' use. Transportation to the lodge from Guatemala City or Antigua is also available.

A number of small lodges have opened up along the road from Iztapa to Monterrico, about 25 kilometers away. The best of these is **Cayman Suites** (Km 10.5, lodge tel. 5529-6518, reservations tel. 2362-1708, www.caymansuites .com.gt, US$85–155 d), set on a spectacular beach flanked by a kidney-shaped swimming pool and open-air palapa-roofed restaurant and bar. Its 22 rooms feature all the usual amenities, some with gorgeous sea views, and include deluxe rooms, junior suites, and spacious, fully furnished suites. All rooms have wireless Internet, satellite TV, and fine hardwood accents. The restaurant serves excellent fusion cuisine and seafood. ATVs are available for rent.

Closer to Monterrico is **Utz Tzaba** (Km 21.8, tel. 5318-9452, www.utz-tzaba .com, info@utz-tzaba.com, US$89 d), which has 10 rooms in a large main building as well as four bungalows. All rooms have tile floors, private hot water bathrooms, wireless Internet, cable TV, air-conditioning, and ceiling fans. The bungalows include two bedrooms and a living room, and come fully furnished with mini-fridge, gas range, kitchen sink, and dining room table. There is a bar by the infinity-edge swimming pool with Jacuzzi, and the hotel's restaurant serves excellent meals including sandwiches, pasta, and seafood in the US$6–10 range. The lodge is closed yearly on Christmas Eve and Christmas Day. Call ahead, as it's also closed for fumigation about every two months.

In **Monterrico,** my favorite midrange accommodations are at **Hotel Pez de Oro** (reservations tel. 2368-3684, hotel tel. 7920-9785, www.pezdeoro.com, US$40 d weekdays, US$52 d weekends), with tastefully decorated rooms built around a swimming pool with wooden deck. The 11 attractive bungalows, all with private baths, feature terra-cotta floors, nice decorative accents, and firm beds. Equally well-decorated and -furnished raised platform bungalows with nice decks (or patios) and hammocks in a separate area with its own swimming pool cost the same. The restaurant here is excellent.

If you're looking for stylish beachside digs look no further than Monterrico's newest hotel, the Italian-owned **Dos Mundos Pacific Resort** (tel. 7762-2078, h2mundos@intelnet.net.gt, www.hoteldosmundos.com, US$80–140 d). This fabulous property features 14 luxurious beachfront villas with terracotta floors, hot-water showers, and air-conditioning in eco-chic thatch-roof structures with private patios. The bathrooms feature artsy ceramic sinks and oversize rain showerheads. The fine restaurant serves excellent Italian cuisine overlooking an infinity-edge swimming pool and the sea.

Heading back west, in the vicinity of **Puerto San José,** the **Soleil Pacífico** (tel. 2277-7777, www.gruposoleil.com) is a huge all-inclusive resort complex on a clean private beach with all the feel of an Acapulco beachside mega-resort. Although it's popular on weekends, you may just have the place all to yourself if you visit during the middle of the week. There are two swimming pools and a variety of dining options. All-inclusive rates start at US$160 per person per night Sunday though Thursday or US$200 on weekends. There are also deluxe suites and bungalows for US$300 and US$400 a night, respectively. You can get a day pass to enjoy the swimming pool and the hotel grounds for US$50 per person, a popular option with cruise ship passengers. Many of the sailfishing outfits also accommodate their clients here. Transport to the hotel is available from Guatemala City and La Antigua with prior arrangement. Its sister hotel is the Soleil La Antigua.

A newer luxury option includes planned hotels at Marina del Sur's **Juan Gaviota** (www.juangaviota.com), an exclusive seaside compound resembling a miniature Miami. It is expected that a U.S. hotel chain will oversee the lodge once it's completed.

If you're exploring the amusement parks near Retalhuleu, your best bet for accommodations is the **Hostales del IRTRA** (tel. 2423-9100, www.irtra.org .gt), encompassing a virtual leisure city with various lodges, restaurants, bars, swimming pools, and a mini-golf course. There are four separate lodging concepts ranging in price from US$40 a night in the simplest accommodations without air-conditioning to US$300 a night for a suite. The newest of the four *hostales,* **Palajunoj,** was inspired by the cultures inhabiting the world's tropical rainforests and is the popular favorite with guests. The five buildings in this complex each have a different theme: African, Polynesian, Thai, Indonesian, and Mayan. All rooms have air-conditioning, cable TV, private bathrooms, and wonderful wooden furnishings. The buildings housing the rooms at Palajunoj are worth a look for their unique architecture. The *hostales* outside this complex feature Spanish colonial, Greek, and rustic cabana architecture.

In Retalhuleu proper, the most atmospheric accommodations can be found at the family-run **Hostal Casa Santa María** (4a Calle 4-23, Zona 1, tel. 5202-8180 or 5205-1132, www.hostalcasasantamaria.com), where eight tastefully decorated rooms in a colonial home come with private hot water bath, cable TV, wireless Internet, air-conditioning, and/or ceiling fan. Room rates are US$25 for a double with fan or US$35 d with fan and air conditioning. There is a nice breakfast room and a café-bar with Internet access and book exchange. The young Guatemalan brother-and-sister team who own it also run Reuxtreme, Retalhuleu's finest outfitter, which operates weekend shuttles to Guatemala City and Antigua, among other services.

Another fine place to lay your head is the friendly **Posada de Don José** (5a Calle 3-67, Zona 1, tel. 7771-0180 or 7771-0841, donjose@terra.com.gt, US$42–55 d), in an attractive two-story building centered around a small swimming pool and courtyard. Standard rooms are spotless and have good beds, cable TV, air-conditioning, ceiling fan, phone, and private hot water bath. The larger suites have a sitting area and some nice furniture.

Food

The region's best restaurants are in the hotels catering to sailfish enthusiasts or in the resorts. In Monterrico, **Café del Sol** (all meals daily), in its namesake hotel, serves up excellent seafood dishes (US$4–8) under an airy palapa or on a pleasant beachside patio. Also in town, on the sandy street parallel to the shore, is **Taberna El Pelícano** (across from Johnny's Place, tel. 5584-2400, noon–2 P.M. and 6:30–9:30 P.M. Mon.–Fri., 6:30–10 P.M. Sat., noon–3 P.M. and 7–9:30 P.M. Sun.). It serves up good pasta dishes and seafood for US$4–8 and has a fully stocked bar.

The restaurant at the new **Dos Mundos Pacific Resort** (tel. 7762-2078, US$8–15), overlooking the sea and an infinity-edge swimming pool, is quite good thanks to its Italian chef. In Retalhuleu, an excellent choice is the restaurant at **Posada de Don José** (5a Calle 3-67, Zona 1, tel. 7771-0180 or 7771-0841), serving up international cuisine with Guatemalan flair.

Sights

Biotopo Monterrico-Hawaii is a protected area encompassing the beaches and mangrove swamps of Monterrico and those of adjacent Parque Hawaii. They are the prime nesting sites for sea turtles on Guatemala's Pacific seaboard, including the giant leatherback and smaller olive ridley turtles. Locals are involved in a conservation project with the local turtle hatchery whereby they are allowed to keep half of the eggs they collect from nests and turn in the other half to the hatchery. Located in the heart of town and run by the San Carlos University Center for Conservation Studies (CECON), the **Tortugario Monterrico** (on the sandy street just behind Johnny's Place, 8 A.M.–noon and 2 P.M.–5 P.M. daily, US$1) encompasses a turtle hatchery right on the beach where collected eggs are reburied and allowed to hatch under protected conditions. There's also a visitors center. In addition to baby sea turtles, the hatchery has enclosures housing green iguanas, crocodiles, and freshwater turtles bred on-site for release into the wild. The staff at CECON is always on the lookout for Spanish-speaking volunteers.

Near the coastal town of Escuintla, heading east on the road to Taxisco, is one of the most unique attractions in Guatemala and indeed all of Central America. At **Auto Safari Chapin** (Km 87.5 Carretera a Taxisco, tel. 5517-1705, www.autosafarichapin.org, US$7 adults, US$6 children) you can drive through grounds harboring a variety of animals, including zebras, hippos, rhinos, giraffes, and a lion. There are also local species like macaws and monkeys, which you can see in a small zoo, and an aviary. You can get up close and personal with the park's giraffes at a rest area partway through the drive. A swimming pool and restaurant round out the list of amenities.

If ostriches are more your thing, check out **Avestruces Maya** (tel. 5608-0835 or 5608-8075, www.avestrucesmaya.com, 10 A.M.–6 P.M. daily, US$3.50 adults, US$2.65 children 10 and over, children under 10 free), occupying 27 acres. It is mostly devoted to raising ostriches but also includes a small petting zoo, plant nursery, and river-like swimming pool where you can relax in an inner tube. A restaurant (open weekends) specializes in ostrich meat, and a small shop sells ostrich leather wallets, boots, purses, and assorted eggshell trinkets. The surprisingly supple leather can be very expensive. The park is located at kilometer 100 along the old road from Guatemala City to Puerto San José. You can camp here for US$3.25.

Guatemala's most popular tourist attractions are not its Mayan ruins or even the colonial city of Antigua. The twin amusement parks of **Xocomil and Xetulul,** just outside of Retalhuleu, receive over one million visitors per year. The first of these, **Parque Acuático Xocomil** (tel. 7772-5780, Km 180.5 on the road to Quetzaltenango, www.irtra.org.gt, 9 A.M.–5 P.M. Thurs.–Sun. most of the year, Wed.–Sun. Nov. 1–Dec. 15, and daily Dec. 15–Jan. 7, US$10 adult, US$7 children) is a wonderful water park on par with the world's best and a must-see if you are traveling with children. Among the attractions are 14 water slides, a wave pool, and a lazy river meandering through the complex of re-created Mayan ruins and monuments. The main restaurant showcases a Mayan pyramid painted in ochre, green, and yellow, as it would have looked in the Classic period. Additional food stands are scattered throughout the park.

The second phase of an eventual four-park plan is **Parque de Diversiones Xetulul** (tel. 7722-9450, www.irtra.org.gt, 10 A.M.–6 P.M. Thurs.–Sun. most of the year, Wed.–Sun. Nov. 1–Dec. 15, daily Dec. 15–Jan. 7, US$27 adult, US$13 children), where a variety of amusement park rides are spread out among seven plazas, each with its own restaurant and gift shop showcasing a variety of replicated world monuments. Among the highlights are Paris's Moulin Rouge, Rome's Trevi fountain, and Guatemala's own Gran Jaguar Temple from Tikal. The park is also home to Central America's largest roller coaster.

IZABAL AND LAS VERAPACES
Accommodations

On the gorgeous Río Dulce, **Hacienda Tijax** (about 1 km east of the bridge on the river's northern bank, tel. 7930-5505, VHF channel 09, www.tijax .com) is one of Guatemala's most enjoyable places to stay. The least expensive rooms are above the restaurant and cost US$13 d with shared bath, though the quaint little A-frame cabins on the riverfront are what this place is all about. Cabins with shared bath go for US$24 d, or US$39 d with private bathroom. There are six private-bath cabins with air-conditioning available for an extra US$10. Spacious bungalows cost US$70 d. All rooms have comfortable beds with mosquito netting and fans. Amenities include an excellent restaurant housed under a large palapa structure, an inviting swimming pool, and Internet access. Activities include a guided tour around the hacienda's working rubber plantation to a lookout tower with gorgeous views of the river and El Golfete, passing a hanging bridge over the forest along the way; two-hour horseback riding tours around the farm; kayaking; and sailing. Tours cost US$10–25 per person. There's a boat marina here.

A fine choice for budget travelers is **Casa Perico** (tel. 7930-5666 or 7909-0721, VHF channel 68), a few kilometers east along the river. Situated beside the Río Bravo, a small tributary of the Río Dulce, the lodge offers rooms in a dormitory above the restaurant/bar for US$5 per person or wooden cabins with private baths for US$15 d. It's a bit out of the way, which is precisely what brings most guests here. The Swiss owners cook good meals (dinner is about US$5–6) and will pick you up from Río Dulce (Fronteras) for free and drop you off at the end of your stay.

Near the Río Dulce bridge, heading west toward the San Felipe castle, **Tortugal** (tel. 5306-6432 or 7742-8847, VHF channel 68, www.tortugal.com) offers a splendid setting, beautiful accommodations, and wonderful attention to details. You can stay in rustically comfortable, tastefully decorated thatch-roof cabins (US$30 d), some with adjoining sun decks, others on raised platforms. Some of the cabins come with tables and chairs, a couch, and hammocks. There are also two dormitories, with beds for US$10 per person, one of which is directly over the water on a raised platform over a dock. All beds have reading lamps. The accommodations all share a bathroom, where the showers are hot and well pressurized. The filtered tap water here is drinkable. There's an excellent restaurant serving vegetarian fare and Guatemalan takes on international dishes in a lovely soaring thatch-roof structure built on a platform over the water. Above the restaurant is a clubhouse where there's a big-screen TV with satellite connection, pool table, and computers with high-speed wireless Internet. Activities include catching some rays on the docks, kayaking (free for guests), sailing, and Rover tours to the jungle hot springs of nearby Finca El Paraíso.

Cobán makes a comfortable base for exploring the neighboring Alta Verapaz wilderness, and its excellent accommodations are a reflection of this fact. In the budget range is one of the best values you'll find anywhere in Guatemala. **Casa D'Acuña** (4a Calle 3-11, Zona 2, tel. 7951-0482 or 7951-0484, casadeacuna@ yahoo.com) lies at the bottom of a steep hill south of the main plaza and has four comfortable dormitories with four beds apiece (US$7 per person) as well as two private double rooms (US$13 d). All rooms have shared bath.

Another excellent value is **Hostal de Doña Victoria** (3a Calle 2-38, Zona 3, tel. 7951-4213, US$25 d), in a 400-year-old colonial home radiating with atmosphere. Its eight rooms centered round a pretty courtyard and café are tastefully decorated and have TVs, desks, and private hot water bathrooms. There is also a shared-bath bunk-bed dormitory where you can stay for US$3.50 per person.

Beautiful **Casa Duranta** (3a Calle 4-46, Zona 3, tel. 7951-4188, info@casa duranta.com, www.casaduranta.com, US$47 d) has 10 tastefully decorated, well-appointed rooms, all with private baths, Guatemalan indigenous blankets, tile floors, and wrought ironworks. Amenities include a TV lounge, a reading area, and wireless Internet throughout the colonial house centered around an appealing courtyard. An on-site café is open for three meals daily.

West of the central plaza is **Hotel La Posada** (1a Calle 4-12, Zona 2, tel. 7952-1495, www.laposadacoban.com, US$50 d), in a 400-year-old colonial mansion with tile floors, Guatemalan accents, and attractively tiled private hot-water bathrooms. Try for a room away from the busy main street on the front end of the hotel. The restaurant here is quite good, though service can be spotty.

If you're traveling north to Semuc Champey, you'll find one of the hippest hotels in all of Central America 500 meters along the road between Lanquín and the village of Cahabón. **El Retiro** (tel. 7983-0009) offers a variety of accommodations for all budgets in a splendid setting beside the Río Lanquín. The so-called "posh block" has tastefully decorated rooms with private baths and electric hot water heaters (US$24 d). There are hammocks out front for taking in the wonderful vistas toward the river and surrounding hillsides. A bed in one of the four-person dormitories costs US$4. Rooms with shared bath are also available, and range from US$10 to US$13 d. You can camp here or sleep in a hammock for US$2. The palapa-style bar plays great music and is lined with rope-swing bar seats. The restaurant serves excellent food, with dinner being a nightly communal experience. There are barbecues on Wednesday night; Saturday night is Mexican. The lodge can arrange a variety of activities for you, including inner tubing on the river for US$1.50 and horseback riding (US$5–16).

If you're visiting the Candelaria caves, namely the Complejo Cultural y Ecoturístico Cuevas de Candelaria, stay at the wonderful **Candelaria Lodge** (tel. 7861-2203, reservaciones@cuevasdecandelaria.com, US$15–20 per person), which serves as the perfect base for exploring the caves and several other local attractions. The comfortable, stylishly decorated cabins (all with shared bath) are set amidst the tropical forest. Delectable French and international dishes (including crepes that are to die for) are served in the lodge's main dining room.

Food

Río Dulce has a number of good eateries centered around the northern end of the bridge. **Bruno's Hotel & Marina** (tel. 7930-5175, www.mayaparadise.com, 7 A.M.–10 P.M.) is especially popular with boaters for its varied menu of international dishes and snacks in the US$5–10 range as well as its TV news and sports in an open-air dining room right by the water. Just up the street, **Restaurante Río Bravo** (tel. 7930-5167, 7 A.M.–10 P.M. daily) serves a similar menu, including good seafood, pasta dishes, and pizzas (US$11) on an open-air deck over the water. There's a full bar and it's a popular place for meeting fellow travelers.

Along a side street 50 meters from the bridge, **Sundog Café** (tel. 5529-0829) has delicious hot sandwiches, including an avocado melt, baguettes, and pastrami sandwiches. There's a 5:20 happy hour.

Whether or not you're staying at **Hacienda Tijax** (tel. 7930-5505, VHF channel 09, www.tijax.com), it makes a great place to eat for its rugged jungle ambiance and delicious sandwiches, seafood, salads, pasta, and steak dishes in the US$5–13 range served in an airy high-ceilinged palapa structure. They brew excellent coffee and have a full bar. Also out this way, about two kilometers downstream from Río Dulce, is **Mario's Marina** (tel. 7930-5569, www .mariosmarina.com), which has a restaurant/bar that is popular with the sailing crowd and serves a variety of seafood and international dishes. Bar patrons can browse the book exchange or enjoy a game of darts.

Closer to San Felipe castle, the restaurant at **Tortugal** (tel. 5306-6432 or tel. 7742-8847, VHF channel 68, www.tortugal.com, 7 A.M.–10 P.M.) is worth a stop for its deliciously prepared, creative menu options and superb location right on the water away from the noise and traffic closer to town. Prepared using fresh ingredients, the menu includes a harmonious blending of authentic Guatemalan cuisine with American and European flourishes. Try the Cannoli de Rosa (US$6), a flavorful Guatemalan crepe stuffed with grilled chicken, sweet onions, peppers, and a salsa cream sauce that will make you swoon. Other dinner options range US$5–12 for items from a quarter pound BBQ burger to seafood stew. It's also a great place for breakfast (US$2.50–6) or lunch (US$4–6). The bar here serves some excellent cocktails, which you can enjoy along with the gorgeous jungle river scenery.

In Cobán, **El Bistro** (4a Calle 3-11, Zona 2, tel. 7951-0482 or 7951-0484, 6:30 A.M.–10 P.M. daily, US$7–15) serves a excellent international dishes, including great pasta, pizzas, meat dishes, homemade breads and pastries, salads, and sandwiches.

Another good place to eat is the café inside **Hostal de Doña Victoria** (3a Calle 2-38, Zona 3, tel. 7951-4213, US$5–10), though the menu is not as intricate as that of El Bistro and leans more toward Guatemalan dishes. It's always a good bet for breakfast.

A good option for fine dining can be found at **Café and Restaurant La Posada** (1a Calle 4-12, Zona 2, tel. 7952-1495, www.laposadacoban.com), inside the Hotel La Posada. The café (1 P.M.–8:30 P.M. Wed.–Mon.) is at the far end of the building and looks out onto the plaza. The fancier restaurant (7 A.M.–9:30 P.M. Mon.–Sat., 7 A.M.–11 A.M. Sun.) is set in an attractive dining room with a fireplace and two terraces facing a garden. The food at both is excellent, though the service is notoriously slow. It's a good place to relax and unwind if you have a few hours to kill or aren't in a hurry. The menu includes Guatemalan and international dishes.

West of the plaza, **Café El Tirol** (1a Calle 3-13, Zona 1, tel. 7951-4042, 7:30 A.M.–9 P.M.Mon.–Sat., US$5–10) is a great place for breakfast or a light meal and coffee enjoyed in a pleasant terrace. The smoothies and sandwiches are particularly tasty.

Sights

The best sights in the region of Izabal and Las Verapaces are natural attractions. One of Guatemala's oldest parks, the waterway connecting the Caribbean Sea with Lake Izabal is protected as **Río Dulce National Park,** covering 7,200 hectares along the river's 19-mile course. Much of the riverbank is shrouded in dense tropical forest punctuated at its most dramatic point by a large jungle canyon with hundred-meter rock faces known as **La Cueva de la Vaca.** The canyon is a 15-minute boat ride upstream from Lívingston. Along this route you'll also come across a graffiti-covered rock escarpment known as La Pintada, with the earliest painting in evidence dating to the 1950s.

In the vicinity of Puerto Santo Tomás de Castilla is **Cerro San Gil,** which encompasses **Río Las Escobas.** This idyllic park, centered around the Cerro San Gil mountain, comprises more than 77 square kilometers (19,000 acres) of lush rainforest. Bathed in rainfall throughout most of the year (averaging 6.5 meters/255 inches) as warm, humid air rises over the mountains from the sea to elevations in excess of 1,200 meters (3,900 feet), the preserve harbors an astounding amount of biodiversity. Among the wildlife protected here are 56 species of mammals, including tapirs and jaguars; 50 species of reptiles and amphibians; and over 350 species of birds, including toucans, black and white hawk eagles, and keel-billed motmots. Over 90 neotropical migrants winter in the area and include the blue-winged warbler and wood thrush.

The park also protects the important watershed of the Río Las Escobas, which supplies water to Puerto Barrios. Part of the watershed is open to visitors (US$8, including guided tour), who can bathe in Las Escobas's cool, clear waters and hike a series of nature trails winding through the park. The park is administered by private conservation group **FUNDAECO** (tel. 7948-4404, www.fundaeco.org.gt), which in partnership with The Nature Conservancy has been able to purchase large tracts of this rainforest ecosystem for preservation. Facilities for visitors include an excellent system of trails winding through the river and waterfalls. The trails include wooden bridges and stops along the way for swimming in stunning turquoise pools. More adventurous types can explore areas deeper into the reserve beginning at a trailhead just up the mountain and going from there to the Río Las Escobas through a dense stretch of forest (one hour), or to Cumbre Las Torres (four hours there and back), or encompassing multiple days of strenuous jungle hiking to the village of Carboneras and down the mountain to Río Dulce. Contact FUNDAECO if you wish to explore these options, as you will need prior authorization. A guided trek of either of the first two options costs US$20 per person. Rates for the longer trip are negotiable.

The park is an increasingly popular day trip with cruise ship passengers, many of whom reportedly state this to be their favorite stop after the crass commercialism of places like Cancún and beaches that all pretty much look the same. The park lies just off the road hugging the coastline from Puerto Santo Tomás de Castilla to the beach of Punta de Palma.

Alta Verapaz department's natural attractions are no less impressive. Also known as the Quetzal Biotope, **Biotopo Mario Dary Rivera** (US$3.50, 7 A.M.– 4 P.M. daily) is a 1,044-hectare (2,580-acre) protected area and one of several biotopes administered by San Carlos University's Department of Conservation Studies (CECON). It's conveniently located along Highway CA-14 at kilometer 160.5, about an hour from Cobán. Though quetzal birds are easier to spot in Sierra de las Minas, the elusive creatures are said to frequent the yards of some local eating establishments (Biotopín Restaurant and Ranchitos del Quetzal), where they like to feast on the fruits of the *aguacatillo* tree. The Quetzal Biotope's convenient roadside location means that if you're on your way to or from Cobán, you should at least stop in for a look. You might just get lucky and see one of Guatemala's most beloved national symbols, with its exotic green plumage, long tail feathers, and bright red breast. Your best chances are between February and September. Plan on being up early if you want to see them.

Semuc Champey Natural Monument and its gorgeous limestone pools (6 A.M.–6 P.M. daily, US$4) lie at the end of a rough dirt road nine kilometers from the town of Lanquín. Although they were once a remote attraction way off

© AL ARGUETA

Semuc Champey Natural Monument is one of Guatemala's most spectacular natural attractions.

the beaten path, they are now one of Las Verapaces' top tourist draws. Accordingly, infrastructure has improved in order to keep up with the rising numbers of visitors. Try not to visit on a weekend, as there are day-trippers in droves from Cobán and vicinity. A giant, 300-meter-long limestone bridge forms the backbone for the descending series of pools and small waterfalls that make up Semuc Champey. The water that fills the pools is the product of runoff from the Río Cahabón, churning as it plunges into an underground chasm from where it re-emerges downstream, at the end of this massive limestone overpass.

Lanquín is home to a series of caves but is also the departure point for **whitewater rafting** trips down the class III–IV **Río Cahabón.** A more impressive cave system is found in northern Alta Verapaz. The **Candelaria caves,** recently awarded national park status, were discovered in 1974 by Frenchman Daniel Dreux and comprise seven separate caves interconnected by the Río Candelaria, spanning 22 kilometers. The caves are 20–30 meters wide in places, with ceilings typically 10–60 meters high.

The northwest corner of Alta Verapaz was once the scene of intense fighting during the civil war, with regular military operations in the neighboring Ixcán jungles, where URNG rebels hid out. Thankfully, all that is now in the past, opening up some wonderful attractions that were once off-limits. **Laguna Lachuá National Park** consists of an almost perfectly circular turquoise lagoon surrounded by protected forest on all sides. The 14,500-hectare park (US$6 admission) is a place of singular beauty, with over 300 species of birds found here, including mealy parrots and keel-billed toucans. Jaguars still roam the park, and you can sometimes see footprints. The lagoon's Caribbean-like waters contain calcium deposits and high levels of sulphur, indicating the probable presence of petroleum beneath its waters. The lake lies partially below sea level, at an altitude of 173 meters above sea level but also 222 meters deep.

PETÉN
Accommodations
The town of **Flores** is still a regional hub for travelers arriving in Petén by air or bus from Guatemala City and making their way to the local attractions. As such, it has plentiful accommodations. For the best value in town head to the local hostel, **Los Amigos** (Calle Central next to ProPetén, tel. 5584-8795 or 5521-2873, www.amigoshostel.com). This backpacker's paradise features a restaurant/bar, security lockers, broadband Internet, and laundry service among its well-rounded list of amenities. The friendly Guatemalan and Dutch owners can also help you plan your travels to other parts of Guatemala. For the ultimate in affordable lodging, you can sleep in a hammock for under US$3

or in dorm beds costing US$3.50. Private rooms with shared bath cost US$8 d or US$11 d with private bath.

The lively **La Casona de la Isla** (Calle 30 de Junio, tel. 7926-0593, US$40–55) is an attractive lakeside house painted in bright yellow and orange hues housing 26 rooms with air-conditioning, cable TV, and private baths. There is a nice outdoor swimming pool, around which the rooms are centered, as well as a whirlpool.

An excellent value is **Hotel Casa Amelia** (Calle Unión, tel. 7926-3328, US$37 d). Its attractive, spotless rooms have original decor incorporating burlap bags for curtains, wooden furnishings, firm beds, ceiling fans, air-conditioning, and large hot water bathrooms. Some of the 10 rooms have nice lake views. All have large TVs with cable.

If you're looking for a bit of seclusion away from town, head to **Chal Tun Ha Lodge** (tel. 7926-3493 or 7867-5499, info@chaltunha.com, US$16 d), located on a three-acre forest preserve west of the town of San Miguel on a bluff with phenomenal lake views. Each of the six charming wooden cabins is set on a raised platform and is fully screened-in with well-ventilated canvas roofing, private hot water shower, and a private balcony. Activities include hiking, canoeing, bird-watching, horseback riding, and mountain biking. Other amenities include laundry service and Internet. There's a swimming pool and a pretty beach known as La Playita nearby.

In Santa Elena, across the causeway from Flores, **Maya Internacional** (central reservations tel. 2334-1818 or direct tel. 7926-2083, www.villasde guatemala.com) has 24 standard rooms and two junior suites ranging in price from US$70 to US$100. One of the area's first accommodations, the recently remodeled property features tastefully decorated rooms with balconies over-looking the lake, tile floors, ceiling fans, air-conditioning, and cable TV. The lodge's Vista al Lago Restaurant offers gorgeous lake views and a varied menu including a Sunday brunch. A swimming pool, great service, wireless Internet, and lovely open-air palapa lobby round out the list of features, making the Maya Internacional a fine choice.

In El Remate, on the shores of Lake Petén Itzá, **La Casa de Don David** (tel. 7928-8469 or tel. 5306-2190, www.lacasadedondavid.com) is a highly recommended establishment owned by a native Floridian transplanted to Guatemala some 30 years ago. His friendly wife and daughter help run the lodge, consisting of 15 rooms with private hot-water baths set amidst nicely landscaped grounds. Eleven of the rooms have air-conditioning; all have fans. Rates range from US$32 d for slightly noisier rooms with fans under the res-taurant to US$52 d for quieter rooms with air-conditioning set farther back from the main house. All prices include one free meal a day. The restaurant serves delicious meals ranging US$4–8 for lunch or dinner. The friendly staff can help you book transportation to virtually anywhere and can answer your travel questions. You can also snag discounted tickets for area canopy tours at the attractive gift shop in the main lobby. The hotel's very informative website is well worth checking out prior to visiting Petén.

Lake Petén Itzá is not without a large resort. **Camino Real Tikal** (tel. 7926-0204, www.caminoreal.com.gt, US$120 d) is a 72-room complex that has been in operation for over 15 years. A planned expansion may soon make it twice as large. The Camino Real has all the comforts you would expect from an international resort chain. The modern rooms are housed in cement structures topped with thatch-roof exterior. There are two restaurants, a bar, a coffee shop, and swimming pool. Recreational activities available to guests include sailing, kayaking, and windsurfing. A large ship does lake tours, and transfers from the Mundo Maya International airport can be arranged prior to arrival via a complimentary shuttle service. Discounted accommodation packages are often available by calling directly or booking via a travel agency.

For Petén's ultimate in style and luxury, head to fabulous **La Lancha** (tel. 7928-8331, www.blancaneaux.com), located farther west along the lakeshore in the village of Jobompiche. Part of movie director Francis Ford Coppola's impressive portfolio of properties, including two other hotels in Belize, La Lancha is Petén's best-kept secret. Its 10 comfortable rooms are housed in lake-view casitas (US$175–260 d) or rainforest casitas (US$110–190 d, depending on season). All rooms have exquisite Guatemalan fabrics and Balinese hardwood furniture. The rooms' wooden decks are graced with hammocks where you can lounge the day away watching the sky's reflection on placid Lake Petén Itzá or order drinks from the bar via your in-room "shell phone." Rates include a continental breakfast, and the restaurant serves gourmet Guatemalan dishes for lunch and dinner for about US$20 per person. There is a swimming pool, but if you wish to cool off in the lake, a short downhill walk leads to the water's edge. Kayaks and mountain bikes are available for exploring at your leisure, and you can book day trips to Tikal. Other activities include sightseeing in El Remate and Flores, fishing on the lake, and bird-watching at Cerro Cahuí.

There are only three hotels within the confines of Tikal National Park. My favorite is the **Jungle Lodge** (tel. 2476-8775, www.junglelodge.guate.com, US$40–80 d), offering decent bungalows with private hot-water baths, ceiling fans, and two double beds as well as a few very basic, less expensive rooms with shared bath. All are set amidst a pleasant tropical garden atmosphere, and there is a swimming pool. The restaurant here serves breakfast (US$5), lunch, and dinner (US$8–10). Tour groups often lunch here. Be advised the lodge is closed every year during the month of September.

Toward the old airstrip just past the museums is the friendly **Jaguar Inn** (tel. 7926-0002, www.jaguartikal.com), where you can choose from nine comfortable bungalows with small front patios with hammocks (US$53 d), a dormitory (US$10 pp), hammocks with mosquito netting (US$5), or camping (US$3.50). You can rent a tent for US$7. The restaurant here is a safe bet, serving up adequate portions of good food three meals a day. Dinner is about US$8. There are laptops available for Internet surfing and checking e-mail (US$5/hour), but the electricity shuts off at 9 P.M.

Next door, **Tikal Inn** (hoteltikalinn@itelgua.com, US$60–100 d) gets consistent praise for its large, comfortable rooms centered around the swimming pool just behind the hotel's restaurant. You can choose from standard rooms or pricier, more private bungalows; all have ceiling fans and private baths. The restaurant serves three meals a day.

Tikal's **campground** is opposite the visitors center, with a spacious grassy area for tents as well as palapa structures for stringing hammocks. There are showering stalls among the bathroom facilities. Hammocks and mosquito netting are available for rent, and there are tiny, two-person basic cabañas for US$6.50 pp. It costs US$4 pp to camp here.

If you're getting to or from Petén by road, you may want to spend the night in the pleasant area of Poptún, in the southern part of the department. Poptún is home to the wildly popular **Finca Ixobel** (tel. 5892-3188, www.fincaixobel .com), which has long drawn travelers coming overland to Petén with its wonderful accommodations and excellent food at moderate prices in an attractive jungle setting. Its wide-ranging activities allow guests the chance to explore myriad attractions nestled in the surrounding cool pine forests and rolling green hills. There are accommodations to suit every taste and budget, including hammocks (US$3), clean, comfortable dorms (US$4 pp), rooms with shared bath (US$13 d), and rooms with private baths (US$26 d). There are more luxurious bungalows and a suite for US$30 and US$36 d. The latest addition to Finca Ixobel's offerings is a series of tree houses amidst spacious grounds. Some have electricity; others are candlelit. Prices range from US$11 d with candlelight to US$17 d with electricity. Only one of the so-called tree houses is actually in a tree, but all are attractive, quite comfortable, and set above the ground. A deluxe tree house with its own bath and electricity is popular with honeymooners and goes for US$23 d.

The restaurant here serves delicious, inexpensive meals largely using ingredients grown on the finca's vegetable garden. Breakfast and lunch are à la carte, while dinner is served buffet style (US$4–8). Breakfast items include homemade yogurt and granola, pancakes, and eggs, with plenty of vegetarian options for lunch and dinner. There is also a bar set beside a swimming pond where you can chill out in a hammock or play a game of Twister with your new friends and fellow travelers.

Any bus traveling the Río Dulce–Flores highway will drop you off at the turnoff to Finca Ixobel. From there, it's just a short 15-minute walk to the lodge. You can arrange minibus transport to Flores and book bus tickets to Guatemala City from Finca Ixobel.

Another option is found nearby in the town of Machaquilá, seven kilometers north of Poptún. **Villa de los Castellanos** (Aldea Machaquilá, tel. 7927-7541, US$25–40 d) is just off the road in a peaceful riverside setting overlooking the Río Machaquilá and set on 12 acres of land encompassing forest and a medicinal plant garden. Its 14 comfortable cabañas all have private baths. There is also a good restaurant, and the owners organize trips to local caves, ruins, and forest preserves.

Food

Flores has a number of decent restaurants. Housed in a tastefully decorated old building festooned with overhanging bougambilia blossoms and painted in bright shades of green and blue, the finest restaurant in Flores is undoubtedly **La Luna** (corner Calle 30 de Junio and Calle 10 de Noviembre, tel. 7926-3346, lunch and dinner Mon.–Sat., main dishes US$6–12). Culinary highlights include stuffed peppers, steak in a black pepper cream sauce, boneless chicken breast in wine sauce, pastas, and vegetarian dishes, including falafel.

Also on Calle 30 de Junio is **Capitán Tortuga** (tel. 7926-0247, 7 A.M.–10 P.M. daily). There is a spacious dining room housed under a large palapa structure and a two-story terrace with lake views where you can enjoy pasta, tacos, sandwiches, chicken quesadillas, grilled meats, and tasty pizzas in addition to a fully stocked bar. For snacks, try the burritos for about US$5.

Across the street is **La Albahaca** (tel. 7926-3354 or 7926-0505, 6–11 P.M. Tues.–Sun.), a cozy little place with a quiet atmosphere serving delicious beef and chicken recipes as well as scrumptious homemade pasta at reasonable prices. There is a nice assortment of Chilean wines.

Café-Bar Las Puertas (corner of Calle Central and Avenida Santa Ana, tel. 7926-1061, 11 A.M.–midnight Mon.–Sat.) serves good espresso beverages and is a popular place, partially on account of its lively atmosphere as a bar with funky decor involving paint-splattered walls. Try one of the many pasta dishes, or if just here for a drink, go with a margarita.

If you're looking for inspiration before an adventure to one of Petén's numerous archaeological sites, head to **Café Arqueológico Yaxhá** (Calle 15 de Septiembre, tel. 7926-0367, 7 A.M.–10 P.M. daily), where you can dine in a pleasant atmosphere featuring colorful Guatemalan tablecloths and photo montages of various Mayan sites, including Tikal, Yaxhá, and Nakúm. Although the chefs do a variety of dishes including steak, chicken, seafood, pasta, and even curry, they specialize in what they call pre-Colombian fare (a variety of Petén-Yucatec dishes), which comes highly recommended.

In El Remate, **El Muelle** (tel. 5514-9785, all meals daily) serves up daily specials for about US$10. The menu is heavy on meat dishes and lake fish, but it also serves pasta, vegetarian fare, and a wide assortment of desserts. The atmosphere is quite pleasant, with views of the lake and the establishment's attractive namesake dock, from which you can take a refreshing plunge into the turquoise waters. There is also a small gift shop selling books, wood carvings, and other knickknacks.

Along the road fringing the lake shore toward the Cerro Cahuí forest preserve, you'll come across **Las Orquídeas** (tel. 5701-9022, lasorquideasremate@yahoo.com, 6 A.M.–10 P.M. Tues.–Sun.), serving decent pizza, pasta, and sandwiches.

For a splurge, head to **La Lancha** (tel. 7928-8331, all meals daily) for gourmet Guatemalan cuisine. You can enjoy an assortment of flavors from the Francis Ford Coppola wineries or your favorite drink from the bar while dining in an airy palapa-style building high above the lake. It's housed in its namesake lodge west of El Remate in Jobompiche.

Sights

No trip to Guatemala is complete without a visit to spectacular **Tikal National Park** (6 A.M.–6 P.M. daily, US$20). The oldest and best-known of Guatemala's national parks, it was

Coatimundis are ubiquitous in Tikal National Park.

© AL ARGUETA

created in 1956 and encompasses 575 square kilometers (222 square miles) of primary tropical forest protecting a vast array of wildlife. Tikal National Park also harbors the remains of one of the Mayan civilization's greatest cities. A visit to Tikal affords the unique opportunity to experience the wonder, mystery, and awe of its enormous historical significance in terms of both natural and human heritage. Owing to its singular importance in the spheres of natural and human history, UNESCO declared Tikal National Park a World Heritage Site in 1979.

Beyond Tikal's borders is the largest protected tropical forest in North America, a 21,602-square-kilometer (8,341-square-mile) park known as the **Maya Biosphere Reserve.** It's Guatemala's last chance for preserving a significant part of the forests that once covered all of Petén. It is gradually gaining notoriety with international travelers for its vast expanses of tropical forest and the remote Mayan ruins that lie buried within. It is hoped that ecotourism here will take hold as a major industry, providing jobs and a viable alternative to ecological destruction, as in neighboring protected areas in Belize and Costa Rica. A cursory glance at a map of Guatemala reveals that the northern third of Petén is a sparsely populated region harboring an unusually high concentration of Mayan sites, remote jungle wetlands, rivers, and lagoons. Those with a strong sense of adventure will find plenty to see and do in one of Central America's last ecological frontiers.

© AL ARGUETA

skyway at Parque Natural Ixpanpajul

If you want to explore Petén's cultural and ecological heritage but don't have the time to visit the area's remote reaches, check out **CINCAP** (10 A.M.–noon and 2–8 P.M. Mon.–Fri.), housed in the Castillo de Arismendi, on the north side of Flores's central park. CINCAP (Center for Information on the Environment, Culture, and Arts of Petén) serves as an information center on *petenero* culture and is run by the environmental group Alianza Verde. There are interesting displays, arts and crafts for sale, and plenty of information on Petén's recreational offerings.

Covering an area of 9 square kilometers (3.5 square miles) and conveniently just off the highway that leads from Flores to Guatemala City, the main attraction at **Parque Natural Ixpanpajul** (tel. 7863-1317, www .ixpanpajul.com, 6 A.M.–6 P.M. daily) is a series of six suspension bridges built over the forest canopy, giving you a toucan's-eye view of the forest. The trip along the forest trail takes a little over an hour and includes a stop at a lookout point to take in the astounding view from the top of the mountain. Other activities include a Tarzan Canopy Tour (zipline), Spot Lighting (nighttime wildlife viewing), horseback riding, mountain biking, tractor rides, and ATV rentals. You can tour the hanging bridges (Skyway) for US$30 per adult or US$22 per child. You also have a choice of mountain biking, tractor rides, or horseback riding ranging from US$5 to US$25. Packages allow you to combine the Skyway with the Tarzan Canopy Tour and/or the Spot Lighting tour for a full day of adventure. You can combine two activities for US$55 or all three for US$75.

DAILY LIFE

MAKING THE MOVE

If after your fact-finding trip you continue to feel Guatemala's magnetic pull, your next order of business is to make the move and establish yourself as a legal resident. Although many expats like to leave the country every 90 days (then re-enter with a fresh 90-day tourist visa so as to bypass immigration laws), becoming a legal resident has several advantages. One perk is that you may be eligible for tax breaks, allowing duty-free importation of your worldly possessions, including a car.

Guatemalan bureaucracy has been notoriously inefficient, though in recent years the state has set out to modernize, and this extends to processes involving immigration and foreign nationals. The country's customs operations have also undergone modernization, and it's now easier and less time-consuming to bring in your household goods. Customs, incidentally, are handled by Guatemala's Superintendencia de Administración Tributaria (SAT), a bit like the U.S. equivalent of the IRS.

© AL ARGUETA

Immigration and Visas

American and Canadian citizens need only a passport for travel to Guatemala. The passport should be valid for at least six months beyond your arrival date. Officially, you may be asked to show proof of an onward ticket and/or sufficient funds for your intended length of stay, though this is rarely enforced by Guatemalan officials. It *is* however, arbitrarily enforced by airline ticketing agents. I'll never forget the time I was flying to Guatemala City on my way back from a magazine assignment in Honduras. At the airport in La Ceiba, I was forced by the TACA airport check-in agent to cough up proof of an onward itinerary beyond Guatemala City or be denied boarding. Quick thinking prevailed. My return ticket to the United States was an e-ticket on Continental Airlines, and I had a copy of the itinerary (with the airline's confirmation number) saved on my laptop. I pulled the record for the agent and was thus allowed to check in, but had I not thought of that I would have had to cough up about US$200 for a one-way ticket to San Salvador (the cheapest international flight out of Guatemala). To this day, I don't know if the agent was trying to scam me or simply doing his job, but what I do know is that it's always a good idea to keep a copy of your onward itinerary when arriving in Guatemala from a neighboring Central American country.

It's possible to extend your stay in Guatemala simply by leaving for at least three days and then re-entering at any official border crossing. In June 2006, Guatemala entered into a border control agreement, known as CA-4, with El Salvador, Honduras, and Nicaragua. This allows travelers to pass freely between the borders of the member nations. So, in order to acquire a new 90-day tourist visa upon re-entry to Guatemala, you'll have to leave the CA-4 region. Your nearby options include Belize, Mexico, and Costa Rica.

It's possible to get a one-time 90-day visa extension from the INGUAT (Instituto Guatemalteco de Turismo) offices in Guatemala City.

Guatemala's immigration laws are fairly relaxed compared to other Central American countries, such as Costa Rica, where many laws aim to discourage or at least regulate the influx of neighboring Nicaraguans. Much like Mexicans seeking work in the United States, Nicaraguans migrate to Costa Rica in droves seeking work in agricultural fields and manual labor.

TYPES OF RESIDENCY
Temporary Residency
Temporary residency allows you to remain in Guatemala for two years with the aim of permitting you to take part in licit economic activities on a temporary

DAILY LIFE

basis. "Licit" activities include a paid job or legitimate in-country financial investments. You can file for temporary residency status before leaving your home country. Temporary residencies can be extended indefinitely for two years at a time, but keep in mind that after two years you may be eligible for permanent residency status.

Filing for temporary residency in Guatemala involves a fair amount of red tape and often takes longer than immigration officials would officially have you believe. Delays of one, two, and up to four years are not unheard of. It may be worth hiring a lawyer to do this for you. If you want to go it alone, your first step is to file for a 90-Day Residency Permit. To do this, you'll need a valid passport, two passport-sized photographs, a letter from a Guatemalan sponsor, and evidence of financial resources for both you and your sponsor. Your sponsor must sign a legal document taking full financial responsibility for you and provide his or her *cédula* (government ID card), a notarized copy of his or her NIT (tax ID) card, SAT forms for the previous tax year, and copies of personal bank account statements for the previous two months showing at least Q15,000 in monthly deposits. Your sponsor may also be the local company with which you are employed, and the requirements for this differ. It usually takes two weeks to issue this visa.

Beyond the 90-Day Residency Permit is what is known as a *visa ordinaria*. It allows the bearer to remain in the country for six months (renewable up to two years). You'll once again need a statement of support from your Guatemalan sponsor in addition to evidence of your financial resources, a report on your Guatemalan police record, a medical report, a police report from your prior place of residence, and a birth certificate authenticated by a Guatemalan consulate. Processing of the *visa ordinaria* officially takes up to two months. Both visas and extensions on the *visa ordinaria* cost Q100 (US$13).

Other visas include those issued to students, teachers, diplomats, and religious workers that are valid for 1–2 years. Guatemalan law also creates a handful of residency categories with added benefits, aimed at attracting the investment of foreign capital. These include *pensionado* and *rentista* residency status.

Pensionado (Pensioner)

Many retired people opt for this type of residency. Status as a *pensionado* requires you to prove monthly income of at least US$1,000 generated outside of Guatemala. Additional family members filing jointly to be claimed under this residency status, including a spouse, will add an additional US$200 to the minimum monthly income required. This income can come from a retirement fund generated by a foreign government, international organization, or foreign corporation. In other words, your source of retirement income can be the U.S. government (Social Security, for example) or the brokerage firm that handles your IRA account. Children under 18 (or between the ages of 18 and 25 enrolled in a university) can be claimed as dependents and receive the same immigration status as their parents.

Pensionados can stay indefinitely in the country and cannot partake in any paid work while in Guatemala, though you are free, in many cases, to own and run your own business.

Rentista (Small Investor)

The income requirements for a *rentista* are the same as those for pensioners. Benefits and restrictions (including the inclusion of spouse and family members) are likewise the same. The main difference in these categories is the source of your income. *Rentistas* are defined as people enjoying a permanent, stable source of income generated outside Guatemala from any of the following:

- Deposits or investments in foreign banks

- Investments in foreign-owned corporations

- Remittances originated from real estate earnings, funded religious work, or academic scholarships

- Investment in Guatemalan state bonds

Benefits and Restrictions for *Pensionados* and *Rentistas*

Pensionados and *rentistas* both enjoy a variety of benefits under Guatemalan law. It's worth noting that Costa Rica abolished many of the same perks, including duty-free importation of household goods and a vehicle, under its revamped immigration laws in 1992.

Although paid work is forbidden, pensioners and small investors are free to start their own businesses. Approved activities include investment in projects involving industry, agriculture, agro-industry, tourism, handicrafts, housing, or others deemed to be of a "national interest." Professional consultants providing their services to government or private entities, universities, and other institutions of higher learning are also free to receive income for their activities.

Pensioners and small investors are free to enter and exit Guatemala as they please but will lose their temporary resident status if they leave the country for longer than 12 consecutive months.

Among the perks provided to *pensionados* and *rentistas* are the following:

- An exemption on import tariffs for household items and appliances brought into Guatemala during the first year of residency. You will still need to pay sales tax (IVA) on new items introduced into the country. Items can be brought in all at once or in subsequent trips

- An exemption on income tax (*impuesto sobre la renta*) on dollar amounts needed to meet your income requirements for residency status

- An exemption on import duties for one vehicle every five years

Beneficiaries of this tax break are also free to buy a car locally without paying import duties on the vehicle. IVA will still be collected on the imported vehicle based on the vehicle's value (CIF). The CIF figure will also be used to calculate the maximum value of this tax break. The value of your vehicle cannot exceed 25 times that of your declared monthly income. If this happens, you will be forced to pay import duties on the difference between this figure and the maximum value of the tax break you are entitled to.

Permanent Residency

Guatemalan law allows the granting of permanent residency status to the following persons living in Guatemala (assuming they are in compliance with immigration laws):

- *Pensionados* (pensioners) or *rentistas* (small investors)

- *Inversionistas* (large investors)

- Spouses and underage or single children of the above

- Family members of Guatemalan citizens who are foreign nationals, including spouses, children, and parents who don't automatically have Guatemalan citizenship

- Temporary residents

- People of outstanding talent and distinguished careers in science, technology, the arts, or sports

THE APPLICATION PROCESS

It's possible to begin the process of applying for residency from your home country. Check with your nearest Guatemalan consulate for specific requirements.

In most cases, you'll begin applying for residency after having spent some time in Guatemala. You'll need to visit the Dirección General de Migración office in Guatemala City (Mon.–Fri. 8 A.M. to 4:30 P.M.). There you can pick up the *Formulario de Solicitud de Residencia Permanente,* which you'll need to complete. It's also available for download online at www.migracion .gob.gt. Click on the link marked Extranjería.

Paperwork for *Pensionados* and *Rentistas*

You can also pick up forms for *pensionado* and *rentista* status at the Dirección General de Migración office in Guatemala City. *Pensionados* and *rentistas* will need the following documents to complete their residency application:

- A passport-sized photo
- Passport and a photocopy of passport, including page with temporary residency stamp, authenticated by a lawyer
- A certificate of validation for your passport issued by your country's embassy or consulate in Guatemala
- Police report (*constancia de carencia de antecedentes penales*) for the country or countries in which you've lived during the five years prior to your residency application
- Documents demonstrating income or pension money totaling at least US$1,000 (For each dependent, an additional US$200 must be added. If the documents are in a language other than Spanish, they must be translated into Spanish by an official, sworn translator.)
- Proof of declared monetary deposits in a Guatemalan bank from overseas

Paperwork for Permanent Residency

Permanent residency, like temporary residency, requires a sponsor. You'll need to provide the following documents along with your application:

- A passport-sized photo
- Passport and a photocopy of passport, including page with temporary residency stamp, authenticated by a lawyer
- A certificate of validation for your passport issued by your country's embassy or consulate in Guatemala
- Police report (*constancia de carencia de antecedentes penales*) for the country

or countries in which you've lived during the five years prior to your residency application

- A notarized letter (*acta notarial*) from a Guatemalan sponsor (or sponsoring company) taking full financial responsibility for person seeking permanent residency

- Certificate confirming previous receipt of temporary residency

If your sponsor is an individual, he or she will need to present the following:

- An authenticated copy of his or her *cédula* (government ID card)

- An authenticated copy of his or her NIT (tax ID) card

- SAT (IVA and ISR) forms for the previous tax year

- Certification of employment and income for the previous two months showing at least Q15,000 in monthly deposits

If your sponsor is a corporation, you will need to get the following from it:

- Financial statements or certification of membership in a trade guild

- Legally authenticated copy of the company's business license

- Authenticated copy of the company legal representative's identification and a document attesting to the person's position as legal counsel for the company

- A letter of employment or offer of employment and work permit issued by the Ministerio de Trabajo

The Process

Applying for permanent residency may look relatively straightforward on paper, but locals who have been through the process tell me it's much more complicated than it looks. You'll need to check back with the immigration office on a regular basis to inquire about the status of your application and see if there are any further requirements. Eventually, you'll receive confirmation of approval for your permanent residency and an interview date will be assigned to you. At this point you'll need to go to the INGUAT (Instituto Guatemalteco de Turismo) office in Zona 4 to pay the Q3,000 residency tax (*pensionados* and *rentistas* are exempt) and return to Migración with the receipt. You must bring your receipt to the interview along with two black-and-white passport photos and the pink copy of your residency approval.

Finally, you must apply for a *cédula* (government ID card) from your local municipality and bring it and your passport, pink slip, and several authenticated copies of each to INGUAT before finally getting your documents back with the permanent residency stamp in your passport. At this point, it's finally safe to break out the celebratory champagne.

In early 2009, Guatemalan authorities were in the process of replacing the *cédula* as the national ID card with the more modern *documento personal de identificación* (DPI) issued by the newly created Registro Nacional de Personas (RENAP). The changes should be fully in place, though the process faced injunctions with the Constitutional Court on the part of losing bidders intent on winning the lucrative government contract to make the new ID card.

Getting Help

It's best to enlist the help of a qualified lawyer to help you through this process. A list of English-speaking lawyers can be found on the U.S. Embassy in Guatemala's home page at http://guatemala.usembassy.gov/acs_legal_information .html. I can personally vouch for the services of Eugenia Méndez Cáceres.

CITIZENSHIP

Opting for Guatemalan citizenship requires you to have lived in Guatemala for at least two years. The first set of conditions for Guatemalan citizenship applies to those who have lived in Guatemala during the previous five years. During this five-year residency, the applicant cannot have left the country for longer than six consecutive months or lapses totaling a year or more. If you have a home in Guatemala and have lived there on and off for a period totaling 10 years, you are also eligible for citizenship. Your final ticket to Guatemalan citizenship is having a home in Guatemala and in-country residency during the previous two years. Under this requirement, you cannot have left the country for longer than one month at a time or periods totaling more than two months. You must also fall under one of the following categories:

- Those who provide important services that contribute to the country's economic, cultural, or social development

- Those who had residency in another Central American country in the three years prior to their residency in Guatemala

- Those with artistic, scientific, or philanthropic merit

- Those of undetermined citizenship

Applicants must demonstrate good conduct and provide police records from Guatemala and any other Central American countries lived in. They must also pass a Spanish-language exam and one on civic considerations that include Central American history/geography and the Guatemalan constitution. Granting of citizenship is determined by the Oficina del Presidente (Office of the President) and carried out in a solemn ceremony presided over by the Ministerio de Relaciones Exteriores (Minister of Foreign Relations).

Moving with Children

Guatemalans love children, and families figure prominently in everyday life. You'll notice this as soon as you reach the boarding area for your flight to Guatemala City, which, regardless of the day of the week, will most likely be carrying several traveling Guatemalan families back home. Although many expats living in Guatemala are retirees or single travelers embarking on a new life adventure, many foreign families move to Guatemala every year for business or diplomatic assignments. This section is primarily geared toward these relocating families.

Schooling will be a major concern for those of you moving to Guatemala with children. The *Resources* chapter contains a list of private schools.

ENTRY AND EXIT REQUIREMENTS FOR CHILDREN
Non-Guatemalan Children

Children of foreign citizenship traveling to Guatemala with only one parent will require permission from the parent or guardian not traveling with the child. This will most likely be in the form of a notarized letter in which the absent parent/guardian agrees to the particular trip. It's also a good idea to carry the child's birth certificate.

© AL ARGUETA

Guatemala is a great place for families with kids.

Guatemalan Children

If your child is born in Guatemala or you or your spouse has Guatemalan citizenship, your child will also have Guatemalan citizenship. Although your child may also have American citizenship and travel on a U.S. passport, the laws applicable to Guatemalan citizens still apply when your child departs the country.

In order to leave Guatemala, the child will need an exit permit issued by Guatemalan immigration authorities. In the case of a Guatemalan-born child residing abroad and traveling to Guatemala with only one parent, the child will need official permission from the absentee parent to leave Guatemala. The rules are inflexible, arbitrarily enforced, and somewhat complicated, so it's best to check with the Guatemalan consulate *before* leaving the United States for specific and up-to-date information.

Moving with Pets

Pets, too, require special care when being brought to Guatemala. You'll find attitudes toward pets here are not quite as sophisticated as in First World countries. Dogs, for example, are often viewed primarily as an additional security measure used to prevent home break-ins. In rural Guatemalan communities, stray dogs are a major concern. You'll see many skinny, mangy animals lurking about, and Guatemalans have no problems kicking or throwing rocks at dogs, which they refer to as *chuchos*. While your dog or cat has had the good fortune of being owned by a resident of the First World, you should take care while walking your dog in areas where there are many strays or of letting your dog roam free. Stray dogs can be notoriously aggressive toward other dogs and cats.

Bringing cats and dogs into Guatemala is fairly simple. Bringing more exotic pets such as birds, reptiles, amphibians, and the like will be much more complicated and may require the services of a professional pet transporter. You can call the nearest Guatemalan consulate to find out specifics for your particular creature. As dogs and cats and small mammals are the most common pets brought in to Guatemala, this section deals with those exclusively.

DOGS AND CATS

Dogs, cats, and small mammals such as hamsters are easily imported into Guatemala. Foremost on the minds of customs and airline agents is the health of your pet, and this needs to be determined via a visit to your veterinarian within one month of your intended arrival on Guatemalan soil. The vet must fill out a health certificate stating that the animal is free of communicable diseases and has been vaccinated against rabies, distemper, hepatitis, leptospirosis, and

DAILY LIFE

MEMORIES OF A CHILDHOOD MOVE TO GUATEMALA

I was 10 years old when my parents decided to move the family to Guatemala in July of 1985. I'm not really sure it was traumatic, but it was certainly life-altering. Perhaps the most difficult thing was leaving my neighborhood friends behind. Back in those days there was no Internet or text messaging, so there was no way to really stay in touch with the people I left back in New Jersey, even if it was just to say hi and hear the latest dirt on my old classmates.

It was a weird time to be moving to Guatemala. The country was still under a military dictatorship, and presidential elections, along with the ratification of a new constitution, had been announced for later that year. I remember food shortages the first week we were there. My sister and I began to wonder out loud why we had moved to Guatemala in the first place. My father had stayed behind tying up some loose ends but joined us about six weeks later. In the meantime, we took a short break from our studies before visiting several schools and taking various admissions tests. My sister and I ended up going to different schools, which I thought was a total joke. Apparently, my grade was completely full at the American School, so I had to go to a different school, one that I always perceived to be of slightly lesser quality. My younger brother would go to the same school a year later when he started his schooling.

Other random memories... I remember street rioting for about a week after public transportation prices went up. The whole city seemed immersed in a chaos I had never experienced. I remember auditing my classes (I had already completed third grade in the United States and was just sitting in on the last few months of the school year). I have some fuzzy memories that involve a final Guatemalan history exam and some haphazard guesses on a multiple-choice basis. I also remember feeling quite isolated during those first few months. I had no friends at school, owing mainly to the fact that I didn't feel I could relate to the people I went to school with. I greatly disliked most of my classmates and just couldn't understand where their strange mentality came from. I later came to understand that this was the mentality of the Guatemalan elite and that it clashed with my American middle-class sensibilities. Odd things like expressing a desire to be a fireman in order to help people were met with ridicule and laughter, and I soon learned I had to censor myself.

Perhaps most difficult during that first year was an intense bout with intestinal parasites. I remember always being tempted to eat the food sold at a little kiosk during school recess but always being wary of the parsley sprinkled over the delicious *tostadas* and *dobla-*

das. Well, I finally gave in to these and other tempting fresh foods. The funny thing is that after a few really bad weeks of needing to be within five feet of the nearest toilet, my stomach finally became accustomed to the local bugs and I could eat pretty much anything – just like all the other kids.

Things *did* get better in other regards, eventually. I made some friends the following year and became better accustomed to the culture. We also moved into a nicer house in the swanky Vista Hermosa subdivision. But I can't say I ever fully liked living in Guatemala, even when I was (by then) 12 years old and my father decided to move us back to the United States. I had often expressed my dislike for living in Guatemala to him and, although I now understand my father had his own demons to wrestle with, I couldn't help feeling like this was all my fault. Of course, it didn't help that my father told me as much, which he still denies to this day.

In any case, this isn't meant to be an essay on parenting mistakes, but it is meant to give you some pointers if you intend to move to Guatemala with your children. Guatemala is obviously quite different today than it was 24 years ago, so many of the issues, such as widespread civil unrest, don't necessarily pertain to a move to Guatemala now. Still, it is my sincere hope that you will communicate to your children why it is you're moving to Guatemala and what they can expect to encounter when they get there. As I discovered, visiting Guatemala over the holidays to spend fun-filled days visiting with family is not the same as living in the country on a day-to-day basis. To this day, I absolutely love Guatemala but am unsure of whether or not I could ever live there again. I dabble with the notion on a fairly frequent basis, but then something stops me. Maybe it's too many unpleasant childhood memories of a place that today might be a very pleasant place for me to live.

Also, please be involved in your children's lives and how they are getting along at school. Ask questions. What did you learn about in school today? How are the kids in your class? Do you feel like you fit in with them? Have you made any friends? This will help ease your children's transition and help them to feel self-assured and supported, even if they're not quite yet fitting in. Your choice of school will also be very important in this regard, as it will influence whether your child is stuck with the children of the elite class and their snobbish ways or at least have kids in class that also come from American families.

I hope you can learn something from my childhood experiences in Guatemala and that it somehow makes the transition for you and your family easier. If so, your child will thank you for it.

DAILY LIFE

parvovirus. This certificate must be endorsed by a Veterinary Service (VS) veterinarian, which your vet may or may not be, so keep that in mind. You then take or mail the certificate to the nearest office of the U.S. Department of Agriculture that approves health certificates for pets. The final step is to have this approved certificate authenticated by the Guatemalan Embassy or nearest Guatemalan consulate. See the *Resources* section for a listing of Guatemalan consulates in the United States. In some cases, airlines require the health certificate issued by the veterinarian to be issued 10 days before travel, which somewhat complicates things. Check directly with your carrier for specifics.

Upon arrival in Guatemala, your pet will be inspected by customs and the proper documentation will be checked. If all goes well, as it usually does, you are then free to enter the country with your pet. If not, the animal may be quarantined for up to 30 days while you weigh your options, including treatment by a local veterinarian.

FLYING WITH PETS

You will most likely bring your pet with you on the plane. If your pet is a seeing-eye dog or small dog, you may be allowed to bring it with you in the cabin. We've all seen little dogs stashed away in big bags along for the ride. In most cases, however, your pet must ride in the plane's cargo hold. The pet traveling as checked baggage has to be transported in a leak-proof cage with handles. The cage should be just large enough to allow the animal to turn around. According to vets, animals should fast for six hours prior to the flight to reduce nausea. It's all right to feed your pet a small snack a few hours before departure if the flight exceeds four hours.

Every airline has different policies, but in general, pets are not allowed to be checked in between May 15 and September 15 because airplane cargo holds are not air-conditioned. Airlines generally will not transport an animal weighing more than 70 pounds.

I've heard good things about Continental Airlines' PetSafe, which requires pets (except small pets and seeing-eye dogs) to travel separately as cargo. You essentially ship your pet as an airport-to-airport QUICKPAK package, which you can track along its journey. Animals are even transported in climate-controlled vehicles through the airline's hubs. Visit www.continental.com/web/en-US/content/travel/animals/default.aspx for more information.

What to Take

Although you can pretty much find everything you need for daily life in Guatemala, prices for many items are much higher than those in the United States. It's best to sort out your belongings and establish early on what you just can't live without and what you won't be able to get, or get for reasonable cost, while in Guatemala. As for the latter, most people tend to bring down needed electronic items such as laptops and personal computers, stereo systems, and other electronics. While they're available through many Guatemala City retailers, the prices for electronics are grossly exaggerated.

Other items such as clothing can be found locally. Several popular clothing brands can be found in Guatemala City shopping malls catering to the country's elite and their U.S.-emulating consumption patterns. Many Guatemalans also take a yearly shopping trip to Miami to find bargains and greater variety on their preferred items. Internet shopping has also grown drastically in recent years via a system allowing you to quickly and efficiently import clothing and other items ordered from Internet vendors in the United States at moderate cost.

SHIPPING OPTIONS

As for getting your items down here, you have a number of options. The first and easiest option is to bring items with you on the plane as part of your checked baggage allowance. Another option is to send items via air cargo. Part of the shipment will be taxed, and you'll need to fill out forms and deal with the importation process. A third option is to ship items by boat to one of Guatemala's Atlantic or Pacific ports. This involves a lot of bureaucracy, but the obvious advantage is that you can fit most or all of your worldly possessions, including a car, into a shipboard container. In some cases this might be relatively affordable thanks to generous tax breaks on import duties for household items and a vehicle that apply to certain categories of temporary residents.

On the Plane

While airlines are limiting the weight of checked bags for flights within the United States and charging for extra bags, these rules (as of yet) do not apply to international flights on most carriers. Most of the airlines flying to Guatemala City allow you to check in two 50-pound bags free of charge. For a little more, you can check in up to 70 pounds. If you have frequent flier privileges such as Continental's Elite Access, you can check two 70-pound bags free of charge. Another perk of Elite Access is free space-available first-class upgrades. If you score an upgrade to first class, you're allowed to check in three 70-pound bags free of charge. Rules and perks vary by carrier, so be sure to check with the airline. These extra bags are really a great deal, as this is the easiest and most convenient way to get your belongings down here without customs hassles. The only paperwork you'll need to fill out is the customs form passed out by flight attendants before landing. If you do show up at the Guatemala City airport with three bags full of clothing, gear, and equipment and are required to see a customs agent, keep in mind you are allowed to bring in the following items duty-free as long as they are portable, used, for your own personal use, and in reasonable quantities:

- Clothing, jewelry, handbags, personal hygiene or dressing table items, medicines, food, instruments, medical devices, and disposable articles related to these items

- A wheelchair (if the traveler is disabled)

- Baby carriages and toys of traveling children

- A photographic camera, a video camera, a sound reproduction device and its accessories, up to six film reels and magnetic tape for each, a broadcasting receiver, a television receiver, and a prismatic binocular

- A personal computer, a typewriter, a calculator, portable musical instruments and their accessories, books, manuscripts, discs, and sound recording equipment

- Engravings and noncommercial photographs

- Tools, equipment, and manual instruments related to the traveler's profession so long as they do not constitute field equipment for offices, factories, laboratories, or similar operations

- Five hundred grams of tobacco; five liters of wine, brandy, or liquor (by travelers of legal age); and up to two kilograms of candies

- Hunting and sport weapons, 500 pieces of ammunition, a tent, and other camping equipment; entry of weapons and ammunition is subject to prior authorization

- Recreational or sport items such as muscle tension equipment, walking machines, a bicycle, surfboard, baseball bat, bags, clothing, footwear, gloves, protective gear

In addition to the above allotments, you can bring up to US$500 worth of goods in your checked baggage without paying customs duties. Your passport will be stamped by customs agents, showing you've used your US$500 exemption. You will be eligible for another US$500 exemption in six months.

Air Cargo

It's possible to send up to 500 pounds as air cargo. Duties differ from items sent in checked baggage, but personal items such as clothing, shoes, books, tools, and some sports equipment will still be duty-free. Everything else will be taxed at various rates determined by SAT.

When your cargo arrives in Guatemala, you will be directed to a bonded customs warehouse where you'll need to present the following in order to pick up your shipment:

- Your passport (Customs agents will be specifically looking for the page with your entry stamp indicating your arrival in Guatemala within 90 days. If you've been in Guatemala longer than 90 days, your shipment will be considered a commercial shipment and you'll be forced to pay duties on everything. So, beware.)

- The air waybill, given to you by your contracted freight handler

- A packing inventory indicating the declared value of your shipment's contents

Assuming all your paperwork is in order, you'll then pay handling and warehouse fees. You can go through the process on your own, ask a Spanish-speaking friend for help, or hire a customs broker.

Shipping by Boat

If you have large quantities of items to ship or have larger items, like a car, shipping by boat is your best option. You can pick from a quarter, half, or full shipboard container, the latter measuring 40 by 8 by 8 feet. Pack your items neatly and securely to avoid the contents of your container shifting during the long sea voyage. Most people hire professional movers to pack their items into the container.

For customs purposes, you also need to inventory all items, including serial numbers for electrical appliances. Based on these serial numbers, SAT agents can determine whether an item is old or new. Make sure to pack only items that are older than six months, or you risk paying duties. You can either meet the ship at its Atlantic or Caribbean port or have your container trucked to Guatemala City. You'll need your passport (showing your arrival in Guatemala within 90 days), the inventory list with declared contents of the container, and the bill of lading to claim your cargo.

Driving to Guatemala

If you're bringing your car down and have only a few items to bring with you, it's worth considering a drive to Guatemala. Thanks to the country's northern location, your border crossings and time on the road getting to Guatemala are greatly reduced compared to the rest of Central America. Most folks who have made the drive say it's a rather pleasant experience.

HOUSING CONSIDERATIONS

Guatemala is in the midst of a building boom. One glance out the window when landing in Guatemala City reveals a number of high-rise condominiums recently built or being built. Still, you seldom hear about Guatemala in real estate terms, with most Americans snapping up property in nearby Nicaragua, Costa Rica, or Panama. It's not that Guatemala lacks any of its neighbors' attractions, but its location as the northernmost country in Central America means that the boom in foreign real estate speculation that began in Costa Rica some 20 years ago has taken some time to make its way north. Fortunately for the would-be Guatemala real estate purchaser, the local market is quite dynamic thanks to the purchasing power of Guatemala's well-to-do. This economic base has ensured the availability of many new housing options, particularly in Guatemala City, Antigua, and the Pacific coast. Far from needing to catch up to its neighbors in terms of sophistication, you'll find Guatemala is still a relative bargain and offers a wide array of housing options.

© AL ARGUETA

Typical homes in Guatemala, aside from the large American-style houses of a wealthy few, can vary drastically from their U.S. counterparts. You may find insulation from this element of culture shock by choosing to live in or build one of these American-style houses, or by seeking shelter in a modern high-rise condominium. Should you choose not to go this route, you'll find yourself adapting to a completely new set of building materials, home interiors, and property particulars. At the same time, those of you hailing from California or the Southwest will find modern Guatemalan homes very similar to homes in your part of the United States.

Building materials aside, you'll also have to decide whether to rent, buy, or build your home. This chapter is designed to help you make an informed decision in this regard and help you as you move along in the process of executing the results of that decision.

GUATEMALAN HOUSES

Traditional Guatemalan homes, particularly in the highlands, are made of adobe. In the poorest areas of the country, especially parts of the northern Petén department, you'll find thatch-roof huts with reed or bamboo walls. Although most expats tend to live in something more closely resembling a modern home, it's nice to have an idea of what some Guatemalans' homes may look like. I've seen some wonderful modern homes blending colonial style with elements of traditional architecture, such as a winding staircase lined with an adobe-brick wall and holes for votive candles.

Most middle-class Guatemalans live in concrete-block homes that are distributed adjacent to each other on city streets. From the outside, they appear flat, with just a window or two and a gate, and are usually painted in vivid colors. Windows are almost always protected with thick metal bars. The tops of walls and the sides of homes often feature barbed wire or broken glass

Flowers adorn the interiors of many Guatemalan homes.

© AL ARGUETA

shards glued to the cement block surface to dissuade would-be home invaders. Roofs are either tile or corrugated steel. Inside, these homes often feature a courtyard or back patio, though little in the way of a yard. A central feature of older Guatemalan homes is the *pila,* a double-compartment washbasin used for washing clothes and dishes. One side is deep and fills up with water. The other side is shallow with a corrugated surface like that of a washboard. These homes feature little or nothing in the way of carpeting, with bare tile floors being the norm.

More modern Guatemalan homes come in a variety of shapes and sizes and more closely resemble what foreigners are used to. Apartments and high-rise condominiums offer everything you'd find in their U.S. counterparts, including connections for washer, dryer, and dishwasher. Bare tile and hardwood floors are typical flooring options, though apartments are sometimes carpeted. In addition to the high-rise condominiums you'll find in Guatemala City and even Lake Atitlán, there are a number of newer subdivisions that often appeal to foreigners because of their affordable prices and modern construction. These often feature a yard with green grass and gardens. Guatemalans are slowly catching up to North Americans in their housing preferences, with more modern designs that incorporate the splendor of Guatemala's outdoor landscape.

In addition to Guatemala's natural grandeur, the richness and diversity of its native cultures makes for some wonderful opportunities for unique home decor. Many opulent Guatemalan homes incorporate modern design and architecture with traditional fabrics and furniture.

RENTING VS. BUYING

Almost every book you'll read on this subject will say the same thing: rent before you buy. This book is no exception. Renting a house or apartment will allow you to get used to local conditions while keeping your options open to build the house of your dreams, buy a property with everything you're looking for, or simply rent something more to your liking. Rentals in Guatemala tend to be very flexible. Unlike in the United States, where you have to give up your firstborn child to get out of a lease, it's fairly easy to find a month-to-month lease. Good negotiating skills always come in handy, but you'll find most landlords very accommodating.

If after being in Guatemala for some time, you decide you absolutely need to buy property here, you'll find you have a number of options. Having rented a place for a while, you will have a better idea of what's available in different neighborhoods as well as different price ranges.

© AL ARGUETA

a tropical home in Izabal

SEARCHING FOR A HOUSE OR APARTMENT

As with many things in life, word of mouth is a great way to get wind of properties available for rent or purchase. As you get to know more and more people in your chosen city of residence, you'll find many an expat who has properties for rent or might run into someone looking for a roommate. You never know who you'll meet. Waiters and other service industry staff are also good people to ask.

A number of regional, tourist-oriented publications are also quite useful in this regard. *Revue* (www .revuemag.com), a monthly magazine published in Antigua, has classified ads covering rentals mostly in Guatemala City, Antigua, Lake Atitlán, and Quetzaltenango (Xela). In Xela, check out XelaWho magazine, found online at www.xelawho.com. The online xelapages.com also has some real estate listings and a helpful discussion board where you might ask around for available properties.

Industry-specific publications, while mostly in Spanish, are also a great place to look. The Spanish-language *Inmobilia.com* monthly magazine and its namesake website are excellent resources, assuming you speak Spanish. In English and particularly helpful for Antigua listings is the website of Century 21 Casa Nova (www.century21casanova.com). Finally, if you can read Spanish, the classifieds in the daily newspaper *Prensa Libre* (www.prensalibre.com .gt) are one of the most popular places to advertise properties for rent or sale. Prices are usually listed in U.S. dollars.

Renting

PRICING

A comfortable two-bedroom home in Antigua generally rents for about US$800 a month. The same amount of money would get you a modern one- or two-bedroom apartment in Guatemala City's Zona 10 or 14. Prices in Guatemala vary widely depending on factors such as what part of town you're looking in, the size of the property, and whether or not the landlord is out to make some extra cash on unsuspecting foreigners. Shop around and ask folks who've been in your town a bit longer about reasonable prices for particular properties. It will be hard to find bargains in places like downtown Antigua or Quetzaltenango. It's hard, but not impossible. The glut of high-rise condos in Guatemala City, on the other hand, means you may be able to find a very affordable apartment in Guatemala City's Zona 10 or Zona 14 at very reasonable rates. A good command of Spanish will certainly help you in this regard, as these types of listings will most often be found in publications geared toward the general populace and not specifically foreigners, such as national newspapers.

You'll also need good negotiating skills. Bargain hard. When possible, try to get apartments that are fully furnished, as the cost of furnishing an apartment yourself can quickly add up to much more than you bargained for. If you're a really good negotiator, you might also get them to throw in some maintenance costs, which can easily add another US$50 or so to your monthly expenditures.

THINGS TO LOOK OUT FOR

Many of the agencies and independent landlords working in popular expat communities are quite reputable. Foreign visitors often have certain expectations that need to be addressed prior to signing a lease, so you'll need to do some fact-finding. This is especially the case if you plan on getting a rental property prior to your arrival in Guatemala.

First of all, living in Guatemala is in many ways no different than living anywhere else in terms of what you get for the money. A US$300-a-month rental property in Antigua, while a good deal, is probably not going to provide the level of comfort you might be used to back in the United States. In this case, expect to be in an old-style Guatemalan home or apartment with tile floors and cement-block construction. You'll most likely have to deal with toilets using ancient pipes unable to process your two-ply Charmin toilet paper, for which you'll need to put a wastebasket next to the toilet. You

DAILY LIFE

GUIDE TO CLASSIFIED ADS

Checking out the Spanish-language classifieds in search of that land plot, home, or apartment? You might find yourself trying to decipher often-cryptic abbreviations and place-names. Here's a list to help you navigate the murky waters of Guatemalan classified ads.

Abbreviation	Spanish Term	Translation
dorms	*dormitorios*	bedrooms
c/s	*con/sin*	with/without
i/	*incluye*	includes
L/telefónica	*línea telefónica*	phone line
L/blanca	*línea blanca*	kitchen appliances
C/U	*cada uno(a)*	each
X/	*por*	per
E/	*edificio*	building or office tower
V/volcanes	*vista a los volcanes*	volcano view
P/estrenar	*para estrenar*	brand-new
M2	*metros cuadrados*	square meters
Q	quetzales	local currency
Vrs	*varas*	unit for measuring land
V2	*varas cuadradas*	square *varas*
T/comodidades	*todas las comodidades*	fully furnished
F/mar	*frente al mar*	ocean-front
F/semana	*fin de semana*	weekend rental

GUATEMALA CITY NEIGHBORHOODS

Abbreviation	Neighborhood
San J/Pinula	San José Pinula
C/Roosevelt	Carretera Roosevelt
V. Hermosa	Vista Hermosa
Carr. Salvador	Carretera al Salvador

also may or may not have a washer and dryer hookup, as most middle-class Guatemalans tend to wash their clothes by hand and dry them out in the sun (quite challenging at the heart of the rainy season). The electrical wiring in older homes may be ancient and unable to handle running your stereo, TV, and laptop all at the same time.

Hot showers may be a luxury you'll have to go without, as many properties in

© AL ARGUETA

a Guatemalan take on the modern bathroom

lower budget ranges feature electric water heaters. If you've done some prior travel through Central America, you'll most likely be familiar with the menacing-looking apparatus (often with protruding wires) that sits atop the showerhead and heats your water. Showers with these electric heaters are often lukewarm at best; it's always a tradeoff between water pressure and water temperature. I've personally been shocked once or twice when attempting to adjust the setting on a unit and accidentally touching the metallic top instead of the plastic switch I was aiming for. There's really nothing quite like being shocked while naked and wet.

These possibilities constitute some of the items you need to look out for when scoping out an apartment. You may or may not be willing to deal with all of the above. Going into a higher price range usually means an upgrade to these living conditions, but you should always make the necessary inquiries. Also beware that rentals, by and large, *do not* include utilities, so budget for that as well. Utilities may include water, electricity, natural gas, cable TV, and even bottled water delivery, so be sure to ask about exactly what is and isn't included. Internet is not usually hooked up in rental properties, as landlords need to sign two-year contracts with service providers and are often unwilling to pay for the service during months when the rental property isn't being let.

Other things to look out for when checking out a rental property include water pressure, the availability of enough electrical outlets with good connections, a functioning telephone, and locks on windows and doors. Also assess how safe you feel in that particular place. Is it in a decent neighborhood? What are the neighbors like? Are there any gaps in the perimeter walls or fences that might allow intruders easy access? Check out entry points to the property and make sure there is sufficient light allowing you to see your way when you might otherwise end up fumbling with your keys and be an easy target for a mugging or break-in. Also, ask the landlord if break-ins have been common, or better yet, ask the neighbors if their homes have been broken into recently. Also factor in issues of daily life such as proximity to bus stops or the ease of getting a taxicab.

RENTAL AGENTS AND LEASES

Independent landlords tend to be fairly flexible regarding leasing terms. It's not at all uncommon to find landlords willing to rent on a month-to-month basis, especially if you're willing to provide a deposit of first and last month's rent. Again, good negotiating skills will get you far. If you are working with an independent landlord, it's a good idea to get everything in writing, so as to avoid misunderstandings that may or may not be genuinely the product of culture and language barriers.

In many cases, you'll be working with an agent acting as a go-between for you and the landlord. This is often the case in larger markets such as Antigua, where you will pay your rent directly to the agent. International debit cards and credit cards are not usually accepted for monthly rental payments, though checks drawn on U.S. banks often are. If paying by U.S. bank check, you must pay your rent at least eight days prior to the due date to provide enough time for your international check to clear. Leases drawn up through agencies are very formal, and breaking a lease will most likely cost you one month's rent.

Going through a leasing agent does have some particular advantages. You'll most likely be dealing with someone who speaks English. Agents can also book you into a property as far out as 30 days prior to your arrival and can receive mail and packages on your behalf (for additional cost). They might also provide pickup service from the Guatemala City airport at reasonable prices and in general be quite helpful during your first few days in your new home. In Antigua, I highly recommend Century 21 Casa Nova (www.century21casa nova.com), which provides all of these services and can also find you a place anywhere in Guatemala.

Buying Property

HOUSING TYPES

Guatemalan homes range from old colonial houses with varying degrees of modern upgrades to ultramodern homes and apartments with everything you'd expect to find in the United States or Europe. The purchasing power of Guatemala's middle and upper classes, along with their tendency to emulate U.S. consumption patterns, translates into a real estate market that offers plenty of options. This despite the considerably smaller gringo presence compared to other parts of Central America.

Houses

In Guatemala City and some other large urban areas, you'll find subdivisions in various parts of the city. The areas of the capital most frequently chosen by foreigners include Zonas 10, 14, 15, 16, and Carretera a El Salvador. It's important to note that most of these subdivisions are protected by gated (and guarded) entry points due to security concerns associated with living in the Guatemalan capital. Antigua, Quetzaltenango, and parts of the Pacific coast also offer many of these gated communities, with homes combining colonial architecture with modern construction. You'll also find many large colonial homes in the downtown city cores. All of the major cities have a downtown core with older colonial homes. These have often been in the hands of local families for generations.

Casa Palopó is a private home turned into a boutique hotel.

It's rare to see freestanding homes in Guatemalan urban areas. In rural areas, you'll see the homes of poorer Guatemalans surrounded by agricultural fields as well as many large hacienda-style homes on coffee plantations, cattle ranches, and the like. There are still some pockets of German influence in the Alta Verapaz region left over from the heyday of German immigration in the early 20th century. Freestanding homes in the style of Alpine chalets, surrounded by green fields, can be found here and there.

Condos

In many cases, housing developments consist of condos or townhouses. Guatemala City's Zonas 10, 14, and 15 also have a substantial number of high-rise condominiums in concentrations not found elsewhere in Central America save Panama. Condos have become an increasingly attractive alternative for young Guatemalan middle-class couples and expats because they provide a certain measure of security. They also provide a certain urban flair not easily found elsewhere in Central America. You can find a nice condo in Guatemala City's Zona 14, for example, with a volcano and city view, for much less than you'd pay in a comparably sized U.S. city, about US$1000 a month for a two-bedroom.

The condo boom hasn't quite yet reached into coastal areas, as the majority of homes there tend to be freestanding or part of exclusive residential communities. One exception is Juan Gaviota, near Puerto San José on the Pacific coast, though the prices there start at about US$300,000.

Another recent trend is the construction of so-called "neo-urban" developments that encompass mixed-use residential and business facilities. These usually include a shopping mall with apartments and houses in the vicinity. There are a number of these being built or recently built in Guatemala City. These projects can also be found in the Pacific coast city of Retalhuleu and the Alta Verapaz city of Cobán.

WHERE TO LOOK

Perhaps the best source for getting information on available housing projects is the monthly *Inmobilia.com* magazine. In addition to advertisements for various housing projects, you'll find classified ads with homes and lots for sale. The magazine also includes commercial property and is generally a great place to get started. The main drawback is that it's in Spanish, though you could easily scour the glossy print ads and make a note of the websites for advertised projects. Many of the companies' websites will also be in English.

In rural areas or smaller towns, you'll certainly come to rely on word of mouth to find available property or houses for sale. Also, keep your eyes peeled along roadways for Se Vende signs put up by private owners. Guatemala's *Prensa Libre* newspaper is another great place to look, but you'll need to know a bit of Spanish.

FINANCING

It used to be that buying property in Guatemala was a purely cash option for foreigners. Nowadays, local banks have smartened up to the increasing number of foreigners buying property here and are willing to work with local realtors to finance your home or land purchase. You'll need a model credit history to qualify. Among the items that may be asked of you are your passport, bank statements for the previous six months, certification of employment history, and a financial statement showing assets and liabilities. Mortgages are available at floating rates about 2 percent above U.S. rates, currently set at about

OCRET: RESTRICTIONS ON PROPERTY ADJACENT TO WATERWAYS

For many, the Central American dream involves buying beach or lakeside property. As is the case elsewhere in Central America, current laws bar anyone from actually owning property adjacent to waterways in Guatemala. Guatemalan law declares that property within 200 linear meters (650 feet) of major waterways (lakes, major rivers, and the ocean) is under the control of the Oficina de Control de Áreas de Reserva del Estado (OCRET) and cannot be registered with sovereign landowners' titles.

The property is public domain and can only be leased from OCRET, typically for a renewable span of 20-30 years. The resident living on the property only has rights of possession and access, not rights of sovereign ownership. The only exceptions to this law are properties with a title registered prior to 1956 or properties that are in declared urban areas.

Should you wish to lease a piece of coastal or lakeside property, you'll need to fill out a form provided by OCRET and provide a map or satellite image of the area you wish to lease. Leases are typically granted for the purposes of tourism development or conservation. It will take about a year to finalize the lease, as OCRET must send inspectors to the area in question to verify the details. The lease is finalized via a legal document, which outlines the land use strictly for conservation and recreation purposes.

As an example of typical leasing fees, a 4,380-square-meter (47,145-square-foot) property would cost about US$300 a year to lease.

Guatemalan law also bars foreigners from owning land designated as a reserve, which includes lands governed by the OCRET statutes. Although this is rarely enforced, a loophole exists in the creation of a foreign-owned Sociedad Anónima to lease the land in question. It's all perfectly legal.

8 percent. Keep in mind you'll also need to front about 30 percent of the appraised value of the property as a down payment. The buyer is responsible for the appraisal once creditworthiness is established. The loan approval process takes about 10 working days.

Many independent home and condo builders provide independent financing for their projects to buyers. If you're interested in buying property from a particular builder, it's a good idea to check out their project history. There are many reputable builders with various projects throughout Guatemala, but it's good to verify the track record of the company you're going with. In some cases, financing for projects is offered through a local bank. This is the best-case scenario.

As for deposits when purchasing property, it's best to have the money go to your attorney's or real estate agent's account. A local bank or escrow service is also acceptable. Beware of arrangements requiring you to put your money directly into the hands of the developer or some other individual unknown to you. As for the timeline for granting access to your deposit money to the developer, it's best to arrange for this to take place after closing or at least after certain agreed-upon purchase conditions are met. A red flag is your developer being able to access the deposit money immediately.

RESEARCHING A PROPERTY

So, you've done some legwork, looked around, and finally found a home or property you think you'd like call your own. The work is just beginning, though, as you must make a number of verifications to ensure that piece of property is every bit as great as you think it is. In this regard, your best bet is probably to hire a lawyer. He or she will know all the ins and outs of working to get the information you need to make an informed decision. A good lawyer will help steer you through the process of buying property in a foreign country and doing business in a culture you might not be completely comfortable with. At the same time, it is entirely possible to research much of what is needed on your own.

Researching a property begins with consulting the national registry, for which you'll need to hire a lawyer, who will check to make sure that the property is registered with all paperwork in order and that there aren't any outstanding liens.

You can ask the seller to provide you with a property map, though this is generally only available for properties in the Guatemala City area. There are plans to complete a nationwide *catastro* (land register) to register and map property throughout the country, but the completion date for such a huge undertaking is still anybody's guess. The Guatemala City municipal offices can provide a property map but will only do so for the property owner.

Guatemala is not without zoning restrictions, and these are heavily in place in Guatemala City and colonial Antigua. You'll need to verify that your land is not located within the confines of a national park or nature preserve. This can be done by checking in with the Comisión Nacional de Áreas Protegidas (CONAP). By the same token, building a house will require an environmental impact assessment. Coastal property has some special attributes, which are discussed in the sidebar on OCRET, the government entity that oversees coastal property rights. It's a good idea to check in with the Ministerio de Comunicaciones y Vivienda (MICIVI) to make sure there are no roads planned to go through the property. This might be a concern, for example, on the outskirts of Guatemala City with a proposed ring road project.

Other considerations include:

- Certifying that all past property taxes have been paid

- Making sure any domestic employees (housekeeper, gardener, etc.) have been paid by their former employer

- Checking for the availability of utilities such as water, phone, and power. This is particularly important in rural areas, where you may find yourself having to bring in electricity

- Knowing who your neighbors are

INSPECTING PROPERTY BEFORE BUYING
Location
Guatemala's spectacular scenery, the charm of its colonial towns, and the opportunity to live in a bustling city or quiet lakeside retreat are all elements that influence foreigners to purchase land here. At the same time, when considering a potential property you'll need to break everything down to its most basic elements to make a proper determination as to its suitability. While the location of a particular property might be excellent, you should also make sure to look around and see what's all around it. Is that fabulous lakeside plot on the shores of Lake Atitlán right next to the hippest new backpackers' hostel? If so, you might be in for some loud neighbors, which may or may not suit your style. The same goes for urban living. The wonderful colonial home you had your eye on might be next door to a popular nightclub or an evangelical church with services five nights a week. In rural areas or smaller towns, you may or may not like being serenaded by

When buying a house, be sure to inspect everything carefully.

roosters at 4 A.M. every morning, so find out what kind of animals your neighbors keep.

Overall Condition

The overall condition of a property includes not only access to utilities such as water, power, and telephone but also road access to remote rural plots or the availability of parking in crowded urban areas. The overall condition of a property will certainly be affected by the quality of its foundation. You should verify that the soil surrounding the property slopes away from the house and that there is sufficient drainage. Check the foundation for signs of water damage. It rains a lot in Guatemala.

Similarly, you should have a look at the roof. If it's a colonial home with clay tiles, check for cracked or broken tiles and inquire as to when they were last replaced. Tile roofs need to be replaced every few years and will shift in storms or seismic events. Roofs made of *lámina,* or corrugated steel sheets, should be checked for rust and possible leaks.

Plumbing

Many parts of Guatemala still experience water outages during certain times of day. It's a good idea to ask neighbors if there is water loss for part of the day. If this is the case, you might find added usefulness for the *pila* found in many Guatemalan homes by filling it at times when water is available in order to have a water supply on hand if needed. Of special note is the fact that older pipes and septic systems in rural areas and some smaller towns and cities can't handle bulky toilet paper. This results in the use of a wastebasket placed next to the toilet for TP disposal. You may or may not be willing to adapt to this system, so find out if this is the case before you sign those papers! On a related note, where exactly is that stuff going? If the house is on a septic system, check out the size of the leach field and its location.

Finally, check the water pressure on showerheads and faucets. Run the shower at full blast with hot water and determine how long it takes for the water to heat up. Is there enough water pressure and hot water to simultaneously run the hot shower and a second faucet elsewhere in the house?

Windows and Screens

Guatemala can be a buggy sort of place, yet it's surprising how seldom you find screened-in windows and doors. Window and door screening will dramatically improve life in your new home. If you've ever been kept up all night by what can only be imagined as a helicopter-sized mosquito buzzing around your ear in the dark, then you know exactly what I'm talking about.

Likewise, check closed doors for an even fit within the doorframe as well as for functional locks that don't stick.

Electrical Wiring

Check out how many outlets there are per room and how far apart they are spaced. Look for grounded outlets with three prongs. The kitchen is a good indicator of the overall quality of electrical wiring. Turn on all the lights and run a few appliances. Look for lights that dim or blown fuses when you turn on the appliances. Check out the master electrical panel. Are all the breakers labeled and well-organized? Many older Guatemalan homes are rated for fewer than 100 amps, which is fine if your use of electric-powered technology resembles that of an early-20th-century homesteader. If, on the other hand, you plan on using modern-day equipment such as air-conditioning, TV, DVD player, computer, washer/dryer, Xbox, and stereo then you're going to run into some problems.

TITLE TRANSFER AND PROPERTY REGISTRATION

Guatemalan law makes no distinction between property owned by foreigners and Guatemalans. Once you and your lawyer have researched the property being purchased, and assuming everything checks out, the next step is to work out the title transfer and property registration. This involves drawing up an *escritura,* a legal document with the terms of the sale. Both parties sign the document and the purchaser presents the money. The buyer will also pay the closing costs, including lawyer fees, at this time. Realtor fees are most commonly the responsibility of the seller, though some agents do work as buyer representatives and will charge fees accordingly. Prior to the actual *escritura,* you may also need to enter into an agreement whereby you formalize your intent to go through with the transaction. This is known as a *compromiso de compraventa* and is quite common. It outlines the timeline for making the deal as well as the general terms of the purchase.

Once the final contracts have been signed, the lawyer then presents the necessary documents to the Ministerio de Finanzas (Ministry of Finance) Dirección de Catastro y Avaluó de Bienes Inmuebles (DICABI), which makes sure all the proper taxes have been assessed. He or she will also send notice to the local municipal government concerning the sale of the property.

CLOSING COSTS
Purchase Fees and Taxes

Your closing costs will include various registration fees, including about Q200 to notify DICABI and the local municipality of the sale. The registry fee varies but is about US$200 for a property valued at US$100,000. Incidentally, all taxes are calculated based on the declared value of the property in the registry, which is most always a grossly depreciated figure. This is a common practice throughout Latin America. Officials recognize this and play the game accordingly. My Guatemalan lawyer provided one example of a Guatemala City home in Zona 14 valued at US$300,000 but registered for US$1.25. The local municipality re-appraised the property for tax and registry purposes at US$20,600, which is still but a small fraction of its real value. Typical estimates for registered property values are between 10 to 30 percent of actual values.

You must pay 12 percent sales tax (IVA) on your property purchase and yearly property taxes, payable in quarterly installments. The latter is known as *impuesto único sobre inmuebles* (IUSI) and is calculated by multiplying the property value by 0.009, for properties valued at over Q70,000.

It bears mentioning that you might want to buy property via the formation of a business corporation known as a Sociedad Anónima (S.A.). Benefits of doing so include easier future title transfer and, in some cases, tax savings.

Lawyer Fees

Lawyers can charge 3 percent of the declared property value for their services but are quite flexible with this. They will often charge half of that with the aim of gaining a happy customer and repeat business.

Real Estate Agent Fees

As mentioned before, realtors usually work with the seller and charge them accordingly. Commissions are typically 5 percent in the Guatemala City metro area and between 5 and 7 percent outside the capital.

RISKS OF PROPERTY OWNERSHIP
Political Considerations

Anyone looking to buy property in Central America will most likely give some thought to political considerations given the region's history of conflict. Guatemala was certainly no exception to the region's fairly recent political troubles, particularly in light of a 36-year-long civil war that ended just over 10 years ago. On the up side, Guatemala has enjoyed democratic governments brought to power by free and fair elections and peaceful transitions of power since 1985. The last coup d'etat was in May of 1993, when then-president Jorge Serrano Elías suspended constitutional guarantees and dissolved Congress and the Supreme Court in a short-lived, Fujimori-styled auto-coup. Guatemala's Constitutional Court ruled against his actions, and Serrano was forced to leave the country just a few days later under international pressure and the widespread outcry of Guatemalan society.

The closest government even remotely resembling a form of socialism was in the 1940s and '50s, during the back-to-back reformist governments of Arévalo and Arbenz. U.S. economic interests put an end to political reform and other supposedly Communist leanings when a land reform threatened extensive landholdings by the United Fruit Company and its powerful allies and shareholders in the U.S. government. Arbenz was deposed by a CIA-orchestrated coup in 1954. In any case, the land reform only applied to large landholdings—hardly the sort of thing that would affect the average foreigners' two-acre lakeside home.

Guatemala's political history, probably more so than any other country in Central America except El Salvador, displays a remarkable pro-capitalist stance. It is a country that has been historically dominated by the interests of a wealthy elite, with this power being enforced by the military. Private property is, and has been, sacrosanct in Guatemala dating to the times of its very heavily entrenched colonial roots. Even the most optimistic analysts of political change will tell you that change is very slow here and it will most likely be quite some time before anything resembling a true democracy takes full hold.

On the other hand, Latin America has displayed a recent affinity for socialist rhetoric, with Venezuela's Hugo Chávez leading the charge against the evils of Yankee imperialism. Still, almost anyone familiar with Guatemalan history and sociopolitics will tell you that Guatemala seems strangely immune to the contaminating effects of such trends. Guatemala is not Nicaragua, where Sandinistas not only once took power by force but were voted out and then back in to office. And let's face it; the Cold War is over.

So, all things considered, you should become familiar with Guatemala's complex history and make researching political considerations a major part of your fact-finding trip to find out if Guatemala is right for you. It's certainly not the United States, but I think there are far riskier places to invest in property than Guatemala.

Economic Risks

The risk factor in this area is considerably less. Unlike in other parts of Central America that have experienced real estate booms powered largely by foreign investors, property values in Guatemala tend to more closely reflect the real value of the land. Because most investors in Guatemalan real estate have historically been local, there is little influence of international investment hype. This isn't Costa Rica or Panama, where foreign investors with deep pockets have edged locals out of significant portions of the country's real estate. Then again, Guatemala is becoming more and more popular, so things may change in the next few years. If anything, your biggest risk in this area is not getting in on the game early.

Legal Risks and Property Titles

This area is a bit tricky. Many Guatemalan properties are not registered, and the government is looking to do a countrywide land ownership analysis (*catastro*) in the next few years, but it's anyone's guess as to exactly when this will happen and when it will be completed. The Guatemala City metro area is one possible exception to the issue of nebulous property titles. Still, the risks of being kicked off your land or falling into a long-standing property ownership dispute are rare, according to a poll of local realtors and family members with Guatemalan property. Courts tend to favor the people currently using the land as long as they can prove they purchased or acquired it in good faith. If you're buying property, properly registering your land title should provide all that you need in the event of a future dispute.

Squatters

Worth mentioning here is the potential for having unwanted guests living on your land. This is most certainly part of the pre-purchase process, which includes verifying that there aren't any outstanding claims to the land in question. But what if someone decides to settle on your land after you've purchased it? This is another case where an ounce of prevention will be worth its weight in gold, as the best scenario is to avoid people moving in on your land in the first place. It should be noted that issues with squatters are rare, but are most often an issue in the remote territories of Quiché, where there are large extensions of land with ancestral claims but no property titles, and Petén.

If you do not plan to build on your property immediately following its purchase, you should hire a full-time caretaker. As always, good references and word of mouth are your best approach for hiring this very important addition to your staff. It's important that your caretaker remains just that, and does not become a squatter. You should document all improvements to your land over the months and years following the purchase.

People living on land without proper title have legal rights to the land after 10 years of living on it continuously, peacefully, and "in good faith," but this time can also be applied retroactively from ancestral claims. Land claims are limited to one *caballería,* or 45 hectares (112 acres).

Building Your Own Home

Building your own home allows you the freedom to build your dream house or at least have complete control over the aesthetics and practical considerations of your new home. You can take full advantage of your land's topography, including any views you might have; put in a swimming pool; and ensure the house has adequate electrical wiring for today's modern electronics. It will probably be more costly than buying a pre-planned home in a residential community, but there are definitely some advantages to building your home from scratch. At the same time, there are many things to watch out for.

a luxury home on the shores of Lake Atitlán

© AL ARGUETA

The general consensus is that you'll need to speak adequate Spanish, be able to spend ample time on-site to verify day-to-day details, know a thing or two about construction, and be able to effectively manage people, especially across cultural and linguistic barriers. It's possible to save some money by working with a qualified independent foreman (*maestro de obras*) to oversee the construction, though most people I spoke to strongly recommended the added expense of working with an architect and a qualified construction company. Ask around and find out how other expats got the home they wanted (or didn't want). Many people are willing to share their experiences in search of the greater good.

BEFORE BUYING A LOT

Prior to building a house on a lot, there are a few things you need to make sure of. First, verify that your land has adequate access to basic utilities such as water, electricity, drainage, and phone service. The latter isn't as big a deal as it used to be thanks to modern devices allowing home telephone service from almost anywhere in Guatemala. If your plot lacks any of these you'll need to get estimates for the costs of installing them. In rural areas, you will most likely need to dig a well or pump water from a nearby source (and treat the water). In many cases, you'll also need to invest in the connection, posts, and cable to hook your house up to the nearest power line.

Next, pay special attention to your land's topographic features, especially if building in remote rural areas. Make sure the property has adequate drainage. Land that's too flat, while great for building, often collects rainwater during the rainy season. Access to and from the plot is important as well. If it's a rural road, chances are it's gravel or dirt. Dirt roads turn to mud when it rains, so you'll probably need a four-wheel-drive vehicle. Mudslides are also common during the rainy season and may affect the roads leading to and from your home. Find out who is in charge of maintaining the roads. Is it the local government or the local property owners?

The final step is to verify that there aren't any building restrictions on your property and to conduct an environmental impact assessment, in order to get a construction permit.

FILING FOR PERMITS

Building permits are controlled by the local municipality and are most strictly enforced in Guatemala City. It typically takes 3–4 months to get a building permit. In many cases, time is of the essence, and builders of condos and shopping malls have been known to start building while their permit is in process. To get a building permit, you must present a completed copy of *formulario*

102, a photocopy of your passport or *cédula* (or that of your lawyer), paperwork in which you officially hire your lawyer, a copy of the property registry, building plans, and various lawyer and architect credentials. Needless to say, you'd be wise to hire a lawyer and an architect to guide you through this rather bureaucratic process.

BUILDING COSTS

Building costs vary widely depending on salaries paid to workers, whether you choose to work with a foreman or a construction company, and the types of finishes you want to use. Estimates range from US$150 to US$750 per square meter (US$14–70 per square foot). The latter would be for an ultra-luxurious home in an exclusive sector of Antigua or Guatemala City, while the former is for a basic home in a rural area using more common materials and cheaper labor. A good benchmark number is about US$450 per square meter (US$42 per square foot). You can expect to pay about 20 percent of the total material and labor costs for an architect. If you're remodeling an existing home, you can do the job on the cheap for about US$40 to US$60 per day. This includes a four-man crew and the foreman.

Keep in mind you'll need to hook up your property to utilities as well as construct perimeter walls and fences. Also, don't forget about landscaping!

Hiring a Crew

The best way to hire a crew is to work with a construction company specializing in home building. Local realtors are also a good source of referrals. Keep in mind, there seems great potential for mix-ups when trying to recruit and hire a building team you have no prior experience with. Word of mouth can be very helpful in this regard, as you'll need someone to vouch for your crew. If you run in to someone who was happy with the results they got from their building team, then your work is laid out for you. The proof is very much in the pudding.

DAILY LIFE

Household Expenses

UTILITIES

Electricity is fairly expensive in Guatemala. For a three-bedroom, 140-square-meter (1,500-square-foot) home, monthly expenses are typically US$135 for electricity, US$15 for water, and US$17 for propane gas. In remote areas, you may need to install your own septic system, at a cost typically between US$500 and US$5,000, depending on the size. To set up water service in your home, contact Empresa Municipal de Agua (EMPAGUA). For electricity, contact Empresa ElÉctrica de Guatemala (EEGSA).

Property Taxes

Property tax, known here as IUSI, is calculated based on a small percentage of the property's registered value. This keeps the tax quite reasonable. A property registered for US$100,000, for example, would pay less than US$1,000 a year in property tax. Keep in mind that a property officially registered with a value of US$100,000 would most certainly be a sprawling mansion under the practice of gross underreporting of property values for registration purposes.

Insurance

Although Guatemala lies in the heart of a volatile earthquake zone, home insurance covering earthquakes, floods, and fires would be around US$500 for a US$100,000 home.

LANGUAGE AND EDUCATION

It's been said that learning a new language is like gaining a second culture, and this is certainly true of the expats I've met who have picked up the local language. A command of Spanish will help ease the transition of living in a radically different culture and provide for a much richer life experience. There are few places in the Americas where Spanish lessons are so readily (and cheaply) available, as Guatemala has become a hub for Spanish-language schools. So there's really no excuse to try to get by in life in Guatemala without at least a basic knowledge of your host country's language.

I had the good fortune, as a toddler, of having parents who spoke to me in Spanish and an older sister who spoke to me in English. True, I didn't speak a word until the age of three (my worried parents had me checked out by a doctor), but as it turned out I was just trying to sort out two languages in my young brain. Once I finally started speaking, it was fully in two languages, and I haven't been able to keep quiet since.

© AL ARGUETA

You may or may not have had the same good fortune, but if not, you're in a good place. You won't have to go very far in Guatemala to find a reputable place to learn Spanish at a reasonable cost. By far the greatest concentration of schools is found in La Antigua, but language schools are also plentiful in Quetzaltenango. They can be found in virtually all of the major tourist cities and destinations.

Learning Spanish

LANGUAGE SCHOOLS

Following is a brief overview of the main language school destinations throughout the country. It will give you a feel for what it might be like learning the language in a given destination.

Guatemala City

Although Guatemala City isn't typically on the radar screens of people seeking

---

CHOOSING A LANGUAGE SCHOOL

Antigua has close to 100 language schools, and the task of choosing the right one can seem downright daunting. It really boils down to the quality of individual instructors, though some schools are definitely better than others. Look around and ask plenty of questions. If you decide midway through a weeklong course that you're just not jiving with the instructor, don't feel hesitant to pull out and ask for a new one. That being said, the following websites can help you out in your search: www.guatemala365.com and www.123teachme.com both have surveys and rankings of individual schools in Guatemala.

In terms of your home stay with a local family, feel free to check out the place where you'll be living, as living conditions can vary widely. Pay careful attention to aspects of security, such as having a separate entrance for your room with its own lock. It's also a good idea to get a feel for the comings and goings of family members, as members of the extended family (such as uncles and cousins) often come and go at their leisure. This may be an issue if you're a single female.

Schools typically range in price US$150-225 per week, including 20-35 hours of instruction and accommodations with a local family. While the schools provide everything you will need to learn the language, it might be a challenge to have a total language immersion experience due to the overwhelming presence of foreigners in major towns such as Antigua and Quetzaltenango. If this is an issue for you, consider taking Spanish classes in Cobán, Petén, or the highland town of Nebaj.

to learn Spanish while in Guatemala, your particular work or living circumstances might dictate you needing to learn the language while living in the capital. Rest assured there are a few serviceable language schools in the Guatemalan capital.

La Antigua Guatemala

Antigua is the hub of Guatemala's Spanish language school scene, featuring a dizzying array of language schools. You'll really need to do your homework here in terms of finding a fit that's good for you in light of so many options to choose from. Some people like Antigua's heavy expat presence, as opportunities for meeting people after class abound. On the other hand, some people find the large foreign presence deprives them of the cultural and linguistic immersion experience. Still, the quality of instruction here is among the best in the Americas, and it's hard to beat Antigua's spectacular setting, conveniently located just 30 minutes from Guatemala City.

Quetzaltenango

Also known as Xela, Guatemala's second-largest city has quickly become the runner-up to Antigua's dominance of the Spanish-language-school market. Among the interesting aspects of learning Spanish in this highland city is the opportunity to combine language instruction with community service. Most schools have some sort of arrangement with local NGOs allowing students to volunteer in community development and environmental projects benefiting communities throughout the highlands. Like Antigua, Xela has a sizable expat community. At the same time, it's a larger city so you still have the opportunity to interact with the locals and gain more of a cultural immersion.

Lake Atitlán

Most of the villages on the shores of Lake Atitlán have at least one language school, though the quality of instruction varies widely. Still, there are few places in the world that can match this gorgeous mountain lake for sheer inspiration. It's all about finding the particular village best suited to your tastes and budget, then locking down a good school and, more specifically, a good instructor.

Monterrico

Want to learn Spanish while working on your tan at the beach? Look no further than Monterrico. This pleasant seaside town and its namesake sea turtle preserve are a great place to get in some beach time, learn Spanish, and help out with efforts to conserve Guatemala's sea turtle population.

GUATEMALAN SLANG: A FEW *CHAPINISMOS*

Following is a listing of a few commonly used Guatemalan expressions and slang terms.

aguas! watch out!

a todo mecate: full speed ahead

babosadas: lies or nonsense

cachito: a little bit

canche: blond or fair-skinned; also was a term used of guerrilla fighters during the civil war

capearse: to play hooky

caquero: arrogant or stuck-up; usually someone of wealth

casaca: tall tales or embellishments

chapparro: person of short stature

chupar: to drink alcoholic beverages

clavos: problems

(tener) conectes: to have influence because of important or powerful friends

cuates: buddies

goma (estar de): to be hungover

güiro: a child

jalón: a lift or ride (in a vehicle)

mango: a handsome man

mordida: bribe

muco: a person of low social class; usually used disdainfully by upper-class Guatemalans in reference to lower classes

pisto: money

salsa: to (mistakenly) think oneself cool and hip

sho (hacer): to be quiet (shut up)

shuco: dirty

shute: nosy

virgo: cool, hip

vonós: "let's go"; a shortened version of *vámonos*

Cobán

The city of Cobán lies in a fertile valley deep in Guatemala's green heartland of Alta Verapaz. The foreign presence is noticeably diminished in these parts, giving you the opportunity for a true cultural and linguistic immersion experience. Among the other perks of studying Spanish in this lovely mountain town is the proximity of magnificent natural attractions such as caves, waterfalls, cloud forests, lagoons, white-water rivers, and Mayan ruins.

Flores and Lake Petén Itzá

Flores is the capital of northern Guatemala's Ohio-sized Petén province, located on a small island just off the shore of Lake Petén Itzá. There are a few language schools here, though the majority of the region's schools are found elsewhere around the lake in a couple of Itzá Maya towns. Many of these community-run schools have managed to combine language instruction with environmental conservation efforts to preserve what remains of the Maya Biosphere Reserve and increase cultural awareness of the Itzá Maya people.

STAYING WITH A HOST FAMILY

Many Spanish students opt to live with a host family while taking Spanish lessons. This is an affordable living option contributing directly to improving the lives of average Guatemalans. Live-ins also benefit from greater opportunities to speak the language, as most host families speak only Spanish. You'll learn the language more quickly from being forced to speak it out of necessity, but you'll also gain a glimpse into the lives of average Guatemalans. In addition to being a great catalyst for learning the language, living with a local family can often lead to life-long friendships.

Most Spanish schools can arrange a home stay for you. Arrangements typically include a room in the family's home and two meals a day. Sometimes laundry service is also included. Housing options vary considerably depending on the particular family and what neighborhood they live in.

Education

Guatemala's public educational system is notoriously lackluster, even by Latin American standards. In this regard, the upside of living in a country dominated economically and politically by a wealthy few is that they have to send their children *somewhere*. This "somewhere" must be able to provide a solid educational foundation that will allow their beloved offspring the opportunity to study in a prestigious American or European university.

If you're moving to Guatemala with children and are wondering if their education will suffer as a consequence of your decision, fear not. There are some excellent bilingual schools here, and the cross-cultural experience they gain as a result of life in Guatemala will make them the envy of many a worldly socialite. Having studied in a Guatemala City private school for two years, I can honestly say the experience made me a more well-rounded person.

The Guatemalan school year runs from January through November, with some private schools adhering to this calendar. There is a two- or three-week break mid-year. Many private schools, including the American School, adhere to the U.S./European calendar, whereby classes begin in August or September. In Guatemala, education is free and compulsory through sixth grade, or between the ages of 7 and 14, at least in theory. Many children in rural areas continue to work to help support their families. When traveling throughout the country, it's not uncommon to see children working or engaged in commerce. There are approximately 9,300 primary schools throughout the country, with about 1.3 million students.

As for colleges and universities, Guatemala has several of these. The degree of sophistication and quality of instruction are often quite good. Guatemala's university enrollment totals about 88,000.

PRIVATE SCHOOLS

If you're bringing your kids with you to Guatemala, there really is no other option but private school. The best schools are, not surprisingly, in Guatemala City, where there is a wide range of schools to choose from. Outside of Guatemala City, many private schools are non-secular.

Over 290,000 students attend private secondary schools in Guatemala. Schools' curricula are overseen by Guatemala's Ministerio de Educación. Most private schools provide bilingual instruction in English and Spanish, but some schools also teach French or German. The Ministry of Education's curriculum is rather progressive, with a strong focus on globalization and multiculturalism. Students learn about international cultures and foreign nations beginning in secondary school, with an emphasis that is much greater than that of the average U.S. curriculum.

The *Resources* section at the end of this book can help you get started with your search for an educational facility for your children, but it is by no means exhaustive. Ideally, you'll scout individual schools (with your child) and speak with staff months before your arrival. It's a good idea to allow children some time to adjust to a new home and new surroundings before they are thrust into a new school environment.

Keep in mind that private schools are not only the preferred educational facilities for the children of expats and diplomats, but also wealthy Guatemalans. As someone who moved to Guatemala at the tender age of 10 with American sensibilities already developed, I can tell you you'll need to temper your child's schooling with some good, old-fashioned parenting. Many of the racist sentiments carried by wealthy Guatemalans are clearly in evidence in private schools. Schools can also be very cliquish, with a strong emphasis on who's wearing what and who lives where. It's very different from a middle-class U.S. public school, for example. Your child will need to get some perspective on things, as it's all too easy to adopt the quite retrograde viewpoints sometimes espoused by Guatemala's elite.

HOME SCHOOLING AND DISTANCE-LEARNING PROGRAMS

Given these conditions, some parents opt to home-school their children. If your time in Guatemala is limited to a few months or a few years, this may very well be the best option for you. Your first step in this direction would be to contact your child's current school district with the goal of getting them to provide a curriculum or the educational standards used. You can then design a learning program so that your child can remain up to speed with his or her peers until your return to the United States.

Another alternative lies in distance-learning programs, also known as cyberschools. A web search will turn up everything from packaged programs from private schools to a variety of guidebooks on the subject. I've heard good things about Rebecca Rupp's *Home Learning Year by Year: How to Design a Homeschool Curriculum from Preschool through High School.*

COLLEGES AND UNIVERSITIES

Guatemala's public university is Universidad de San Carlos de Guatemala (USAC). The main campus is in Guatemala City's Zona 12, though its origins date back to Antigua Guatemala, where it was the third university to be established in Latin America, in 1676. It is still considered one of the finest universities in Central America. USAC offers undergraduate and graduate studies in several areas of science and humanities. During Guatemala's civil war (1960–1996), it was a hotbed of opposition to government repression. Students and faculty were often prime targets of the government's dirty war against Communist subversion. Thousands of USAC students and faculty were the victims of forced disappearance. My dad, a USAC alumnus, has vivid memories of student protests in Guatemala City streets during the turbulent 1960s.

Today, things have been toned down a bit, though students still put on the annual Huelga de Dolores, a sort of parade marked by somewhat comical political satire and even a bit of hazing. Participants wear hoods and march through the streets to protest all the latest government foibles.

USAC has branches in a few Guatemalan cities, most notably Quetzaltenango.

Aside from USAC, there are a number of excellent universities based mostly in Guatemala City. Among the private, secular universities worth mentioning is Universidad Francisco Marroquín (UFM). UFM features a splendid campus and a sylvan setting on the edge of a ravine in Zona 10. Among its many outstanding facilities are the Ixchel and Popol Vuh museums and the excellent Ludwig von Mises Library. Established in 1971, it is probably the most modern university in all of Central America. Admissions requirements are Guatemala's most stringent and there are about 2,700 students enrolled in various undergraduate and graduate degree programs. Course texts and guest lectures given by internationally acclaimed speakers are often in English.

STUDY ABROAD PROGRAMS

Guatemala is not a big destination for study abroad opportunities, which is somewhat surprising given its rich cultural and ecological traditions, as well as the top quality of several Guatemala City universities. That being said, college students seeking a study abroad opportunity have a few options, including the University of Arizona (www.studyabroad.arizona.edu), which in partnership with the Antigua-based Centro de Investigaciones Regionales de Mesoamerica (CIRMA, Center for Mesoamerican Research) offers semester and year-long programs focusing on intensive Spanish language instruction and Central American history, politics, and culture. Northern Arizona University (international.office@nau.edu) offers semester and year-long study abroad opportunities in partnership with Universidad del Valle de Guatemala in Guatemala City.

© AL ARGUETA

Antigua is popular with Spanish-language students.

HEALTH AND SAFETY

As the old saying goes, "An ounce of prevention is worth a pound of cure." This advice goes far regarding health in Guatemala. Many of the ills to which travelers and foreign residents succumb to are easily preventable. At the same time, your system will require some time to adapt to new germs and bacteria commonly found in food products to which locals have developed immunity. It's all part of the process of making Guatemala home.

Guatemala's status as a poor, developing nation translates into a variety of health and safety risks for the foreign traveler or resident. Many of these are directly related to poor hygiene. When it comes to safety and law enforcement, the Policía Nacional Civil (created by the 1996 peace accords), has not lived up to its expectations as an efficient, incorruptible, and professional police force. On a positive note, the tourism police (Politur) have demonstrated proficiency in helping travelers as well as making areas somewhat safer with patrols and group escorts. Private initiatives, as they almost always do in Guatemala, have stepped in to fill the gaps, also providing some measure of protection for foreign visitors.

© AL ARGUETA

With this in mind, I offer you some tips to stay healthy during your stay in Guatemala, but if you're here for the long haul bear in mind things may get worse before they get better, specifically in regards to gastrointestinal health.

Guatemala's safety situation is covered at the end of this chapter. We'll take an honest look at crime statistics in what can sometimes be a dangerous country, with the intention of exposing foreigners' propensity for becoming victims of crime and providing practical suggestions to avoid becoming a target.

Preventive Measures

BEFORE YOU GO

Officially, no vaccinations are required for entry into Guatemala, though it's a good idea to be up-to-date on rabies, typhoid, measles-mumps-rubella (MMR), yellow fever, and tetanus shots. A hepatitis vaccine is now widely available and is probably also a good idea. If you plan on taking preventative medications against malaria, start taking them a few weeks before potential exposure to the disease. The Centers for Disease Control and Prevention (CDC) maintains an international travelers' hotline, which can be reached at 888/232-3228, and a travel health home page found at www.cdc.gov/travel.

AVOIDING COMMON AILMENTS

There are certain measures you can take to avoid succumbing to many of the most common ailments affecting foreign travelers and residents alike. Washing hands frequently and drinking only bottled water will help keep you free of stomach ailments, as will consuming only cooked foods or peeled fruits such as bananas and oranges. Lettuce and strawberries are two common culprits often leading to severe gastrointestinal distress. Likewise, stay away from ice cubes unless you have complete assurance that they come from purified water. By law, all ice cubes served in Guatemalan restaurants must come from purified water—a good idea in theory but certainly not always the case. I've often had my doubts even about supposedly purified ice cubes in restaurants after falling ill. When in doubt, leave the ice out.

Be careful not only with what you eat, but where you eat. Stay away from street stalls selling cheap food, referred to jokingly by locals as *shucos* (literally, "dirties"). While Guatemalan stomachs have developed immunity over the years to nasty food-borne bugs, the average gringo's has not. While living in Guatemala, I became suddenly ill after about the third month. As it turned out,

I had amoebic dysentery. After treatment with strong antiparasitical medications, my stomach eventually adjusted to the local bugs and I was able to eat almost anything, much like someone who had lived in Guatemala their entire life. Unfortunately, I later moved back to the United States and have since been unable to recapture my former immunity during frequent, short visits.

Guatemala's phenomenal year-round weather makes it a great place to start a vegetable garden. You'll have the peace of mind that everything grown on your plot is free of pesticides and is irrigated with potable water, as much of the produce consumed locally has been irrigated with water from questionable sources. If you do buy local produce, be sure to carefully soak all your fruits and vegetables in clean water with an iodine solution (available in stores) or with a solution of one teaspoon of household bleach per quart of water, for 15–20 minutes. Certain fruits and vegetables are more susceptible to contamination than others. These include leafy greens such as lettuce, spinach, and cabbage; berries; and fleshy vegetables such as tomatoes and peppers.

HEALTH INSURANCE

Travelers and short-term foreign residents might want to consider purchasing traveler's insurance before heading to Guatemala. Several different types of insurance with varying degrees of coverage are available in the United States, Canada and Europe.

A relatively new Guatemalan initiative offering assistance to foreign travelers is ASISTUR (Asistencia al Turismo), which provides services via the purchase of its ASISTUR Card. You can buy policies for one day, 15 days, 30 days, or one year costing just US$1 per day. Included in the coverage is round-the-clock telephone assistance for issues including legal and medical situations. Security escorts, roadside assistance, helicopter evacuation from remote areas such as volcanic summits or jungles, and special assistance in case of robbery (including provision of hotel room and meals) are also provided to those insured by ASISTUR. Other coverage options (extra cost) include life insurance, coverage of medical expenses, and theft insurance. The card is available at the INGUAT kiosks at the Guatemala City and Flores/Tikal airports. ASISTUR can be reached from anywhere in Guatemala by dialing 1500 or 1-801-ASIST. As this is a new venture, you could probably give them a call if you find yourself in a bind, even if you haven't purchased coverage. An ASISTUR agent might be nearby. Crimes against tourists are a great concern to Guatemalans in general, and their gracious hospitality dictates their desire to help out a traveler in need. That being said, for US$1 a day, the coverage and peace of mind are certainly worth it.

DAILY LIFE

DAILY LIFE

International Health Insurance

Before arrival in Guatemala, you'll need to verify what sort of international coverage (if any) your stateside health insurance may provide. If your policy does provide international coverage, be sure to carry your insurance identity card and a few claim forms, just in case. The latter are easily downloadable in pdf format from most companies' websites. Also, verify whether or not you can file claims from Guatemala or whether you'll have to save receipts and wait until returning to the United States to file a claim. Thanks to the rise of medical tourism in Guatemala, many local clinics are willing and able to work with U.S. insurance agencies to determine how what part of treatment costs might be covered by insurance.

I have heard good reports about international coverage under policies with Blue Cross/Blue Shield and Aetna, but you'll need to do some homework and shop around to suit your specific needs.

Medical Services

DOCTORS AND HOSPITALS

Medical services in Guatemala City are generally top-notch, particularly in many private hospitals. Outside the capital, there are several private hospitals providing quality medical care in urban areas. Public facilities such as the Instituto Guatemalteco de Seguridad Social (IGSS) should be avoided, as they are set up to cater to low-income people with no other alternative and are notoriously understaffed and underfunded. Rural areas are extremely lacking in health care, which has resulted in the presence of Cuban doctors in parts of the highlands who have arrived to help bridge the health care gap. I simply can't bring myself to advise treatment of foreign residents in public Guatemalan facilities in light of the poor quality of care, the misallocation of already thin resources, and the availability of alternatives at reasonable cost. ASISTUR can help locate excellent English-speaking doctors for those under its insurance coverage.

DENTISTS

There are some excellent dentists in Guatemala, particularly in Guatemala City and Quetzaltenango. Many uninsured Americans have begun making trips to Guatemala as a less expensive treatment alternative for root canals, crowns, and periodontics, among others. In Guatemala City, I can personally vouch for the services of Dr. Oscar Cuellar. Dr. Cuellar speaks fluent English and

MEDICAL TOURISM

A new niche industry has emerged as the result of an increasing number of Americans who lack health insurance. Thousands of Americans now travel every year to Central America seeking treatment in modern clinics at a fraction of U.S. prices for procedures that include dental work, plastic surgery, heart procedures, and eye surgery. All this is perfectly safe, as many Central American doctors are U.S.-trained and speak fluent English. Facilities are generally on par (or better than) what you find in the United States.

While much of this niche market goes to Costa Rica, Guatemala has also started capturing its share of the medical tourism market. Perhaps the greatest obstacle to locking in a greater percentage is a general perception of Guatemala by Americans as Third World. This misperception easily crumbles within minutes of arriving in Guatemala City's modern airport and checking in to one of the city's comfortable hotels. The Guatemalan capital is easily the region's most modern, and its private health care facilities

outshine anything its neighbors have to offer.

Adding to the allure of medical procedures at a fraction of the cost is the opportunity to recover in a peaceful environment. Many travelers, for example, combine plastic surgery with a stay at one of Antigua's health spas and return home looking and feeling completely refreshed. It's a great way to have your cake and eat it too.

At least one company provides a one-stop shopping experience for those wishing to make the trip down to Guatemala for medical procedures. **Angels Abroad** (Avenida La Reforma 7-62, Zona 9, Edificio Aristos Reforma, Oficina 401, tel. 2382-8811, www.angelsabroad.com) can provide information and recommend English-speaking doctors in a variety of fields. They will also pick you up on arrival in Guatemala, drive you to and from your appointments, book hotels and airline tickets, provide you with a cell phone for communicating with loved ones back home, and offer general assistance. Prices for their services are quite reasonable.

is a member of the American Dental Association. There are significant savings involved in having dental work done in Guatemala. I recently had a root canal performed at Cuellar's state-of-the-art clinic in Guatemala City for about US$200. Back home in Austin, the same procedure would have cost me just over US$1,000! I cashed in some frequent flier miles for the plane ticket.

MEDICAL RECORDS

It's useful during your stay in Guatemala to have documented evidence of your medical history in order to facilitate care on behalf of your new health care provider. Important records include a list of immunizations and pre-existing medical conditions, recent dental X-rays and a list of known allergies. Also, make sure to bring with you any needed prescription medications in their original plastic bottles. It's useful to have the name of their generic equivalent, in case the standard version is unavailable locally.

DISABLED ACCESS

Access for people with disabilities is still a bit difficult outside of Guatemala City. Most modern buildings, including the newly remodeled airport, are user friendly for the disabled. Outside of the capital, things can get tricky. Crumbling sidewalks (where they exist) and older architecture rarely feature ramps or inclines and will certainly present a challenge to those with limited mobility. Still, you're likely to find a great deal of compassion and people willing to lend a helping hand. Guatemalans generally treat senior citizens with a great deal of courtesy and respect. They often have limited mobility, so the same care naturally applies to people of all ages with disabilities.

PHARMACIES AND PRESCRIPTIONS

In many cases pharmacists serve as de facto doctors, as prescriptions are not necessary for medications in Guatemala. Patients will often describe symptoms and take something on the pharmacist's recommendations. Still, it's always best to see a doctor. Many drugs can be found more cheaply in Guatemala, as they are produced locally by a handful of pharmaceutical companies.

In almost every town, at least one pharmacy will be open all night thanks to a system known as *farmacia de turno* (on-call pharmacy), in which the local pharmacies stay open on a rotating basis. Local newspapers publish a listing of these pharmacies, and sometimes the outlets themselves have a neon sign stating as such.

Health Hazards

FOOD- OR WATER-BORNE DISEASES

Despite taking precautions, many Guatemala newbies might find themselves experiencing a classic case of "the runs" as their digestive tracts adjust to new flora. This usually lasts only a day or two. If the problem persists, it may be a sign of more serious issues. In some cases, it may be food poisoning, which can occur just as easily back home. If this is the case, drink plenty of water and get some rest. You'll probably end up just having to ride it out for a few days and may want to take an antidiarrhea medicine such as Pepto Bismol or Lomotil.

Travelers' Diarrhea

In addition to diarrhea, symptoms of this often-acquired malady include

DAILY LIFE

Guatemala abounds in fresh produce, but be sure to wash it properly.

nausea, vomiting, bloating, and weakness. The usual culprit is *E. coli* bacteria from contaminated food or water. It's important to stay hydrated. Drink plenty of water and clear fluids and keep your strength up by eating bland foods such as crackers or steamed rice. As with food poisoning, you may want to take some over-the-counter antidiarrhea medication.

Dysentery

Characterized by many of the same symptoms as described above along with the possibility of bloody stools and generally prolonged malaise, dysentery comes in two flavors: bacillic (bacterial) and amoebic (parasitic). The onset of bacillic dysentery is usually sudden, characterized by vomiting, diarrhea, and fever. Treatment is via antibiotics, to which it responds well. Amoebic dysentery, on the other hand, has an incubation period and symptoms may not show up for several days. It's also harder to get rid of. It is usually treated with a weeklong course of Flagyl (metronidazole), an extremely potent drug that will wipe out all intestinal flora—good and bad. It also has some marked side effects, such as a bitter taste in the mouth, irritability, sweatiness, and dizziness. You should avoid alcohol while taking this drug, as the combination will make you violently ill. An expensive alternative is Tindamax (tinidazole, 500 mg), which must be taken four times a day for three days. If you've ever had to take amoeba medication for a week, you might be willing to cough out the extra cash to cut the treatment time in half. You should eat plenty of yogurt or take probiotics while on either of these medications. Your tummy will thank you.

As with all gastrointestinal issues, it's very important to stay hydrated. Also, see a doctor in order to get an exact diagnosis. Because of the prevalence of gastrointestinal diseases among Guatemalans, most cities have at least one clinic where they can take a stool sample and diagnose the exact nature of the problem.

Cholera

Not entirely unheard of in Guatemala, cholera can be an issue in poorer neighborhoods lacking adequate sanitation, which are usually not visited by foreign travelers. Today's cholera strains are not nearly as deadly as those of

GETTING (AND STAYING) PARASITE-FREE

Almost everyone who spends a significant amount of time in Guatemala ends up developing some sort of gastrointestinal issue. This goes for locals too, as health authorities estimate a good portion of the population is infected with parasites as a product of poor sanitation and limited access to potable water.

In most cases the offending parasite is an amoeba, which are commonly found in produce such as lettuce and berries. Many Guatemalans do a yearly cleanse to rid themselves of parasitic problems and are familiar with the symptoms of amoebic dysentery. Excessive tiredness, a metallic taste in the mouth, and weird cramping on the outer parts of the stomach usually signal the presence of this unwelcome visitor. Although they can cause loose stools, that's not always the case. Symptoms tend to be delayed in onset and only get worse with time. Fevers are also common.

While prescription medications such as Flagyl can and will do the trick, anti-parasitic medications have some serious side effects. Many people prefer a more natural approach, using herbal remedies. In Antigua, **La Tienda de Doña Gavi** (3a Avenida Norte #2, tel. 7832-6514, noon-7 P.M. daily) sells an herbal concoction known as Jacameb, which you take twice a day with hot water. I've only had limited success with the product, though I have had better luck with a product known as Paranil. The latter consists of an herbal pill concoction that you take on an empty stomach in the morning for about a month. Paranil is available online from www.drnatura.com.

As always, it's best to see a doctor. As necessity is the mother of invention, there are many doctors in Guatemala specializing in gastrointestinal health. Unlike doctors in First World nations who are unaccustomed to diagnosing and treating parasitic problems, doctors in Guatemala have a very good handle on the issue and are an excellent resource.

In addition to doing a yearly cleanse, you'll need to be very careful about your consumption of raw fruits and vegetables while in Guatemala. It's best to only eat these if you've properly sanitized them yourself or are absolutely sure they've been properly washed and disinfected. It's also best to consume only ice cubes made in your own home from water you are absolutely certain is purified.

the past, though there have been outbreaks in Guatemala in years past. It's best to avoid raw fish and ceviche, a marinated raw seafood salad popular throughout Latin America.

INSECT-BORNE DISEASES

Mosquitoes are the main carriers of insect-borne illnesses common throughout tropical areas around the world. The best approach to avoiding malaria and other mosquito-borne illnesses is to avoid being bitten by mosquitoes in the first place. Mosquitoes are most abundant during the rainy season, so take special care to protect against mosquito bites during this time of year. Some travelers favor liberal application of bug spray with DEET as the active ingredient, which seems to be the most effective at keeping the critters at bay. Plant-based bug sprays seem to be less effective. It's also possible to buy clothing treated with permethrin, a bug-repellent chemical. It's also possible to buy it separately and treat your clothing with it. Treated garments are scentless in addition to being highly insect repellent. You can find these products in camping and outdoor stores.

Malaria

Malaria is transmitted by the female *Anopheles* mosquito and is prevalent in the Caribbean lowlands and Petén jungles, though not in the highlands. Anopheles mosquitoes tend to bite at night. Flu-like symptoms of malaria include high fever, chills, headaches, muscle pain, and fatigue. It can be fatal if left untreated.

Some travelers also opt to take antimalarial drugs, available locally without a prescription (and quite cheaply). The most widely used is chloroquine, known by its brand name Aralen. Although chloroquine-resistant strains of malaria are found in other parts of the world including South America, this is not the case in Guatemala. You'll need to start taking the drug (500 mg) a week before arriving in malarial zones, weekly while there, and continue to take it once a week for at least four weeks after you've left the malarial zone. Other travelers opt to take two 500 milligram doses with them to use if and only if the disease strikes.

Some people experience marked side effects while taking chloroquine, including nausea, headaches, fever, rashes, and nightmares. A newer antimalarial drug, Malarone, was approved by the FDA in 2000, supposedly with fewer side effects than traditional drugs, and it does not need to be taken for as long. It is not yet widely available in Guatemala.

Dengue

Dengue is also transmitted by mosquitoes and is prevalent in lowland areas, though it is far less common than malaria and only rarely fatal. Although there is no treatment, most people recover from its debilitating symptoms, which include a fever that can last 5–7 days, headache, severe joint pain, and skin rashes. The disease may last up to another week after the fever has lifted. Tylenol can help reduce the fever and counteract the headaches. Dengue is transmitted by a mosquito that bites during the daytime, the *Aëdes aegypti*. A far less common, though potentially fatal, form of dengue is hemorrhagic dengue. It needs to be treated within a few days of the apparition of symptoms, which are a carbon copy of regular dengue symptoms until severe hemorrhaging sets in, making medical treatment well-advised at the first sign of dengue.

Chagas' Disease

Spread by the bites of the conenose and assassin bugs living in adobe structures and feeding at night, Chagas' disease is most common in Brazil but also affects millions of people between Mexico and Argentina. Curiously, Panama and Costa Rica are Chagas-free, probably owing to the absence of adobe structures from local construction styles. Chickens, dogs, and rodents are thought to carry the disease. Avoid sleeping near the walls of an adobe structure and wear DEET-containing bug spray to bed. The only time this may be a consideration for the average traveler is if trekking across areas of the western highlands and staying with local families, who tend to live in adobe structures. Chagas-carrying bugs also tend to be found in dried palm leaves, which makes mosquito netting a must for the traveler sleeping under thatch-roof structures that are not insulated by wire mesh.

The disease usually starts off as a swollen bite accompanied by fever, which eventually subsides. Chagas may eventually cause heart damage leading to sudden death, and there is no cure for this disease. Only about 2 percent of those bitten ever develop Chagas.

In 2008, the World Health Organization declared Guatemala to be Chagas-free.

BITES AND STINGS
Sand Fleas and Sand Flies

Among the more annoying *bichos* (bugs) are sand fleas, which are virtually imperceptible but can leave a trail of welts on feet and ankles. The best way to avoid bites is by washing off after walking on sandy areas. Annoying and also extremely painful are the bites of sand flies known as *tábanos,* which inhabit coastal areas, mostly on the Caribbean coast. They look like a cross between a bee and housefly. You may not feel them on you until it's too late, as they have a knack for landing gently on their victims. *Tábano* infestations are worst during the dry months when breezes off the ocean are greatly reduced. If traveling to remote beaches, go prepared with pants, long sleeves, bandana, hat, and bug spray. It may seem silly going to the beach with pants and long sleeves, but it sure beats the very unpleasant experience of being bitten and pursued by these persistent critters (I speak from experience).

Snakes

Lowland Guatemala is home to some of the world's deadliest snakes, including the aggressive fer-de-lance, a pit viper also known as *barba amarilla* for the yellow coloring under its mouth. It's easily distinguishable by its diamond-shaped head and intricate diamond patterns on its skin. It is fairly common in Petén, Izabal, and the Verapaces. Bites are usually fatal unless the victim receives medical attention within a few hours. Other poisonous snakes include rattlesnakes; the red, black, and yellow-banded coral snake; and the eyelash viper, which you should be particularly wary of, as it tends to blend in to vegetation, especially palm trees.

Wear high boots and long pants for hiking in the jungle. Always watch where you step and be particularly careful of woodpiles and rocks. Snakes tend to hang out near jungle watering holes and gaps created by fallen trees. For extended trips into the jungle, it's a good idea to go with a guide. Let them lead the way, as their eyes are keenly attuned to the presence of snakes and they are usually armed with a machete.

HIV/AIDS

AIDS is a growing concern in Guatemala, particularly due to widespread prostitution in a society ruled by machismo. Certainly not making things any better is prostitutes who continue working after being infected. If you plan on engaging in intercourse with a stranger or friend met in your travels, be sure to use a condom, available almost anywhere and known as *preservativos* or *condones*.

DAILY LIFE

Environmental Factors

Guatemala has a certain wild feel to it, and living here means a return in some measure to a more earthy lifestyle. Even in the modernity of Guatemala City's concrete jungle, you're still in plain view of the country's volcanoes, serving as a constant reminder of the tectonic forces at work just below the earth's surface. You're very much at the mercy of the elements here, including seismic activity, torrential downpours often leading to mudslides, and the ill effects of inadequate sanitation often found in developing nations.

EARTHQUAKES AND TREMORS

Unless you hail from California, it may take some time to adjust to the frequent earth shakings of Guatemala's terrain. Although there are thousands of tremors per year, most of these are barely felt, as the epicenters are often located off the Guatemalan shores deep below the earth's crust and the quakes reach intensities of only 3 degrees or so on the Richter scale. Sometimes stronger tremors are felt, usually in the vicinity of 5 degrees on the Richter scale, but you'll also get used to these. It's not uncommon to find yourself in the middle of one of these tremors while out eating dinner. Most patrons just continue eating and drinking while light fixtures sway gently. If you're new to this, you can take a cue from your surrounding patrons. Still, it can be very disconcerting when these earth rumblings last well over 30 seconds.

Guatemala's last major earthquake, registering 7.5 on the Richter scale, was in 1976. Thousands of lives were lost when the adobe walls of many villagers' homes collapsed. In Guatemala City, most of the business sector's concrete-and-glass buildings were built after 1976 and are built to ride out strong earthquakes. I've talked to many people who live and work in these towers and they say tremors feel a lot like being on a boat gently swaying on ocean waves. Some high-rises, especially in Zona 10, have been around since before 1976 and have proved their earthquake worthiness.

If you are in an earthquake, it's best not to run out of the house or even go for a doorframe, a common misconception. It's best to seek shelter under a desk while adopting a crouched position protecting your head. Falling objects and walls will crash upon furniture, but you should be safely protected in the pocket created underneath the structure.

AIR QUALITY

Air quality in Guatemala City can often be abysmal, as you'll notice while flying in during the height of the dry season. Thermal inversions often envelop the city in a thick haze. Many allergy sufferers, myself included, begin to feel the ill effects of poor air quality within hours of arrival. Symptoms usually include runny nose, sneezing, and a scratchy throat. Over-the-counter allergy meds such as Claritin or Allegra are available locally and usually do the trick. Even in rural areas, fresh air can often be polluted by the presence of intracity buses spewing out diesel fumes. Areas near major highways often have pollution levels well beyond acceptable limits.

In rural areas, particularly the northern Petén province, smoke from seasonal forest fires and agricultural burning can add to the poor air quality, with smoke from larger forest fires sometimes drifting as far north as Texas.

The rainy season brings with it a whole new cast of characters, making the lives of allergy sufferers all the more interesting. If, like me, you're allergic to mold spores, you'll find the months of September and October almost unbearable in tropical areas. There's nothing quite like hiking through a tropical jungle with humidity in the range of 90 percent and temperatures in the 90s while dealing with a runny nose and watering eyes. Allergy meds can provide some relief, but I have yet to find something that cures my symptoms entirely. If staying in an older colonial home or hotel housed in a colonial building, you may find yourself needing a dehumidifier, as the plaster walls, wood beams, and tile floors tend to trap moisture and feed the aforementioned problems.

WATER QUALITY

Guatemala has some serious water issues, with only about half of Guatemalan households having access to water services. According to the Pan-American Health Organization, as of the year 2000, only 25 percent of water in urban systems was disinfected, while only 1 percent of all collected sewage water was being treated. Sewage water often runs into rivers, locally known as *aguas negras*. These rivers of untreated sewage also run into lakes, such as Lake Atitlán. Many of the ravines crisscrossing Guatemala City contain such rivers. In coastal areas, untreated sewage runs into the ocean in many towns and villages.

It's a good idea to carry a water filter or iodine tablets when camping. You'll also need to buy bottled water for household consumption or install a home water filter, even in Guatemala City where water is (supposedly) treated. Several companies, such as Agua Salvavidas, can deliver a five-gallon water jug to your home weekly.

SMOKING

Smoking is still rather socially acceptable in Guatemala compared to the United States, though you'll find it's frowned upon in public places such as banks, airports, and office buildings. With this in mind, smoking in public places, including restaurants and bars, was officially banned in February 2009.

SOLID WASTE

Solid waste disposal is a big problem in Guatemala. The capital's dump has long been a source of revenue for hundreds of people living in its vicinity trying to eek out a living collecting discarded bottles, papers, and plastics. Trash at the Guatemala City dump is often burned, and the toxic fumes are often carried by the winds to neighboring Zonas 5, 7, and 11. Recycling as we know it in the Unites States is virtually unheard of in Guatemala, and you'll sometimes come across piles of trash lining roads and highways, a rather disconcerting sight.

SUN EXPOSURE

The Guatemalan sun can be quite brutal thanks to the country's location at tropical latitudes. In highland areas encompassing much of the country, you also have the added factor of altitude and a correspondingly thinner atmosphere to deal with. All this translates into plentiful quantities of skin-scorching UV rays, and so adequate protection is needed. If you're fair-skinned, it's a good idea to bring high-SPF sunscreen to Guatemala with you, as it can be sometimes hard to find anything above SPF 15 in local stores. Guatemalans tend to be darker-skinned, which is one obvious reason for this. A hat and sunglasses can also go a long way in keeping the sun's harmful rays at bay and will help prevent you from developing cataracts later in life.

Safety

POLICE

The Policía Nacional Civil (PNC) was created after the civil war with help from Chilean and Spanish security forces but has not been the efficient security force it was hoped it would be. In addition to widespread allegations of corruption, it is perceived as being grossly inefficient. Corrupt agents are suspected of involvement in everything from drug trafficking to highway holdups, as many robberies occur shortly after travelers are stopped at police checkpoints, and perpetrators are often described as wearing police uniforms. Despite these conditions, if you are stopped by police it is best not to offer a bribe, as straight cops will not hesitate to throw you in jail. It's best to go through the usual mechanisms and pay the fine (if applicable). After being stopped, be particularly mindful of your surroundings and especially on the lookout for vehicles that might be following you a little too closely. If you have hired the services of ASISTUR, you may want to give them a call and let them know you've been pulled over. There may be an agent in the vicinity who could accompany you the rest of the way to your destination.

The Guatemalan military sometimes jointly patrols areas with police forces due to the latter's demonstrated inability to provide a security presence tending to dissuade criminal activity. This has led to criticism because the joint patrols (as they're called) run counter to the peace accords allowing for the creation of a professional civilian security force. The involvement of high-ranking police officers in the assassination of three Salvadoran diplomats and their driver in February 2007, in addition to denunciations that police forces harbor death squads within their ranks, may have served as the needed impetus for a systematic purge and revamping of the police forces (once again) from the ground up.

In contrast, the tourism police (Policía Turística, or Politur) are generally helpful and have been dispatched to patrol tourist areas. They have been particularly effective at curbing robberies in areas where criminal activity was once getting out of hand including, Tikal National Park and areas in the vicinity of Antigua.

CRIME

Crime has been a problem throughout Guatemala in the aftermath of the civil war, though statistics show most foreign travelers and residents enjoy their time in the country without incident. As far as statistics go, 24 American citizen residents and 6 U.S. tourists have been murdered in Guatemala since 1999, when the Guatemalan government named a special prosecutor to investigate all American citizen murders. Suspects have been tried and convicted in only two cases. But, as many veteran Guatemala travelers and residents like to point out, you're still safer here than in many large U.S. cities.

Private security forces guard a variety of Guatemalan businesses.

HOW SAFE IS GUATEMALA?

This is a tough question, but one which you will have to ask yourself before embarking on your Guatemala adventure. The question might be better phrased as, "Can I live in a country where I know the potential for danger is always just around the corner?" For many, this is the deal breaker when considering Guatemala (and much of Latin America) as a place to live. Let's face it, the State Department and U.S. Embassy reports don't paint a pretty picture; going into detail in country reports about murders, gang violence, robberies, and kidnappings. Ask around, and things don't look much better. Many Guatemala expats I've talked to have been victims of some type of crime, ranging from pick-pocketing to highway banditry. I have personally been robbed three times in Guatemala. Only once was it violent, and I was technically on the Mexican side of the border along the Usumacinta River. I was once pick-pocketed in Guatemala City and also fell prey to robbers upon leaving La Aurora International Airport. They absconded with my laptop and passport. It bears mentioning that I only live in Guatemala part-time. Maybe it was bad luck, as all of these happened in the same year (2004) and I haven't had anything happen since then.

On the other hand, you may also talk to people who have never had anything happen to them. In many cases, folks who've been victims of crime simply shrug it off and explain that it's all part of living in a developing country with a legacy of violence and a failed State. All in all, it really does take a special kind of person to live here. I've said it once and I'll say it again. Guatemala isn't for everyone. You might be willing to play the odds; you might not. At the same time, there are certainly things you can do to protect yourself and to avoid becoming a victim of crime. You're not completely defenseless and at the mercy of the country's security conditions.

If you love Guatemala you'll probably find that the rewards of living here far outweigh the uncertainty of what may or may not happen to you. At the end of the day, nothing in life is 100 percent safe, is it?

Among Guatemala's urban areas, Guatemala City has by far the greatest prevalence of crime. Recently, much of the crime against foreign travelers and residents has consisted of robberies targeting arriving passengers heading in to the city from La Aurora International Airport. Private vehicles, taxis, and shuttle buses have been targeted indiscriminately. Authorities were investigating suspected groups while simultaneously opening security checkpoints and police kiosks to provide greater police presence along this route. It remains to be seen whether large-scale infrastructural improvements involving roads adjacent to the airport (as part of the airport renovation project) will make conditions safer for arriving passengers. Incident reports show that passengers arriving on early morning flights are more likely to be targeted. Most of the red-eyes into Guatemala arrive from LAX, so be especially careful if you are arriving on one of these flights.

For more on this topic, read the U.S. government's Consular Information Sheet, found online at www.travel.state.gov. Another useful site is that concerning recent incidents of crime against foreigners in Guatemala available at http://guatemala.usembassy.gov/recent_incidents.html. It will give you an idea of what can happen, but try not to let it alarm you.

Gang violence is also a growing concern. The groups, known as *maras,* operate in parts of Guatemala City not usually frequented by international travelers as well as in some urban areas throughout the country.

Drug Trafficking

Guatemala is a major transshipment point for cocaine coming into the United States from South America, as evidenced by the many clandestine landing strips found in isolated areas of Petén department. Marijuana is grown in remote lowland areas of Guatemala, and poppies (the basis for heroin) are grown in the western highlands, particularly in the department of San Marcos.

High-ranking military officials have been implicated in drug smuggling, working with local cartels linked to Colombia's powerful Cali cartel. U.S. drug officials have begun referring to Guatemala as *la bodega* (the warehouse), as it houses a large portion of the cocaine continuing north to Mexico, from where it makes its final entry into the United States. Among the local cartels, the most prominent are based in the eastern lowlands near Zacapa (not an area frequented by foreign tourists or residents), Izabal department, and the southern portion of Petén department near Sayaxché. Some travelers have reported run-ins with local drug traffickers on private lands, but you're unlikely to be harmed as long as you adopt a live-and-let-live attitude.

Cocaine consumption is an increasing problem among affluent Guatemalans, particularly in Guatemala City nightclubs. Drug use is strictly forbidden by law and you will be thrown in jail without hesitation for violations. If you arrive into Guatemala by air from elsewhere in Latin America, drug-sniffing dogs will probably be on hand to greet your flight, and you may be questioned by authorities after clearing immigration procedures.

Extortionary Kidnapping

Kidnappings for ransom reached an all-time high after the civil war, usually involving prominent citizens held for ransom and sometimes returned to their families, depending on whether or not the ransom money was collected. They seem to have subsided in more recent years and rarely, if ever, involve foreigners. Most kidnappings occur in Guatemala City, with residents of affluent neighborhoods most often targeted. Some of these, known as "express kidnappings," are intended to have a quick turnover and involve smaller sums of money, usually in the tens of thousands of dollars.

Unlike cases involving attempted robbery, which you should never resist, some kidnappings have been thwarted by resistance from intended victims. Keep in mind, kidnappers most likely have to grab their intended victim from a public place, so making a scene and running away from would-be captors makes some degree of sense. I've heard many tales of a good scream throwing kidnappers off guard and preventing their plans from coming to fruition.

Many prominent Guatemalans hire bodyguards to protect them, and you will often see these heavily armed personnel waiting for their clients outside gyms, restaurants, and other haunts of the well-to-do. If you are worried about potential kidnapping or just want professional risk assessment, contact Yantarni S.A. (www.yantarni.com.gt). In addition to providing protection and risk assessment, the company can also provide tactical training taught by British security experts.

Theft and Armed Robbery

Theft is a common problem in Guatemala and comes in several varieties: the more secretive forms, such as pickpocketing and vehicle break-ins, and the outright violent forms, such as carjackings and home break-ins involving armed men. In terms of the former, you should avoid carrying a wallet in public places where large crowds of people might brush up against you. Buses are a favorite hangout of pickpockets, and you should never step onto a bus with your wallet in your back pocket. You should also never leave valuables inside a parked vehicle. As for violent robberies, many Guatemalans have resorted to packing heat in the face of authorities' inability to provide adequate protection or bring perpetrators to justice. In Guatemala City's affluent Zona 15, there have been recent reports of robbers shot dead by their intended victims. Again, I refer you to the services of agencies, such as Yantarni, that provide security services for training and equipment.

A related issue is that of highway holdups on rural roads, a very unpleasant topic that I must nonetheless cover here. Sometimes, groups will use bends in the road and speed bumps to their advantage, stopping vehicles as they slow down and robbing passengers of valuables. In the most spectacular cases of highway banditry, pickup trucks carrying armed men pursue a vehicle and then pass it. Another car might come alongside the victim's vehicle while the car in front shoots at it, in an attempt to make the driver stop the car. In addition to taking the passengers' possessions, perpetrators occasionally drag the car's occupants out of the vehicle, tie them up, and steal the car. Rapes and assaults are sometimes perpetrated.

Guatemalans who sniff out an impending carjacking on rural roads have been known to speed up as would-be perpetrators signal them to slow down, not without significant risk of being harmed by the bullets that are often landed on the car by frustrated assailants. If you are stopped and robbed, it's best to remain calm and give them what they want. Opposing a robbery will only make matters worse, as the thieves will only see this as an invitation to use greater force. (I speak from a personal experience in Mexico.) Robberies in which the victim resists often end with the victim being shot to death.

It's hard to predict where robberies may occur, though certain areas do seem more prone to this type of crime than others. Among these areas are RN-11, along the eastern side of Lake Atitlán, the road to El Salvador outside the Guatemala City area (Salvadorans are a favorite target), and some rural Petén roads, including a remote dirt road leading to the ruins of Yaxhá.

Common Scams

It's good to be aware of a number of common scams used by con artists to relieve unsuspecting citizens of their valuables. At the moment, passengers arriving at Guatemala City's La Aurora International Airport seem to be an easy target, perhaps because of the ongoing reorganization of neighboring roads leading in to the city. According to incident reports, most robberies take place once the victims have arrived near their intended destination within the city. Keep an eye out for anyone who might be following you.

If you're picking someone up or are being picked up at the airport, it's a good idea to inspect the car's tires prior to leaving the parking lots adjacent to the airport terminal. A common scam involves a "Good Samaritan" who approaches you while you're on the road out of the airport to inform you of a flat tire. Drivers who stop to address the problem on the open street are quickly relieved of their valuables, often at gunpoint. You can stop at a nearby gas station to address the problem there, but beware of distractions and crooks aimed at getting inside your vehicle while you are unaware. Lock the doors and keep an eye on the inside of your vehicle. Better yet, have someone stay inside the car. Favorite items include laptops, so it's best to carry these in an inconspicuous backpack or other carry-on bag. The traditional laptop shoulder bag all but broadcasts that you are carrying a computer with you. I speak from experience.

Another common scam involves a person or persons coming in to a restaurant and asking the potential target to move his or her car for supposedly blocking someone's exit. Once the unsuspecting victim is outside, he or she is robbed at gunpoint. Know where you parked your car, and under no circumstances should you walk out of a restaurant or public place with someone alleging wrongdoing on your part.

Staying Safe

During your time in Guatemala, there are a number of common sense measures you can take to avoid becoming the victim of street crime. Don't walk around wearing flashy jewelry, and carry only the amount of cash you need for the day in a concealed place. Use safety deposit boxes for important documents like passports and plane tickets. In crowded cities, carry your backpack in front of you and be aware of your surroundings at all times. Keep car doors locked while driving and roll up windows, especially in Guatemala City. Always keep an eye on your luggage at the airport, bus terminals, and hotels. At night, take a cab and don't go walking out and about after dark. At the beach, be sure not to bring too many things that might tempt thieves while you're in the water. Also, be careful not to walk along isolated stretches of beach, particularly around the Caribbean city of Lívingston.

If you plan on exploring Guatemala's gorgeous backcountry during your time here, you'll be happy to know there are still many areas of the country that remain relatively crime-free, particularly the western highlands region of the Ixil Triangle, where you can still explore freely. Before embarking on a backcountry hike or volcano climb, always inform someone who is not going with you of your plans and when you plan to return. It's never a good idea to climb volcanic summits without a guide, particularly those around Antigua and Lake Atitlán, as these are especially prone to robberies. Some volcanoes are more infamous than others. Always inquire locally about current conditions.

EMERGENCIES

You can phone the police from any part of the country by dialing 120, or the fire department by dialing 122 or 123. However, don't expect an ambulance to come whisk you away immediately. A better option is ASISTUR, which can be reached by dialing 2421-2810 or 1-801-27478. Another useful number is that of the U.S. Embassy's American Citizen Services section, which can be reached at 2326-4405. The after-hours emergency numbers are 2331-2354 and 2331-2354. It's a good idea to register with the U.S. Embassy once you've had a chance to settle down. This can be done easily online at http://guatemala. usembassy.gov/acs_information_residents.html.

If you are robbed, be sure to file a police report as soon as possible and contact the U.S. Embassy. You'll need a copy of the police report to get a new passport, if it's been stolen. Technically, you should also get your entry stamp into Guatemala re-issued by Migración, which costs nothing, though passports are no longer checked by immigration authorities upon exiting the country from La Aurora Airport.

EMPLOYMENT

Guatemala is one of the poorest countries in the northern hemisphere, though there is no lack of resources and opportunities for new personal ventures abound. Although there is great poverty here, there is also great wealth. Those with an entrepreneurial spirit can do quite well in Guatemala, as you will see unmet needs and potential business ideas everywhere you look. Adding to the allure of doing business in Guatemala is the opportunity to create jobs and share your know-how with a largely uneducated populace. The Guatemalan government is in the process of revamping foreign investment laws as well as providing new tax breaks and other incentives for foreigners opening busi-nesses in this country. New ventures relating to tourism and reforestation are especially welcome and encouraged with tax incentives. Specially demarcat-ed free trade zones (*zonas francas*) also offer tax breaks to businesses located within their borders.

Those of you looking for a more traditional 9-to-5 job might have a harder go at it, but you are encouraged to look for opportunities with government

© AL ARGUETA

agencies, multinational corporations, and NGOs working in Guatemala. There are many opportunities to volunteer or work with aid organizations, thanks to a substantial amount of effort being poured into social justice and environmental causes in the aftermath of the 36-year-long civil war. Guatemala has traditionally been a place where people go to mellow out or get a change in perspective, so it's not surprising that it can be a bit challenging to find gainful employment. There are some jobs available with multinational corporations based in Guatemala City, but competition for these few jobs is fierce and the local workforce often gets first dibs.

Investment law reforms aside, Guatemala is still very much a closed society where the wealthy few control the vast majority of the country's resources. A lot of patience and some good contacts will help you out in the long run. The government officially welcomes foreign investment, and the country's future economic success in the world's increasingly globalized economy will depend largely on the influx of foreign capital and know-how.

Self-Employment

Entrepreneurs will see opportunities almost everywhere they look in Guatemala. Although red tape, archaic bureaucracy, and deeply ingrained nepotism might stifle your initial enthusiasm, you can take comfort and inspiration from the knowledge that you are in many ways a pioneer teaching Guatemalans how to do business in a global capitalist economy. I personally think one of the best things that could happen to the local economy is a large influx of American capital, business ethics, and material know-how much like what has been fueling the economies of Costa Rica and Panama in recent years. It's not that Guatemala lacks economic activity, it's just that the economic power is so heavily concentrated in the hands of a wealthy few.

Foreign aid agencies and the

Agriculture is still Guatemala's largest employer.

© AL ARGUETA

DR-CAFTA AND GUATEMALAN BUSINESS

The Dominican Republic-Central America Free Trade Agreement (DR-CAFTA) took effect in June 2005. A recent study commissioned by the Guatemalan Finance Ministry and financed by the United States Agency for International Development (USAID) shows some very promising developments for a variety of local businesses. The study was conducted by IDC Consulting, with the results being presented in December 2008. IDC provided a case study of six companies doing business in Guatemala that have managed to dramatically increase their sales. The study also cites remaining challenges to doing business in Guatemala.

Here is a brief synopsis of highlighted sales and employment figures for several of the companies before and after DR-CAFTA, along with the challenges faced by these companies, as reported in Guatemala's *Prensa Libre*.

CTL

CTL is a Guatemalan agro-chemical company that began opera-

tions in 2005; its sales increased from US$100,000 in June 2005 to US$1.3 million in June 2008. In the same period, its exports increased from 5 to 80 percent of sales.

ACCESORIOS TEXTILES

This company makes labels for the garment industry. Sales increased from US$569,000 in June 2005 to US$2.8 million for the same month in 2008. The number of employees increased from 110 to 160, and the number of export clients rose from 10 to 47.

DHL

The Guatemalan office of this international shipping corporation saw a 157 percent increase in sales from June 2005 to June 2008. During the same period, transported cargo increased from 17,900 tons to a whopping 113,200 tons.

TRANSACTEL

At Transactel, one of several call centers that have established operations in Guatemala in recent years, sales multiplied by a factor of 18

Guatemalan government publicly recognize that the country's future economic potential rests largely in the development of small and medium-sized independent businesses with greater potential for more equitable wealth distribution. So, dear reader, it is very much my hope that these pages might inspire you to look past the challenges of doing business here and look forward to reaping the economic and emotional benefits of pioneering your business endeavor here in Guatemala.

SOCIEDAD ANÓNIMA (S.A.)

Starting a business in Guatemala is relatively easy and there is a particular legal framework allowing you to set up shop, with rules and benefits similar to those of a limited liability corporation (LLC) back home. Known as Sociedades Anónimas (Anonymous Societies), S.A.s are everywhere in Guatemala after the ratification of DR-CAFTA. It now employs 2,800 people, which is a significant increase from its original 400 employees.

ONGOING CHALLENGES

Many challenges to doing business in Guatemala remain, as exemplified by comments made by company executives interviewed for the study. Among them is Paul Kronick of Caoba Doors, a producer of wooden doors and window frames that exports 92 percent of its annual sales. "It's not easy doing business in Guatemala," he said. "The high cost of electricity, lack of security, and trying customs procedures are cause for worry." He added that disorganization prevails at the Superintendencia de Administración Tributaria (SAT) and much time is wasted when documents frequently disappear and new ones must be obtained.

CTL reported similar challenges, citing that the export process requires an average of 15 days. Company CEO Guido Azzari said, "The main problems are in customs (SAT) because they put up unfounded roadblocks and hold up the process." Accordingly, DHL Guatemala manager Arnoldo Carranza believes operations at the country's ports demonstrate extreme disorganization because they operate under their own board of directors in the absence of a unified strategy or governmental plan.

In other cases, obstacles to free trade arise not from government bureaucracy and inefficiency but from remaining trade barriers imposed by the U.S. government and U.S. companies. Sergio de la Torre, of Accesorios Textiles, says his company's biggest barrier is obtaining certification for Guatemalan clothing labels from companies like Target, Wal-Mart, and JCPenney. In the case of decorative plant exporter Plantas Ornamentales, U.S. laws prohibiting the importation of foreign soil prevent the company from exporting fully germinated plants. They must instead export seeds, meaning a huge loss in potential profits.

DAILY LIFE

and commonly follow the name of a company much like "Inc." does in the United States. Liability with an S.A. is limited to how much money has been put into the corporation. Many people use S.A.s to purchase property.

To form a Sociedad Anónima, two people appearing before a lawyer execute the articles of incorporation, including a minimum initial investment of Q5,000. This is generally done via a deposit into one of the local banks linked to the financial system. Each shareholder subscribes to at least one share of stock. The business can be headed by a sole administrator or additional shareholders designated to positions such as president and vice president. The framework also gives you the opportunity to name your company's legal representation. Foreigners are free to form S.A.s but cannot constitute the legal representation to one unless they have Guatemalan residency.

Once the articles of incorporation have been met before a lawyer, he or

BEING A *BUEN PATRÓN:* GUATEMALAN LABOR GUIDELINES

You may or may not be starting a business that will employ several Guatemalans, but chances are you'll at least have some domestic help while living here. This being the case, it's a good idea to get a feel for the local labor laws.

The first thing you should be aware of is that Guatemalan laws and tradition provide workers an additional two months' salary. The first of these is the *bono 14*, which is one month's salary paid as a yearly bonus in July. The second of these is the *aguinaldo,* paid in December prior to the 15th and also the equivalent of one month's salary. It's traditionally used to purchase gifts and help with other holiday expenses.

Work days are limited by law to 8 hours daily, and total hours worked are not to exceed 48 in a single week. Labor laws also limit the number of hours worked during evening shifts (6 P.M. to 6 A.M.) to 6 hours daily and no more than 36 hours per week. The workweek culminates in a paid day off, usually Sunday. This "extra" day is commonly just factored in to a weekly pay rate. In addition to the bonuses, there are a dozen or so paid holidays in Guatemala. All workers who have worked a minimum of 150 days in a single year are allotted a two-week (15-day) paid vacation. The minimum salary in 2008 was around US$200 a month – slightly less for farm workers. There is also a Q250 (about US$33) monthly incentive bonus on the books.

If your business employs three or more people, you will need to register with the Instituto Guatemalteco de Seguridad Social (IGSS) in order to provide your workers with certain benefits such as health care and retirement benefits when they reach the age of 60. The employer must pay 14.67 percent of the gross monthly payroll as the *cuota patronal* (employer's contribution). A smaller portion, 4.83 percent, is deducted from the employee's paycheck and paid into the IGSS fund.

Things become complicated should you need to fire one of your staff, as you will need to demon-

she will then register your company in the Registro Mercantil General de la República (Mercantile Registry). Once registration is complete, the respective shares are officially issued to company shareholders and the respective company accreditations are issued. A tax ID number (NIT) is also issued. The final step is the issuance and legalization of the company's books—a total of six covering accounting and legal issues. A seventh book documents shareholders' meetings. All of these are presented to the Superintendencia de Administración Tributaria (SAT) for review and legalization. These books, once legalized, document the company's internal affairs and stock transfers; they are privately kept by the company shareholders.

Corporation Tax (ISR)

Guatemalan business taxes are fairly straightforward, though there are myriad strate just cause for doing so or be willing to pay the employee a hefty *indemnización* (compensation). Guatemalan laws are very much on the side of the laborer, so it's important to keep good records of employee labor conditions. Everything a laborer says in court will be taken at face value unless the employer can prove otherwise. If the employee says he makes US$500 a month and there is no data to say otherwise, then that is what he makes. Should you fire someone without just cause, you must provide a severance package that includes the monthly Q250 bonus, severance pay of one month's salary for each year worked (up to 5 years), prorated *bono 14* and *aguinaldo*, and vacation pay up to five years. If the dispute lands in court, you are responsible for paying 1–6 months' salary, depending on the length of the trial.

If the employee quits or is fired with just cause, he or she is still entitled to certain irrevocable rights including unused vacation pay and prorated *bono 14* and *aguinaldo*.

Your flexibility and personal relationships with staff come into play here, as they may be willing to work for you on holidays for extra pay or work through their vacation time for additional wages. Keep things open but professional and formal. It's a good idea to have employees sign off on received paychecks and to keep a log of sick days and vacation time. You want to keep a happy balance between the two extremes of looking like a pushover and appearing like a gringo taskmaster who exploits Guatemalan workers. This should be easy if you keep in mind that you are here to provide jobs for people who may otherwise not have them and to break new ground in a land that offers as many opportunities as it lacks. You have much to learn from your employees, and they will most certainly learn a lot from you. My mother opened a boutique during my family's two-year-stint in Guatemala during the 1980s and still recalls it being one of the most rewarding times in her life.

deductions that can be taken for particular businesses. It's a good idea to have an accountant or other tax professional with a certain amount of savvy regarding local tax laws prepare your business taxes for you. Taxes for businesses are similar to those for individuals and are applied as *impuesto sobre la renta* (ISR). In oversimplified terms, your company's gross income minus all business expenses yields your *utilidad neta* (net income). Taxes are then calculated as a percentage of this number according to a chart established by the Superintendencia de Administración Tributaria. As in the United States, companies are responsible for withholding part of employees' gross income for tax purposes.

INCENTIVE LAWS

Guatemala's foreign investment laws date to 1989 and are generally considered obsolete by the local business community, which is pushing to have the laws

CREATING YOUR OWN PHILANTHROPIC OPPORTUNITIES

Anyone who has spent a fair amount of time in Guatemala will probably find it hard to ignore the landscape of poverty. Part of settling in Guatemala involves coming to grips with the country's constant contradictions and, in many cases, trying to do something about it. Many expats volunteer with various charitable organizations, but you may also be inspired to go out and start your own philanthropic organization according to your interests and the unmet needs you see. Following is a brief first-person account by one such expat volunteer. This person has chosen to remain anonymous, but the account can give you some things to look out for if you decide to start your own project. Specific place-names have been omitted to protect the source's anonymity.

A PHILANTHROPIST'S STORY

I went to Guatemala several years ago and enrolled in a Spanish school. I'd intended to do the full-day immersion program for the entire summer but quickly realized that I couldn't focus after about four hours – that my brain turned to mush. I inquired about volunteer opportunities and the school referred me to a project that had a dental chair and small setup but relied solely on volunteer dentists. I went to them and ended up working every weekday afternoon, bringing my Spanish teacher with me to translate and later to coach me in practicing my Spanish.

I enjoyed the project so much that I started thinking bigger than just me volunteering. I questioned the staff and administration about their needs and proposed me going home and raising the money to pay a dentist, assistant, and public health worker (the idea was to hire Guatemalan staff who would provide services all year). The project put together a budget and I came home and identified a donor interested in health care.

The pitch was that the donors

reformed. It is no secret that Guatemala's free trade zones and industrial parks pale in comparison to facilities in neighboring countries, something the new laws will need to address in order to attract more investment dollars.

LABOR LAWS

Guatemalan labor laws are very much in favor of workers' rights. Before embarking on any business venture, get familiar with various aspects of the labor code, including employer contributions to health care, vacation pay, and severance pay.

DAILY LIFE

could provide care to 1,000-plus individual children for a pittance (US$25,000). They agreed with the caveat that I oversee the project funds in a hands-on manner since there is a lot of graft due to the poverty in Guatemala. I agreed.

The project with the funding I set up went for two years. At that time I started to suspect there was graft, and with some investigation it turned out to be on the side of the American charity counterpart. The problem was that because of the way it was all set up, there was no accountability in the United States or in Guatemala. At that point, knowing that the services were being provided but that a percent was being skimmed off for who-knows-what, I decided to break with that project.

By then, I had made enough contacts in three years and a total of 8-9 months in-country to start helping other smaller projects that were conceived and run totally by Guatemalans. The catch was that American donors couldn't/wouldn't get a tax break. I was able to contact a couple of churches here in the United States who were committed to the type of work I was doing, and they were willing to accept the donations of Americans wanting the tax write-off and then turn around and send the money to Guatemala.

So, that is my story. In speaking to a lot of foreigners down in Guatemala, it seems the theme resonates. Foreigners, and sometimes *chapines*, start projects with honest and good intentions, and then later greed or narcissism and ego creep in.

The moral is that despite all this, good works are being done. The other point is just to do the good deeds and watch and ask questions, and if you think there is graft don't completely give up, just modify. Often the graft is due to the extreme poverty in Guatemala. There is no middle class; it is the poor in gradations (even the dentist we hired made just US$500 a month) and then the ultra-rich who more or less control everything in Guatemala.

The Job Hunt

As I mentioned before, people don't usually come to Guatemala to take a job; they come here because they love the country and its people. You can certainly make money here, but it probably won't approach what you can make back home. The cost of living here *can* be lower, depending on how you live, but it won't be that much lower. Keep in mind, Guatemalans travel to the United States in droves to work and send money home, so this isn't exactly the healthiest job market. But, if you know some people, have a marketable skill or two or a great business idea, and know how to sell yourself (and your ideas), you can certainly find something to pay the bills or indeed do very well down here. In addition to work with multinational corporations and NGOs, perhaps the next-most-popular employment option for foreigners is teaching English.

JOB-HUNTING TIPS

Word of mouth is still the best way to find a job in most places, and Guatemala is no exception. Business here is very relational, and people will want to meet you and get to know you before they will even consider you for an open position. That being said, it's better to err on the side of formality when making initial contacts. Dress your best.

Jobs are most plentiful in the Guatemala City area, as this is the country's economic engine. Popular tourist areas or cities with large expat communities, such as Antigua, Lake Atitlán, and Quetzaltenango, are also good places to look.

You may need to translate your résumé to Spanish. Also, be sure to have certified copies or original documents such as diplomas and other certifications with you and available for scrutiny. Employers will want to see these documents, which is a trait very much in line with the pomp and circumstance of Guatemalan business culture. You may also be surprised to find job ads requiring not only your résumé or CV (curriculum vitae), but also a passport-sized photograph of yourself. Posted job ads often have strict age requirements and may be limited to a particular gender.

WHERE TO LOOK

In addition to word of mouth, expat communities often have bulletin boards or particular publications widely circulated among foreign residents. It's a good idea to browse these advertisements periodically as well as to post a job wanted ad of your own. There are a number of local job websites advertising openings in Spanish. Daily newspapers such as *Prensa Libre* and *Siglo XXI* have help wanted classifieds where openings at multinational corporations and other positions requiring native English speakers often appear in English.

A growing number of Guatemalans are employed by the tourism industry.

© AL ARGUETA

WORK PERMITS

Nonresident foreigners can easily secure work permits allowing them to work in the country legally. The Ministerio de Trabajo (Ministry of Labor) tends to favor the applications of foreigners with a Guatemalan spouse and/or children. If this is the case, you'll need to present a written offer of employment, police records, children's birth certificates, marriage certificate, photocopy of temporary visa or residency visa (or documents showing these have been applied for), and a written request addressed to the Ministerio de Trabajo. Foreign residents without a Guatemalan spouse or children must make the same request via a form available from the Ministerio de Trabajo. It is then the employer's responsibility to submit the necessary paperwork on the employee's behalf. Eligible foreigners can expect to get their work permit in 2–3 weeks.

Working for a Nonprofit

Guatemala tends to attract a rather benevolent crowd, and many people visiting the country are here to do charitable work. In some cases these are paid positions but most of the time these are volunteer assignments that range in duration from a week to several months. In most cases, you will be asked to commit to a particular time frame and will need to pay your way. A variety of NGOs (nongovernmental organization is *organización no gubernamental* or *ONG* in Spanish) have projects in Guatemala and you'll need to do some homework to see where you best fit in.

VOLUNTEERING

Those willing to work for free will have no trouble finding opportunities to volunteer with local organizations. The *Resources* chapter at the end of this book includes a list of suggested volunteer opportunities, but they are certainly not the only ones available. Most organizations require a commitment of at least two weeks, and not all can provide room and board. In many cases, you must pay for these separately. It is of utmost importance that volunteers have at least some command of Spanish and a high degree of cultural sensitivity. Technical skills are a definite plus. Before deciding to work with an organization, it's a good idea to get a feel for its long-term vision as well as sort out its religious or political affiliations. Most places aren't pushing a particular agenda, but it's a good thing to look into before you get too deep into the process.

Many Spanish-language schools have well-established programs seeking to match students and nonstudent volunteers with local projects. Most Spanish language schools in Xela, for instance, have a strong service-learning component. These programs take much of the guesswork out of trying to find and arrange your own opportunities while also providing an opportunity to meet other foreign volunteers.

ORGANIZATIONS

Several NGOs are working in Guatemala in the aftermath of the civil war. Many of these are based in and around Quetzaltenango and work in the western highlands on a variety of community development projects. A number of environmental organizations also have offices in Guatemala, with particular concentration on the lowland tropical forests of Petén and Izabal departments. Among the latter are Conservation International, The Nature Conservancy, and World Wildlife Fund. The best way to find work with these agencies is to visit their websites. Different positions may be on offer, such as field director or communications officer. Get in touch with one of the many NGOs working in Guatemala and inquire about available positions. This will probably involve pounding the pavement in Guatemala City and Quetzaltenango.

FINANCES

Many people are drawn to Guatemala as a cheap retirement option or as a place to live a simpler lifestyle than that offered in North America or Europe. It's best to figure out during your fact-finding trip exactly how you picture your new life in Guatemala. You can certainly live a lifestyle similar to that offered in the United States, with a condo, car, cell phone, cable TV, and the like, but you'll find this costing about the same as your life back home. On the other side of the spectrum, you can live very much like a local for far below what you ever thought possible. Adding to the variables is whether or not you'll be making your income in U.S. dollars or Guatemalan quetzales.

This chapter is designed to help you know beforehand what you can expect to pay for basic living expenses such as rent, food, fuel, entertainment, household help, and taxes. Armed with this information, you'll have a better estimation of how much you'll need to make ends meet. The second part of this chapter gives you the low-down on financial ins and outs such as local banking, taxes, and investment.

Cost of Living

It's really up to you how much or how little you can get away with spending on a monthly basis. Many expats living in Guatemala are looking for a simplified version of their life up north. You can rent a simple room, shop at local markets, eat your meals at home, forgo extras like a car, cable TV, and cell phones and live for about US$600 a month here. Most of us tend not to simplify quite that much and require a budget of about US$1,200 a month. If you're a couple, add another 30 percent to that. This should provide an adequate budget allowing you some frills here and there. Keep in mind that some Guatemalan cities are more expensive than others, particularly Guatemala City and La Antigua.

As far as Latin American capitals go, Guatemala City is supposedly among the least expensive to live in. This is certainly relative, as the temptation toward consumerism can be a huge factor in determining how much money you keep in your wallet. The Guatemalan capital has excellent restaurants, shopping, and other splurges that can quickly add up. So, while you might be spending less on rent than if you were to live elsewhere, you might be tempted to eat out more or consume more easily available U.S. goods, which quickly adds up. On the flip side, living in a remote mountain town would yield fewer options for consuming expensive imported goods and thus be easier on your budget.

SHOPPING

Visitors to Guatemala are often surprised by the proliferation of shopping malls and U.S. franchises. It used to be that only Guatemala City had a decent selection of shopping options, but you can now find most of what you'll need in larger towns and cities throughout the country. Still, the best selection and prices for household goods and luxury items are available in Guatemala City at a variety of shopping malls, warehouse shopping outlets, and hardware stores.

Among the best stores to shop for items in bulk or just plain hard-to-find items (like Dr. Pepper) is the U.S. chain PriceSmart. There are four or five of these in the Guatemala City metro area. A locally owned version known as ClubCo might also yield some finds. Hiper Paiz is Guatemala's version of Wal-Mart and was recently purchased by this North American retail giant. Expect the name to change gradually over time. Paiz is owned by the same company and is a grocery store with branches throughout the country. As elsewhere, prices and selection vary widely from one location to the next. If you are looking for imported U.S. goods and a better overall selection of

© AL ARGUETA

Guatemala City is the country's undisputed financial center.

products, your best bet is to shop in the areas frequented by Guatemala City's well-to-do. These include shopping malls in the Guatemala City suburb of Carretera al Salvador, such as Pradera Concepción, Zona 10's La Pradera, and the Zona 11 retail district centered around Mall Miraflores and Parque Comercial Las Majadas.

Guatemalans like to dress well and you'll find no shortage of options for clothing retailers. Many of these are successful local chains, such as Saúl E. Méndez. Foreign brands represented in several of the shopping malls include Tommy Hilfiger, Lacoste, and Spanish retailer Zara. The latter offers relatively good value for the money and some stylish threads.

Electronics can also be found in stores adjacent to or within shopping malls. Max is probably the best place to go for selection.

Simán, a Salvadoran-owned department store chain, has all the look and feel of a Macy's back home and is your best option for department store shopping. There are three locations in the Guatemala City area.

As for housewares, your options include Sears and Cemaco, among several others.

BASIC EXPENSES
Food

It's easy to find inexpensive fruits and vegetables in Guatemala, thanks to an abundance of locally cultivated produce. At the same time, quality is sometimes an issue because, much like coffee, the best of the crop is exported. Shopping for groceries at chain supermarkets such as Paiz, Hiper Paiz and PriceSmart will

GETTING YOUR FEDERAL BENEFITS IN GUATEMALA

It's possible to continue receipt of your federal benefits, including Social Security, while in Guatemala. Benefits are handled by the Federal Benefits Unit (FBU), an arm of the American Citizen Services Unit of the U.S. Embassy in Guatemala City. Questions about Social Security and other federal benefits are answered weekdays 1-3 P.M. Social Security checks are distributed each month on the 10th and 11th (or the next business day) during the same hours, at the consular section. The FBU processes Social Security number applications; Social Security Administration claims for retirement, disability, and survivor benefits; changes of address; and issues involving direct deposit or non-receipt of Social Security checks. The FBU also handles benefit programs for the Department of Veteran Affairs, Office of Personnel Management, Department of Labor, and Railroad Retirement Board.

The American Citizen Services Unit can be reached by phone at 2326-4405 or via email at AmCits-Guatemala@State.Gov. For more information, visit the website of the U.S. Embassy in Guatemala at http://guatemala.usembassy.gov/federal_benefits.html.

be more expensive but you'll find a good selection of harder-to-find imported vegetables and fruits, such as kiwi. You'll find health food stores, including GNC, in several Guatemala City shopping malls. Zona 10's Gourmet Center is a great place to go for hard-to-find items, including kosher food.

You can expect to pay about US$200 per month on groceries, plus an extra US$100–150 per additional person on your shopping list. You may find yourself buying certain items in bulk and other items in more conventional sizes, for which your initial grocery bill might be significantly larger. If you have domestic help, enlist their assistance to stretch your grocery budget as far as possible, as Guatemalans often have a knack for making do on substantially less money than North Americans ever thought possible. They will often cook quite tasty local specialties using local ingredients that can be bought cheaply.

Entertainment

This varies widely from person to person depending on what floats your boat. Movies in Guatemala are relatively inexpensive, at about US$5 per show. There's even an IMAX theater at Pradera Concepción (though it's more expensive). Taxi rides can be expensive in Guatemala City, but in small towns you have the option of motorized rickshaws, or *tuk tuks.*

Beer is generally cheaper than at bars back home, at about US$1.25 a bottle. There are good local brews, but imports can cost closer to US$3. Guatemala also produces some fine rums; the best-known is Zacapa Centenario, at about US$35 a bottle.

There are decent bowling alleys and mini-golf courses in Guatemala City and prices are generally cheaper than back home.

Fuel

Expect fuel costs to be a major part of your monthly budget. Although Guatemala produces a small amount of petroleum, its low quality makes it suitable mostly for producing asphalt. Thus, the country is subject to volatile oil prices on the international market. Prices at the pump are generally 30 percent higher than the U.S national average. In January 2009, a gallon of regular unleaded gasoline cost an average of Q27.39 (about US$3.65) in Guatemala. This was down from an average price of Q35.41 (US$4.72) in July 2008. Diesel fuel cost Q27.29 per gallon, on average, in January 2009. This was a considerable price decline from its all-time high of Q36.95 (US$4.93) per gallon in July 2008.

Many homes use propane gas for cooking stoves. In September 2008 the price for a 25-pound propane tank was Q125 (US$17), while a 100-pound tank cost Q500 (US$67). Propane prices in Guatemala are the second-highest in Central America.

Housing

Much like everywhere else, housing costs vary considerably depending on location. Almost everywhere in Guatemala, you'll have the option of living very much like a local or in greater comfort (and safety) in newer homes or condos in nicer neighborhoods.

Domestic Employees

Most middle- and upper-class Guatemalans hire domestic help to assist them with the day-to-day affairs of cooking, cleaning, and child-rearing. A handyman and gardener are also sometimes part of the payroll. More than a show of wealth, this is generally a cultural phenomenon, as prosperous Guatemalans enjoy lovely gardens and well-manicured lawns as much as the next person but typically don't enjoy the manual labor involved in creating them. To put this another way: Why toil in the hot tropical sun when you can pay someone next to nothing to do it for you, all the while feeling good about giving him/her a job? (I speak from a Guatemalan standpoint here.)

In some cases, the domestic help is split into those who do the cooking and cleaning and those who mind the children. Most Guatemalan families simply have what's called a *muchacha*. She cooks, cleans, makes the beds, does laundry, and maybe walks the kids to and from the bus stop. In some cases the *muchacha* is like another member of the family and will travel with the family on holiday. I've seen middle-class families who treat the domestic help quite badly, but have also seen wealthy folks who treat their nannies and cooks quite well. In the best cases, it seems to be a symbiotic relationship where there is some give and take on both ends. Guatemalans typically don't eat with their staff. The staff tends to eat afterwards in a separate eating area in the kitchen.

As for costs, you can expect to pay about US$200 a month for a good live-in *muchacha*. Those not living on the premises are paid slightly less but are reimbursed for transport. A gardener costs about US$25 per week.

As the old saying goes, it *is* hard to find good help. Your best bet is to enlist the help of friends and family, as word of mouth is the best way to find reliable and honest staff.

Banking

CURRENCY

Guatemala's currency is the quetzal, named after the country's elusive national bird. The quetzal is pegged to the U.S. dollar and denoted by Q. In March 2009, the exchange rate was about Q8 to US$1. It has remained at about the same rate for several years now. Bills come in denominations of 5, 10, 20, 50, and 100 quetzales. The Central Bank, Banco de Guatemala, recently issued new Q1 bills printed on a polymer hybrid paper. Plans called for new Q200 and Q500 notes that might be in use in 2009. Coins come in denominations of 1, 5, 10, 25, and 50 centavos (Q0.01, Q0.05, Q0.10, Q0.25, Q.50) and Q1, though other than the 1 quetzal coin they are more of a nuisance than anything else. It is increasingly rare to even see 1 centavo coins anymore. Often, if your change is just a few centavos, the merchant will keep it.

In smaller towns and villages, you might have trouble breaking Q100 (or larger) notes, so bring smaller bills with you if possible.

EXCHANGE

Travelers and expats have the option of getting by with cash U.S. dollars (which you will need to at least partially exchange for local currency), travelers checks (American Express being the most widely recognized and accepted), wire transfers (most expensive option), Visa or MasterCard cash advances (watch those interest rates), or through ATMs linked to international networks (recommended). You can exchange euros in most banks in Guatemalan cities, though they are rarely accepted for cash payment outside of hotels and stores in tourist areas.

Travelers Checks

Still the safest way to carry money while traveling through Guatemala is with travelers checks, although you'll only be able to exchange them in urban areas and tourist destinations with full-service banks. There's also a bit more bureaucracy involved in exchanging travelers checks, and you might be asked to show your original purchase receipt. American Express is by far the most widely accepted type of travelers check.

Wire Transfers

Due to the widespread phenomenon of remittances sent home by Guatemalan nationals living abroad, several wire transfer companies have set up shop all over Guatemala. This may be your best bet if you run short of cash while trying to get a steady income stream to finance your new life abroad. Many local banks and businesses are Western Union affiliates. For a list of these affiliates in Guatemala, visit www.westernunion.com. You can also send money via American Express MoneyGram. Keep in mind these companies make their money off exorbitant fees charged for their services in addition to a poor exchange rate for the money, which you'll end up getting in local currency.

Credit Cards and ATMs

Credit cards have become more and more commonplace in Guatemala, though they are still accepted mainly in urban centers, major tourist attractions, and luxury hotels or expensive restaurants and shops. Some smaller merchants may charge a fee, usually 7–10 percent of the transaction amount, the justification being that they are charged this amount by the credit card companies and can't afford to absorb the cost because of their smaller sales volume. Visa and MasterCard are the most widely accepted.

ATMs in Guatemala are hooked up to international networks, and most travelers have no problems accessing their bank accounts in this way. It's always a good idea to keep an eye on your transactions online and report any inconsistencies to your bank immediately. You will never be required to enter your PIN on a pad to enter an ATM kiosk, a common scam to steal card and PIN that has fooled some travelers. Always be aware of your surroundings and try not to visit the ATM at night or unaccompanied.

DAILY LIFE

You can search for Visa ATM locations in Guatemala online at http://visa. via.infonow.net/locator/global/jsp/SearchPage.jsp and MasterCard ATMs at www.mastercard.com/atm. A useful listing of Banco Industrial Visa ATMs throughout Guatemala can be found at www.bi.com.gt/Cajeros-BI_body. htm. This will give you an idea of the availability of ATMs in your particular neck of the woods.

BANKS

Banks in Guatemala tend to keep long hours, typically 9 A.M.–6 P.M. Monday–Friday and 9 A.M.–1 P.M. on Saturday. Changing money and travelers checks at banks is relatively painless and routine, though you'll probably be asked to show your passport or at least a photocopy of it for identification. If you're a resident, you'll need your *cédula*. You'll also notice that banks, like convenience stores and other businesses, are heavily guarded by armed watchmen.

In border areas, you'll typically be approached by money changers offering slightly better rates than local banks. It's perfectly safe to change your money with them, though it's probably a good idea to exchange only what you might need for the first day or two in the new country. Refrain from pulling out a wad of bills for all to see.

OPENING AN ACCOUNT

Opening a Guatemalan bank account is fairly straightforward, though specific requirements may vary from bank to bank. In most cases you'll need to provide a valid passport (or *cédula* if you have gained residency) and a utility bill from the home in which you live. You can open an account in U.S. dollars or Guatemalan quetzales. Foreigners without residency status are barred from opening local checking accounts unless a Guatemalan cosigns on the account.

Taxes

GUATEMALAN TAXES

The Guatemalan equivalent of the IRS is the Superintendencia de Administración Tributaria (SAT). Following the 1996 peace accords, there have been efforts to reform the Guatemalan tax system, which has one of the lowest taxation rates in Latin America based on percentage of GNP. In addition to a hefty 12 percent sales tax, taxes are assessed on imported goods, real estate, and of course, income.

In Guatemala, income tax is known as *impuesto sobre la renta* (ISR). Tax laws are complicated and ever-changing, so it's a good idea to get someone to help you prepare them, especially if it's your first time dealing with the Guatemalan tax system. Taxes are collected by SAT. In the most basic terms, your gross income minus all deductible expenses yields your *total renta neta* (total net income) for the year. Taxes are then calculated as a percentage of this number according to a chart established by SAT.

Among the tax deductions allowed by Guatemalan tax laws is a standard Q36,000 deduction for essentials such as housing, clothing, medicines, and food. You don't have to prove these expenses, so everyone just knocks Q36,000 from their tab right off the bat. In addition to this standard deduction you can also deduct health care costs, 401K contributions (known here as a *fondo de prestaciones*), insurance premiums (life insurance, accident insurance), lab costs, child support, charitable donations, bail, and even sales tax at 100 percent. You'll need to save your receipts for these deductions, on which there is no limit.

The deduction on yearly sales tax (IVA) further complicates matters, as you'll need to save receipts for everything you buy during the course of the year and enter it into a *planilla,* or spreadsheet declaration. These are due yearly on January 15, and SAT offices nationwide are flooded with contributors rushing to get their *planillas* in as the deadline approaches. The spreadsheet is now available in electronic format, but the first page of the declaration still needs to be completed on the government-issued SAT form. Deductions for IVA cannot exceed 12 percent of your total *utilidad neta* (net utility). An ongoing tax reform may eventually (and gradually) phase out the IVA deductions.

If, after all these deductions, you break even or report a net loss, you're done with the process and don't need to pay taxes. If you show a profit, you'll need to refer to a table established by SAT, which determines your rate of taxation. So, even if you may not be completely ready to go out and file your Guatemalan taxes, this brief description should at least allow you to understand why Guatemala's taxation rates as a percentage of GNP are among the lowest in Latin America.

U.S. TAXES

The long arms of the IRS reach well into Guatemala, so setting up shop in your new home country doesn't necessarily mean you're off the hook with your dues to Uncle Sam. The IRS imposes taxes, including inheritance tax, on all Americans regardless of their country of residence. As a result, a growing number of expats around the world have begun renouncing their U.S. citizenship so as to reduce their tax burden. This is a decision that should be taken only after full consideration of the consequences, as there are laws currently in place that are aimed at prosecuting this perceived form of tax evasion.

There are some perks to filing your taxes while living abroad, however. For starters, the normal April 15 filing deadline is automatically extended to June 15. Simply send in your return by April 15 and write, "Taxpayer living outside the USA" and "Qualifies for automatic two-month extension," across the top of the tax return. Be advised that interest and/or penalties may apply if you owe more than US$1,000 in taxes. Income tax returns can be filed through the U.S. Embassy in Guatemala City. You can also use online tax preparation software to file your claim from anywhere in the world.

Your second possible tax advantage while filing abroad is the Foreign Earned Income Exclusion. The rules on this one are somewhat complicated and you'll need to file paperwork to apply for it, but if you qualify you'll be eligible to exclude up to US$80,000 of income earned abroad from taxation. You will need to have been abroad more than 330 days, and the exclusion does not apply to capital gains, interests, dividends, gambling winnings, pensions, or annuities. You should probably hire a tax professional to walk you through the ins and outs of this particular exclusion. Also keep in mind you still need to file a return.

A final possible tax break comes in the form of a housing deduction for which you may be able to knock off up to US$12,000 in housing expenses.

Investing

Foreign investors will find Guatemala largely virgin territory. While a number of *maquiladoras* and call centers have set up shop in recent years thanks to tax breaks and other incentives, the country's huge potential in the technology, agro-industrial, tourism, and service industries remains largely untapped. Investment laws in Guatemala are fairly straightforward, and much of the bureaucracy stifling investment in neighboring countries is absent, at least on paper, thanks to a 1998 Foreign Investment Law. Following the 1996 peace accords, there were a number of structural reforms put in place, including the deregulation of the telecommunications and electricity sectors and trade liberalization. There are eight free trade zones in Guatemala and incentives largely targeting the mining, tourism, forestry, and petroleum sectors. Foreign investment has also been facilitated thanks to the recent adoption of the Dominican Republic–Central America Free Trade Agreement (DR-CAFTA). Guatemala has the largest economy in Central America.

Despite Guatemala's attractive offerings for the foreign investor and the relative ease of doing business here, the country still manages to capture only a relatively small percentage of foreign investment in Central America. Although there is a sufficient skilled labor pool, Guatemala has yet to cash in on the technology industry in a way even remotely approaching Costa Rica, which has been home to several technology companies, such as Intel, for several years now. One of the reasons often cited for the glut in foreign investment is the issue of safety in urban areas such as Guatemala City.

Investment scams aimed at foreigners are largely unheard of here, thanks to the country's relative obscurity compared to some neighboring Central American nations in the collective consciousness of the investing American public. Still, be wary of investment scams, which are indeed present here, as many Guatemalans can attest to.

For more information on Guatemalan investment opportunities, visit the web page of Invest in Guatemala at www.investinguatemala.org.

DAILY LIFE

COMMUNICATIONS

If you thought moving to Guatemala meant losing touch with friends and family back home, think again. With Internet access readily available almost everywhere and cheap cell phone service to the United States, you'll be able to stay in touch as often as you'd like. Telephone, Internet, and postal services are far more efficient and economical in Guatemala than elsewhere in Central America thanks to deregulation and free market economics, a distinct advantage for technologically inclined expats looking to settle down here.

I still remember the days when making a phone call to family in Guatemala meant putting up with a crackly connection and having to be wary of possible wiretaps by military intelligence personnel in their quest to eliminate Communist subversion in Guatemala. Thankfully, those days are behind us. Peacetime and free market economics have brought about the privatization of the formerly state-run telephone company and opened the market to competition from international phone companies. Wireless

© AL ARGUETA

PHONE HOME: KEEPING IN TOUCH WITH FRIENDS AND FAMILY

For some, moving to Guatemala is a way of cutting ties and starting afresh in a new place, but most people will want to stay in touch with folks left behind. Luckily, keeping in touch is fairly inexpensive and easy to do from Guatemala. First, there's the inexpensive and widespread use of cell phones with calling rates to the United States in the vicinity of US$0.12 per minute. You can also send and receive text messages to and from the United States for pennies.

Depending on your phone carrier, calls from land lines are also very affordable and start at US$0.06 per minute (on nights and weekends). At other times, you'll need a special three-digit code to get the best rates, which you must dial from the outset of your call. For Telgua, the three-digit code is 147. For Telefónica, it's 130. To call the United States, dial 00 + 1 + area code + number. To call Guatemala from the United States, dial 011 + 502 + eight-digit number. There are no city or area codes for Guatemala. The country code is 502.

Calls to Guatemala from the United States can be very expensive, often around US$1 a minute if you just pick up your phone and dial. Special calling cards with low rates to Latin America are available in grocery stores and are one option. Rates to Guatemala are usually around US$0.35 a minute with these cards. Special rate plans are available for international calling with the U.S. phone companies, but you'll need to ask your carrier and enroll in a plan for the discounted rate.

Calling collect from a pay phone and using calling cards for international calls from a pay phone are slightly less popular options, but are options nonetheless. To call collect from a Telgua (Ladatel) pay phone, dial 147-120 and you will be connected to an operator. For calls from a Telefónica pay phone, dial 130-120. You can also use these numbers to call collect from any land line.

A number of privately owned telecommunications centers have sprung up in many towns and cities popular with tourists. You can call almost anywhere in the world for US$0.10–0.40 a minute. After establishing the number to call, an agent dials it for you and then directs you to a glass booth where you can take the call.

service is even more competitive, with cheap call rates to the United States, excellent coverage, and even video call capabilities available from your own cell phone. Taking advantage of Guatemala's competitive telecommunications sector, many U.S.-based corporations have established call centers in Guatemala, providing another form of foreign investment and a source of new jobs.

Telephone Service

Guatemala's original phone company, a government monopoly known as Guatel, was privatized in the 1990s during the government of Alvaro Arzú. Several other companies have moved into the market in the aftermath of telecommunications deregulation. Now known as Telgua and 70 percent owned by Mexican company Telmex, the former state-run telephone company competes primarily with Spanish telecommunications giant Telefónica. Both offer competitive prices and service. The companies also have branches that provide wireless phone service. Claro is Telgua's wireless service, while Movistar is Telefónica's cell phone service provider.

Friends and family tell me getting a phone line is a relatively painless process, with the phone companies sometimes offering special deals whereby you can get a second line for next to nothing. Telgua also offers packages whereby you can get telephone, Internet, and cable TV for one low price. Its Internet arm is Turbonett, while cable is provided by Claro TV.

LAND LINES

Telgua is Guatemala's main provider of fixed-line services and is widely known to have the widest coverage area. To get a line, you'll first have to verify coverage in your area. Once coverage is verified, installing a new line costs about US$83. You must provide a water or electric bill for your home and sign a three-year contract. In the event that you need to reconnect an already existing line, there needs to be a two-month period during which the line is not in use. Reconnection costs US$13.

Telgua offers two monthly calling plans. The first of these, known as Plan 4480, includes 200 minutes of domestic airtime for Q44.80 (US$6). The alternative is Plan 85 and includes 500 minutes of domestic airtime for, you guessed it, Q85 (US$11.50). Additional minutes cost US$0.05 per minute. Calls to the United States cost as little as US$0.40 per minute from 7 p.m. to 7 a.m. on weekdays and US$0.06 per minute on weekends. You can pay your bill online or at any Telgua store.

A novelty with Telefónica is its so-called Línea Fácil, which is particularly useful in remote areas without traditional telephone coverage. Available with six different phones, the pre-paid, pay-as-you-go service is easy to use (as its name, "easy line," indicates) and simply plugs in to an electrical outlet. It involves minimal initial setup and you can be up and running in minutes. It's also a great option for international calling. Incoming calls are free, while calls to the United States and Canada cost US$0.10 per minute. You need to dial 130 before the usual 00 + 1 + area code and number when dialing the United States to get these rates. In-network local calls to other Telefónica users cost US$0.06 per minute and US$0.08 for local calls to other carriers' phone lines. Other services available at no additional cost using Línea Fácil include call waiting, incoming text messages, caller ID, and voicemail. Airtime for voicemail is charged at US$0.06 per minute.

You can buy your phone from any Telefónica store. They also sell phone cards for recharge minutes, or you can recharge from your own phone by dialing *123 and charging the minutes to your credit or debit card.

CELL PHONES

Cell phone service in Guatemala is much more competitive than elsewhere in Central America, and the quality of the signal received, even in mountainous areas, is actually quite impressive. To that end, it seems cell phone towers have been installed almost everywhere you look.

The main players in the cell phone market are Tigo, Claro, and Movistar. Of these, Movistar is linked to its land-line equivalent Telefónica, while Claro is affiliated with Telgua. You can often get special deals if you sign up with one of these carriers for your land line and then add on cell phone, Internet, and even cable TV. I can personally vouch for the service and coverage area of Tigo, which also has coverage in neighboring Honduras and El Salvador, allowing you to roam on their local networks.

If you're an iPhone enthusiast or your phone uses the latest 3G technology, you'll be happy to know that both Movistar and Claro sell the iPhone locally. All three carriers have 3G networks with various rate and data plans to suit your needs. Prices are comparable to those in the United States. In the area of videophone capabilities, all three companies offer this service on phones equipped with this feature. See their websites for more details.

Getting a permanent cell phone line is very straightforward and involves a visit to any of the wireless providers' stores located in Guatemala City or Quetzaltenango. If, like many expats, you find yourself spending time in Guatemala seasonally you can also pay as you go. If you have a GSM cell phone compatible with one of the local networks, you can localize your cell phone by buying a SIM card from a local carrier at a cost of about US$7. You can then add airtime by purchasing prepaid phone cards almost anywhere. Sometimes, cell phone companies offer double or triple points, so if you buy a Q100 phone card and apply it to your account on a day with *doble saldo* (double credit), you'll have Q200 worth of airtime credited to you. Things will certainly begin to change with the recent arrival of 3G technology and the gradual phase-out of GSM phones, but you can certainly use your 3G phone on Guatemala's network.

Calling rates for GSM service are very similar to those for land lines; about US$0.12 to the United States at any given time and US$0.06 for domestic calls.

INTERNET CALLING

Internet phone connections provide a novel and affordable method for staying in touch. Using voice-over-Internet protocol (VOIP), it's possible to use services such as Skype (www.skype.com) to make a phone call from your computer. If both users have Skype accounts, the call is free. You'll need a headset to plug into your computer so that it can be used as a phone. Internet calling is often available from Internet cafés for additional charge.

PAY PHONES

While coin-operated pay phones were once plentiful, these have been almost entirely replaced by those requiring the purchase of a phone card. Pay phones are operated by both Telefónica and Telgua, so you'll need to buy a phone card from the correct company. Phone cards are widely available from automated dispenser machines and from the ubiquitous corner store. They come in several denominations. Telefónica booths are painted navy blue and green, while Telgua booths are grey with a collage of various Guatemalan scenes painted onto their sides. Telgua prepaid phone cards are licensed under the name Ladatel and come in denominations of Q20, Q30, and Q50.

FAX SERVICES

Fax service is widely available from office supply stores in Guatemala City or from one of the many Internet cafés found in smaller cities or rural areas.

Email and the Internet

INTERNET ACCESS

You'll find Internet access throughout most parts of Guatemala is readily available and features fast connection speeds. In Guatemala City and other urban areas, connection speeds are similar to those in the United States. Unlike in other Central American countries, Internet service in Guatemala is not provided via a government monopoly, so free trade has resulted in better conditions for consumers.

Many government agencies, including local municipalities, have Internet sites, as do the vast majority of private companies doing business here. Email is widely used as a form of contacting businesses and staying in touch with friends and family. Guatemala's Internet code is gt.

On the Road

Guatemala's popularity as an international tourist destination in vogue with backpackers and the younger crowd has resulted in the proliferation of Internet cafés. Depending on the location and how many different setups are in town, prices range from as little as US$0.75 an hour to about US$2 an hour. Many hotels in all budget ranges also provide Internet service in their business centers or in your own room.

In Your Home

There are a variety of Internet service providers, all of which can be located in your local yellow pages. I can personally vouch for the services of Turbonett, which is fast, dependable and reasonably priced. As with most utility setups, getting Internet access is usually quick and painless in the Guatemala City metro area but might be somewhat more time-consuming in smaller cities and towns.

Turbonett offers wireless broadband Internet with connection speeds as fast as 1.5 mbps with prices starting at US$47 per month. A compatible modem with USB port sold by Turbonett will set you back another US$49, but it's a one-time expense. Less expensive plans for connections with more basic Internet cable cost US$25 or US$30 depending on the connection speed.

Postal Mail and Shipping

EL CORREO

Guatemala's national postal service has been vastly improved since Canada Post took over its operations in the 1990s as part of a widespread privatization of government services. As long as you stick to mailing items that are not considered of value, it's okay to send things through the mail. When mailing items to Guatemala via the U.S. postal service, the letter or package will be delivered locally by El Correo. The same applies for items mailed in the reverse fashion. It costs about US$2 to send a large, 8-ounce envelope first class with the national postal service, but it may take up to two weeks to reach its destination. Letters sent to Guatemala via the U.S. Postal Service using Priority Mail will take about three days to arrive.

PRIVATE MAIL SERVICES (P.O. BOXES)

An increasingly popular option with many expats and well-to-do locals is the use of post office boxes provided by a number of local companies. These companies generally have a mailing address in Miami to which you can have packages mailed for delivery in Guatemala. The packages clear customs, with the appropriate duties being assessed, and are then available for pickup. Fees go by weight and your monthly dues for this service usually provide an allowance of a few pounds.

These services are especially useful if you wish to order items online from the United States and have them delivered to you in Guatemala. I have a friend who likes to order books on Amazon in this fashion. He gets his order in three days, with all customs fees already accounted for by the time he has the package in his hands. Guatemala's SAT, the local equivalent of the IRS, has undergone substantial modernization, ensuring that packages spend minimal time in customs (one hour or less) after arriving in Guatemala. It has been praised as one of the most efficient systems in Latin America.

NATIONAL POSTAL SERVICE

The main post office (8:30 A.M.–5 P.M. Mon.–Fri., 8:30 A.M.–1 P.M. Sat.) is in downtown Guatemala City (7a Avenida 11-67, Zona 1). There are also branches at the airport and the corner of Avenida La Reforma and 14 Calle, Zona 9, with the same hours. This is certainly your least expensive option for shipping things home, but it should be used only for nonvaluable items and maybe books.

INTERNATIONAL COURIERS
DHL

DHL has several locations in Guatemala City as well as an office in Antigua. The courier is particularly popular with people in the Guatemalan departments, as their coverage area is not limited to the Guatemala City metro area. Overnight service is available to Miami and other Central American capitals with service beyond Miami to the continental United States requiring an extra day.

FedEx

FedEx has several options for shipping packages to and from Guatemala. Their presence in Guatemala, however, is limited to the Guatemala City metro area. They have offices in Zona 10, open 9 A.M.–6 P.M. Monday–Friday.

UPS

UPS is another popular shipping option from Guatemala and is widely used by crafts stores in Antigua to ship items to the United States. It takes about 5–10 business days to receive a box shipped from Guatemala via UPS Express shipping.

Media

NEWSPAPERS AND MAGAZINES

Prensa Libre is Guatemala's most widely circulated newspaper and is highly respected. You can find the online version at www.prensalibre.com.gt. Other excellent newspapers include *Siglo XXI* (www.sigloxxi.com) and *elPeriódico* (www.elperiodico.com.gt). All of these are tabloid, rather than broadsheet, in format. A tabloid in the sense of being filled with plenty of yellow journalism, scandal, and not much else of use is *Nuestro Diario,* which nonetheless seems to be somewhat popular in the country's interior. Guatemala's respectable newspapers are an excellent source of information and make a great way to practice reading Spanish. They have a long tradition of investigative reporting and have done a wonderful job of uncovering numerous scandals Guatemala's corrupt politicians would probably get away with (at least without public knowledge) were it not for the work of these intrepid journalists. Journalism can still be a dangerous occupation in Guatemala, though press freedom has come a long way since the dark times of the civil war.

Published in Antigua, the monthly *Revue* magazine has tons of helpful tips and contact information for hotels, restaurants, and businesses in Guatemala as well as parts of Honduras and El Salvador. There are also well-written stories on topics of interest to locals and visitors alike. It's available in tourist shops, hotels, and restaurants free of charge.

Also published in Antigua, by the owners of Café No Sé, is *La Cuadra,* featuring a very engaging mix of stories of particular interest to travelers and expats including local travel service recommendations, humorous editorials, and coverage of the arts. It recently upgraded to a glossy paper format.

TELEVISION

Guatemala has its very own cable TV channel, Guatevisión, which can also be seen in the United States. It features a morning show based in Guatemala City as well as some fairly humorous entertainment programs providing a glimpse of the nightlife and outdoor recreation scene throughout the country.

GUATEVISIÓN, GUATEMALAN CABLE TV

Not surprisingly, Guatemala's network television channels leave a lot to be desired. Programming consists largely of foreign soap operas, gory newscasts highlighting the daily carnage on Guatemala City streets, and badly dubbed-over movies. While you can certainly escape to the cable TV stations carrying every English-language network your American heart may desire, you may also want to explore Guatevisión, Guatemala's cable TV channel.

While the channel also airs its fair share of Spanish-language soap operas and talk shows, it has a fairly interesting programming assortment of locally produced TV shows, which provide a fascinating glimpse into Guatemalan idiosyncrasies. While I'm a big advocate of getting out there and exploring Guatemalan culture first-hand, some of Guatevisión's shows may actually serve as practical teaching aids in smoothing the transition into your new home culture. You'll certainly pick up some of the local slang and acquire an appreciation for the Guatemalan pronunciation of the Spanish language.

First, there's the morning show, *Viva La Mañana*, with its energetic hosts and interesting mix of programming to help kick-start your morning. Guatevisión also features the country's most dependable and professional newscast in *Noticiero Guatevisión*, which airs four times a day on weekdays and at 8 P.M. during the weekend. There are also sports and entertainment shows, but my personal favorites are programs that provide a glimpse into Guatemalans' unique ways of speaking and acting. These include the weekly (Wednesday) shows *Punto G* and *Expedición GT*. The first of these is definitely a show for the younger crowd, as much of it revolves around trips to Guatemala City and Antigua bars and nightclubs to capture the local party scene. Still, it captures the fun-loving spirit of Guatemala's youth and also features some very charismatic hosts. *Expedición GT* features adventurous trips to Guatemala's lesser-known natural wonders as well as less orthodox-yet-practical information, such as how to hire a bodyguard and basic rules of weapons handling, as I saw recently on one episode.

All in all, Guatevisión makes an excellent alternative to the local Spanish language programming and will certainly help you in your quest to blend in to the local culture. If it all gets to be too much, you can always flip the channel to CNN.

Guatemala even has a celebrity newscaster of sorts, Harris Whitbeck, formerly of CNN, who reports events around the world in English and Spanish. One of his more recent projects is a local TV show, *Entrémosle a Guate* (Let's Get in on Guate), with profiles of everyday Guatemalans who make the country a special place.

There are a number of local TV channels, with programming that runs the gamut from Brazilian and Mexican soap operas to the nightly news. The newscasts are slightly less glamorous than those of cable TV channel Guatevisión, and the nightly newscasts on most of these tend to focus heavily on acts of violence in Guatemala City and less on investigative reporting.

If you do opt for getting cable television, you should be aware that you won't have all the networks you'd see in the United States. The main channels include U.S. television networks (ABC, NBC, CBS, and FOX), but many channels, such as HBO, Discovery Channel, and Cinemax, feature different programming aimed at the local Spanish-speaking population. If you want your U.S. premium channels in their pure form, your best bet is to go with a satellite dish or DirecTV.

TV reporter Harris Whitbeck

You can hook up DirecTV locally with Telgua, but sources tell me you can also contract the service in the United States (if you have a U.S. billing address) and bring the hardware down with you to install.

RADIO

Radio is not a big player in the local media, at least not to the extent that it is in some other Latin American countries. Still, there are plenty of radio stations transmitting mostly from Guatemala City and featuring both Spanish and English-language programming. There is also a fairly heavy concentration of Spanish-language Christian radio. If you miss hearing English-language rock music, tune in to KISS FM, 97.7 on your radio dial.

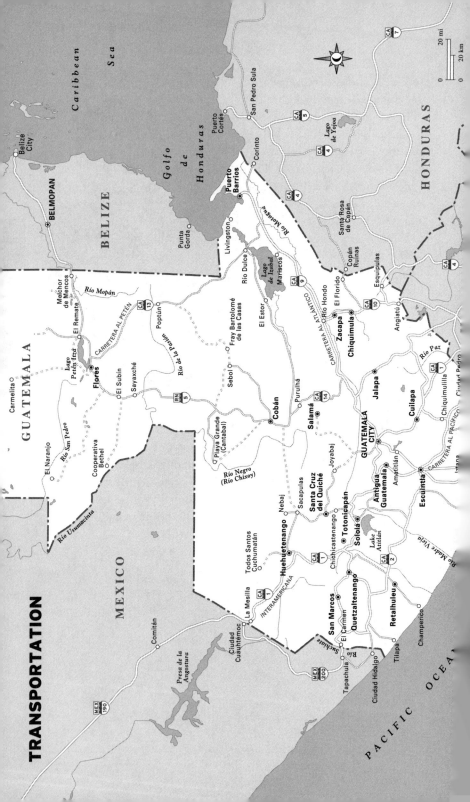

TRAVEL AND TRANSPORTATION

Getting to Guatemala is easy enough, but getting around can be a bit tricky. While distances might seem short when looking on a map, you have to take into account the mostly mountainous terrain, the serpentine nature of the country's roads, and ongoing road improvements when figuring out the logistics of road travel. On a positive note, Guatemala's road network, as a whole, is much better than that of its Central American neighbors.

If you're not getting around on your own steam, options for transportation range from the budget, so-called "chicken buses" favored by locals to tourist shuttle vans and first-class buses. A relatively new phenomenon, still in the works, is a nascent domestic air network covering major destinations using a system of newly created air terminals inherited from the presidency of Oscar Berger.

© AL ARGUETA

Getting to Guatemala

BY AIR

Most international travelers to Guatemala arrive by plane. Several factors have worked together to make Guatemala more easily, though not always cheaply, accessible in this regard. First, Guatemala has become increasingly popular as a travel destination. Tourism statistics show the country has been welcoming over a million visitors since 2004. The Guatemalan government has recognized this and has invested millions of dollars into remodeling the country's two international airports while developing local airports for the creation of a domestic route network. U.S. carriers have stepped up their presence in Guatemala in recent years and are expected to continue this trend, particularly with the vastly improved infrastructure at Guatemala City's La Aurora International Airport and the Mundo Maya Airport in Flores/Tikal.

In addition to increased tourism, more and more Guatemalans have family living in the United States, which means this is easily one of the fastest-growing markets on U.S. carriers' radar screens. As for cost, the market is very elastic. The arrival of a new carrier into Guatemala often signals an all-out pricing war as seen with service startups by Delta in 1998 and US Airways in 2005, when flights from the United States to Guatemala hovered around US$300 roundtrip. Demand quickly catches up with supply, however, and prices double as carriers see little reason to discount flights in a market where planes are already flying full.

The future of aviation looks uncertain, however, as airlines attempt to do business amid record-high oil prices. Rising fuel costs have forced airlines to charge for services such as baggage handling, meals, and even seat selection. Airline routes worldwide are being cut in an attempt to streamline operations and reduce operating costs. In 2008, new flights from Mexico City via Interjet and Aeromexico were cut almost as quickly as they were added. U.S. carrier ATA went the way of the dodo bird just days before it was set to begin service to Guatemala City from Miami. The year also saw the departure of United Airlines from the Guatemalan market after a 17-year presence and an almost year-round occupancy rate of at least 80 percent on its daily flight from LAX. US Airways, which shared airport staff with United, left at the same time.

As for airfares, the price of an average plane ticket from the United States to Guatemala varies widely depending on the route and season but ranges from about US$350 to US$750 roundtrip. Still, deals can be had if you know where to look and are willing to give up some comforts like advance seat selection and ticket changeability. Internet sites offering discounted tickets and air ticket consolidators are worth checking out if this describes you. A particularly useful tool for comparison shopping is kayak.com.

Guatemala has an open skies agreement with the United States, meaning that any carrier from either country can fly to any point in the other. Guatemala once had an official flag-carrier, Aviateca, but Salvadoran-owned TACA has since absorbed it. Domestic flights between Flores and Guatemala City are officially operated by Aviateca, but this appears to be a mere formality, as the aircraft livery, ticket jackets, and related travel documents all clearly make it known that you are flying TACA. TACA operates the majority of flights into and out of Guatemala, flying nonstop from a handful of gateway cities in the United States as well as via its hubs in San Salvador and San José, Costa Rica. The U.S. carriers also have a strong presence here. Several Latin American carriers, some of them noteworthy, operate here as well. The only European airline serving Guatemala at this time is Iberia, the Spanish flag-carrier.

When departing Guatemala on an international flight, you'll need to pay a US$2.75 security fee in cash at the airport prior to passing through the security checkpoint. A US$30 departure tax is also collected but is included in the taxes you pay at the time you purchase your airline ticket.

Airports

Most international travelers flying to Guatemala arrive via Guatemala City's La Aurora International Airport (GUA). La Aurora could not be more conveniently located for Guatemala City residents, lying in the heart of the city just minutes from the business and hotel district. A recent renovation and expansion has brought the once-obsolete La Aurora into the 21st century, though the transition to a new government in early 2008 delayed the project's completion and put planned future phases in limbo. In any case, the new glass-and-steel north and central terminals are vast improvements over La Aurora's former facilities and feature a number of good restaurants and duty-free shops. The check-in lounge, with its high, angular ceiling somewhat resembling an egg carton, is actually part of the original construction dating back to the 1960s. It has been given an updated look and restored to full functionality.

Car rentals have been operating rather informally, with agents awaiting arriving passengers holding identifying corporate signage. It can be a bit chaotic when exiting La Aurora, as families of arriving Guatemalans tend to like to load up cars (and sometimes entire buses) to welcome a returning loved one. The same goes for departing family members. As you make your way out of the terminal (before merging with the crowds outside) you'll see an INGUAT tourist information kiosk. The English-speaking agents can provide maps

DAILY LIFE

GUATEMALA CITY'S NEW AIRPORT

It's been a long time coming, but it finally happened. Guatemala City finally got an airport worthy of its stature as Central America's largest city. Gone are the days of walking down dark corridors and waiting in cramped boarding areas. It's quite a pleasant surprise to walk into a bright, modern, glass-and-steel terminal upon disembarking from your arriving aircraft. Somehow, it just doesn't feel like the Guatemala I've been flying to all these years.

The first phase of the modernization and expansion of La Aurora International Airport was completed at a cost of US$100 million and includes a completely revamped main terminal building with a covered access ramp fronted by a three-story, 480-car parking garage. Inside, the refurbished terminal houses new check-in facilities under a high-vaulted ceiling that evokes the wonder of flight and harkens to the golden days of aviation.

La Aurora opened in 1968 as one of the finest air terminals in Latin America. It was once a hub for Pan Am's Latin America network. The recent renovations do a fine job of capturing the terminal's lost splendor while bringing it fully into the 21st century. Outside, it retains original sculptures by famed Guatemalan artist Efraín Recinos, which line the terminal's glass sides.

New construction includes the North Finger, housing 12 gates with spacious waiting areas. Arriving passengers enter the terminal and immediately ascend to an elevated walkway above the departure gates from which there are fabulous city views toward Zona 14 to the east.

The original international departures hall running out from the main terminal was demolished to make room for the six-gate Central Finger, adjacent to the main terminal, with capacity for four large aircraft like 747-400s and Airbus A340s. Spanish carrier Iberia flies A340s to Guatemala five times per week.

Future runway improvements will allow for simultaneous takeoffs and landings with the separation of the main taxiway from La Aurora's runway 01-19. A new cargo facility is also planned as part of the second phase. The final phase will be the construction of an additional five-gate complex known as the South Finger, bringing the total number of gates to 23. It's a substantial increase in capacity from La Aurora's original eight gates.

In June 2007, La Aurora was elevated to category 1 status by the FAA, meaning its facilities and safety measures are in compliance with the agency's standards.

While the new airport is certainly a vast improvement over the formerly obsolete facilities, not everyone is happy with the price paid for progress. The government of Álvaro Colom, which took office in January 2008, has repeatedly made the new airport a scapegoat and used it as a centerpiece of its populist rhetoric. President Colom has made frequent mention of a multimillion dollar transfer of funds from the Ministry of Education, in 2007, to finance the project. It should be noted that the funds had returned to the Treasury's common fund after not having been utilized by said ministry, and so, were up for grabs. Still, Colom likes to say that the airport was built with money that should have gone toward health and education.

Shortly after taking office, the new government put the brakes on the project, alleging gross overspending and corruption. It should be noted that the much-respected International Civil Aviation Organization (ICAO) oversaw the project's completion, including technical and financial aspects, in its entirety. A long, drawn-out audit was conducted by Guatemala's Finance Ministry. When no financial malfeasance was found (big surprise), Colom had to eat his words and kindly ask ICAO to retake the reins for the project's continued execution. The first phase of the project was finally completed in late 2008, almost a year after its original due date.

For now, it looks like the second phase of the project, including the new taxiway and cargo facility, will break ground at the end of 2009.

La Aurora's aging facilities had received substandard maintenance and minimal infrastructural improvements during the 1980s and '90s. While the improvements have brought Guatemala's main port of entry up to international standards, authorities realize the airport will eventually need to be moved out of Guatemala City altogether. A commercial district at its northern end and a deep ravine to the south hedge in La Aurora's sole runway and limit its expansion. In addition to several mountains and volcanic peaks making the approach into GUA difficult for pilots, Guatemala City's office buildings and condos flank the surrounding areas, leading to fears of a runway mishap of tragic proportions.

La Aurora's convenient location within the confines of Guatemala City is clearly a double-edged sword. Runway overruns, some fatal, have occurred in the past.

The most notable include the non-fatal 1993 TACA crash of a Boeing 767, which attempted to land in a rainstorm, and a Cubana DC-10 crash in 1999 killing 26. Its safety in light of its location right in the heart of the city has always been questioned.

The new airport project has been talked about for decades, but it may be scheduled for takeoff in the next few years. The Japan International Cooperation Agency (JICA) has donated feasibility studies for the new airport, including the determination of the best location based on several criteria, as well as blueprints for the terminal's architectural design. Authorities have announced Masagua, in the coastal department of Escuintla, as the ideal site for the new facility. The new site offers several advantages, including the absence of urban congestion, a runway at sea level to allow long-haul flights from Europe and Asia, more room to build facilities, and the opportunity to turn the airport into a magnet for economic development outside of the capital. The main disadvantages appear to be the project's hefty US$565 million price tag and the greater distance from the capital. Authorities will need to incorporate public transportation and new access roads to the airport, which would be completed sometime in the next 15–20 years, when La Aurora is projected to definitively exceed its capacity even with the recent improvements. It may take 10 years just to implement structures for the project's execution, including the purchase of needed lands, formalizing of design plans, and contracting the necessary construction work.

La Aurora International Airport, Guatemala City

and answer basic questions about ground transportation. Taxis and shuttles also operate out of the arrivals area. A taxi to Zona 10 or Zona 14 costs about US$8, more for trips to Carretera a El Salvador or elsewhere beyond the city limits. Most of the Zona 10 hotels have courtesy shuttles to and from the airport. A shuttle bus to Antigua costs about US$11.

The situation on the ground will hopefully have changed by the time you read this, as airport authorities allocate space to taxi companies, car rental agencies, and shuttle companies with the completion of La Aurora's new arrivals area.

Flores/Tikal (FRS), officially known as Mundo Maya International Airport, serves the northern department of Petén and the ruins of Tikal. Its renovation is also in progress, a project inherited from the previous government. Flights arrive several times daily from Guatemala City, Cancún, and Belize City. The flight to Flores from the Guatemalan capital takes about 30 minutes. Most travelers arriving here head straight for the ruins of Tikal about an hour away via numerous minivans, or to the city of Flores, just five minutes away, by taxi. A *colectivo* van to Tikal costs about US$4. A taxi to Flores costs about US$2. Arrival procedures are fairly straightforward thanks to the airport's smaller size. Departing passengers will be happy to know the airport was recently fitted with air-conditioning, a feature long overdue in the hot, humid Petén climate.

Flights to Guatemala City

The majority of nonstop flights come from a handful of North American hub cities including Atlanta, Chicago, Dallas/Ft. Worth, Fort Lauderdale,

Houston, Los Angeles, Miami, and New York/Newark. San Salvador and Panama City are becoming increasingly important as connecting points for flights from South America on TACA and Copa Airlines, respectively. Madrid holds the distinction of being the sole European city with direct service to Guatemala City, this being a nonstop flight five times per week on Spanish flag-carrier Iberia.

Among the U.S. carriers, American Airlines flies nonstop three times daily to Guatemala City from Miami and daily nonstop from Dallas/Ft. Worth. It code shares with British Airways on flights from the U.K. as well as offering excellent European connections of its own.

Continental Airlines has three nonstops a day to Guatemala City from Houston Intercontinental (IAH) as well as two Saturday-only nonstop flights from New York/Newark (EWR). They sometimes operate additional frequencies from EWR on weekdays.

Delta Airlines flies daily from Atlanta to Guatemala City with additional service from Los Angeles on an ever-changing frequency. At last check, flights from LAX were operating Thursday, Friday, and Sunday. The newest U.S. carrier to arrive on the scene, Spirit Airlines flies daily nonstop to Guatemala City from Fort Lauderdale.

Salvadoran conglomerate Transportes Aéreos del Continente Americano, or TACA, flies daily nonstop to Guatemala City from Miami and Los Angeles with three or four weekly nonstops each from Chicago, New York JFK, and Washington, D.C. Other nonstops include flights from Mexico City, Cancún, and San Pedro Sula. There are numerous daily flights from TACA's hubs in San Salvador, El Salvador, and San José, Costa Rica, with onward connections to/from South America. In July 2008, TACA introduced nonstop service to Lima three times per week.

Flights to Flores/Tikal
Flights to Flores/Tikal arrive primarily from Guatemala City, Belize City, and Cancún. Continental Airlines operated weekly service to Flores from its hub in Houston for just over a year, but the flights were discontinued in November 2006. It may have been an idea ahead of its time. Maya Island Air is a Belizean carrier flying to Flores/Tikal from Belize City.

BY SEA
Cruise ships dock at Puerto Quetzal, on the Pacific Coast, and Puerto Santo Tomás de Castilla, on the Caribbean side. Cruise lines offer a variety of activities for those wishing to disembark and explore Guatemalan shores, including

visits to local resorts and beaches near Santo Tomás and inland trips to Antigua, Tikal, and Lake Atitlán or deep-sea fishing in the Pacific waters. For those wishing not to travel inland, there is not much to see and do in the immediate vicinity of either port of call, although the pier is usually packed with vendors selling everything from bags of Guatemalan coffee to colorful textiles and clothing. A land-based activity close to a port of call worth mentioning is hiking in the Cerro San Gil forest preserve near Santo Tomás de Castilla. Puerto Quetzal boasts a nearby ostrich farm.

Ferry and water taxi services connect the Guatemalan town of Lívingston with Punta Gorda, Belize (2.5 hours, US$35), and Omoa, Honduras (1.25 hours, US$16), both offered by Exotic Travel on Tuesdays and Fridays. Transportes El Chato has a daily boat to and from Punta Gorda costing US$16 and taking roughly an hour to make the trip. A US$10 departure tax applies when leaving Guatemala by sea.

If you're coming in to Guatemala on your own boat, you will most likely arrive on the Caribbean side and will need to check in with immigration officials in Lívingston before sailing up the Río Dulce, the most popular route with boaters.

BY RIVER

The most popular route into Guatemala by river is via the Usumacinta River, which divides Mexico and Guatemala. Boats travel from the Mexican town of Frontera Corozal to La Técnica and Bethel, in Guatemala's northern Petén department. This is the route of choice for travelers wanting to combine visits to the Mexican sites of Palenque and Yaxchilán with trips to the various Petén ruins. Yaxchilán lies on the Mexican bank of the Usumacinta and is highly recommended. Buses from Palenque to the Mexican border are available via Transportes Montebello and Autotransportes Rio Chancala. From La Técnica, buses leave for the Petén departmental capital of Flores at 4 A.M. and 11 A.M. (US$4, five hours). Buses leave Bethel for Flores at 5 A.M., noon, 2 P.M., and 4 P.M., cost US$4, and take four hours to make the trip. Package trips encompassing bus and boat transportation are available from various travel agencies in Palenque and Flores for travel in either direction for about US$35.

It is also possible to travel from Benemérito, south of Frontera Corozal, up the Río La Pasión to Sayaxché, Guatemala, and via the Río San Pedro between La Palma and El Naranjo. These routes lack scheduled passenger service and are not recommended as they are increasingly being used as transshipment points by the growing drug and illegal immigrant trade between Petén and Mexico.

BY LAND

Many travelers enter Guatemala by bus, as part of larger explorations encompassing neighboring countries. If traveling by car or bus, try to make the border crossing as early in the day as possible, as there are few serviceable hotels and restaurants in border towns and they are notorious for their seedy atmosphere. Onward bus service tends to wind down further into the day, so try to get a move on while you can.

Overland from the United States

When I was 10 years old, my parents decided to move the family to Guatemala from New Jersey. A year later, we took a trip back north with the mission of driving our Toyota van, left in the care of friends, down to Guatemala. I don't remember much about the trip, quite honestly; just a lot of highways, countless hours in a van with my family, a diet of fast food, and nights spent in roadside motels. Once we crossed the border into Mexico, I do remember staying at some pleasant hotels where we would relax in swimming pools after a long day of driving. The trip also served as a good lesson in geopolitics, as the wealth disparities between the United States and Mexico became readily apparent as soon as we crossed the border. Another oddity was the unavailability of unleaded fuel in Mexico in 1986, which caused our van to make a loud clickety-clack noise during our entire run through Mexico. I remember Guatemala felt somewhat more civilized than our northern neighbor simply because we had gas stations other than Pemex and (gasp) unleaded fuel.

Many folks make the overland trip to Guatemala. The country's location in the northernmost reaches of Central America keeps border crossings to a minimum. Rest assured, unleaded fuel is now available in Mexico. The advent of the Internet has also made it easy to find information for planning your road trip.

Most people cross into Mexico from the United States via Brownsville and then take the route through Mexico along the Pacific coast. You can also travel via Mexico City or along the Atlantic side, but the Mexican capital's traffic and inferior roads on the Atlantic side make the routes less desirable. You'll need to get a tourist visa to travel through Mexico (US$25) or a *transmigrante* visa, but many experienced road-trippers discourage others from getting the latter, deeming it unnecessary and more difficult to process. For Mexican vehicle insurance, some travelers have recommended Sanborn's Insurance (www.sanbornsinsurance.com). More detailed information for planning the drive to Guatemala is available in the *Gringo's Guide to Driving Through Mexico and Central America,* found online at www.drivemeloco.com.

In Guatemala, you will also find many people make a living from bringing used American cars into the country, known as *vehículos rodados,* and then selling them locally. See the section on *Driving* later in this chapter for the ins and outs of importing a vehicle into Guatemala or buying a used car locally.

If you're just driving a car to Guatemala but don't plan to leave it or sell it there, you'll need to have the following documents with you to get the car into the country:

- Passport
- Driver's license
- Vehicle registration
- Vehicle title
- Photocopies of all the above

Be aware you must leave the country with the vehicle you entered with originally.

In terms of fees and paperwork for getting your vehicle into the country, you'll need to get a tourist permit (US$1.50), a vehicle entry form (RP-131) and sticker (US$5) and, sometimes, fumigation (US$3). The vehicle entry sticker is valid for 30 days (no extensions) and will be marked "SAT," which stands for Superintendencia de Administración Tributaria. This is the Guatemalan equivalent of an IRS/customs hybrid. After you've presented all the necessary paperwork, SAT agents will look through your car and you may be required to wait a few hours while your vehicle awaits processing.

It is at this point where most foreigners have issues with the entry process, as you've already presented all the necessary documents and are mentally ready to be on your way. While an opening exists for corrupt government officials to collect bribes in an attempt to expedite your claim, SAT has made serious inroads in recent years to reduce waiting times for customs transactions and has generally done quite well at cracking down on corrupt officials. In June 2008, 24 SAT officials at the El Carmen border were relieved of their duties after *Siglo XXI* newspaper reporters working undercover revealed they were collectively charging about US$8,000 a day in illegal processing fees.

Be patient and you'll soon be on your way. Also be advised that, once in Guatemala, you may run into military checkpoints a few kilometers down the road from the border crossing. If you are flagged down to stop, present all the required documents and be courteous and friendly.

From Mexico

The main border crossings on the Pacific flatlands are Ciudad Hidalgo/Tecún Umán and Talismán/El Carmen, near Tapachula, Mexico. On the Pan-American highway, the border crossing is at Ciudad Cuauhtemoc/La Mesilla between Comitán, Mexico, and Huehuetenango, Guatemala. Many travelers recommend this last route as the best entry point into Guatemala from Mexico when traveling in your own vehicle. All of these border towns have frequent bus service to nearby cities within both countries.

There is direct bus service to Flores from Chetumal on Linea Dorada and San Juan Travel. Both services stop in Belize City en route with a total trip duration of about eight hours.

A new road is being completed from western Petén into Mexico via El Ceibo, so it will soon be possible to travel overland between Petén and Mexico's Tabasco state. Check locally for the latest.

From Belize

The Belize border crossing into Guatemala is at Benque Viejo del Carmen/Melchor de Mencos. There is twice daily bus service from Belize City to Flores via Linea Dorada. The trip lasts four to five hours and costs US$15. San Juan Travel also has a daily bus covering the route.

A less expensive option is to take Novelo's or Batty's buses from Belize City to the border and make onward connections to other points in Guatemala on frequent buses and minibuses from Melchor de Mencos.

From Honduras

The main border crossings are at El Florido (between Copán Ruinas, Honduras, and Chiquimula, Guatemala), Agua Caliente (between Nueva Ocotepeque, Honduras, and Esquipulas, Guatemala), and Corinto (between Omoa, Honduras, and Puerto Barrios, Guatemala). There are shuttle minibuses running between Copán, Guatemala City, and Antigua, as well first-class bus service to Guatemala City from the main Honduran cities. Hedman Alas has daily service to Guatemala City via the El Florido border from Copán, San Pedro Sula, Tegucigalpa, and La Ceiba.

From El Salvador

El Salvador's numerous borders with Guatemala are at Las Chinamas/Valle Nuevo (Highway CA-8), La Hachadura/Ciudad Pedro de Alvarado on Pacific Coast Highway CA-2, San Cristóbal/San Cristóbal on the Pan-American Highway CA-1, and Anguiatu/Anguiatu (Highway CA-10). Several bus lines operate service between Guatemala City and San Salvador, mostly via Las Chinamas, including Pullmantur. Moon-Ray Tours offers direct bus service between Antigua and San Salvador on comfortable, brand-new buses.

To and From Points South
Ticabus connects Guatemala City to San Salvador, Managua, San José, and Panama City, taking several days to make the trip and stopping in the listed capitals along the way. A one-way ticket from Guatemala City to San José, Costa Rica, costs about US$50.

Getting Around

BY AIR
The only scheduled domestic service within Guatemala is between Guatemala City and Flores, although ongoing improvements to local infrastructure at many smaller airports may mean a small network of local flights may soon be up and running. Some of the flights to and from Flores operate using smaller aircraft, so unless you enjoy the cramped space and longer flight time of a ride in an ATR-42, pay careful attention to the equipment being used on the flight. Airfares for this domestic service have recently skyrocketed and are surprisingly expensive, particularly when taking into account the short distance involved in flying within Guatemala.

All of the domestic carriers flying out of Guatemala City operate from their private hangars, located on the east side of the runway, opposite the main terminal building. The only airline operating its domestic service from the main terminal at La Aurora airport is TACA.

New domestic airports with passenger terminals are complete or nearing completion in Huehuetenango, Quetzaltenango, Puerto San José, Coatepeque, and San Marcos. Plans call for terminals at the Pacific coast leisure destination of Retalhuleu and the existing paved runway at Puerto Barrios. Cobán has a functional airstrip, though there is no scheduled service. Flights from Guatemala City to all of the above may become a reality once the terminals are complete and investors make inroads into a market with certain potential. During the late 1990s, TACA subsidiary Inter operated domestic air service between Guatemala City and Cobán, Quetzaltenango, Huehuetenango, and Puerto Barrios.

Airlines
TACA operates two daily flights between Guatemala City and Flores using

Airbus A319 aircraft. Additional flights on certain days of the week make the trip on an ATR-42. TAG (800/528-8216 toll-free U.S. or 2332-1897 Guatemala, www.tag.com.gt) has a daily flight to Flores from Guatemala City leaving at 6:30 A.M. The return trip from Flores is at 5 P.M.

BY LAND
Bus

Most travelers get around Guatemala by bus or shuttle bus. The majority of inter- and intracity buses are "chicken buses," as travelers have dubbed them, recycled U.S. school buses painted in lively colors. Cargo and carry-on baggage often consists of live animals, hence the name. Please be aware that robberies, including pickpocketing and armed hijacking, are increasingly common on these inexpensive public buses serving the interior. The U.S. State Department Consular Information Sheet cites the death of over 100 bus drivers and passengers in armed robberies during 1996 alone. Chicken buses are also poorly maintained and frequently involved in traffic accidents where the bus plunges into a ravine or makes a blind pass into a head-on collision. For the intrepid, the chicken bus is still an easy way to see Guatemala and get to virtually any part of the country cheaply.

Tourist shuttle buses plying the main tourist routes, though more expensive, have become increasingly popular for safety reasons and are highly recommended. Additionally, shuttle buses sometimes offer door-to-door service. Recommended shuttle buses are ATITRANS, Turansa, and Grayline Tours.

The "chicken bus" can get you almost anywhere in Guatemala.

Also reliable are first-class buses that run between Guatemala City and major cities such as Quetzaltenango, Huehuetenango, Puerto Barrios, Cobán, and Flores. Prices are comparable to shuttle buses, but service is aboard large luxury coaches, often with restrooms and onboard food service.

Pickups and Minivans

Another common form of getting around, particularly in remote rural areas with infrequent bus service is via (roughly) scheduled service aboard pickup trucks. Minivans have also replaced cumbersome chicken buses in many rural areas with poor roads.

Highway Overview

Roads in Guatemala are surprisingly good in some places, particularly on well-trodden paths like the Pan-American Highway. They are much better, overall, than the roads in neighboring Belize and Costa Rica. Roads in and around tourist areas are generally well marked, some courtesy of the Guatemala state tourism agency, INGUAT (Instituto Guatemalteco de Turismo). If while driving, you come across a large tree branch in the middle of the road, be prepared to stop. This is Guatemalans' way of officially signaling that danger lies ahead, usually in the form of a car stopped by the side of the road. Whether it be by bus or by car, do not travel on rural highways in Guatemala after dark.

Guatemala has several main highways with which it might be useful to get acquainted. The Pan-American Highway (CA-1), also known as the Interamericana, runs from the Mexican border at La Mesilla through much of the western highlands, to Guatemala City and east to El Salvador at San Cristóbal border. This is the road taken (at least for much of the journey) from Guatemala City to many of the main travel destinations, including La Antigua, Lake Atitlán, Quetzaltenango, and Huehuetenango. CA-1 is being expanded to four lanes from Guatemala City all the way to the Cuatro Caminos junction near Quetzaltenango.

© AL ARGUETA

Guatemala City is the country's travel hub and all major roads pass through it.

The Pacific Coast Highway (CA-2) crosses the Pacific slope from the Mexican border at Tecún Umán all the way to Ciudad Pedro de Alvarado and El Salvador. A new, wider Pacific highway is currently in the planning stages.

Highway CA-9 runs from the Pacific coast to Guatemala City, encompassing the country's only toll road: a good, fast *autopista,* or freeway. From Guatemala City it heads east to Puerto Barrios and is currently being widened to four lanes from the capital to El Rancho Junction. CA-14 branches north from El Rancho into the departments of Baja and Alta Verapaz.

Continuing east along CA-9, the next junction is at Río Hondo, where CA-10 branches southeast to Zacapa and Chiquimula before linking up to eastbound CA-11 for Copán, Honduras. Back on the main branch of CA-9, CA-13 is the designation given to the road branching off at La Ruidosa junction, just before Puerto Barrios, heading north to Río Dulce and continuing to Petén. It arrives in Flores and then branches eastward to the Belize border at Melchor de Mencos.

A road crossing the country from Izabal department west all the way to Huehuetenango is also planned for the near future and will be called the Franja Transversal del Norte. Also in the works is a Guatemala City Ring Road project circumscribing the city's metro area and allowing heavy cargo traffic between Pacific and Atlantic coast ports to bypass the already traffic-congested capital.

Rental Cars

Rental cars are plentiful in Guatemala, and can be rented in Guatemala City, Panajachel, Antigua, Quetzaltenango, Cobán, and Flores. Some local agencies are also available.

Taxis

Taxicabs are available in almost any town or city. When in smaller towns, the best way to find a taxi is in the central square, or *parque central.* In Guatemala City, taxis are available at the Zona 10 hotels, shopping malls, or (as a last resort) can be hailed from street corners. It's always best to call a cab, as certain city zones get more taxi traffic and not all companies are reliable. These taxicab companies are recommended for getting around the capital: Taxis Amarillo Express (tel. 2332-1515) requires you to call for a cab and will need an exact address to pick you up. Another option is Taxis Blanco y Azul (tel. 2360-0903). As a final word of caution, the U.S. Embassy discourages travelers from hailing cabs off the street in Guatemala City.

In smaller towns and villages, you'll also find the Asian-style *tuk tuks,* or motorized rickshaws powered by a motorcycle engine. These offer a lower-cost alternative to standard taxicabs and are great if you're traveling without luggage over short distances.

If you're checking out places to live and need to get around for days at a time, it might be worth renting a taxi by the day or week. This is particularly the case in Guatemala City, where there are so many neighborhoods tucked into the varied terrain and certainly some places you'll wish to avoid. It's also nice to have someone else driving while you take in the surroundings and decide if you like the areas you're looking at.

Many taxi drivers are willing to negotiate a daily or hourly rate, somewhere in the vicinity of US$10 an hour or US$75 a day. You can often get a really good deal if you negotiate for multiple days. Most Guatemalan taxi drivers are friendly and helpful, making great sources of conversation to gauge opinions on issues of daily life for the average Guatemalan. It seems almost everyone has a friend or a friend of a friend who is a taxi driver, and they may be able to recommend someone to you.

Hitchhiking

Though hitchhiking in its traditional form is not widely practiced in Guatemala, a local adaptation exists in remote rural areas where there is limited or nonexistent bus service. People with pickup trucks will often give you a ride in the back of their trucks. The fee is usually nominal, if anything at all.

Boat

In some areas, getting around by boat is the most practical option. This is particularly the case on the shores of Lake Atitlán, where regular ferry service and small motorboats make their way across the lake from Panajachel to the outlying villages. Boat service is also a major form of transportation in coastal areas, particularly in Izabal department along the Río Dulce, on Lake Izabal, and in coastal areas such as Lívingston and Puerto Barrios. On the Pacific side, motorboats traverse the Canal de Chiquimulilla, which separates the Pacific seaboard from the Guatemalan mainland along much of the coast.

Driving

RENTING A CAR

There's nothing like the freedom of having your own wheels when you're set on exploring new surroundings. Renting a car allows you to go wherever Guatemala's roads will take you. With that in mind, it's probably best to rent a four-wheel-drive vehicle. The only exception to this is if you plan to stick to urban areas such as Guatemala City and Antigua or along the Pan-American Highway. A compact car will run you about US$300 a week, while a four-wheel-drive vehicle can cost as much as US$400–600 a week. You might find better deals online. It sometimes pays to reserve something through an online booking service and then call around locally to get their best rates and comparison shop. Most cars in Guatemala are stick shift, with automatic transmission often costing a bit more.

Make sure to purchase additional insurance if your credit card doesn't offer you adequate coverage. Coverage provided by credit cards such as Visa and American Express usually doesn't apply if you go "off-road," which you likely will. Coverage varies from one credit card company to the next but usually excludes personal liability (damage to property or other vehicles) and theft. Also, if you stick to basic coverage offered by the rental agency, your credit card will have to cover the outrageous deductibles in the vicinity of US$750–1,500. Purchasing full coverage from the agency can run in the vicinity of

DAILY LIFE

© AL ARGUETA

Renting a car will allow you to explore Guatemala's scenic back roads.

US$25 a day and really adds to the final bill, but some find it a small price
to pay for peace of mind.

Before leaving the car lot, make sure to check the car over, paying attention to every minute detail. Rental agents will go over the car with you and
document any scratches, dings, and dents. They'll inspect it again when you
return the vehicle. Any new damage (or previously undocumented damage)
might cost you dearly.

Never leave a vehicle parked on the street overnight and never leave personal
belongings inside an unattended vehicle.

BUYING A CAR

Issues with safety and the unreliability of public transportation have forced
many Guatemalans to purchase their own vehicles. You'll see everything from
1970s jalopies to brand-new Ferraris cruising along Guatemalan streets. The
most popular brands are Toyota, Nissan, BMW, Volvo, and Mercedes Benz.
Guatemala is actually one of Latin America's top importers of luxury vehicles,
with BMW leading the pack. There are Porsche and Ferrari dealerships in
Guatemala City. Ironically, some high-end versions of Japanese autos, such as
Lexus, Infiniti, and Acura, aren't sold locally by dealerships. If you buy a used
vehicle of this type or bring one in from the United States, you'll likely need
to special-order parts from dealerships or import parts through the mail.

If you're looking for a used car, it's best to buy one from a dealership, a friend
of a friend, or some such other arrangement. Classified ads are another good
resource, as listed vehicles are usually for sale by their owners. This allows you
to get an idea of how well the car has been taken care of by interviewing the
source directly. Most of the vehicles brought in to Guatemala and sold in used
car lots are brought in under salvage titles, and the rolling back of odometers
is common. Bringing cars in for sale is a virtual cottage industry with little
consumer protection afforded to the buyer.

Just as you'd do back home, have a trusted mechanic check out the vehicle
before you seal the deal.

High import tariffs make buying a car in Guatemala very expensive. If you
choose to bring your own car to Guatemala from the United States and leave it
here, you'll likely find yourself paying close to half its value in import fees.

Finally, car theft is quite common in Guatemala and is on the rise, particularly in Guatemala City. Vehicle thievery isn't limited to break-ins, but
also comes in the carjacking variety. Target vehicles aren't limited to luxury
brands, either. I have a cousin who was carjacked in her Volkswagen on a busy
Zona 9 street in broad daylight. Oh, and remember the family van we drove

down from the United States? It was stolen at gunpoint just outside my dad's Guatemala City Zona 10 office, also in broad daylight, about a year after we got it to Guatemala. As with any armed robbery, do not resist the perpetrators. Your life is worth much more than any car. That being said, theft insurance is a good idea, but expect to pay a premium.

IMPORTING A CAR FROM THE UNITED STATES

There are two ways to import a vehicle into Guatemala. First, you can drive it down (the least expensive option), or you can have it shipped overseas by container. Driving cars down through Mexico is by far the most popular alternative. Shipping a car from Florida to Guatemala's Caribbean port will cost you about US$1,000—more from the West Coast. This does not include the various duties you'll have to pay when you pick the car up in Guatemala, among them a flat US$800 *flete* (tax assessed for shipping) on vehicles brought in by sea.

If you choose to overland option, you'll need your passport, vehicle title and registration, an invoice from a recognized dealership showing the purchase price, and your driver's license. If you don't have the original invoice or one from a recognized dealership, Guatemalan authorities will use the Guatemalan Blue Book value to determine duties. Import duties are assessed by Guatemala's SAT, which is quite modern by Central American standards. Its web portal (http://portal.sat.gob.gt) will give you an idea of how much you'll pay in duties. The web portal uses the example of a 2001 Toyota Corolla valued at US$5,400. For automobiles brought overland, a US$500 *flete* applies, in addition to a US$50 insurance charge. These charges are added to the car's value, giving us a total of US$5,950. On this figure, a 20 percent duty is charged (US$1,190), bringing the total to US$7,140. Sales tax of 12 percent (US$856.80) is applied to this last figure and added to the final bill, bringing the grand total to US$2,046.80 in import tariffs. That's almost 40 percent of the car's value! Be aware that cars older than 10 years are taxed more heavily.

Selling the car locally involves a mountain of tedious paperwork purposely designed to discourage foreigners from selling cars in Guatemala.

As a final recommendation, it often makes more sense to simply bring in the vehicle on a 30-day permit and then go through the hoops of importing your vehicle through SAT in Guatemala City with the help of a decent lawyer.

DRIVER'S LICENSES

You can use your valid, state-issued U.S. driver's license during your initial 30-day entry permit for driving in Guatemala. After that, things get a little

TRAFFIC CITATIONS, ACCIDENTS, AND BREAKDOWNS

Guatemala City and some of the larger urban areas are equipped with a Policía Municipal de Tránsito (Municipal Transit Police). Their duties include directing traffic during rush hour and issuing citations for traffic violations. Some of the most common violations committed by foreigners include turning right on a red light (technically illegal, though many people here do it) and talking on a cell phone while driving, which is also illegal. You'll find most Guatemalan drivers do it anyway, as long as there isn't a Transit Police officer nearby.

If you're issued a citation, you'll have to pay it at a local "Muni" office. As elsewhere in Latin America, you may sometimes be given the opportunity to buy your way out of a violation, though you should never offer a bribe outright as it may land you in even more trouble. A more subtle way to get around this might be to politely ask if there "isn't anything that can be done." It's sneaky, I know, and giving in to bribes only serves to perpetuate the legacy of corruption. Still, this rather open-ended question might also get you off the hook with a warning instead of a full-fledged fine.

Outside of urban areas, cops are more concerned with citizen safety in light of Guatemala's legacy of highway banditry. They're not usually looking for speeders. Foreigners do often attract the attention of police in rural areas, and you may be asked to stop. I've been stopped almost every time I've rented a car, despite the fact that I do not at all fit the gringo profile. I've never been issued a citation, as police are usually just interested in making sure your documents are in order. In isolated

more complicated. Your options are to use an International Driver's License, avail yourself of a temporary driving permit (*permiso*), or get a Guatemalan driver's license.

Guatemala recognizes the International Driver's License, available in the United States from the American Automobile Association (AAA). You should also carry your state-issued driver's license with you when driving.

Guatemala's Policía Nacional Civil (PNC) issues temporary driving permits to foreigners with valid driver's licenses who need to drive in Guatemala beyond their initial 30-day entry permit. *Permisos* cost US$4 per month and are issued for a period of time not to exceed the length of your authorized stay in the country as stamped on your passport. As with the International Driver's License, you'll need carry your valid, state-issued driver's license with you at all times. To get a *permiso*, visit the Departamento de Tránsito in Guatemala City. You may also enlist the help of a *tramitador* in facilitating the process.

If and only if you've gained Guatemalan residency status, you may get a Guatemalan driver's license through the PNC's Departamento de Tránsito.

cases, particularly near Lake Atitlán, foreigners have been stopped by cops on rural roads shortly before being robbed by bandits, leading to suspicions that local police are in on the scam. It's a good idea to get an officer's name and badge number if you are stopped, just in case.

Breakdowns do sometimes happen, so it's best to be prepared if and when they do. Rural roads are patrolled by local police forces and also by Provial, which offers free roadside assistance. Provial can be contacted by calling 2422-7878. Local police can also help.

Defensive driving is your best defense against being involved in a traffic collision, but if you are involved in an accident, there are a few things you should know. First, in fatal accidents both drivers will be taken into police custody until a judge can determine culpability via a reconstruction of events. You are essentially guilty until proven innocent. If you are involved in an accident, phone the police by dialing 120, or the fire department by dialing 122 or 123. You should also refrain from moving your vehicle, as you are then tampering with the accident scene.

In the event of an accident or breakdown, beware of "Good Samaritans" who might stop and offer help. They may be out to help themselves to your belongings. Lock your vehicle and don't lose sight of it. I once witnessed a gruesome accident on the Pan American Highway near Chimaltenango, with a long line of cars forming in the aftermath. Waiting vehicles included intercity buses with unscrupulous passengers who had no qualms about getting off the bus and seeing what they could get their hands on.

DAILY LIFE

To apply for a license, you'll need to fill out the proper form and provide six passport-sized photos, a photocopy of your passport or Guatemalan *cédula* (soon to be replaced by a new card known as DPI), and a valid driver's license (so as to avoid taking written and road driving tests). You'll also need to take a vision exam, provide your blood type, and inform authorities whether or not you are allergic to penicillin. Fees for new licenses depend on the length of their validity and range US$13–32 for periods of 1–4 years.

Guatemalan driver's licenses were recently redesigned with all the bells and whistles of modern ID cards in an attempt to stop the increasingly popular falsification or alteration of these documents.

RULES OF THE ROAD

To the untrained eye, it may appear that Guatemalans drive like crazy people. After you've been here a while and get used to things, you'll realize there is a method to the madness. In recent years, the painting of lanes on Guatemala City streets has helped bring some measure of order to traffic patterns, whereas in the past folks just sort of drifted across the pavement and improvised the number of lanes. Pedestrian crossings at intersections are also a phenomenon only implemented in the last decade or so.

Most Guatemalans drive aggressively, and you'll find they weave in and out of traffic in an attempt to get places in the quickest time possible. In urban areas, city buses and truck traffic add to the chaos, though Guatemala City has wisely limited truck traffic through the capital to certain off-peak hours. Another feature of Guatemala City driving is numerous one-way streets, with directions sometimes changing on a whim. Get used to planning your maneuvers well in advance, as you'll need to be in a certain lane to go a certain direction through the city's many overpasses. There's nothing like the frustration of trying to cut through four lanes of rush hour traffic to get into the right lane or taking a turnoff onto a highway overpass and finding you've ended up going the wrong way. As always, practice makes perfect.

In many places, you'll find a stop sign in front of a traffic light. In these cases, the traffic light has arrived more recently on the scene and takes precedence over the older street sign. Why they don't remove the old signs is anyone's guess. But if the light is green, go for it. You'll also notice that traffic lights blink green before turning yellow. Unlike in the United States, there's no lapse time between a yellow-light-turned-red on one street and the granting of a green light on the other, opposing street. Keep this in mind before pulling the old "gold rush" through a yellow light.

If you drive a large vehicle, you might be surprised by the narrow size of parking spaces in parking lots, particularly those at shopping malls. Although there is a Hummer dealership in Guatemala City, I honestly can't see why anyone here would own one. Parking the darn thing would be a nightmare, not to mention driving it outside the city on narrow rural roads or paying about US$5 a gallon to fill its thirsty tank.

In rural areas, be aware of animals and cattle obstructing roads. Mountain roads can be very dangerous with many a blind curve and intercity buses with imprudent drivers at the wheel. It's best to drive within posted speed limits, which are sometimes enforced on major highways. While it's tempting to drive fast on straightaways in lowland areas like Petén and the coasts, you'll find obstructions such as fallen coconuts, sleeping dogs, pigs, chickens, and livestock often come out of nowhere. Swerving to miss an obstruction is the cause of many an accident when drivers are simply going too fast.

Perhaps one of the most annoying elements of driving on Guatemala's rural roads is that they often pass through small towns and villages, which never envisioned such high levels of traffic. Bypasses are few and far between, especially in the highlands. You'll often find yourself driving through the narrow streets of small towns trying to find your way back (or keep from losing it) to the main road leading out of town. A command of Spanish always helps, though it's often hard to get good directions from folks who don't drive and are therefore unaware of one-way streets and other particularities.

Road Signs

Major highways are generally well-marked, especially by Central American standards. The way to major tourist attractions is often marked by bright blue INGUAT signs, taking much of the guesswork out of trying to find a turnoff leading to your destination. Signs announcing scenic lookouts, for example, are depicted with white binoculars on a bright blue background. Another example is the turnoff to Lake Atitlán from the Pan-American Highway, which is marked with a blue INGUAT sign depicting a volcano and water.

© AL ARGUETA

DAILY LIFE

Watch out for wildlife when driving in Tikal National Park.

On major roads and highways, green road signs point the way. They look much as they do in the United States. Directional road signs sometimes hang over the road or highway but more often are smaller, rectangular, and found on the right side of the highway. On major highways such as the Interamericana, you'll see distance markers on the sides of the road. If you find yourself driving at night (not a good idea), you'll find that the road to Antigua and parts of the Interamericana are lined with reflective tabs along the center stripes and sides. These can also be especially helpful when driving at higher altitudes where low-lying afternoon clouds clinging to mountainsides tend to creep in and make driving all the more challenging. It's basically a thick fog.

Stranded cars sometimes carry reflective triangles, but it's more common to see a pile of tree branches announcing that danger lies just around the corner.

PRIME LIVING LOCATIONS

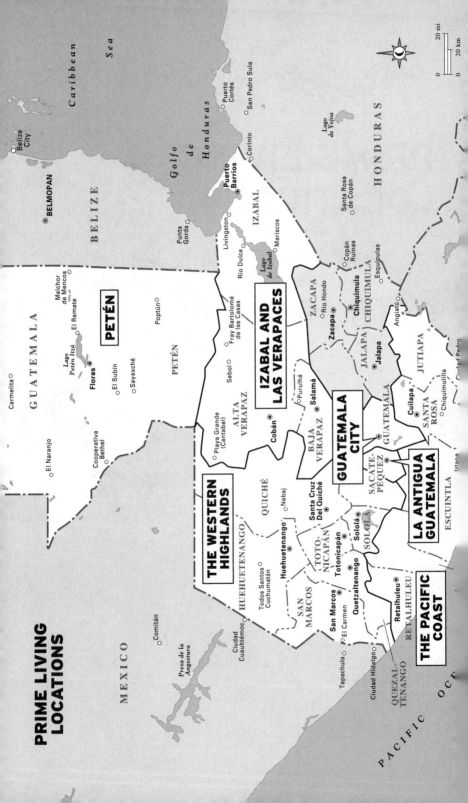

PRIME LIVING LOCATIONS

PETÉN

IZABAL AND LAS VERAPACES

THE WESTERN HIGHLANDS

GUATEMALA CITY

LA ANTIGUA GUATEMALA

THE PACIFIC COAST

OVERVIEW

The hardest part of your move to Guatemala may be deciding where you want to live. With so many wonderful attractions and decent weather almost everywhere, you'll probably find yourself needing to sit down and consider your numerous options. Certain locations are markedly more popular than others, and these have become traditional expat locales. There are certainly other options open to you depending on your personal preferences. While many foreigners live in colonial Antigua, some might prefer the sand and surf of the country's hot and humid coastal areas or the chilly mountain air of Quetzaltenango. There really is something for everyone here.

Strategically, it might make sense to start with the most popular expat havens and then explore less traditional locales. You might spend a few days in Guatemala City and Antigua or Lake Atitlán before heading off to the more remote reaches of pleasant Cobán or the Pacific coast beach town of Monterrico. Doing so will allow you to assess the greater level of comfort available in and around Guatemala City and balance that with infrastructure considerations in more rural settings.

GUATEMALA CITY

The largest city in Central America, Guatemala City has a long history of being overlooked by travelers, who tend to make a beeline to neighboring Antigua. If you're living in Guatemala for business or diplomatic reasons, you will most likely find yourself residing in "Guate," whether you like it or not. While some guidebooks talk about the place in disparaging terms, it is my sincere opinion that the country's capital has a lot to offer and is actually much more livable than any of the other Central American capitals. The way I see it, if you're going to live in a city, you might as well take advantage of all that urban life has to offer you. I find that in most of the other Central American capitals, the feeling of being in an urban area is just not quite there. San José and Managua, for example, feel like overgrown towns.

In addition to serving as the country's major transportation hub, Guatemala City is the country's economic and political center. Among its attractions are numerous recommended museums, vibrant nightlife, and a range of excellent dining and accommodations options. The downtown area is undergoing a promising restoration and is once again becoming a hip place to congregate. Closer to the airport, the Zona Viva is the place to go for nightlife, pleasant streetside cafés, and some of Latin America's finest restaurants.

If you prefer to have all the conveniences of a modern capital nearby but would rather live in greater tranquility, you will probably want to consider living in the suburban hillsides to the east of the capital. These areas are the Guatemala City equivalent of Beverly Hills, with luxurious homes, sweeping views of the urban area, and all the comforts afforded to the city's elite residents.

LA ANTIGUA GUATEMALA

One of the former capitals of Guatemala (there have been three besides the current capital), La Antigua, as it's more commonly known, is a UNESCO World Heritage Site. It features Guatemala's loveliest town plaza, graced by the elegant facade of the Catedral de Santiago and the former colonial-era government buildings. Antigua harbors the ruins of the third-largest Latin American colonial capital, after Mexico City and Lima, with its collection of convents, churches, and monasteries. Along the city's pleasant cobblestone streets, you'll find a sublime assortment of restaurants, accommodations, and shops housed in beautiful old houses dating to colonial times and painted in an array of bright colors. La Antigua is at once colonial and contemporary, which makes for many charming juxtapositions.

The city's numerous Spanish language schools have been beckoning travelers for years, and this is still one of the best places in Latin America to pick up the language. Enclosed in a valley by volcanoes and green mountains draped with coffee plantations, the city's surroundings are perfectly suited to outdoor activities including hiking, mountain biking, and touring farms and villages.

Not surprisingly, Antigua is one of Guatemala's most popular places for resident foreigners thanks to its near-perfect climate, stunning setting, and convenient location just 45 minutes from Guatemala City. It makes a more peaceful alternative to Guatemala City while still being close enough to all the capital's conveniences and the international airport. Homes range from original colonial-era constructions to more modern neocolonial homes, townhouses, and apartments. Adding to Antigua's allure is its large expat community, which helps ease the culture shock of moving to this exotic land.

THE WESTERN HIGHLANDS

The western highlands boast not only Central America's highest mountains and volcanoes, but also its most authentic and vibrant indigenous culture. Here you'll find colorful Mayan markets, quaint mountain villages, and gorgeous alpine scenery. Also in this region is spectacular Lake Atitlán. On its shores are three volcanoes and a dozen or so Mayan villages where you can take in the local culture or simply relax and unwind. The lake has been hosting foreign travelers and residents for decades. Each of the villages has its own unique feel, and they all cater to the whims of different residents, from those wanting to live on the cheap to those seeking lakeside luxury. Guatemalans have been in on Lake Atitlán's gorgeous real estate for quite some time, but foreigners are just now getting wind of this mountain paradise.

From a junction near Lake Atitlán, the Pan-American Highway continues west to Quetzaltenango. Also known as Xela, Quetzaltenango is Guatemala's second-largest city. It combines the feel of a Western European city with the serenity and crisp mountain air of the highland valley in which it lies. Like Antigua, Xela effortlessly combines Old World charm with New World cosmopolitan flair. It, too, has a growing expat community largely involved in humanitarian activities with numerous NGOs that have set up shop here.

THE PACIFIC COAST

Guatemala's Pacific coast has long been overlooked by travelers and would-be residents, though recent developments have begun reversing this trend. Only one hour from Guatemala City or Antigua by a fast, four-lane freeway, the tropical coast is easily accessible and a world away from the temperate highland valleys where Guatemala's current and former capitals lie. Lying closest to the capital is Puerto San José, a popular getaway for folks from the capital looking for some beach time. The crown jewel of Guatemala's Pacific coast is the residential community of Marina del Sur, with luxury homes befitting of Miami's finest subdivisions.

The port town of Iztapa, farther east, is home to Guatemala's nascent saifishing scene, with a number of operations geared toward this lucrative sport. Iztapa also has some pretty beaches and affordable beachfront real estate. A 26-kilometer road leads east from Iztapa to Monterrico, originally established as a sea turtle preserve and now Guatemala's most popular beach town, with a range of housing options. The real estate market along this Iztapa-Monterrico corridor has been heating up in recent years. West of Puerto San José, the sleepy village of Sipacate offers the coast's best surfing waves and is popular with surf enthusiasts. The rugged coastline continues west past the port of Champerico and on to the Mexican border.

In the western part of the Pacific lowlands, Retalhuleu has grown by leaps and bounds in recent years thanks to the construction of world-class amusement parks in its vicinity that are now Guatemala's top tourist attraction. It has always been a playground for wealthy ranchers and farmers and has decent hotel infrastructure. New real estate projects have made it increasingly appealing as a place to live amidst tropical breezes and swaying palm trees.

While Guatemala's Pacific coast lacks the crescent moon, white-sand beaches found farther south, it certainly has its charms. Much of it is covered by mangrove forests, and the sand here is dark brown and volcanic in origin. The beaches are very similar to the black-sand beaches found on Hawaii's Big Island.

IZABAL AND LAS VERAPACES

East of Guatemala City, the hot, arid, cactus-studded plains of the region known as El Oriente give way to the humid tropical flatlands of Guatemala's Caribbean coast. Its main port, Puerto Barrios, is not so much a tourist attraction but more of a gateway for adventures into the more remote reaches of the Guatemalan Caribbean coast. These include untamed Punta de Manabique, the seaside Garífuna town of Lívingston, and the Belize cayes.

Across the Bahía de Amatique fronting Puerto Barrios, Puerto Santo Tomás de Castilla will (according to plans) soon house a new cruise ship terminal. Day-trippers on cruise ships currently come ashore to enjoy the verdant Cerro San Gil rainforest and the waterfalls of Río Las Escobas. Traversing the forested mountain chain north of here, lovely Río Dulce connects Lake Izabal, the country's largest, with the Caribbean Sea. Río Dulce is also the name of the town at the lake's confluence with its namesake river. It's a popular destination with the sailing crowd and there are a number of marinas. Many of the luxurious homes of Guatemala's elite dot the shores of the river and adjacent tributaries.

The region collectively known as Las Verapaces comprises the departments of Alta and Baja Verapaz and is the green heartland of Guatemala. Here you'll find the country's best-preserved cloud forests in the Sierra de las Minas Biosphere Reserve. It's a good place to visit if you want a shot at glimpsing Guatemala's national bird, the resplendent quetzal. If you'd like to explore the cloud forests but aren't a hard-core naturalist, then the newly created Cloudforest Biological Corridor should suit you just fine. Including numerous jungle lodges and the Biotopo Mario Dary Rivera, the corridor runs along the road heading north from Guatemala City to the town of Cobán.

Cobán enjoys a pleasant mountain setting amidst green hills and coffee farms, making an excellent base for trips into northern Alta Verapaz. Cobán is easily one of Guatemala's most pleasant cities to live in, with a temperate climate, good services, and a pleasant provincial atmosphere. It has a long history of expat residency, as German coffee planters set up shop here in the early 20th century. Although most German families were kicked out of Guatemala during World War II (at U.S. insistence), you will still see plenty of German influence in the local architecture and in the faces of some of Cobán's residents. The city's small shopping mall is built in German style, as are many of the local homes and coffee farmhouses. The combination of European influence and lush mountain setting give Cobán some striking similarities to parts of Costa Rica.

Cobán also serves as a convenient gateway to the region's phenomenal natural attractions, including the spectacular limestone pools of Semuc Champey, white-water rafting on the Río Cahabón, the Mayan site of Cancuén, the impressive Candelaria caves, and splendid Laguna Lachuá. It makes an excellent place to live for outdoor enthusiasts or those looking to establish ecotourism operations. It is also considered one of Guatemala's safest regions.

PETÉN

Petén is to Guatemala what the Amazon rainforest is to Brazil. In this lowland jungle frontier, you'll find the remains of several Mayan cities, with new ones being discovered via satellite imagery almost yearly. The best-known Mayan site is Tikal, a must-see for anyone with even a casual interest in the Mayan civilization. In addition to the impressive temple pyramids, Tikal is a refuge for varied wildlife in the protected forests surrounding the ruins. These extend for several miles into the larger Maya Biosphere Reserve, with Tikal being just one of several parks encompassing this vast protected area. Another Mayan site of note is Yaxhá, made famous in *Survivor Guatemala*.

At the center of the department is the island city of Flores, on Lake Petén Itzá, a transportation and services hub that is part of a larger urban area encompassing the neighboring town of Santa Elena. Flores is the base of many NGOs working in Guatemala to protect Petén's endangered forests and wildlife. It is also home to an international airport and a shopping mall. Along with El Remate, found along the road to Tikal, it hosts most of Petén's foreign visitors and residents. Although Flores might sound rather modern given this description, it's actually a very sleepy traditional town. Its quiet streets are lined by pretty, pastel-colored houses, and many residents still pack up for the traditional noon siesta, mostly because of the stifling midday heat. Living conditions outside the semi-urbanized areas are very primitive, so if you've got a fair amount of gumption and the endurance to stick it out, Petén's forests and lakes make a great place to live a simpler life in a tropical environment.

El Remate has of late stolen some of Flores and Santa Elena's allure. Unlike Flores, it affords the opportunity to live right beside the lake, surrounded by forests unencumbered by the constraints of a small island. A number of expats have established lakeside eateries or small lodges here. You might soon join them.

On Petén's southeastern fringes is the small town of Poptún. Surrounded by pine forests and a karst landscape dotted with caves, rivers, and Mayan ruins, it lies at a much cooler elevation of 610 meters (2,000 feet) and is popular with travelers going overland to and from northern Petén. It has a number of good local lodges from which to explore the wonderful terrain.

GUATEMALA CITY

The nation's capital and largest city is a bustling urban agglomeration of four million inhabitants. At first glance Guatemala City, or "Guate," as it's more commonly called by locals, can seem overwhelmingly crowded, polluted, noisy, and downright dodgy. The same can be said of New York, however. It's all just a matter of getting acquainted with your surroundings and discovering the more pleasant aspects of life in this mountain city. Among these are a temperate spring-like climate, a splendid volcanic backdrop, excellent dining and entertainment options, and the opportunity to live in relative comfort with all the amenities of a First World city.

The newly remodeled La Aurora International Airport serves as a fitting gateway to Central America's most modern capital. Just minutes from this port of entry, you'll find most of the areas frequented by Guatemala's well-to-do and foreign residents. Scattered among forest-clad ravines and sprawling east into neighboring mountainsides are Guatemala City's business, retail, and residential sectors. The northern part of the city is home to its downtown core, which

© AL ARGUETA

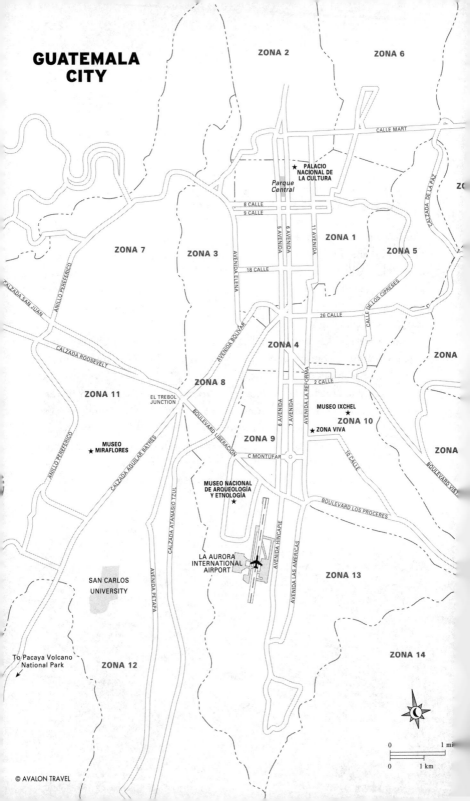

has unfortunately seen better days as a colonial capital but is also the ongoing focus of some much-needed gentrification. Tumbling out into surrounding ravines and plateaus in the vicinity of the downtown core are the city's slums, while its industrial sectors lie mostly to the south and west.

If you're in Guatemala on a business or political assignment, you'll probably find yourself living in Guatemala City. Although it's much maligned by first-time and short-term visitors, you'll find that it grows on you after a while. There are a number of very pleasant areas in this city and its outskirts; you just have to know where to look. As far as Latin American capitals go, you could certainly do worse. I actually find the other Central American capitals, including San José, Costa Rica, less livable. As the region's largest and most cosmopolitan city, it has a greater variety of living options suited to tastes, needs, and pocketbook.

The Lay of the Land

Guatemala City's sprawl occupies about 400 square kilometers, filling a large valley scarred by deep ravines (known locally as *barrancos*) and surrounded by mountains and volcanoes. Its terrain gives the city a patchwork kind of feel when viewed from the air, with parts of the city meandering fingerlike into the scarred landscape. The urban sprawl has also started migrating east and west into surrounding mountains. A large plateau atop the mountains

PRIME LIVING LOCATIONS

© AL ARGUETA

La Aurora International Airport is a fitting gateway to cosmopolitan Guatemala City.

THE VIBE IN GUATEMALA CITY

Your first glimpse of Guatemala City will most likely come from the window of an aircraft flying over the urban sprawl as it prepares to land at La Aurora International Airport. Guatemala City tends to feel huge when first seen from the air. It might also feel quite intimidating and downright scary, depending on whether or not people have told you horror stories about the city's crime or its pollution and noise. All of these are true, and certainly worth considering, but you've made it this far, so you should probably check things out for yourself and see it through your own eyes.

Guatemala City is in fact quite large. It is Central America's largest city, with an approximate metro area population approaching four million inhabitants. The capital lies spread out across a broad valley surrounded by mountains and volcanoes and crisscrossed by ravines. Its setting is really quite spectacular. The good news concerning the city's size is that you really have no reason to venture into more than about a third of the city's area. Much of the sprawl composing the sizable metro area is found outside the official city limits and is composed of Guatemalan working-class subdivisions, industrial parks, and slums. The nicer parts of town are also conveniently located adjacent to each other, in the eastern third of the city near the airport. The downtown core lies to the north of the city's newer sectors.

Perhaps most fascinating about Guatemala City are the constant juxtapositions evidencing this vibrant capital's status as a microcosm of Guatemala's larger wealth and class disparities. Tin-roofed shacks cling to forested hillsides just out of view from the wooden decks of US$500,000 homes. Buses trundle slowly down tree-lined boulevards while late-model BMWs zip by in the passing lane. Mayans from the highlands dressed in traditional garb wait for these buses under steel-and-glass bus stop shelters advertising French perfumes.

If you're coming from elsewhere

abutting the city to the east is traversed by the Carretera a El Salvador (Road to El Salvador) and is one of the fastest-growing suburban sectors. The surrounding landscape is accentuated by the presence of active Pacaya volcano, often visible at night, to the south. To the southwest, the cones of Agua, Fuego, and Acatenango volcanoes can be seen rising above the mountain separating Guatemala City from neighboring Antigua.

The city itself is divided into 21 zones, or *zonas*. Only a few of these hold any interest for the foreign visitor or resident. Zonas 1 and 2 encompass the downtown sector, with Zona 4 serving as a kind of transition zone between the original city core and newer business and residential sectors. Zona 10 harbors the homes of wealthy elite, high-rise condominiums, hotels, restaurants, nightclubs, banks, and embassies. Moving south and abutting the airport, Zona 14 is home to a large concentration of wealthy neighborhoods and high-rise condos. To the east and heading up the slopes of surrounding in Central America or have been there recently (especially San José and Managua), you may be surprised to find that locations here have actual street addresses as opposed to general directions the likes of, "two blocks north of the pink church across from the house with purple bougainvillea." Guatemala City also tends to feel more like a real city and not an overgrown town (sorry, San José), with actual buildings occupying a somewhat impressive portion of the urban sprawl. These buildings house condos, banks, hotels, and office buildings, giving the city a very modern feel. You'll see Guatemala's well-to-do frequenting the cafés, bars, restaurants, and hotels found in these sectors, along with travelers and foreign residents. Guatemalans love to be seen dining out in fine restaurants and shopping at exclusive stores for the latest fashions.

A darker side of Guatemala City's flashy displays of wealth is the shotgun-toting guards you'll find stationed outside of banks, gas stations, and fast food franchises. The congregating of suit-wearing bodyguards outside gyms, restaurants, and private schools would be downright comical were it not such a flagrant reminder of the specter of extortionary kidnapping. And then there's the barbed wire — lots of it — and iron bars adorning many of the city's houses, which lie bunkered away in cordoned-off neighborhoods guarded by access gates staffed by security personnel. It all takes some getting used to, but we're fairly adaptable as a species.

Good or bad, love it or hate it, Guatemala City is what it is. If it all gets to be too much, just head up into the hills east of the city and look at it from above. It seems a lot more peaceful that way, framed by low-lying clouds and its gorgeous volcanic backdrop. Spend a few minutes picking out your favorite locations and seeing how many different parts of the city you can identify. You'll feel a lot better, believe me.

PRIME LIVING LOCATIONS

mountainsides lie residential Zonas 15, 16, and Carretera a El Salvador. Several of the city's *zonas* are separated from each other by natural boundaries, such as forested *barrancos*.

CLIMATE

Foreigners are often surprised by Guatemala City's climate, as it can be much cooler here than its location at a tropical latitude might suggest. This is a product of its altitude at about 1,500 meters (5,000 feet) above sea level. Like the rest of Guatemala, the capital is prone to a variety of seasonal weather patterns. Although it's easy to divide the weather into rainy and dry seasons (as elsewhere in Central America), there are also some lesser-known subdivisions within these two major seasons.

That being said, the rainy season runs from May to October, with the dry season being from November to April. The beginning of the dry season between the months of November and February sees cooler temperatures and tends to feel a lot like a North American autumn. Skies are crisp and clear with daytime highs in the 60s and 70s. Sometime around March, things start to warm up and the air gets hazy. Daytime highs hover around the mid-to-upper 80s during March and April. This is what Guatemalans commonly refer to as *verano* and it coincides with the weeklong revelry known as Semana Santa (Holy Week), a sort of nationwide spring break. If you have allergies, be aware that the particulates during this dry, hot time of year can often reach unholy levels. Making matters worse are thermal inversions that often blanket the city in a thick haze. Guatemala City during March through May tends to look a lot like Los Angeles.

Sometime around the middle of May, the first rains arrive. It takes a few weeks for the parched hillsides to regain their verdant splendor, but they eventually do. The air also clears up as the constant rains begin to wash away atmospheric pollutants. The rainy season often consists of bright sunny mornings with warm temperatures that give way to afternoon thunderstorms lasting an hour or two. May to October is also the Atlantic hurricane season. While the mountainous terrain tends to deflect the full power of a hurricane often experienced in low-lying coastal regions, tropical storms often drench Guatemala's highland regions (and Guatemala City) with downpours lasting multiple days and resulting in flooding and mudslides. September and October tend to see the rainiest weather, with these fronts often keeping the skies over Guatemala City socked in for days. By the time things clear up again in November, you'll be begging to see the sun again.

Daily Living

Life in Guatemala City can tend to look a lot like life in a North American city. Make no mistake, however; it retains its own unique flavor. Along with nearby Antigua, Guatemala City has the largest population of foreign residents, though the city's size and sprawl make it easy for foreigners to feel like they're few and far between.

Perhaps one of the biggest things you'll need to get used to while living in the Guatemalan capital is the constant need for vigilance. It's a city very much on the move, and the potential for danger certainly exists. Carjackings, kidnappings, and the occasional street shootout are par for the course. In this regard, it bears striking similarities to Mexico City and even Los Angeles. This heightened sense of vigilance, it should be noted, does not apply exclusively to Guatemala City. The same can be said for living anywhere else in Guatemala, or Central America, for that matter.

HEALTH

Health care in Guatemala City is generally quite good. It boasts some of Central America's most modern health-care facilities, and many Guatemalan doctors are trained in the United States. Among the best local hospitals are Hospital Herrera Llerandi, Hospital Bella Aurora, and Hospital Centro Médico.

Lately, Guatemala City has become a destination for uninsured Americans traveling to receive medical treatment in state-of-the-art facilities at a fraction of U.S. prices. I personally have my dental work done in Guatemala City at the hands of a trusted dentist. Medications are widely available here and are often less expensive than in the United States. In most cases, you don't even need a prescription to pick up basic items such as antibiotics. Local pharmacists, for the most part, do a great job of providing information on drug side effects and prescribed dosages.

SCHOOLS

Wealthy Guatemalans send their children to one of the many top-notch private schools in and around the capital, as do most foreign residents. Particularly popular with Americans are the Colegio Maya and the American School. Tuition for private schools in Guatemala City can be quite high, starting at about US$6,500 per year for pre-kindergarten and rising to about US$10,000 per year for high school.

SHOPPING

You can find almost anything you might possibly want or need in Guatemala City. In addition to many modern shopping malls stocked with the latest fashions and electronics, there are a number of department stores for household appliances and cosmetics. For grocery shopping, the local giant is Paiz, which was recently taken over by Wal-Mart. You can shop in bulk and enjoy greater discounts at its Hiper Paiz mega-centers. U.S.-style warehouse shopping is available at PriceSmart, or a number of local chains. Guatemalans love U.S.-made goods, which is easy to see given their wide availability.

You can also save big money by purchasing your fruits and vegetables from the local farmers markets. The largest market is in downtown Guatemala City, though its distance from residential areas preferred by foreigners and the somewhat dangerous neighborhood might put off some foreign residents from shopping here.

If you'd rather have someone else cook your meal, there is no shortage of places to eat out. From ubiquitous fast-food joints like McDonald's and Burger King to slightly fancier places like T.G.I. Friday's and Applebee's, there is no shortage of restaurants to satiate your cravings for "gringo food."

Housing

Guatemala City differs greatly in terms of housing from most other Central American capitals, as a significant portion of its population lives in luxury high-rises. Zona 14 is often referred to as Guatemala City's "Little Manhattan." Many foreigners have chosen the safety and convenience (and fabulous volcano views) of life in a high-rise Guatemala City apartment. A recent building boom means these types of properties are plentiful and reasonably priced for rent or sale. Low-rise condominiums and town homes are fewer in number but still an option.

Guatemala's capital also has a variety of gorgeous colonial homes, particularly in Zona 10, and savvy buyers can often snap one of these up if their timing is impeccable. If you have the money, there are also spacious and newer properties available within the Guatemala City limits in Zonas 14, 15, and 16. Many of these are neo-colonial or American in style and are priced at levels comparable to U.S. cities. Some will prefer to live away from the city limits in the suburbs of the surrounding hillsides, where sizable plots of land are sold in subdivisions much like in the United States.

Adding to the mix of Guatemala City's housing offerings are some current projects following neo-urbanism trends that combine living areas with shopping and office facilities somewhat resembling a small town. These projects can be found in Zonas 10 and 16 and the southwestern suburb of Mixco. Neo-urbanism is a recent architectural trend involving a return to the simpler days when people lived, worked, and shopped in a relatively small area. It seems to be taking off in Guatemala, particularly with today's gas prices and ever-increasing traffic congestion.

Some less expensive housing options can be found in downtown Zona 1, where a number of lofts have been built. This is also the case in Zona 4, though safety conditions in both of these areas are markedly worse than parts of the city considered more livable by expats and Guatemalans alike.

Where to Live

Until the safety situation shows great improvement, the downtown area (Zonas 1 and 2) should best be avoided as an option for living in Guatemala City. Perhaps the ongoing restoration projects will help clean up the downtown's image and result in a much-needed economic revitalization. The Zona 4 area in the vicinity of the pedestrian thoroughfare known as 4 Grados Norte is fairly livable, though it is still not one of the areas most likely picked by foreign residents. It thus will not be discussed here in detail.

This leaves us with the areas of the city most often chosen by foreign residents, including Zonas 10, 14, 15, and 16. To the east of these areas in the surrounding mountains and adjoining plateau are Santa Catarina Pinula and San José Pinula, along the road known as Carretera a El Salvador. On Guatemala City's western fringes, along the road to Antigua, lies the more middle-class suburb of Mixco.

CITY NEIGHBORHOODS (*ZONAS*)
Zona 10

Zona 10 is Guatemala City's financial district, but there are also plenty of shopping malls, fancy restaurants, and museums. Nestled in between all these are several options for housing, including high-rise condos and some older, very elegant homes. The latter might prove more difficult to find, and if you really have your heart set on a home in Zona 10, it might require some patience. On the other hand, if you're looking to live in a Zona 10 condo, you can choose from a variety of different properties, including loft apartments, which have just recently made their appearance on the Guatemalan real estate scene. Although Zona 10 is the heart of Guatemala City's business and commercial district, it is bordered to the east by a ravine, which separates it from Zona

Zona 10 is Guatemala City's financial district.

© AL ARGUETA

GUATEMALA CITY'S HIGH-RISE CONDOS

One look at the Guatemala City skyline and the city's high-rise condominium construction boom becomes obvious. The reasons for the overwhelming demand for high-rise real estate are many, not the least of which are security considerations. There are few places where you'll be safer living in Guatemala City than up above the city's streets. Access to apartments is strictly controlled, parking lots are secure, and buildings are quake-resistant to ride out Guatemala's frequent tremors. Adding to the allure of a high-rise apartment are some incredible city and volcano views.

The fact that so many of these properties have been built so recently means many of them have all the comforts you would expect from life in a First World city. It also translates into a wide variety of price ranges, and you may be able to get a good deal if you have some negotiating prowess. Rental properties in high-rise condos are plentiful, as many wealthy Guatemalans purchase condos as an investment and then rent them out to foreigners.

When looking for a place to call home, there's certainly no substitute for looking around on your own. To get you started, I've sampled a few of Guatemala City's newer properties in a few parts of town and provided you with the basics.

LAS PILAS

Las Pilas is nearing completion and is located in Zona 15 at the top of Bulevar Vista Hermosa, overlooking the traffic circle that connects to Carretera a El Salvador. The materials used in the construction, including the finishing touches, were all of good quality and included granite countertops. Bedrooms are spacious, as are the kitchens. The building's location at the top of the hill translates into phenomenal views over the city and surrounding hillsides. If you have deep pockets, consider the penthouse apartment, priced at about US$700,000.

ORLEANS

About midway down Bulevar Vista Hermosa, Orleans is a smaller complex set in a quiet Zona 15 residential sector and has a more low-key feel to it. The apartments here are also quite spacious, and it feels very much like a middle-class U.S.-style apartment building. It may not have

15. This gives parts of Zona 10 a very suburban and slightly "out of the city" feel, particularly if you are fortunate enough to find a home or apartment bordering the ravine and looking out over this natural greenbelt.

Zona 10 is also home to Guatemala City's "Zona Viva," a nightlife and entertainment district located between 10a and 16 Calle (north to south) and Avenida La Reforma and 6a Avenida (west to east). On Friday and Saturday nights it can feel a lot like Austin's Sixth Street, with cars jamming the streets and revelers in droves enjoying a night on the town. This may or may not be to your liking, though if you're in a high-rise apartment you may hardly notice the noise down below.

Bordering Zona 10 to the west is Zona 9. Both zones lie separated from dramatic city views, but it certainly doesn't lack comfort or style. It's only about 10 stories high. A two-bedroom apartment here rents for about US$1,000 a month.

ATRIUM

This is my personal favorite of the Guatemala City high-rise condos I visited, mostly for its style and sophistication. The interiors feel spacious, modern, and luxurious. The building is also centrally located on a prime stretch of real estate along Zona 10's Diagonal 6. The complex is composed entirely of loft apartments, a concept which I understand was difficult to sell Guatemalan buyers on. It looks to have eventually caught on, as the building was almost completely sold when I visited. Another hard sell was the hefty price tag, with one-bedroom lofts starting at about US$225,000. You can also rent a one-bedroom unit for about US$1,600 a month. On the building's top level, there is a wonderful infinity-edge swimming pool looking out over the surrounding cityscape and mountains. It feels fabulously Los Angeles.

PLENUM 14

Nearing completion and well-located in Zona 14, Plenum 14 is another great condo option featuring modern facilities and some nice finishing touches, including hardwood floors and marble-floored bathrooms. It is also more affordably priced, starting at about US$147,000.

© AL ARGUETA

Atrium offers luxury loft apartment living.

each other by Avenida La Reforma, a wide, tree-lined boulevard devised early in the 20th century in emulation of French urban planning patterns. It is one of the city's busiest arteries, but also one of its most pleasant, complemented by many streetside cafés and monuments adorning the green grass of the wide central traffic divider. It has a very park-like feel. Many of the neighboring apartment buildings feature views of Avenida La Reforma.

The boulevard continues south, away from Monumento a Los Próceres, where it becomes Avenida de Las Americas. The latter separates Zonas 13 and 14. North of Zona 10 lies Zona 4.

The Zona 10 sector is especially popular with embassy staff. Among the most sought-after neighborhoods is Oakland, in a quieter part of Zona 10, where you will frequently find apartments and houses for sale or rent. Expect to pay about US$1,000 a month for an unfurnished two-bedroom apartment. Maintenance is often not included in the price and will cost about US$100 more. Tucked away into the forested hillsides heading east from the city are a number of very exclusive Zona 10 neighborhoods with houses in the US$500,000 range. It's Guatemala's answer to Beverly Hills. The views are wonderful and access is via gated-off roads that wind their way up the steep mountainsides.

Neo-urban tendencies whereby commercial, business, and residential facilities are combined into a single area resembling a self-contained town have also taken hold in Zona 10 with the recent construction of Fontabella Plaza, located at 12 Calle and 4a Avenida. The project involves a shopping mall with exclusive stores and restaurants in addition to a small residential area, all in Spanish colonial style.

Zona 14

Guatemala City's boom district, Zona 14 has grown by leaps and bounds in recent years thanks to a plethora of new condos and office buildings being built in this area. The sector's main feature is Avenida de Las Americas, which is really just a continuation of Zona 9/10's Avenida La Reforma and boasts the same sylvan landscaping interspersed with monuments to Columbus and other historical figures. At the end of this avenue is a steep drop-off and Plaza Berlin, from which there are good views of the city's southern sprawl

Zona 14 is one of the city's fastest-growing areas.

and Pacaya Volcano. Avenida Las Americas also parallels La Aurora Airport's runway 01-19. Branching off from the main artery are a number of side streets and residential areas. Two-story houses now share these streets with 20- and 30-story commercial and residential buildings.

Like Zona 10, Zona 14 also abuts a ravine. Using the isolation afforded by this natural boundary is the neighborhood known as La Cañada, one of the city's most exclusive. Prices for condos in Zona 14 vary greatly but are similar to those found in Zona 10 and start at about US$100,000.

Living in Zona 14 is very much an urban experience due to the dense concentration of high-rise condos. If that suits you, you'll have no trouble finding an apartment for sale or rent, as listings in real estate magazines and the newspaper classifieds are plentiful. According to a February 2009 report in Guatemalan daily *elPeriódico,* Zona 14 has the highest concentration of apartments in Guatemala City, with 798 units. Average prices for apartments in Zona 14 range US$1,200–1,350 per square meter. Apartments typically lease for US$700–1,200. An overabundance of apartments on offer, coupled with the world economic crisis, may mean significant savings for apartments in this sector.

Zonas 15 and 16

I have pleasant memories of the two years I lived in a Zona 15 home as a boy. From the bathroom, I could see the city below and watch planes flying in and out of the Guatemala City airport. From my bedroom, I had a view of a forested hillside and often awoke to the mooing of cows from a dairy farm across the ravine fronting our backyard. Much has changed in the 20 years since I lived in Zona 15, but the sector remains one of Guatemala City's nicest. Zona 15's dominating man-made feature is Boulevard Vista Hermosa, which runs uphill and southeast from Zona 10. On either side of the boulevard lies Colonia Vista Hermosa, an enclave of Guatemala City's well-to-do since the 1970s. The project is divided into three sub-sectors, and rental properties are abundant.

In recent years, the city's deteriorating safety conditions have made the streets of this quiet residential area prone to home break-ins, resulting in the cordoning off of entire blocks and the hiring of security personnel to monitor entrance to the individual neighborhoods. Realtors assure me the situation has improved in recent months with these measures, and it's now more common to see folks out walking the dog on the neighborhood streets. Much of Guatemala City can feel like an area under siege, and although Vista Hermosa has lost some of its early luster, it still makes a very suitable place to live.

Although once limited to one- and two-story houses, Vista Hermosa now boasts

© AL ARGUETA

There is still a lot of greenery in Guatemala City's Zona 16.

several high-rise condos of its own, with prices to match those of Zona 10 and 14. The city views from high-rises in Zona 15 are extraordinary, owing to the area's location in the foothills of the mountains lining the Guatemala City valley.

From Boulevard Vista Hermosa, a smaller road meanders its way up into a neighboring plateau and on to Zona 16. This is a much newer sector of the city and there are a number of projects being planned or executed here. Zona 16 feels very much like parts of Southern California, with wonderful city views, a fabulous golf course with adjoining residential areas, and the feeling that you're in the city but not engulfed by it. Adding to the allure of this sector is the presence of several private schools, including the American and Austrian schools, and two universities.

As for the caveats of living in Zona 16, keep in mind the access roads to this area are limited thanks to the city's fractured topography. Local residents often complain about the traffic and how long it takes them to get up and down the mountain to other parts of town. Here too the neo-urbanism model has taken hold, and a standout is the multi-phase Ciudad Cayalá. Created by a team of 10 Guatemalan and 23 foreign architects, the project has a construction timeline spanning the next 15 years and will encompass residential and commercial sectors spanning approximately 160 hectares (400 acres). Construction has already begun on the first phase, 44-hectare (108-acre) Paseo Cayalá, which will be built in the style of an old European city and encompass office buildings, houses, apartments, and lofts. The project abuts a substantial forest reserve, which developers say will be preserved intact.

SUBURBS
Carretera a El Salvador

From Boulevard Vista Hermosa, the road winds out of the city and up a mountainside heading southeast, eventually making its way to neighboring El Salvador. The first 35 kilometers or so of this Carretera a El Salvador are Guatemala City's suburb extraordinaire. After climbing up the mountains to the east of Guatemala City, the road eventually traverses a plateau, providing the perfect topographic conditions for the establishment of a virtual satellite city. The area around Carretera a El Salvador is also prime agricultural farmland. You'll find countless subdivisions springing up all over this fast-growing area, giving it all the feel of a U.S. suburb. The plateau lies at an altitude of about 2,135 meters (7,000 feet), so it's a bit cooler than Guatemala City and it also receives more rainfall during the rainy season.

Prices in this part of town vary greatly, as it's a fairly sizable area and there are homes of many different sizes. I've heard of three-bedroom condos that rent for US$500 a month, but also some that go for five times that amount. The sprawl in this area has grown to incorporate the once-sleepy towns of San José Pinula and Santa Catarina Pinula. Those familiar with San José, Costa Rica, might find this area very similar to the Escazú suburbs near that city.

Catering to the ever-increasing numbers of Guatemala City residents fleeing to the surrounding suburbs, the area has at least one sizable shopping mall in Pradera Concepción, which adjoins Condado Concepción shopping district. Between them, they boast a number of restaurants, PriceSmart warehouse

Alta Vista Golf Club lies east of the city in San José Pinula.

a luxury subdivision near Carretera a El Salvador

shopping, Wal-Mart, Sears, banks, car dealerships, and even an IMAX movie theater. The selection of goods in local supermarkets is more upscale (with prices to match), so a lot of folks looking for favorite import items do their shopping up here. This area is also home to two of Guatemala's most upscale golf courses and one of the city's finest hotels.

I have a cousin who lives in this area, and I have to admit, it can often be difficult to see her when I'm in town. The distance from the rest of Guatemala City is substantial and the self-contained nature of the area means she very rarely needs to go into the city proper. This may or may not suit your taste. Living out here provides the opportunity to enjoy surroundings very similar to what you'd find on the outskirts of a major U.S. city. Housing prices can also be quite similar to what you'll find in the United States, and the popularity of this area can be easily ascertained while perusing newspaper classifieds. This is Guatemala City's newest sector, so houses are typically more modern and incorporate aspects of urban planning such as landscaping and surrounding greenery that Americans hold dear and won't be found in many other parts of concrete-heavy Guatemala City.

Traffic here can be a bit of a problem. Although the road is a four-lane highway, it is the sole access road between the plateau and the city. Add to that heavy truck traffic and commercial vehicles heading to and from El Salvador and it's easy to see why traffic has reached a point of saturation. Then again, you don't really need to leave the area unless you work in the city, and traffic gridlock is endemic to Guatemala City's poorly planned urban infrastructure throughout the metro area. There's really no escaping it.

Mixco

Yet another option for those wishing to be out of the city limits is the south-western suburb of Mixco. While not as luxurious or sylvan as Carretera a El Salvador, it nonetheless makes a suitable place to live. It's also on the way out of town toward La Antigua, so if you find yourself visiting the old colonial capital frequently, then this might work to your advantage. Mixco was once a separate city, but it has been all but engulfed by Guatemala City in recent years. The traffic and urban planning here are somewhat chaotic and the area is most easily accessed from Guatemala City by both Calzada Roosevelt and Boulevard San Cristóbal. The latter serves as the access road for San Cristóbal, one of Mixco's larger and best-known neighborhoods, with a variety of construction phases and price ranges in accordance.

Guatemala City's original, failed ring road project harks back to the 1970s and is known as El Periférico. It also provides access to parts of Mixco, including a recently unveiled neo-urbanistic project known as Condado Naranjo. Like similar projects elsewhere in the city, it encompasses stores, offices, and some rather smallish homes in Spanish neo-colonial style. Prices for houses range from US$105,000 to US$168,000, while apartments go for anywhere between US$60,000 to US$120,000.

Getting Around

Guatemala City is no stranger to traffic gridlock. An ever-increasing population purchasing an ever-increasing number of cars, coupled with a historical lack of city planning, has put the Guatemalan capital's road network on the verge of collapse. Not all is lost, however, as city planners have recently come up with a few bright ideas including the construction of a Guatemala City ring road and the beginnings of a mass transit system for the city's large commuter population. The ring road project will allow heavy truck traffic to altogether bypass the city when driving between the country's Caribbean and Pacific ports.

The urban sprawl is best navigated by car, as the current public transportation system composed of old buses painted bright red has become dangerous to ride on and is not recommended. Gang members often board buses and demand "taxes" from drivers in exchange for a measure of freedom from ongoing harassment. Armed robberies of passengers are also common. As many Guatemala City residents now carry guns, would-be robbers are sometimes foiled on the scene, but not before an ensuing gun battle, often claiming the lives of innocent bystanders.

PRIME LIVING LOCATIONS

Most foreign residents end up buying their own cars or riding taxis, but if you find yourself living on the southern outskirts or along Calzada Aguilar Batres, the new Transmetro transport system might be just the ticket for you. It offers a much safer alternative to public buses but is in its infancy and therefore offers a limited coverage area.

Driving in Guatemala City can be quite chaotic and you'll find Guatemalan drivers very aggressive. It takes some getting used to. Just follow along and know that it's all part of the process of adapting to your new environment.

In addition, various nuances make navigating Guatemala City's streets all the more interesting. While road signs are available to guide you, the traffic patterns that dictate how to get anywhere are often complicated. You may find yourself missing your exit a few times if you're not in the correct lane. As always, practice makes perfect. In some places, you may see contradicting traffic signals, such as a stop sign and a traffic light at the same intersection.

STAYING SAFE IN GUATEMALA CITY

Guatemala City can be a dodgy place, though certain *zonas* are certainly more prone to crime than others. Most of the areas frequented by tourists are relatively safe, though the downtown area (Zona 1) is by far the country's purse-snatching and pickpocketing hub. Exercise common sense and caution when in public areas. Riding public buses is not usually a good idea, though the newly unveiled transit system, the Transmetro, has proven much safer. Pay careful attention when using ATMs. Some thieves have been so ingenious as to set up fake keypads at the entrance to ATM kiosks asking cardholders to enter their PIN numbers in order to gain access to the machine. You should never enter your PIN number anywhere other than on the ATM keypad itself.

It's a good idea to drive around with locked doors and windows rolled all the way up. (Make sure your car's air-conditioning system is working properly so as to avoid the temptation to roll down the windows when it gets hot out.) Avoid talking on a cell phone while driving. It will keep you alert to your surroundings and will not draw undue attention from potential thieves. Cell phones are a favorite target. Do not wear flashy jewelry. Recently, some parts of the city have become prone to robberies whereby the perpetrators (usually on motorcycles) target cars stopped at traffic lights. In most cases, the victims have been talking on their cell phones or are women traveling alone and wearing expensive jewelry. For this reason, many Guatemalans tint their windows to keep prying eyes away from the contents of their car. If you are the victim of a robbery or witness one, dial 110 from any phone.

You should never leave valuables in a parked car. Avoid flashing expensive items such as laptops and cell phones in public places.

Watch out for a common scam,

In this case the traffic light takes priority, so a green light with a stop sign at the intersection means keep on keeping on. The stop sign is usually just a leftover from a time before the traffic light was installed.

TAXI

Getting around by taxi can be tricky, as it's best not to hail cabs off the street the way you would in any other city. Gypsy cabs are common and robberies do sometimes occur. There is really only one reliable taxicab company in Guatemala City and it requires you to call for a pickup if you wish to hire its services. It can be inconvenient for first-time visitors, but if you're living in Guatemala City, you will most likely have a cell phone to use for this purpose. Taxis Amarillo Express (tel. 2332-1515) is also one of the only companies to use meters. Otherwise, the airport taxis and those at the Zona Viva hotels are generally reliable.

particularly in the vicinity of the airport, whereby a "Good Samaritan" informs you of a flat tire on your car. If that is indeed the case, pull over in a well-lit, public place, if you can, but do not stop in the middle of the road to change the tire. They may try to carjack you. If you are able to make it to a public place such as a gas station, have someone in your party stay inside the car or keep an eye on it yourself while you have someone change the tire for you (it's common for gas station attendants to change tires in Guatemala). The important thing is not to lose sight of the inside of your vehicle for a moment. Believe me when I tell you, thieves can be extremely crafty at distracting you and getting into your car while you take care of the urgent business at hand. Locked doors may be a deterrent but are not going to stop the thieves at this point if they've targeted you. For information on other precautions and common scams to watch out for while traveling in Guatemala, see the State Department's Consular Information Sheet online at http://travel.state.gov/travel/cis_pa_tw/cis/cis_1129.html.

In November 2008, the U.S. Embassy issued safety warnings for certain Guatemalan roads. Among the areas mentioned was the road east of kilometer 13 of Carretera a El Salvador. Due to its popularity with the city's wealthy residents, it appears this sector has become the scene of several violent robberies, carjackings, and kidnappings. The embassy recommends avoiding travel beyond kilometer 13 between 9 P.M. and 6 A.M. The document also recommends avoiding travel on the following roads outside Guatemala City: Routes 4 and 11 in the vicinity of Lake Atitlán and Route 14 between Antigua and Escuintla.

For this and other pertinent information, visit http://guatemala.usembassy.gov/warden_information.html.

looking east toward Carretera a El Salvador

TRANSMETRO

The newly unveiled Transmetro offers a glimmer of hope for Guatemala City's public transportation system and is expected to be fully in operation by 2020. The first phase, including the first transfer center (in Zona 12) for out-of-city buses coming in from other parts of Guatemala, opened in February 2007. The Transmetro consists of long, train-like interconnected green bus units that bring travelers from the transfer center to the downtown area via Calzada Aguilar Batres. The buses follow a path along the central part of the artery and do not intermingle with street traffic.

More transfer centers are currently in the works, with the transfer center for buses coming in from eastern parts of the country currently under construction. The next Transmetro route to be constructed will follow the length of Calzada Roosevelt and provide access between the city and its Mixco suburb to the west. Another route will head south from downtown along 6a Avenida all the way to the airport.

The system promises to provide Guatemala City residents with a safe, comfortable, and fast option for getting around the city. Buses stop only at designated locations, bus drivers will no longer trundle the streets competing for passengers, and the prepaid system eliminates on-board cash. Transmetro buses and stations are guarded by cameras and plainclothes police officers, making it a very safe system to ride. It seems a good idea, in theory at least, though opponents believe Guatemala City's substantial population requires more drastic measures. Alternative proposals call for an underground subway system or one in which train cars travel along elevated paths over crowded city streets. Some believe the Transmetro will be obsolete before it's even completed.

METRO

Guatemala City's sheer size and dense population, along with the diversity of its terrain, make it a very good candidate for a subway system. Residents and authorities have talked about this possibility for years, but in July 2008 Vice President Espada visited Santo Domingo to study the city's subway system and get a feel for the execution of such a grand project. Early reports claim the Colom administration might be planning to build the project before it hands power over to the next administration in 2012.

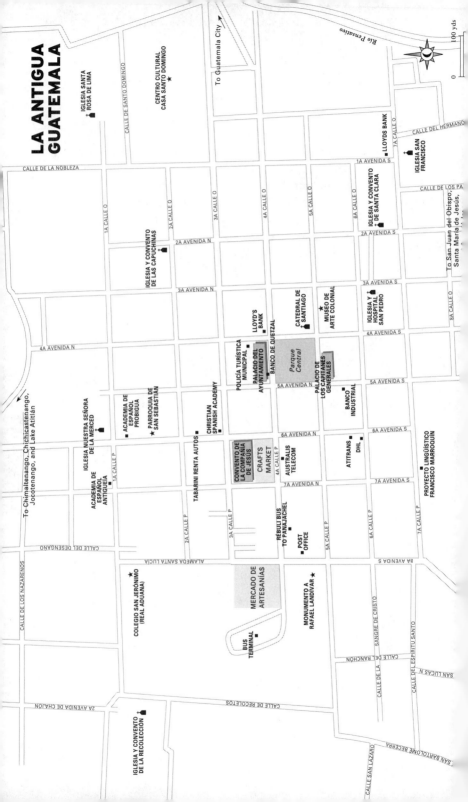

LA ANTIGUA GUATEMALA

La Antigua Guatemala is Guatemala's former colonial capital, destroyed by earthquakes in 1773. Better known simply as "Antigua," it is Guatemala's premiere expat destination for reasons that become obvious when you first set foot in this pleasant valley surrounded by coffee-studded mountains and smoking volcanoes. Just a 40-minute drive from Guatemala City's international airport, La Antigua is a world away from the Guatemalan capital. It's comparatively quiet, colonial, paved with cobblestones, and downright charming. Many expatriates live behind the walls of Antigua's bougainvillea-clad, pastel-colored colonial homes, and those seeking a community of mostly English-speaking fellow travelers, artists, and international adventurers will soon find themselves feeling right at home.

In Antigua, it's possible to live in a delightfully antique colonial home in splendid Spanish style or in more modern constructions built in neocolonial style. The small-town atmosphere can be easily balanced with the more rural elements of life in the surrounding hills and villages or tempered with periodic

© AL ARGUETA

trips to nearby Guatemala City for supplies or a dose of the 21st century. After a few days in Antigua, it's easy to feel swept away to another continent. It's a lot like being magically transported across time and space to a Spanish town in the 1700s.

HISTORY

The former capital of Guatemala, now known as Ciudad Vieja, was built on the slopes of Agua volcano and was the first of Guatemala's capitals to suffer merciless destruction at the hands of nature. An earthquake on the evening of September 10, 1541, unleashed a torrent of mud and water that came tumbling down the volcano's slopes and destroyed the city. The new Muy Leal y Muy Noble Ciudad de Santiago de los Caballeros de Goathemala, as it would officially come to be known, was established on March 10, 1543, in the Panchoy Valley. The new capital would be no stranger to the ravages of nature, its first earthquake being endured by its inhabitants only 20 years after the city's founding.

An earthquake in 1717 spurred an unprecedented building boom, with the city reaching its peak in the mid-18th century. At that time, its population would number around 60,000. Antigua was the capital of the Audiencia de Guatemala, under the jurisdiction of the larger Viceroyalty of New Spain, encompassing most of present-day Mexico and all of Central America as far south as Costa Rica. The Viceroyalty's capital was in Mexico City, which, along with Lima, Peru, would be the only other New World cities exceeding Antigua's political, cultural, and economic importance. Antigua boasted Central America's first printing press and one of the hemisphere's first universities and was known as an important center of arts and education. Among its outstanding citizens were conquistador and historian Bernal Díaz del Castillo, Franciscan friar and Indian rights advocate Bartolomé de las Casas, bishop Francisco Marroquín, artist Tomás de Merlo, English priest/traveler Thomas Gage, and architect Juan Bautista Antonelli.

Antigua's prominence came crashing down in 1773. The city was rocked throughout most of the year by a series of earthquakes that later came to be known as the Terremotos de Santa Marta. Two earthquakes occurred on July 29. The final blows would be delivered on September 7 and December 13. The capital city was officially moved the following year to its present location in modern-day Guatemala City. Basically, the whole town up and left and moved to present-day Guatemala City, where a new capital was established.

Antigua lay in ruins occupied mainly by squatters, its monuments pillaged for building materials for the new capital. It wasn't until the mid-19th

© AL ARGUETA

Agua volcano lies south of La Antigua.

century that it became once again populated and its buildings restored, in part with the money from the region's newfound coffee wealth. The city was declared a national monument in 1944 and came under the protection of the National Council for the Protection of Antigua Guatemala in 1969. It was declared a UNESCO World Heritage Site in 1979. The council has done a fairly decent job at protecting and restoring the city's cultural and architectural heritage, though building code violations are not at all unheard of. Still, many power lines have gone underground and truck traffic has been effectively banned from the city's streets, greatly reducing noise pollution.

The Lay of the Land

Antigua lies at an altitude just over 1,500 meters, in a valley separated by a mountain from the larger valley occupied by Guatemala City. Its setting is truly spectacular, flanked to the south by the sentinel cone of 3,750-meter Agua volcano, and to the southwest by twin-cratered, 4,235-meter Acatenango and active Fuego volcanoes. The surrounding hillsides are planted largely in coffee and offer excellent opportunities for recreational pursuits such as hiking and mountain biking. Although the area feels landlocked, Guatemala's Pacific coast is little more than an hour away via a good paved road skirting the western slopes of Agua volcano. The city's colonial monuments and museums, along with a lively arts scene, provide excellent sources of cultural entertainment.

Arco de Santa Catalina is an example of La Antigua's colonial architecture.

ORIENTATION

Getting around Antigua is fairly straightforward. True to its colonial foundations, it was laid out in a grid pattern surrounding the central plaza with *calles* running east–west and *avenidas* running north–south. The plaza is bounded by 4a Calle and 5a Calle to the north and south, and 4a Avenida and 5a Avenida to the east and west. Street addresses are labeled according to their direction relative to the plaza: *norte* (north), *oriente* (east), *sur* (south) and *poniente* (west). Most streets are known by this method, though all have names dating back to colonial times. Only a handful of streets are known solely in this manner.

CLIMATE

Antigua's climate is remarkably similar to that of Guatemala City, which is easy to ascertain given their proximity to one another. There are distinct dry and rainy seasons and temperatures tend to be just a little bit cooler in light of Antigua's slightly higher elevation. Daytime highs are generally in the low 70s for the cooler months of November through February and in the mid-80s for the warmer months of March through May. June through October see high humidity levels with daytime highs typically in the high 70s or low 80s. During the rainy season (May–October), it generally rains for an hour or two in the afternoon or evening, though it can sometimes rain for days on end at any time during the aptly-named rainy season. During the height of the dry season in March and April, expect Antigua's surrounding mountains and volcanoes to be veiled by thick haze from dust and agricultural burning.

CULTURE

The local cast of characters here is most certainly interesting and you'll likely have a great time navigating Antigua's human landscape. There are the folks who have been here for years and can tell you all about Antigua before everyone came in and "ruined" it, and there are also those who are more recent arrivals in town and are just glad to have found this little cultural oasis tucked in between Guatemala's volcanoes. Then there are the locals, who have adapted to the influx of gringo travelers and residents, all while holding fast to their traditions. Antigua is in many ways a microcosm for variables that have been set in motion throughout Guatemala in the aftermath of its civil war, as parts of the country are exposed to outside influences and globalization. Personally, I find Antigua to be a fascinating mix of local culture and outside influences.

Perhaps my favorite thing about Antigua is the fact that it feels a world away from anything in the United States. Beyond its quaint atmosphere, charming colonial architecture, and cobblestone streets, it's reassuring to know that just 30 minutes away over the next mountain is a cosmopolitan world capital. Should I need my fix of Dr. Pepper and warehouse shopping (not typical), I can easily drive to Guatemala City. You may find that after spending a few weeks in Antigua, much of the rest of the world feels downright ugly and over-industrialized.

Daily Living

Antigua is easily one of the most rewarding places to live in all of Latin America. In addition to it spectacular natural setting, pleasant spring-like climate, and splendid colonial atmosphere, it offers a relatively sophisticated lifestyle in close proximity to all the comforts and conveniences afforded by Guatemala City. It's also a rather progressive city, which nonetheless vehemently protects its valuable historical heritage. In February 2009, Antigua became Central America's first "digital city" by providing free Wi-Fi Internet access within a 1.5-kilometer-radius of the town's central square. In short, Antigua is a world away from the hustle and noise of Guatemala City yet literally lies just over the next mountain.

Because of Antigua's popularity with expats and its status as a hub for Spanish schools, English is widely spoken. This can be a double-edged sword if you're earnestly trying to learn Spanish, but it can certainly be a source of comfort and camaraderie during your initial time in Guatemala, when you're trying to get comfortable with the local culture. Local English-language magazines and

EXPAT PROFILE:
JOHN REXER AND MIKE TALLON

As the story goes, a few years ago John Rexer and Mike Tallon, formerly of New York City, were flying down a moonlit dirt road in the back of a pickup truck somewhere near the Guatemala-Mexico border surrounded by bottles of booze. The moon was high in the gloriously clear desert sky. And so was the driver. A deranged Mexican *mezcalera*, she had spent the day sampling product with her *norteamericano* business associates, who were now being flung about like grinning rag dolls.

The truck rounded a curve much too fast and the driver yanked the steering wheel violently to compensate. In the bed of the truck, John and Mike slid across the metal and smashed into a few crates of Ilegal Mezcal, the high-quality booze John has been importing into Guatemala from Mexico and then exporting to the United States and Europe. Mike turned to his friend and said, "We're both in our 40s. We both had sort-of-successful careers in New York City. We're both pretty smart guys. . . ." John finished Mike's thought adding, "And now we're barreling down a dirt road in Mexico, heading for the border and hoping we make it home alive." "Yup," Mike responded. "I don't know about you, but it feels like I've finally done something right with my life."

John first came to Guatemala about six years ago after deciding to escape the New York rat race and 9/11 memories. In early 2002 he started traveling through Mexico and Central America while writing a novel. But by the time he'd gotten to Antigua, his cash supply had dwindled to nonexistence and he realized that his two choices were sucking up the pain and heading back to America for a "real job," or risking what little he had left on starting a business in a foreign country. The result of that risk, half a decade later, is Café No Sé, the best bar in Antigua and the epicenter of several other quixotic business ventures.

One of those businesses is Ilegal Mezcal. Since backpacking through southern Mexico twenty years ago John has had an ongoing love affair with *mezcal*, a drink similar to tequila but with a much richer taste and history. "Most people north of Juárez don't know a thing about *mezcal*. They think it's tequila with a worm in it. With Ilegal we want to educate people up north as to what *mezcal* is really all about. It's kind of a messianic mission – to bring traditional *mezcal* from the beautiful little villages of Oaxaca, Mexico, to a global market. The most important thing is that people learn that this is not just a delicious and potent drink, but a cultural history being poured from a bottle into their glass. If they miss this, then they really have not experienced *mezcal*."

Another business that grew from

© NORA HILLEN

John Rexer, left, and Mike Tallon, right

Café No Sé is *La Cuadra* magazine. John started *La Cuadra* a few years back, after a number of conversations with his friend and Mexican pickup partner, Michael Tallon. Mike, a former high school teacher in Brooklyn, was on a year-long trip through Central America back in 2004 when, "A series of inexplicable events turned my life into a Benny Hill-credits-rolling, kazoo-orchestra chase scene. Long story, I'll tell you some other time. I knew I didn't want to head back north, but I also knew I needed a place to land for a while. That turned out to be Café No Sé in Antigua."

Soon after arriving in town he began bartending at the café and plotting with John to launch a progressive, satirical, and political magazine for the English-speaking audience of Guatemala – and ultimately, all of Central America. He is now co-publisher with John and the editor-in-chief of the rag.

He explains the reasons for starting the magazine in Guatemala: "Both John and I are drinkers with writing problems, as Brendan Behan would say, but up in New York there's no outlet. The costs of starting up a magazine are prohibitive, and trying to get a magazine, other than, maybe, the *Utica Area Journal of Progressive Hayseeds*, to print previously unpublished writers is next to impossible. So we figured, screw it, let's make our own magazine – one that keeps its tongue firmly in its cheek, its middle finger in the air, and its arms open to writers with talent and an interesting story to tell. If you're in Antigua, swing by Café No Sé. We'll have a drink and trade some more stories."

John's advice for others thinking of taking the expat route and starting a business: Always remember you are a guest in someone else's country. Remember why you left. Laugh a lot and have patience. *Things are not going to go according to plan* – and that's the fun of it.

Mike says, "write what you think, then raise a glass and never look back."

Thanks to John Rexer and
Michael Tallon

PRIME LIVING LOCATIONS

restaurant bulletin boards can point you in the direction of religious services offered in English and even AA meetings in your native tongue.

HEALTH

Antigua has a few serviceable hospitals but its proximity to Guatemala City's excellent health-care options makes the latter the most viable option for medical treatment. Local English-language publications such as *Revue* can point you in the direction of Antigua-based English-speaking doctors and even mental health practitioners.

SCHOOLS

Antigua, in terms of its expat population, tends to cater mostly to retirees and young independent travelers. Expat families with school-aged children will most likely find the search for suitable schooling somewhat frustrating. Again, the proximity of Guatemala City and its substantial educational offerings will mean families with children may end up needing to live in Guatemala City or commute to school from Antigua.

If you're in Antigua to learn Spanish, then you're certainly in luck. There are close to 100 language schools packed into this small city. The hardest thing about language school in Antigua is settling on which one to go to.

SHOPPING

Antigua is a mecca for traditional Guatemalan handicrafts, with a number of outdoor markets. Its central market contains an area exclusively for the sale of handicrafts, in addition to extensive offerings of flowers, fruits, and vegetables. There's really nothing quite like getting a big bag of oranges for US$5 and taking it home to squeeze your own fresh, homemade orange juice. There are some small grocery stores in the area for basic sundries.

Antigua offers a number of fancy handicraft, jewelry, and clothing shops and is home to several excellent wrought-iron workshops. Wicker and wooden furniture are local specialties as well.

For modern household appliances, electronics, and all your First World needs, you'll most likely need to go to Guatemala City. The closest supermarkets and shopping malls are less than 30 minutes away in the western Guatemala City suburb of Mixco.

Housing

Let's face it: Antigua's overwhelming popularity with Americans and Europeans means it is not the place to go shopping for a real estate bargain in Guatemala, as that ship has already sailed. That being said, if you have deep pockets and just have to get your hands on a piece of Antigua's much sought-after real estate, then welcome to one of Central America's hottest markets.

Strict building codes designed to protect Antigua's status as a UNESCO World Heritage Site dictate the types of buildings (and the materials used) within city confines. At the same time, it is precisely Antigua's colonial charm that draws so many people here, so it's almost unthinkable that anyone would want to build something not in sync with the town's colonial vibe. Still, they've tried, and it's certainly a good thing these laws are in place and vehemently enforced.

Colonial homes tend to be large, typically around 300 square meters (3,200 square feet), and built around breezy interior courtyards. Many of these homes will have already been owned by savvy expats who got in on the market early in the game. The advantage to these more expensive properties is that plumbing and electrical wiring have often been brought up to standards expected by a former resident of the First World. Older colonial homes in the hands of non-expats may not always have the most aesthetically pleasing renovations performed on them in the years leading up to your purchase. The plumbing and wiring may need some upgrades, but these properties are usually less expensive.

More recently, Antigua has seen a surge of neocolonial style housing developments catering mostly to Guatemala City elite looking for a second home. These gated communities are good in that they make provisions for the country's security situation and are a particularly convenient option for retirees. Housing developments often include a community swimming pool and clubhouse, and because building restrictions are less stringent, you can build a two-story house (unlike in central Antigua).

Some analysts believe the abundant supply of these properties will result in significant price decreases in the coming years. At the same time, they've been saying that about Guatemala City's condo market for a long time and the bottom still hasn't dropped out. As long as Guatemala's rich keep getting richer, which I don't foresee changing anytime soon, market prices will probably hold. Another factor is the increasing presence of foreigners, who will most certainly continue buying property here.

Finding a real estate agency to work with here is easy, and many international

A CONVERSATION WITH ANTIGUA REALTOR BRIAN WILSON

I sat down with Antigua realtor Brian Wilson, president of Century 21 Casa Nova Real Estate, to get the scoop on Antigua's booming real estate market.

Antigua is obviously Guatemala's hottest real estate market, but what are some of the country's other real estate investment opportunities and what makes them attractive?
The Río Dulce area is attractive for people who like boating and fishing. A few new high-end hotels are being built for weekend visitors from the capital and international tourism. Ecotourism is starting to catch on throughout Guatemala, and Petén seems to be attracting some investment in this regard as well.

Going back to Antigua, what specifically attracts real estate investors?
Great appreciation in real estate prices, the fact that it's a beautiful historic city, proximity to services such as health, an international airport, and shopping. It's also a good market for rental property. Re-sales are very quick, so liquidity is not a big problem.

What are some of the hottest projects going on in Antigua and throughout Guatemala right now?
Close to Antigua, in neighboring Alotenango, La Reunión Antigua Golf Resort has been created around a Pete Dye-designed 18-hole PGA-rated golf course. The site offers golf course lots with a prestigious clubhouse and pro shop. The purchasers can develop their own unique housing designs. There is a big project in the Lake Atitlán area geared to foreign and local investors, complete with helipad facilities and large recreation areas. On the Pacific coast, several new developments are in place catering to foreigners interested in deep-sea fishing, such as Marina del Sur in the Puerto San José area, which is 45 minutes from Guatemala City and Antigua.

It's no secret that the vast majority of Americans looking to purchase property abroad come to Central America in search of sun, sand, and surf. These haven't traditionally been Guatemala's strongest offerings. How do you see Guatemala competing with its Central American neighbors in terms of its attractiveness to would-be real estate investors? What are its distinct advantages? Is there a market for the sand and surf crowd in Guatemala?
The climate is the big selling feature here. Temperatures are ideal! Guatemala is really Central America's undiscovered jewel, though many people mistakenly think of the country as a backward "banana republic." This is soon dispelled once people spend a few weeks touring the country.

Sadly, the tourism office has a very limited budget for promoting the country abroad, so the news doesn't get out to potential investors or tourists, unlike Costa Rica. Guatemala has tremendous cultural offerings thanks to its Mayan legacy. The other Central American countries are, in my opinion, little more than an extension of East L.A.; there is no distinct culture to speak of.

There are beaches here, but the sand is volcanic so they're not the typical white-sand beaches most visitors normally picture. The market here is for sport fishing, big business, and world-class resorts.

In the years you've been in business, what are some of the more recent trends you've noticed concerning foreigners' interest in acquiring property in Guatemala?

The main comments we receive concern the current U.S. political situation, plus the high cost of living and taxes. A lot of people are moving here because they can afford to live a comfortable lifestyle for 70 percent less than they are spending at home.

What are some of the unique challenges of investing in Guatemala? What should potential buyers be aware of?

Investors looking to build residential or commercial properties should be aware of numerous restrictions in the Antigua area. There are strict guidelines that need to be followed to ensure that anything being built adheres to architectural standards imposed by Antigua's cultural preservation laws. Finding available land to develop isn't an easy task, either. Many landowners don't want to sell.

Anyone buying property needs to have a reputable lawyer review all pertinent documents to be sure that the property is properly represented. Don't deal with people who are not part of the real estate chamber, as they may have a vested interest in selling the property they are representing.

What services does Century 21 Casa Nova Real Estate perform for foreign investors interested in Guatemala, and what kinds of issues/ problems are you set up to solve?

In a nutshell, we do it all. We have several people in place to handle any situation that may arise so that the investor can dictate his or her wishes and we can perform the required functions to make it work.

Are Americans buying property in Guatemala mostly as second homes, or are you seeing an increase in people buying business property as well?

It's a 50/50 split as far as second homes go. Buyers who are still employed are buying second homes here, while retirees have increasingly become permanent residents. We haven't seen any real volume in terms of business buyers due to the high cost of land or existing buildings in areas that make the best business investments.

I recently read a story in a U.S. travel magazine about an investor who purchased property for cacao cultivation in the region of the Verapaces. Are American investors getting in on the local commodities markets such as coffee and cardamom (traditionally dominated by Guatemala's elite)?

Much of this activity pertains to programs of NGOs. Cacao is being reintroduced in several areas of Guatemala due to the high quality of the product, with NGOs setting up fair trade deals to help local farmers. Cattle and exotic fruits have also shown good growth. Guatemala is a great country for specialty farming, as land in agricultural areas can be quite inexpensive.

What is your favorite Guatemalan coffee?

Sorry, but I don't drink coffee.

PRIME LIVING LOCATIONS

names, including Century 21 (Casa Nova Real Estate) and Re/Max, have a presence in Antigua.

RENTAL APARTMENTS

Apartments for rent are plentiful in Antigua, though it's best to book far in advance of your intended stay for the best deals. Apartments in the downtown core are more expensive than in outlying areas. Many foreigners have the mistaken notion that a US$300 a month apartment in Antigua is like one that costs double anywhere else. This is simply not true and you'll find that, much like anywhere else, you get what you pay for. Sure, you can find US$300-a-month apartments for rent, but they may not provide the level of comfort your North American tastes are used to. That being said, Guatemala certainly tends to attract a Bohemian crowd, and it seems there will always be a market for no-frills rentals. Just be sure that is what you really want before signing that lease.

Where to Live

For colonial gems, the best place to look is in the city center. Of course, these homes tend to be more expensive. The farther out you go from the downtown core, the less expensive things tend to get. Many Antigua-area residents choose to live outside the city core in one of the surrounding towns and villages, where housing prices are substantially more affordable. Each scenario has its own advantages and disadvantages.

You'll notice building styles change as you leave Antigua's central core and head into adjacent towns and villages. Tile roofs often give way to more economically accessible corrugated tin roofs and concrete block construction. It's a good idea to spend some time studying the various neighborhoods within Antigua and checking out the surrounding towns. While many of them are more affordable, they will often lack the colonial charm that makes Antigua proper so enticing.

CENTRAL LA ANTIGUA

Should you want to be close to the action, your best bet is to live in Central Antigua. Despite the city's popularity, you can still find rentals for fairly decent prices. A one-bedroom apartment typically costs between US$400 and US$550 a month. The main issue here is availability, so you'll need to plan far in advance in order to get the best rates and even have a chance of finding

LA ANTIGUA'S NEW GOLF RESORT

Antigua now has its very own golf resort thanks to forward-thinking Guatemalan investors willing to plunk down US$80 million to provide Antigua with something its world-class offerings once lacked. Opened in 2008, La Reunión Antigua Golf Resort lies 17 kilometers from Antigua in neighboring Alotenango on the road to the Pacific coast. The setting of the 70-hectare (173-acre), Pete Dye-designed 18-hole golf course is truly spectacular, flanked by Agua, Fuego, Acatenango, and Pacaya volcanoes and lush green fields. An existing 30-room boutique hotel will soon be joined by a 100-room hotel to be managed by an international hotel chain. Originally home to a 560-hectare (1,382-acre) coffee farm, the project will eventually encompass a spa, church, convention center, commercial area, equestrian center, and a forest area for canopy zipline tours, and rappelling.

In addition to the golf resort, the extensive property will also serve as an exclusive community. In its first phase, already 500 lots with 450 villas have been sold to wealthy Guatemalan families. A second phase will involve the sale of 20 exclusive villas for foreign investors. Prices range US$400,000–600,000, and the villas come totally equipped and furnished.

The golf resort's creators are also very much concerned for the well-being of surrounding communities. A percentage of the hotel's gross sales and the sale of villas will go to local community development projects. For more on the project, check out the website at http://www.lareunion.com.gt.

something in town for a reasonable price. A recent look at rental properties revealed many properties to choose from but few that were available for move-in within six months of my search. A decent, basic two-bedroom home or apartment starts at about US$650 a month, but if you're looking for something in a gated community with amenities such as a garage and laundry room, you're probably looking at paying closer to US$1,100 a month.

If you're looking to buy, prices are still relatively modest compared to elsewhere in Central America and very modest by U.S. standards. I recently looked at a gorgeous, brand-new, 230-square-meter (2,500-square-foot), three-bedroom neocolonial home that was going for US$265,000.

Central Antigua is certainly not as quiet as it used to be. Buses trundle from the central market heading out to Guatemala City and many other highland towns. On weekends, the children of Guatemala City's elite like to come party at Antigua's hopping bar scene. Still, during the week it feels very relaxed.

AROUND LA ANTIGUA

Abutting Antigua's central core are a number of smaller towns and neighborhoods, some of which merge seamlessly with the colonial city. Many of these neighboring towns are popular locations for neocolonial housing developments.

Jocotenango lies just northwest of Antigua and was actually a city *barrio* until the early 19th century, when it became a municipality of the Sacatepequez department. It has a few colonial residences that may be upgraded to the 21st century if you know where to look and have the patience (and money) to invest in some heavy remodeling. There are also some newer gated communities here. One drawback of living in Jocotenango is the heavy bus and truck traffic that passes through town on the way out to Chimaltenango and the Carretera Interamericana.

Antigua Gardens is one of the area's newest subdivisions.

Just southeast of Antigua is Santa Ana, which also merges with the city core. It feels a lot quieter than central Antigua or Jocotenango. New three-bedroom houses in the vicinity of 200 square meters sell for US$150,000–200,000 or rent for US$650–700 a month.

Heading southwest from Antigua is the former colonial capital of Ciudad Vieja. While the town itself is nothing to write home about, there are a number of luxurious gated communities in its vicinity. One of the nicest gated communities I've looked at is Hacienda San Jerónimo. It's only four kilometers from Central Antigua on the road to Ciudad Vieja and nestled among tall trees and coffee farms with splendid views of Agua volcano. Colonial courtyards with fountains and cobblestone streets complete the Old World feel. Prices are in the vicinity of US$250,000. Along this same road, which continues to the Pacific coast town of Escuintla, is the town of Alotenango. It's home to Antigua's first golf resort, with its own gated community, and a neighboring subdivision known as Antigua Gardens.

If you're interested in checking out housing options for rent or purchase, I highly recommend Casa Nova Real Estate (www.century21casanova.com). The company website features an interactive map of the Antigua area, along with neighboring villages and neighborhoods. You can click on the particular area you're interested in and see properties for sale or rent.

If living in a gated community just isn't your style, you might want to look in some of the more rural outlying towns such as San Miguel Dueñas and San Pedro Las Huertas, where there are rural lots for sale surrounded by agricultural fields and little in the way of planned development communities. My advice to you is to rent a car for a week and explore all the outlying towns and villages in order to get a feel for the unique geography of each (volcano views vary, for instance) and see what best suits your tastes.

Getting Around

Antigua is a very walking-friendly city, and many of its residents living within the city confines tend to forgo car ownership unless they make frequent trips outside of town. You can walk from one end of town to the other in about 30 minutes. *Tuk tuks,* or motorized rickshaws, make getting around very easy and inexpensive within short distances. Taxis are also readily available for longer trips to nearby towns or Guatemala City. Buses heading to a variety of highland destinations convene at the city's bus terminal, on the west side of town. A number of car rental agencies also have offices here. Be aware that parking can be limited on Antigua's streets, some of which are closed off to vehicles during the weekends, when Guatemala City residents flock here to party.

The quaintest option for getting around is traditional horse-drawn carriages, which feel right at home on Antigua's cobblestone streets. These are strictly a sightseeing venture, but it may make for a fun time, nonetheless, and give you a feel for the Antigua of centuries past.

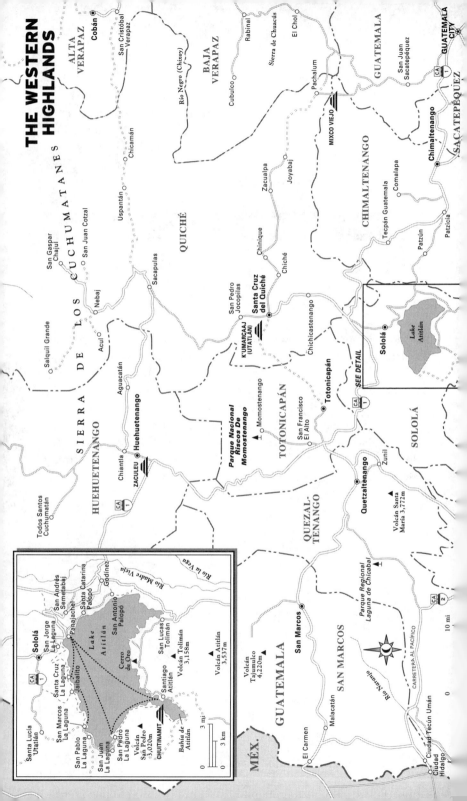

THE WESTERN HIGHLANDS

The western highlands are much of what make Guatemala unique. While other Central American countries also offer tropical beaches, swaying palm trees, and sunny skies, nowhere else in the region do cultural wealth and scenic beauty meld into the very fabric of everyday life quite like they do in the mountains of western Guatemala. Dotted by hamlets and agricultural fields, mountain lakes, volcanoes, chilly plateaus, and pine forests, the highlands are a region still recovering from Guatemala's civil war and trying to arise from the endemic poverty largely responsible for the conflict. Still, visitors continue to flock here, and more and more foreigners, particularly in the area around Lake Atitlán, have started calling this region home. While wealthy Guatemalans have been buying property on the shores of Lake Atitlán for many years, foreigners started dropping in during the hippie days of the 1960s. The lake and its shoreline villages still tend to attract a rather eclectic mix of wanderers and New Age enthusiasts, but it has more recently become the haunt of journalists, well-known novelists, and North American retirees.

GUATEMALA: FAST-FORWARD

For decades, intrepid travelers have come to Guatemala to experience this mythical pocket paradise: a compact, diverse nation in the middle of the Americas with 33 volcanoes, Lake Atitlán, "the most beautiful lake in the world" [according to both Aldous Huxley and D.H. Lawrence], steamy jungles, ancient Mayan temples, and colorful indigenous villages.

The volcanoes are still here; the lake is still here; much of the steamy jungles are still here, with their enigmatic ancient Mayan temples. However, the villages of Guatemala's highlands are experiencing a major transition thanks to remittance money sent back from Guatemalans working in the United States.

White-washed adobe houses with terra-cotta tile roofs are being exchanged for concrete-block walls and corrugated tin roofs. Electricity, indoor plumbing, rebar, satellite dishes, asphalt, and concrete are just some of the newcomers to these villages.

In one of my favorite, rather remote highland villages, Chajul, young women in traditional regalia blithely sip Coca-Cola and chat on cell phones in Ixil Mayan. Boys play soccer in the street wearing Beckham jerseys, Yankees baseball caps, calling to each other in Ixil, Spanish, and English. In Sololá, speakers broadcast evangelical radio shows that compete with hip-hop and rap coming from the local fruit market. It appears that more people own pickup trucks, cell phones, and televisions than toilets.

Why the dramatic change? Guatemala welcomes US$3.5 billion annually from the Guatemalan workforce living in the United States. Thanks to these greenbacks, traditional, often indigenous communities are on fast-forward, hurtling into a brave new modern world. All this has happened in the past few years, and perhaps because of the distance between what was and what has become, the results can be overwhelming: sometimes wonderful, sometimes painful, often humorous, and always interesting for the traveler, especially to those who are students of human nature.

Enrique V. Iglesias (former longtime president of the Inter-American Development Bank) lauds the direct and democratic attributes of remittances. However, witnessing remittances in action, I do not find it always pretty what they are doing to village life in Guatemala. It sounds so good on paper: Courageous Guatemalans enter the US, work hard, send money home, and

For the more altruistic crowd, the highlands offer a fascinating venue for opportunities to work in the promotion of social justice, a fact which quickly becomes evident from the number of NGOs working in and around Quetzaltenango. Whether you're looking to return to a simpler state of being surrounded by natural beauty or lend a helping hand, the highlands are among Guatemala's most attractive regions to settle down in.

Guatemala's volcanic chain forms the spine of the rugged highlands, though nonvolcanic mountain chains, most notably the glaciated peaks of the 3,800-meter Cuchumatanes mountains, also give this region its topography. The help to sustain their country – direct, democratic, family-to-family. However, early stage capitalism produces the most voracious consumers, and with limited leadership, law enforcement, zoning, education, or planning, these new dollars create new consumers who are left to learn as they go.

Yet, as travelers today, count your anthropological blessings – you get to be voyeurs on a whirling dervish of change and culture clash. While it is not always beautiful or charming, if you are from the developed "first" world, it is strangely fascinating and perhaps even important to see.

I have interviewed Guatemalans living in the United States who say (some with great relish, some with dejected nostalgia) that they no longer recognize their villages. They tell me that the families they left (to better support by working in the United States) have used their hard-earned cash to transform the highlands into something new. But few know just what that is.

The signs of progress are everywhere: a proud grandma's adobe house is now a three-story concrete house faced in shiny tile and paned with reflective glass. Old-time swimming holes have become water parks. Pagan shrines and ritual have diminished as evangelicals reweave the religious fabric and build Christian churches in these communities. A pickup truck is much easier to carry products with than a forehead tumpline but one notices expanded waistlines. Televisions provide a window to the war in Iraq, China's environmental issues, American pop culture, giraffes in Kenya.... Women do not spend hours hand spinning wool blankets anymore; the ones arriving from China are much cheaper and just about as warm.

One of the great Guatemala travelers explains it to me this way: "The Guatemala I met 20 years ago was a slow, enchanting melody. Guatemala today is the same melody, it is now just being played on fast forward."

After living in and writing about Central America for almost 10 years, I still encourage travelers to go to the Guatemala highland villages: look, explore, listen, absorb. No longer for their simple charms, but as a fascinating window into the fast-changing lives and vernacular of Central America.

Contributed by
Catherine Docter, writer and
consultant, contributing editor,
Departures magazine,
Antigua, Guatemala.

Cuchumatanes are home to a vast highland plain covered largely in grasses posing similarities to the Peruvian Andes. The city of Quetzaltenango partially occupies one of the highlands' largest valleys. A few of the region's volcanoes are active, including Santiaguito, Fuego, and Pacaya.

CLIMATE

The climate here is temperate and, in many places, downright chilly. Quetzaltenango frequently sees freezing temperatures between December and February, the coldest months. The highest volcanic peaks in this region, nearly 4,000 meters, are sometimes coated with a light dusting of snow or ice. During the summer months, temperatures tend to get a bit warmer, though a damp chill often sets in following the afternoon rains. The southern shore of Lake Atitlán tends to get more rain than the northern shore, thanks to warm, humid air that rises and cools as it hits the volcanoes on the lake's southern flanks.

Quetzaltenango (Xela)

Guatemala's second-largest city once rivaled Guatemala City for political and economic wealth until an earthquake and a volcanic eruption in 1902 curtailed its emerging power and secessionist dreams. Today it remains a strong center of regional identity. Quetzaltenango is also a strong contender in Guatemala's Spanish-language school market, second only to Antigua, and is a regional hub for various NGOs working with highland Maya communities in the aftermath of the country's civil war. You'll find a well-established and ever-increasing expat community in this urban area of roughly half a million inhabitants. Better known as Xelajú, or simply "Xela," Quetzaltenango offers many of the cosmopolitan aspects of life in larger cities but retains a markedly provincial atmosphere.

THE LAY OF THE LAND

Nestled in a broad valley dominated by the cone of Santa María volcano and her spawn, active Santiaguito, Xela lies surrounded by agricultural fields rich in volcanic nutrients. Xela is the main population center of the country's K'iche' Maya and sits at a rather high altitude of 2,300 meters. It can be correspondingly chilly. Xela has a rather cosmopolitan feel to it and can feel similar to a highland European city. It is considerably safe for a city of its size and has a lively cultural scene peppered by the ever-increasing presence of foreign visitors and residents. There are good local restaurants, along with ubiquitous American casual dining franchises, and interesting day trips to neighboring highland Mayan villages that still adhere strictly to the old ways. Nearby natural attractions include a wonderful crater lake, climbs to the surrounding volcanoes, and soaking in warm hot springs. If you really start to long for the warmer climates, the sweltering Pacific coastal lowlands are just about an hour away, and beaches lie not much farther.

Quetzaltenango lies a few kilometers south of the Cuatro Caminos junction, found along the Pan-American Highway. Its Zona 1 downtown core houses most of its important monuments, as well as the bulk of its tourist services and

© AL ARGUETA

Xela's Parque Centroamérica

is laid out in the standard grid pattern. *Avenidas* run roughly north–south and *calles* run east–west. Zona 2 covers an area to the northeast, while Zona 3 sprawls to the north and northwest.

Like the rest of Guatemala's important urban centers, Xela is built around a central park. The city's sprawling Parque Centroamérica is lined with government offices, museums, and a shopping arcade, among other buildings, and is itself splendidly shaded by trees and adorned by neoclassical monuments and flower beds. Its decidedly European feel is enhanced by the presence of several Greek columns, and it makes a fine place for people-watching or enjoying the warm afternoon sun amidst the surrounding buzz of activity. An artisans' market is held here the first Sunday of every month.

At the western end of the park, between 12 and 13 Avenidas, is Pasaje Enríquez, a pedestrian thoroughfare and commercial arcade originally built to house fine shops but now home to several good bars and restaurants. One of these is on the second floor, from which there are wonderful views of the plaza below.

On the eastern end of the park is the original facade of Iglesia Catedral del Espíritu Santo, which dates to 1535 and was constructed by Bishop Francisco Marroquín. The facade is all that remains of the original church, as a new church was erected behind it in 1899 and was almost entirely destroyed in the earthquake of 1902. The current cathedral building is the latest reconstruction. The neighboring Municipalidad (City Hall) was likewise reconstructed after the 1902 earthquake in grand neoclassical style.

Outside the City Center (Zona 3)

The legacy of maniacal dictator Manuel Estrada Cabrera's quest to emulate all things European, the neoclassical Templo Minerva is a monument to the Greek goddess of wisdom. It stands at the corner of Calle Minerva and Calle Rodolfo Robles. The temple looks over the city's bus terminal and busy market.

Farther along, in Parque Minerva proper is the Parque Zoológico Minerva, where there's an unimpressive collection of animals housed in cages. Buses to this part of town leave from Pasaje Enríquez at 13 Avenida and 4a Calle Zona 1.

Formerly the Zona Militar 1715, the old building that once served as the train terminal for the defunct Ferrocarril de los Altos was slated to be the new home of the museum dedicated to its memory. It should be quite nice, if a similar museum in Guatemala City is any indicator. It's now known as the Centro de Desarrollo Intercultural y Deportivo de Quetzaltenango, and there are plans for several other museums to open here in the coming years. Already housed in this complex is the Museo Ixkik' del Traje Indígena, housing a collection of indigenous costumes.

HISTORY

Quetzaltenango was originally a Mam-speaking Mayan town prior to coming under the influence of the K'iche'-speaking Maya of K'umarcaaj during their 14th-century expansionist wars. K'iche' leader Tecún Umán was defeated by Spanish conquistador Pedro de Alvarado in 1524 at a site known as Llano del Pinal, southwest of town at the base of Santa María volcano. The town became quite prosperous during the 19th-century coffee boom. Its newfound prosperity coupled with the abatement of Spanish power in the aftermath of independence to create strong separatist sentiments shared with highland areas to the west. Guatemala City would bring the renegade region back into the fold in the latter part of the century, though Quetzaltenango remains a strong focal point for regional identity.

Like other Guatemalan population centers, it is no stranger to earthquakes, having been rocked by an earthquake and a volcanic eruption courtesy of Santa María volcano in 1902. It was subsequently rebuilt, largely in neoclassical style. Its strategic location at a crossroads for trade and transport between the highlands and agriculturally rich Pacific slope have continued to ensure the city's prosperity despite any setbacks along the way. A regional railway once connected Xela to the Pacific slope, but natural disasters and political manipulation from Guatemala City made the railway, known as the Ferrocarril de los Altos, extremely short-lived.

DAILY LIVING

Xela is very similar to Antigua in terms of basic living conditions. While Xela is not outright colonial in style, it has a certain Old World feel and charm to it. It is also similar to Antigua in its strong expat presence and the popularity of language schools. Quetzaltenango has some very modern aspects to it as well, and in this way is a bit of a hybrid between Guatemala City and Antigua.

Health

Xela's pharmacies are generally well-stocked, owing to its importance as Guatemala's second-largest city. There are a variety of health-care practitioners throughout town, many with overseas training. The city's best hospital is Hospital Privado Quetzaltenango, though there is also a public hospital. For traveler's diarrhea, you may want to take a stool sample and have it analyzed at a local laboratory to find out the specific bug causing the problem and implement the proper treatment plan. Tom at Xelapages.com recommends Laboratorio Aguilar, on Calle Rodolfo Robles, a half block from the Galgos bus station.

Schools

Much like Antigua, Xela caters mostly to independent travelers, so expats with families including small children may be hard-pressed to find adequate schooling. There are a number of private schools in Quetzaltenango, many with religious affiliations, but none that offer the quality of education found in Guatemala City's private schools. If you're an independent traveler looking to study Spanish while in Xela, you'll have no trouble finding a Spanish school.

Shopping

As a local trading and services hub, Quetzaltenango has a fair amount of products on offer. Local markets are stocked with an abundance of fruits and vegetables, and there are several large supermarkets in and around town. Although local handicrafts are nowhere near as abundant or sophisticated as those found in Antigua or even Panajachel, they are available.

Xela also has at least two shopping malls, located on Avenida Las Americas. The best of these is Pradera Xela. U.S. casual dining chains such as Pizza Hut, Chili's, and Applebee's are in the vicinity.

WHERE TO LIVE
Downtown

Xela's downtown sector is home to many older colonial homes. Much like in Antigua, you'll find many of these homes and apartments are available for rent by locals who have owned the properties over several years. Local websites such as Xelawho.com and Xelapages.com are the best way to get wind of properties for sale or rent. As always, word of mouth works too.

PRIME LIVING LOCATIONS

You'll find many older colonial homes in Quetzaltenango, as well as a few that have been upgraded with modern amenities. Xela has yet to catch up to Guatemala City in terms of high-rise condos, so you won't find this option available. Zona 3, in and around the zoo and Pradera Xela mall, has some well-located middle-class neighborhoods with more modern homes. A one-bedroom apartment with kitchen and bath typically rents for about US$400 a month.

When searching for an apartment or home, keep in mind Xela is downright cold at night and mornings during much of the year. You will most likely need a space heater and may even want to install carpeting, which is virtually unseen elsewhere in Guatemala.

Outlying Suburbs

Much like Guatemala City, Xela has grown by leaps and bounds in recent years, though it still lacks true suburban sprawl in the traditional sense. The surrounding towns and villages occupying this huge valley have grown along with Quetzaltenango and serve as residential areas for many people working in the city. Most affluent *quetzaltecos* have farms and/or homes in rural areas outside of the city, but planned communities have only recently started to spring up on the outskirts of town. Among the most impressive projects are Xela Gardens, just off the road heading to the Pacific Coast, and Nueva Ciudad de Los Altos, a huge planned community about four kilometers northwest of town. The latter has its own boulevard leading to and through the project and is another neo-urban concept encompassing shops, residential areas, and recreation as a stand-alone community. It also has some nice views of the city below. This might be the place to look if you plan on staying in Xela long-term. Prices for plots average about US$75,000, depending, of course, on the size of the lot.

GETTING AROUND

Getting around Xela is relatively easy. Minibuses leave from Zona 3's Minerva bus terminal heading to the city center at the south side of 4a Calle. You can also catch downtown minibuses at the Rotonda (traffic circle) on Calle Independencia. City buses make their rounds around town along fixed routes. There are plenty of taxis throughout the city, and there's a taxi stand at the north end of Parque Centroamérica. Bike rentals are also locally available if that's your preferred method of transportation.

Lake Atitlán

Lake Atitlán has been attracting wanderers for centuries. Among its most famous advocates was writer Aldous Huxley, who wrote glowing reviews of the mountain lake during his travels through Central America, declaring it "The most beautiful lake in the world." Today's resident journalists include former CNN correspondent Harris Whitbeck and author Joyce Maynard, to name just a few. Although Huxley's opinion of Lake Atitlán has been quoted countless times, it bears repeating, as words cannot begin to describe the magic felt when seeing the lake for the first time, its waters shimmering in the afternoon light. Picture Italy's Lake Como, only with volcanoes and quaint Mayan villages.

The villages on the shores of this peaceful lake harbor fascinating Mayan culture intermingled with the influences of more recently arrived expatriate residents. Each of the towns on the lake shore has a different vibe and feel, so it's worth exploring all of the major towns to see which one best suits your particular personality. The towns on the northern shore of the lake all feature panoramic views of the three volcanoes to the south, but if you want to get up-close and personal with these dormant volcanic peaks your best bets are the towns of San Pedro and Santiago Atitlán, built on their very slopes.

Lake Atitlán enjoys a delightful spring-like climate thanks to its elevation at about 1,500 meters. Its somewhat chilly waters are deep and mysterious, while plant and bird life on its shores are abundant. Its origins can be traced back

© AL ARGUETA

Guatemala's spectacular Lake Atitlán and its three volcanoes some 85,000 years to a volcanic eruption that created the collapsed caldera that the lake now fills, also spreading ash over a thousand-mile radius. The lake was created when drainage to the Pacific Ocean was blocked following the emergence of the more recent Tolimán and Atitlán volcanoes. It covers 125 square kilometers, being 30 kilometers long and 10 kilometers wide. Its maximum depth is over 320 meters, though the 1976 earthquake that rocked much of Guatemala may have opened a drainage point somewhere, as the water level has been gradually declining ever since. A third volcano, San Pedro, is somewhat lower than the other two but still offers a challenging climb on a path straight up its slopes.

Atitlán earns high marks from retirees seeking a slower pace of life and an escape from frenetic lives lived in North American or European cities. It is one of the best places in Guatemala to enjoy unspoiled nature and spectacular scenery. Its potential as a world-class expat retirement community has barely begun to be exploited.

Local Dialects

Guatemala's status as a pluricultural and multilingual country is very much in evidence at Lake Atitlán, which is practically split in two along ethnic and linguistic lines distinguishing its modern-day Mayan inhabitants. Villagers on the south side of the lake, including those living in San Lucas Tolimán, San Pablo La Laguna, San Juan La Laguna, San Pedro, and Santiago Atitlán, speak Tz'utujil. Speakers of Kaqchikel include the inhabitants of north shore villages such as San Antonio and Santa Catarina Palopá, Panajachel, Sololá, Santa Cruz, and San Marcos.

Property Restrictions

Ownership and use of lakeside property is governed by OCRET, a government office charged with the protection of state lands. Technically, Lake Atitlán is a protected area. OCRET laws stipulate that outright ownership of lakeside plots is forbidden in favor of a renewable 20- or 30-year-lease. Exceptions to this law include properties that were titled before 1956. Among these is the San Lucas Tolimán-area subdivision known as Yacht Club Atitlán, situated on land originally owned by a wealthy Guatemalan family with a pre-existing land title.

THE LAY OF THE LAND

The south side of the Lake Atitlán basin is dotted with three conical volcanoes: Tolimán, Atitlán, and San Pedro. Beyond the volcanoes is the Pacific coastal plain, with its coffee and cotton plantations. Warm, moist air blows in from the ocean and rises on the slopes of the volcanoes, making the area almost perpetually rainy. Due to the rugged, mountainous landscape, temperatures in the Lake Atitlán basin, as elsewhere in the highlands, can get downright chilly during the winter months of December through January.

Most of the Atitlán basin's prime real estate is found on the northern shores of the lake, owing to the simple fact that the villages located there enjoy the best views of the volcanoes on the lake's southern shore. Of the main tourist settlements, only San Pedro La Laguna and Santiago Atitlán are on the southern shore, clinging to the fringes of their namesake volcanoes.

DAILY LIVING

Living in the vicinity of Lake Atitlán means getting back to the basics in some ways. Although there is no shortage of luxury homes built on its shores, it is still very much a rural area where people go to get away from it all. This may change in the next few years as more and more expats buy property here, but for now it remains, for the most part, pleasantly provincial.

Prices for property in the Lake Atitlán basin vary widely. You can rent a place for as little as US$350, or as much as US$3,200, per month. Lake Atitlán has long been the haunt of wealthy Guatemalans, many of whom rent out their luxurious villas on a weekly or monthly basis. At the same time, Atitlán has attracted many folks from North America looking to embrace a simpler life. They have, accordingly, built many simpler homes. The end result is a wide array of housing types on offer, with prices in accordance.

Health

The larger towns, and in particular Panajachel, are relatively well-stocked with medications. A number of health-care providers can be found in Panajachel, and there is at least one reputable medical clinic for emergencies, though it is advisable to seek medical attention for more serious conditions at a hospital either in Guatemala City or Quetzaltenango.

Schools

Again, the region tends to cater to independent travelers, so the best schools will be found in Guatemala City. This not withstanding, a search on the U.S. Embassy in Guatemala's web page revealed the existence of at least one private school in the Lake Atitlán area. Located in Panajachel, the Robert Muller LIFE School is a bilingual international school established in 1989. It offers instruction from pre-Kinder to middle school.

As elsewhere in Guatemala, Spanish schools are popular in the Lake Atit-lán region. Virtually all of the villages catering to foreign visitors and expats have at least one language school.

Shopping

As the lake's most cosmopolitan town, Panajachel has at least one grocery store stocked with the imported products expats seem to prefer. All of the surrounding towns and villages have local markets stocked with produce and local items for sale. Small *tiendas* (grocery stores) also provide many daily necessities. Panajachel is a major center for handicraft exports, and you'll find no shortage of these items on display throughout town. There are not, as of yet, any shopping malls in this region, though some basic electronics can be purchased in Panajachel.

WHERE TO LIVE
Panajachel

The lake's main tourist town has always been Panajachel. It was once a requisite stop along the "Gringo Trail" (as it was known in the 1960s), the path of American and European backpackers making their way down to South America. There are incredible views across the lake from "Pana," as it's often referred to by locals. In recent years several of the outlying villages have started receiving their own fair share of visitors and residents. Many foreigners prefer the more peaceful atmosphere of the other villages surrounding the lake. As one expatriate living in San Pedro put it, "Twenty minutes in Panajachel is enough for me." Still, if you plan on living at the lake you will likely find yourself visiting Panajachel fairly frequently for supplies, as it's the most developed of the lakeside villages and also serves as a transportation hub.

Pana's main street is Calle Principal. Most buses coming in to town stop at the intersection of Calle Principal and Calle Santander, which leads directly to the lakeshore. Santander is lined with a plethora of banks, shops, restaurants, hotels, and other tourist services. The town hall, church, market, and a few other restaurants and hotels are found a half-kilometer northeast along Calle Principal from the Calle Santander junction. East of Calle Santander and running parallel is Calle Rancho Grande, which also has some accommodations. Running roughly between the two along the lakeshore is Calle del Lago.

Foreigners are spread out into many areas of town, but one of the most popular residential sectors is Barrio Jucanyá. Numerous one- and two-story condominiums and homes in gated communities are scattered along areas mostly abutting the lakeshore. Prices here are comparable to those in Antigua.

Plan on spending about US$500 a month to rent a one- or two-bedroom apartment. Prices for homes vary widely, depending largely on proximity to the lakeshore, among other considerations. A two-bedroom, 195-square-meter (2,100-square-foot) home can cost US$100,000 inland but easily fetch US$300,000 by the lakeshore.

A road runs northwest outside of town past the Reserva Natural Atitlán to Bahía San Buenaventura and a pair of high-rise towers vaguely reminiscent of Honolulu. After being left abandoned for two decades, the buildings were completed a few years ago and converted into a hotel and condominiums.

San Andrés Semetabaj

Heading northeast from Panajachel, the road crosses over a bridge and continues on to nearby towns and villages. After the road crosses the bridge, a turnoff leads up the steep slopes framing the edges of the lake basin and onto a high plateau to the town of San Andrés Semetabaj (on the road to Godinez). Here, too, are a number of gated communities from which there are spectacular panoramic views over the lake below. These include Vistas Teresita and Santiago del Lago. Santiago del Lago is a brand-new development, with 0.4-hectare (one-acre) plots costing US$100,000–200,000.

It gets a few degrees cooler up here than down by the lakeshore, and rainy season afternoons usually see low clouds and fog. Many northerners prefer this area for its tranquility, sylvan setting, and temperate climate, not to mention the views.

Santa Catarina Palopó

Five kilometers east of Panajachel, after a right turn at the turnoff beyond the bridge, is the quaint lakeside village of Santa Catarina Palopó, a collection of adobe houses with tin and thatch roofs built into the surrounding hillsides. The streets near the church and the road leading to the lakeside are excellent places to pick up some of the colorful textiles and handicrafts produced here. Many of the villagers still sport their traditional attire.

In recent years the outskirts of Santa Catarina Palopó have become somewhat of a luxury neighborhood, with many of Guatemala's well-to-do building weekend homes here. Among the local celebrities is CNN's Harris Whitbeck. There is also at least one excellent boutique hotel, Casa Palopó, that is worthy of mention. You'll find many of the large houses constructed here are built into the mountainside, as lakeside properties were snatched up long ago. Many of the area's newer homes lie separated from the lakeshore by the main road leading to Panajachel. The chief advantage to this arrangement is a bit

Santa Catarina Palopó

of privacy and seclusion, as the houses sit atop the surrounding countryside accessed by private driveways meandering up the vertiginous slopes. Home prices for lakefront homes are in the range of US$100,000–300,000. In addition to private homes, condos have recently begun springing up in the area near Casa Palopó.

San Antonio Palopó

San Antonio Palopó is the next town over heading southeast along the lakeshore. Real estate here is just finding its footing, so it's a good place to look for bargains. San Antonio Palopó can feel very much off the beaten path, but the volcano and lake views from its shores are as good or better than elsewhere around the lake. Affordable lakeside plots are still widely available here.

Among the local highlights in terms of gated communities is Villas de Santiago, which enjoys a prime location on a bluff above San Antonio Palopó, easy road access, gently sloping terrain, and incredible views. Lot sizes range 200–450 square meters and cost US$25,000–56,000.

Santa Cruz La Laguna

West of Panajachel and only accessible by boat is the quiet village of Santa Cruz La Laguna, more commonly referred to simply as "Santa Cruz." It's understandably popular with the backpacker crowd, thanks to a number of small lodges that set up shop here years ago. For this same reason, lakeside plots in Santa Cruz are increasingly hard to come by. You may have better luck in the surrounding hillsides, if that suits your fancy. Santa Cruz tends to

© AL ARGUETA

boat dock at Santa Cruz La Laguna

feel remote because of the lack of road access, but it has a fairly sizable expat presence for a town of its size. There are several hotels and restaurants catering almost exclusively to foreign travelers. Home prices can vary widely here, with modest homes for US$100,000 and more luxurious offerings going for US$500,000.

Jaibalito and Tzununa

Farther west along the lakeshore from Santa Cruz is the village of Jaibalito, which is even smaller than Santa Cruz and is also only accessible by boat or foot trail from Santa Cruz or the road to Sololá. Many properties here are literally built into the rocky cliff sides hugging the shoreline. Because of its topography, you'll be hard-pressed to find an available lakeside plot.

Land, and particularly lakeside plots, is more readily available in neighboring Tzununa, which enjoys a spectacular location on a small bay. A casual glance at real estate listings in the Lake Atitlán area will reveal this region's suitability for those looking for undeveloped land for purchase.

San Marcos La Laguna

San Marcos is a unique lake town in that it harbors a strangely esoteric vibe, aided by its prominence as Guatemala's New Age center. It's about a three-hour walk from Santa Cruz and two hours from San Pedro. Most visitors arrive at a boat dock located beside Posada Schumann, though boats stop first at the main dock a few hundred meters east. A road runs beside the lodge into town; it and a parallel street 100 meters west form the main pedestrian

FINDING SOLACE IN LAKE ATITLÁN

Foreigners have recently started getting in on Guatemala's superb real estate offerings, but the area has long been the haunt of well-to-do Guatemalans. Among the latter is former CNN correspondent Harris Whitbeck, who has established his private retreat in Santa Catarina Palopó, away from the demands of his Mexico City base and the rigors of life on the road covering wars and natural disasters.

While covering his lakeside home for a magazine assignment, I take in the view from the patio overlooking Lake Atitlán and its three sentinel volcanoes. It at once becomes obvious why Whitbeck would choose this location for his place of solace. The rainy season has just arrived, and an ethereal afternoon mist blankets the upper reaches of the mountainside behind his multistory, tile-roofed home.

"This place is my anchor; it helps keep me grounded," Guatemalan-born Whitbeck tells me. The product of a marriage between a southern belle and a Guatemalan aristocrat, Whitbeck grew up in Guatemala City and has been coming to the lake since he was a young boy. His grandmother, affectionately nicknamed "Mutty" (MOO-tee) by her grandchildren, owned a home up the hill in San Andrés Semetabaj. The family still congregates in her home, and Whitbeck recalls fond memories of weekends spent with

© AL ARGUETA

Harris Whitbeck's lakeside retreat

his aunt Lucy, a travel writer, who would engage him with tales of faraway lands. These tales would later inspire Whitbeck to follow in her footsteps.

Whitbeck's home, designed by a Guatemalan architect, was built in 2003 while he was embedded with an American combat unit in Iraq. While in the field, Whitbeck would receive frequent e-mail updates on the construction's progress. With bombs and artillery fire blasting all around him, knowing that his tranquil lakeside home awaited his return gave him peace of mind, Whitbeck says. His lake-

arteries into town. San Marcos is also accessible via a road that branches down from Santa Lucía Utatlán.

Despite its New Age feel, the hills surrounding San Marcos have their fair share of homes owned by wealthy Guatemalans. Land here is still fairly abundant, and there were, at last check, several large plots of land on the market for very reasonable prices. A lakefront plot with 20 meters side retreat also provides a welcome respite from the mayhem of Mexico City, where he's a former CNN Bureau Chief, and where he's lived since 1994.

It's been two years since my last visit to Whitbeck's home, and he's added to his collection of knickknacks gathered from travels around the world. The wooden table and chairs he had been painting in bright shades of sapphire and turquoise on my previous visit are now finished and there's a blue U.N. peacekeeper beret added to an existing collection that includes an Iraqi passport, Mayan beads, Thai figurines, and fossilized shells from the Galapagos Islands. It turns out the patio fronting the pool, with the blue wooden table and chairs, is his favorite spot in the house. "I've had the most interesting conversations at that table," he says, adding that it seems to have a certain energy that causes people to open up with their deepest, darkest secrets. There was the high-level U.N. diplomat, for example, who spoke candidly over a glass of Zacapa Centenario rum about the inherent difficulties of trying to convince a certain Central American military general of the need to curb drug trafficking in the region.

The patio does in fact have a certain mystique. The elegant infinity-edge pool looks over the lake and provides sweeping views of the volcanoes and nearby Santa Catarina. Inside, the two-bedroom lakeside retreat is decorated with colorful Mayan textiles from Guatemala's extraordinary legacy of traditional weaving. Cala lilies, beautifully arranged by the house's very attentive caretaker, Mario, adorn the dining room table. But my favorite feature of Whitbeck's home is the charmingly traditional adobe-brick wall lining the multi-tier staircase dominating its north face. It provides the traditional feel of a Mayan home to a structure that manages to effortlessly mesh comfort and refinement with rustic allure. Many highland Maya still use adobe blocks as the main building material for their homes. The blocks used in Whitbeck's home were made from dirt dug up during its construction.

From the table with the blue chairs, I ponder the flickering light of sunset dancing upon the surface of the swimming pool. It seems I have time for some reflections of my own. Were someone to ask me what I'm thinking, it would go something like this: It seems ironic that a country so often remembered for its history of violence is now also a place of peace and beauty, where the traditional and the modern exist side by side in relative harmony and people come to get away from a world gone mad. It seems it's all part of Guatemala's newfound allure.

of beachfront goes for about US$60,000. A two-bedroom home with a 1,300-square-meter plot near the lake shore will run about US$140,000. San Marcos town proper has seen a bit of a tourism boom in recent years and has a fair amount of services available. An abundance of villas owned by wealthy Guatemalan families means you can rent an entire home for as little as US$500 a month.

PRIME LIVING LOCATIONS

San Pablo and San Juan La Laguna

Serene San Pablo and San Juan La Laguna are relative late-comers to the tourism and real estate scenes. Either makes a good stop if you'd like to see a fairly sizable lakeside village that remains largely untouched by international tourism. The towns are accessible by boat or via a road that comes from San Marcos.

There are some good real estate deals in this area, especially along the road leading from San Marcos to San Pablo. One of the main advantages here is that many of these plots have road access and sit on hills overlooking the lake, offering some phenomenal views. The area between San Pablo and San Juan is almost virgin territory. It's also worth noting that while much of the surrounding lakeshore is rocky, a fair number of sandy beach areas with reed plants line the shores in the vicinity of these two towns. Land plots in the surrounding hillsides go for as little as US$15,000.

San Pedro La Laguna

On the lake's southwest corner and accessible by frequent boats or road, San Pedro is second in popularity with the expat crowd only to Panajachel and has a hip international atmosphere. The town, with a population of 13,000, is a bit on the scruffy side and seems to have sprouted from the lakeshore almost overnight. If you're not already feeling decidedly immersed in the Third World, you soon will as you walk along some of the side trails leading into the heart of the village from the main road through town. San Pedro has increasingly become home to a number of language schools, some of dubious quality, collectively offering some of Guatemala's least expensive tuition rates. While it was originally a backpacker Shangri-La, there have been recent additions to the hotel infrastructure, making for suitable accommodations to house the non-backpacker crowd.

Most of the tourist hotels and services are between two docks, on the southeast and northwest sides of town, and in the areas adjacent to them. The first one serves boats to/from Panajachel and the rest of the lake towns; the other is for boats to Santiago Atitlán. They are about one kilometer apart. The area in between them is known as "El Otro Lado." Street numbers and names are not generally in use here. From the Santiago dock, turn right to get to El Otro Lado and continue to the Panajachel boat dock. From the latter dock, turn left to get to the other side of town.

Perhaps because of its rustic atmosphere, most available property in San Pedro tends to be in town or very near it. The lakeshore here is nice and flat, unlike the rockier areas on the opposite side of the lake. Although San Pedro lies in the shadow of its namesake volcano, you won't find spectacular volcano views over the lake because the town is quite literally on its slopes and the volcano lies behind you when looking out onto the lake.

Santiago Atitlán

Santiago Atitlán is a more traditional sort of place and has a very different feel from San Pedro. It's spectacularly set in an inlet with gorgeous views of San Pedro volcano just across this small body of water. Atitlán and Tolimán volcanoes rise up behind it. It is the main enclave of Guatemala's Tz'utujil-speaking Maya, whose wonderful painting and handicrafts can be seen along the main street coming up from the boat dock, which is lined with art galleries and craft shops. On display is a very distinct form of painting depicting various elements of indigenous life such as agricultural harvests and festivals.

Santiago suffered greatly during the civil war, as the area was a hotbed of activity for ORPA guerrillas who established themselves in this strategic area between the highlands and the Pacific coast. The Guatemalan military established a base here and began systematically searching for guerrilla sympathizers, killing hundreds. Among them was American parish priest Stanley Rother, who served here from 1968 to 1981, when his life was brutally ended inside his chambers by a paramilitary death squad. Rother, an outspoken critic of the Guatemalan military, had witnessed injustice for decades and had increasingly been unable to silently stand by as many of his parishioners fell prey to a similar fate.

© AL ARGUETA

view of San Pedro volcano across the bay from Santiago Atitlán

As the civil war waned, the military's presence became increasingly unnecessary, as was the case throughout much of Guatemala, and villagers became increasingly resentful of its presence. On the night of December 1, 1990, drunken soldiers shot a villager and fled to the army barracks outside of town. Indignant, some 2,000 unarmed villagers went to the army barracks, seeking justice, but were greeted by gunfire. Thirteen people were killed, including three children, and another 20 were wounded. The massacre unleashed a flood of international pressure, as well as pressure from within the village, to close the military garrison. A petition with 2,000 signatures was presented to the Guatemalan government asking for the base's closure, which was soon granted.

More recently, Santiago made world headlines in October 2005 after a number of devastating mudslides in the wake of Hurricane Stan left close to a thousand victims. The neighboring village of Panabaj was completely wiped out by the mudslides, and the scars can still be seen on the mountainside. Many international organizations are still working in the area, and Santiago has become a popular center for volunteer activities in the tragedy's aftermath.

Another Santiago curiosity is the presence of a highland Maya deity known as Maximón, housed in the home of a different member of the local *cofradía,* or Catholic brotherhood, every year. The effigy is a wooden figure clad in colorful silk scarves and a Stetson hat, smoking a big cigar and receiving offerings of moonshine, cigarettes, and rum. Local village children will offer you their services to go see the idol, which you can photograph for a fee. It is not surprisingly a sore point between the Catholic syncretists and the increasingly prominent evangelical Christian churches that have won over many of Santiago's residents.

Santiago's colorful market really gets going on Fridays and Sundays, when the town's streets are filled with vendors and Mayan women dressed in the town's spectacular purple costume. The men wear interesting striped shorts, though it seems in fewer numbers every year. Standing prominently in the central plaza, the Iglesia Parroquial Santiago Apóstol was built between 1572 and 1581.

Santiago has a fascinating history, but it remains a very off-the-beaten-path kind of place. Expats not working with NGOs are few and far between here. While land is available, it is not one of the lake's real estate hotspots.

San Lucas Tolimán and Vicinity

San Lucas Tolimán is probably the least attractive of the lakeside villages, though the adjacent area is as gorgeous as the rest of the lake. It makes a good place to get away from it all. Again, the volcanoes are behind you as you look out to the lake. Another noteworthy feature is the proximity of Guatemala's Pacific coastal plain, with a road running from San Lucas Tolimán to the settlement of Cocales. The road leading to the coast from here is notorious for highway banditry.

GETTING AROUND

Most people living in the Lake Atitlán area get around by boat. There is frequent boat service between the various villages. Don't be surprised if boat operators charge you, the foreigner, a few *quetzales* more than locals. It's a standard practice. For villages lying close to or adjacent to each other (such as Panajachel and Santa Catarina Palopó), taxis or *tuk tuks* can get you around cheaply and easily. Of course, you'll need to consider that not all villages are accessible by road, but these inevitably enjoy frequent boat service as a result.

THE PACIFIC COAST

Guatemala's identity as a mostly mountainous country of cool lakes, evergreen forests, and wandering rivers has meant the coasts (Caribbean and Pacific) have traditionally been omitted from the collective consciousness in favor of its better-known, more traditional attractions. This general eschewing of coastal living seems to apply just as much to Guatemalans, the wealthy few who can afford second homes near the beach having settled mostly on a handful of urbanized subdivisions in the vicinity of Puerto San José. Very few of the Pacific coast's black-sand beaches are inhabited, the chief economic activities along the seaboard being fishing, shrimp farming, and loofah production. The actual sand beaches are separated, along much of the coast, from mainland Guatemala by a narrow channel known as the Canal de Chiquimulilla, running the length of the coast from the town of Sipacate east to Las Lisas, near the Salvadoran border, traversing Puerto San José, Iztapa, and Monterrico along the way.

Things have started to change in recent years with the growth of Guatemala's tourism industry, as visitors and foreign residents seek new places to explore beyond the well-trod path. The Pacific port of San José has always been popular with Guatemala City residents as a place for sun and surf, though foreign visitors will find more acceptable places to visit and live in elsewhere along the Pacific seaboard. It's just 90 minutes from the capital via a four-lane toll road. Adjacent to Puerto San José is the newer Puerto Quetzal, best known for its cruise ship terminal hosting an increasing number of seafaring visitors to Guatemala.

More recently, the beaches found in and around the area of Monterrico and its namesake sea turtle preserve have become the site of vacation homes and new resort hotels. Unlike in Puerto San José, most of the properties in and around Monterrico can be found right on the beach. Nestled in between these two poles lies Iztapa, Guatemala's original colonial seaport, which in recent years has gained notoriety as word gets out about world-class sailfishing in Guatemala's Pacific waters.

Guatemala is also Central America's surfing frontier, with some excellent breaks on many of the coast's empty beaches, particularly around the village of Sipacate and farther west toward Mexico. Things get more primitive the farther west you head from Sipacate, though the port of Champerico might soon become a magnet for coastal development owing to ongoing infrastructural improvements specifically aimed at capturing more tourism investment. Champerico is a satellite of nearby Retalhuleu, a haunt of the Pacific coast's

© JULIO PEREIRA

a tropical home in a Pacific coast subdivision

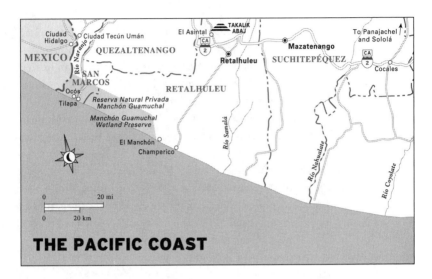

THE PACIFIC COAST

farming and ranching community and now the site of a large-scale amusement park that is Guatemala's most-visited tourist attraction.

Guatemala's relative obscurity as an expat destination in light of the popularity of neighboring Central American countries becomes quite obvious when you consider that the vast majority of Americans buying overseas property are in search of sand and surf. Were it not for the investment power of wealthy Guatemalans, the Pacific coast would have very little to offer in the way of urbanized settlement. As is the case elsewhere in Guatemala, local money has filled the void left in the absence of U.S. investment. What does this mean for potential foreign investors and expat residents? It means there's still plenty of cheap land available on exotic black-sand beaches that are often comparable in quality to those found in better-known Central American locales. I've personally never found the Costa Rican beach towns of Jacó or Dominical particularly impressive (nor their coastlines), yet they haven't failed to attract millions of dollars in U.S. real estate and tourism investment. Factor in nice beaches, cheap land prices, good road access, and Guatemala's newfound popularity as a world-class sailfishing destination, and you'll see why the Pacific coast is probably the country's region of greatest untapped potential. If you're a surfer, sport fisher, beach bum, or all of the above, it might be a great time to get in on some of Central America's cheapest beach front property.

THE LAY OF THE LAND

The mountains and volcanoes forming Guatemala's rugged spine yield to the fertile coastal plains lining the entirety of the country's southern Pacific coast. This

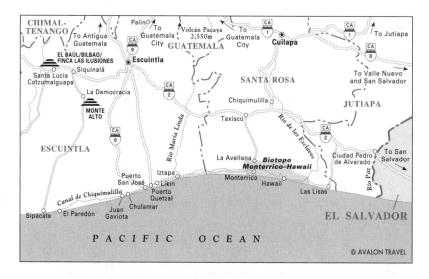

is Guatemala's most fertile agricultural area, blessed with volcanic soil, abundant sunshine, and plenty of rain. It's a hot, humid tropical region where the cultivation of coffee, cotton, and sugarcane figure prominently into the region's economy—and its identity. The Pacific coast plains are bisected by Highway CA-2, which runs west to east from the Mexican border all the way to El Salvador. The closest seaside community to Guatemala City, Puerto San José is connected to the capital by Highway CA-9, though a newer toll road is now the preferred way to go.

Local Property Restrictions

Ownership and use of coastal property is governed by Oficina de Control de Áreas de Reserva del Estado (OCRET), a government office charged with the protection of state lands. OCRET laws apply to coastal lands within 200 meters of the high tide mark and stipulate that outright ownership is forbidden in favor of a renewable 20- or 30-year lease.

DAILY LIVING

Life on Guatemala's Pacific coast is in many ways life on the frontier. Only a few of the towns covered in this section offer anything in the way of comforts most North Americans are accustomed to. Many of the communities in the vicinity of Puerto San José harbor the weekend homes of wealthy Guatemalan families. Although they have all the standard amenities, there's really not much to see or do in the immediate vicinity. They're designed solely for the purpose of rest and relaxation and are virtual islands of development in a sparsely populated sea of underdevelopment.

There are a few pharmacies in major towns such as Puerto San José and Retalhuleu, but little elsewhere. Schools are virtually nonexistent in coastal regions, and there are no bilingual international schools in the region. Retalhuleu has a few private schools offering instruction in Spanish. The only town in the region with a Spanish-language school is Monterrico.

As for shopping, Retalhuleu has three surprisingly decent outdoor shopping malls with at least one well-stocked grocery store. There are a few small grocery stores in and around Puerto San José and Monterrico, but you may find yourself visiting the departmental capital of Escuintla if you're seeking harder-to-find items. For those really hard-to-find imported items, you'll need to make the drive to Guatemala City. Markets selling abundant local produce and foodstuffs are everywhere.

Of the towns covered here, Monterrico is the only one with any sort of expat community. Many of the town's expats own lodges, restaurants, and other tourism-related businesses. Iztapa, given its status as a sportfishing hub, also has a few expats who run local businesses.

Puerto San José and Vicinity

Puerto San José has long been Guatemala's default location for Pacific beach property thanks to its proximity to the capital via a fast, four-lane highway. It's possible to be at the ocean in just 90 minutes from Antigua or Guatemala City. Most of the subdivisions in the vicinity of Puerto San José tend to be older and not directly on the beach. Most homes in these communities front artificial canals built to accommodate property owners' boats. Well-known communities include Likín and San Marino, though they will not be covered here due to the availability of better, newer living options near Puerto San José and elsewhere along the Pacific coast. In any case, available properties in these communities are few and far between, as many have been owned by wealthy Guatemalan families for generations.

A shining star, if you have deep pockets, is the newer development of Juan Gaviota, west of Puerto San José. Even farther west is the coastal town of Sipacate, on the fringes of Sipacate-Naranjo National Park's protected mangroves. It is also Guatemala's surfing mecca, specifically the nearby settlement of El Paredón.

WHERE TO LIVE

It's important to note from the outset that Puerto San Josá isn't somewhere you actually go to live. It's a dusty Guatemalan port town that I can barely even recommend for a visit. The communities housing the weekend homes of wealthy Guatemalans, like Likín and San Marino, are found along the stretch of road leading east from Puerto San José to the more modern shipping terminal of Puerto Quetzal. Heading west from Puerto San José, the road takes you to the neighboring communities of Chulamar and Juan Gaviota. Even if you don't have the deep pockets to afford a home in Guatemala's luxurious Juan Gaviota community, it's one of the easier places to locate villas for rent.

Chulamar

About five kilometers west of Puerto San José, Chulamar is a residential development for Guatemala's wealthy. Anchoring the real estate project is the large Soleil Pacífico resort, formerly the Radisson Villas del Pacífico. Homes here are in a gated community with round-the-clock security. There's not much else around here, as it's basically a self-contained community—a bastion of civilization literally in the middle of nowhere.

Juan Gaviota

Juan Gaviota, a huge planned community spanning 15 kilometers of beachfront located 12 kilometers west of Puerto San José, is the newest enclave of Guatemala's elite and has all the feel of a Miami subdivision. The first of several construction phases encompassing this ambitious project is Marina del Sur, which features a central clubhouse with a restaurant fronting the Pacific Ocean in addition to swimming pools, tennis courts, soccer fields, and beach volleyball courts. Along with luxurious single-family homes and villas are a number of six-story condo buildings with ocean views. Altogether, there are close to 300 residential units. Prices for homes run in the US$200,000–300,000 range. The area is expected to become a magnet for future development, and several undeveloped land plots adjacent to the sizable complex are now for sale.

Juan Gaviota is equipped with a boat marina, and future plans call for a golf course, timeshare condos, and hotels. If you're looking to build a house in Juan Gaviota, you'll be happy to know that a new subdivision known as Casas Punta Caracol (www.casaspuntacaracol.com) is currently in the works. Housing plans depict tropical luxury living with four different home models to choose from. Future phases of Juan Gaviota will also offer slightly lower price points.

A few homes are available for rent. The best place to look for beach villa rentals in this neck of the woods is on the website of Antigua-based Century 21 Casa Nova. Homes here rent for about US$700 a week, or US$400 for a weekend. Again, this is a self-contained gated community and you won't find

JUAN GAVIOTA: GUATEMALA'S PACIFIC PARADISE

While Guatemala's Pacific coast hasn't yet attracted the attention of foreign investors, it doesn't mean the region lacks infrastructure comparable to that of its better-known neighbors. Local investors, as they always do in Guatemala, have stepped in to fill the void. The planned community of Juan Gaviota began in the late 1990s as the dream of a group of five Guatemalan investors who were able to purchase a sizable land plot with 15 kilometers of beachfront.

The development essentially sprang up out of nowhere. A trail crisscrossing the property had to be upgraded to a serviceable road, a canal was dredged (along with a bridge to cross it), and electricity had to be brought in. The latter, at a cost of over US$4 million, now benefits nearby communities in addition to residents of Marina del Sur. Wave breakers had to be installed in order to provide a safe haven for boats and facilitate the construction of the marina. Several thousand tons of rock also had to be brought in. The first phase of Marina del Sur alone is estimated to have cost over US$130 million.

The project has a 20-year master plan, made in conjunction with a local consulting firm. The next phase encompasses a golf course and three hotels, opening Juan Gaviota to foreign investors and visitors. It is rumored the hotels are being built by a U.S. investment firm.

The community is in some ways an ecological preserve. Juan Gaviota's creators left local mangrove swamps undisturbed in their quest to maintain the local ecological balance. Poaching of sea turtle eggs and iguanas from the property is strictly prohibited. Private ownership of the vast property and the presence of private security forces to patrol it ensure closer compliance of these restrictions, something which is not easily replicated in coastal communities elsewhere in Guatemala.

Juan Gaviota's developers have placed their eyes upon Lake Petén Itzá and Antigua Guatemala as locales for future development projects on a similar scale.

much of anything in the way of surrounding communities in this sparsely populated area of the Pacific coast.

Sipacate

West of Juan Gaviota is the sleepy seaside village of Sipacate, home to Guatemala's nascent surfing scene. It is accessed via a road turning south from Highway CA-2 at the town of Siquinalá. Real estate and tourism development are still very much in their infancy here, but it's a good place to look for cheap beachfront plots. The atmosphere here is still that of a sleepy village where chickens and pigs run around on dusty streets. The beaches are among Guatemala's finest, with gently sloping sands leading to the ocean and some great shore breaks.

The nearby village of El Paredón, a few kilometers east of Sipacate, is home to at least one surf camp and some of the coast's best surfing waves.

GETTING AROUND

As elsewhere along the Pacific seaboard, your best bet for getting around is to have your own wheels, be it your own car or a rental. Parts of the road communicating Puerto San José with its western enclaves are unpaved. It's best to have a four-wheel-drive vehicle. Roads in the immediate vicinity of communities like Chulamar and Juan Gaviota are paved, but you'll still need to cross areas of unpaved road to get there. A paved road leads from a turnoff at highway CA-2 to the town of Sipacate.

Monterrico and Vicinity

Monterrico is by far Guatemala's most popular seaside destination with foreign travelers, though there are honestly better beaches to be found elsewhere along the Pacific seaboard. The shore break here is rather abrupt but tends to smooth out as you head west toward Iztapa and east toward Las Lisas.

Iztapa is connected to Monterrico via a paved two-lane road and is the capital of Guatemala's nascent sailfishing industry. Along this road you'll find many small seaside hotels and private properties, some for sale. Rumor has it a golf course is planned somewhere along this corridor. Heading east from Monterrico toward the Salvadoran border is another turtle preserve at the village of Hawaii, sparsely inhabited save for the homes of a few wealthy Guatemalans. The region in the vicinity of Monterrico has all the feel of the next Central American real estate frontier and is certainly one of the prime locations to check out if you're interested in buying beach property in Guatemala.

WHERE TO LIVE
Monterrico

Monterrico was a quiet seaside village populated mostly by shrimp fishers and loofah farmers as recently as 10 years ago. The construction of weekend homes by Guatemala's elite, along with about two dozen hotels, has translated into a small real estate boom centered around the small town and its namesake sea turtle preserve. Monterrico is in many ways an overgrown seaside village. Its sand streets are still very quiet during the week, when urban-dwelling

YOU *CAN* SURF IN GUATEMALA

While neighboring countries like Costa Rica, Nicaragua, and even El Salvador have acquired relative status as Central American surf spots, Guatemala has remained relatively obscure in this regard. Although the country's Pacific shores have perfectly surf-worthy breaks, the coast has always taken a back seat to the scenic and cultural wonders of the highlands, among other areas. A relative lack of tourism infrastructure in this region has also contributed to keeping the Pacific coast on the periphery of Guatemala's emerging status as a destination for outdoor-loving, adventurous travelers.

The newfound popularity of beach destinations such as Monterrico and Iztapa has resulted in the corresponding development of coastal areas near these beach towns. As more and more people visit, locals and foreigners alike are discovering that you can, in fact, surf in Guatemala. The Guatemalan surfing community can be found mostly in small villages along the coast and numbers only about 100 people, according to local estimates. Surfing Guatemala's breaks means you won't have to share a wave with 20 other people, as is the case with other, more popular regions along the Central American coast. The best surfing beaches in Guatemala can be found at Iztapa and Sipacate, both of which have more-than-adequate accommodations.

U.S. travel magazines have put the word out concerning El Paredón Surf Camp, a bare-bones surfing paradise on one of Guatemala's best breaks. Still, you wouldn't know it cruising around the sandy streets of this quiet village, where chickens roam freely and you can still show up on almost any given day with nary another surfer in sight.

The biggest waves can be found during swells occurring between mid-March and late October with wave faces sometimes as large as 18 feet. During other times of year, waves average 3–6 feet, with the occasional 10-foot swell.

If you want to check out the surfing scene in Guatemala, a useful website is www.surfingua-temala.com, established by Pedro Pablo Vergara, a local surfer who co-started Maya Extreme Surf School and offers trips to Guatemala's surf spots. The site lists about 20 breaks along the Pacific coast, with area maps to help you find them along with information on accommodations ranging from budget surf camps to stays in private villas. They can also arrange transportation for you and your surfboards to various surf spots from Guatemala City.

Along with Maripaz Fernandez, Vergara started Maya Extreme Surf School (www.mayaextreme.com) in 2001, and Maya Extreme Surf Shop (Centro Comercial Pradera Concepción Local 308, Guatemala City, tel. 6637-9593), in 2005. The shop sells the company's own brand of "G-land surf boards" and is based in one of Guatemala City's nicest shopping malls. A one-day "learn to surf" package costs US$125, including transfers, food, equipment and instruction.

In 2006, Robert August (of *Endless Summer* fame) traveled to Guatemala with his crew to surf the Pacific coast's waves. The result is *The Endless Journey Continues*, a movie chronicling their surfing trip to Guatemala.

Guatemalans are at their jobs. A few expats own local businesses such as hotels and restaurants.

As for daily life, there's little to see and do in and around Monterrico. The main attraction here is the beach itself. The local sea turtle preserve hosts volunteers interested in contributing to ongoing efforts to protect sea turtles, and especially their eggs, from poaching. Tours to the surrounding mangrove forests offer an alternative to beach activities.

Monterrico's popularity with locals and foreigners in recent years means prices have gone up in inverse proportion to the availability of beachfront land. Still, it's a deal compared to elsewhere in Central America, especially when you consider the area's future growth potential. You'll find lots for sale on hand-painted signs, real estate magazines, and websites. Keep in mind prices for properties advertised on websites (usually by real estate agencies) may be considerably higher than those for properties offered by local vendors. You'll find prices in and around Monterrico generally fall in the vicinity of US$6–15 per *vara cuadrada*.

It's a good idea to rent a property for a week or two in order to get a feel for what it might be like to live here. I've heard good things about Casa Karina, an American-owned villa that rents for US$600 a week.

Along the Monterrico-Iztapa Road

A paved, two-lane, 25-kilometer road connects Monterrico to Iztapa, to the west, and runs parallel to the seashore. As you go from Monterrico to Iztapa,

PRIME LIVING LOCATIONS

a sea turtle in Monterrico

THE SAILFISH CAPITAL OF THE WORLD

A unique swirling of ocean currents between Mexico and El Salvador creates an eddy unusually rich in pelagic fish (such as herring and mackerel) right on Guatemala's doorstep, where billfish, including sailfish and marlin, gather to feed along with large concentrations of dorado, yellow-fin tuna and wahoo. The end result is some of the world's best sailfishing waters.

Enthusiasts of Guatemala's emerging sailfishing scene are quick to point out that it is the true "Sailfish Capital of the World" and have the numbers to back up their claims. The world records for conventional and fly-fishing single-day catches have been set here, at 75 and 23. In March 2006, a single vessel carrying five anglers caught and released a whopping 124 sailfish. While the records are indeed impressive, anglers plying the Guatemalan Pacific coast need not worry about any "feast or famine" phenomenon, as catch-and-release numbers are quite consistent. In terms of billfish releases per angler, a statistic compiled by The Southwest Fisheries Science Center in California, Guatemala ranks at the top. Its catch per unit of effort (CPUE) for Pacific sailfish in 2005 was 5.83, compared to Costa Rica's 2.57 and Panama's 2.25. On average, you can expect to catch between 15 and 20 fish per boat per day, but catches of 25 fish aren't uncommon.

Guatemala's strength is certainly in its numbers. Unlike most of its competitors, it's not known as a beach destination with impressive resort accommodations. All that is starting to change, however, and there are now some very comfortable accommodations where you can stay right on the beach and relax after a long day at sea. Some of the outfitters accommodate anglers in their own lodges; otherwise there are private luxury villas on the beach or the large Villas del Pacífico resort. Many outfits combine fishing packages with a round of golf on one of Guatemala City's excellent golf courses. All of the outfitters listed here practice catch-and-release and use circle hooks, as mandated by Guatemalan law.

Fishing is active year-round, but most anglers come between November and May seeking a respite from colder climates. Prices for fishing packages vary by the size of the boat used and can be fairly expensive in Guatemala, as boats generally travel 40–80 kilometers offshore to a deep, 600-meter basin where sailfish tend to congregate around its rim, translating into higher fuel costs. Boats heading out this way are usually in the 28-foot range, but there are also a few 42- and 43-foot boats. Expect to pay about US$2,100 per person for two people on a two-day/three-night fishing package on a 28-foot boat. Most packages include food and drink, accommodations, boat and captain, gear, and transfers to and from the Guatemala City airport. Anglers often spend their last night in Antigua or Guatemala City.

the first settlement you'll come across is Aldea El Pumpo. There are a few hotels here and a number of properties and houses being developed.

All along this corridor, interspersed with loofah farms you'll find many hand-written signs advertising properties for sale. Rumor has it a golf course may be in the works somewhere along the coastline. The beaches from here all the way to Iztapa are among the prettiest on Guatemala's Pacific seaboard. A number of small beach hotels have sprung up along the way, a sure sign that new real estate development isn't far behind.

Among the new projects along this road is Villa Los Cabos, located at kilometer 11.5. The large, horseshoe-shaped complex encompasses 26 four-story villas built around a large swimming pool. Each villa houses three apartments, ranging in price US$130,000–158,000. The two buildings on either end of the horseshoe are two-story private villas that fetch US$250,000 apiece.

Farther east and closer to Monterrico, at kilometer 20.6 is a project known as Islas Monterrico, which appears to be in its early stages as a planned seaside community.

Development along this stretch of road is still very much in its infancy, but it's a good place to look for property if you want to get in on the game early. The area has huge growth potential.

Iztapa

Iztapa is Guatemala's original seaport, used by Spanish conquistador Pedro de Alvarado as his departure point for onward journeys to Peru. The town itself is as dilapidated as any along the Guatemalan Pacific coast, but Iztapa's allure lies offshore in the waters richly abundant in sailfish, marlin, yellow-fin tuna, and other prized species popular with anglers. The beaches, separated from town by the Canal de Chiquimulilla, are some of the Pacific coast's prettiest. They are clean and gently sloping.

On the beach, there are a few homes of Guatemala's wealthy elite and at least one excellent lodge catering to sportfishing enthusiasts or anyone with the cash to hang out in its posh digs. Check out Sailfish Bay Lodge, owned by American expat Robert Fallon. He is a wealth of information on Guatemala, having made the move here from Costa Rica a few years ago.

GETTING AROUND

There are buses between Iztapa and Monterrico, but if you want to check out the real estate scene your best bet is to rent a car and travel along the corridor between the two towns. From Iztapa, you'll need to take a car or passenger ferry from Colonia 20 de Octubre across the Canal de Chiquimulilla to the

Sailfish Bay Lodge, Iztapa

barrier island harboring the road to Monterrico. This is the recommended way to go. The ferry crossing takes about five minutes. Closer to Monterrico, there's also a much longer car and passenger ferry crossing (about one hour) leading to the Pacific slope town of La Avellana.

Most everything in Monterrico is within walking distance either through town or along the beach. *Tuk tuks* are available in Monterrico and Iztapa to take you around town for a few quetzales. They can also take you to and from the ferry crossing in La Avellana. Secure parking for vehicles is available at the better hotels in town. If you arrive with your own vehicle, you'll probably find yourself parking it for the duration of your stay.

Retalhuleu and Vicinity

Moving east from the Mexican border, the first town of any real interest to visitors is a rather pleasant place with a newfound importance as the gateway to some increasingly popular tourist attractions. The most prominent of these are also Retalhuleu's newest: the twin amusement parks of Xocomil and Xetulul, just a few minutes outside of town. The parks attract over two million visitors annually, mostly from within Guatemala. Adding to its prominence as the southern coastal region's new recreational hub is the town's proximity to the ruins of Takalik Abaj and some decent stretches of beach within a relatively short distance.

Commonly referred to as "Reu" by locals, the town has always been the playground of local coffee and sugarcane farmers, a fact that will be readily apparent by the prevalence of roadside hotels with sparkling swimming pools and pleasant outdoor restaurants. The weather here is warm year-round, but you can always find shelter from the scorching sun under the abundant palm trees, as you will see from the palm-lined boulevard leading to the town center from the main highway.

Reu is becoming increasingly attractive as a hub for exploring this once seldom-visited area of Guatemala. Although I don't yet know of any expats living here, people have settled in stranger places. Even if amusement parks aren't your thing, the town's location on the humid coastal plain near beaches, coffee farms, and volcanoes might suit you just fine.

WHERE TO LIVE
Retalhuleu

Retalhuleu is pleasant enough, as far as Guatemalan coastal cities go. The amusement parks and the numerous hotels housing their visitors are located outside the city limits, along the road leading to Quetzaltenango. The city proper is accessed via a palm tree-lined boulevard bordered by stately mansions. It can make quite an impression on the first-time visitor.

As Retalhuleu is not exactly an expat enclave, there is virtually nothing in the way of local real estate companies working with foreigners to rent and buy property. The city's popularity with local agricultural elites, along with its newfound status as a tourism destination, however, translates into a decent amount of real estate development offering what expat residents are usually looking for.

La Trinidad is a shopping and housing complex near the town's bus depot. The modern outdoor shopping mall has a number of good restaurants and even a Radio Shack. Behind the shopping mall is a large housing complex, known as Villas La Trinidad, which will eventually encompass 200 homes. The project was designed and is being built with help from U.S. architectural firm Seth Harry & Associates, known for designing several planned communities in Florida. They have also designed several of Guatemala's other neo-urban communities. Villas La Trinidad looks like something straight out of South Florida and features swimming pools, tennis and squash courts, a clubhouse, gym, and spa. Home prices start at US$103,000.

Champerico

Along the western Pacific coast near the Mexican border is the old port town of Champerico, a sort of coastal satellite of Retalhuleu. This area is still relatively undiscovered and may be another place to look for beach-front bargains. The Dutch and Guatemalan governments are jointly financing the construction of a new marina near Champerico's dilapidated pier. The project is expected to foster tourism growth by allowing Champerico to become a new sailfishing enclave. For now, Champerico retains a certain Third World charm.

Other local attractions include the coastal Manchón Guamuchal wetland preserve and the nearby beach of El Tulate.

Infrastructure in and around Champerico is still quite primitive compared to Monterrico-Iztapa and Puerto San José, but it doesn't look like it will stay that way for long. Its proximity to Quetzaltenango and Retalhuleu may make it an important regional center in the years to come.

GETTING AROUND

Most buses plying the Pacific Coast Highway (Carretera al Pacífico) stop in Retalhuleu's main bus depot, located at 7a Avenida and 10a Calle. There are regular buses to Guatemala City, Quetzaltenango, the Mexican border, and Champerico. *Tuk tuks* and taxis are the best way to get around town if you don't have your own wheels. A good, paved road connects Retalhuleu to Champerico.

IZABAL AND LAS VERAPACES

The departments of Izabal and Alta and Baja Verapaz occupy the bulk of the eastern portion of Guatemala. The region is a rugged land of mountains, cloud forests, remote Caribbean beaches, tropical lakes, and sweltering rainforests. Izabal and Las Verapaces are a paradise for nature lovers, though they are also among the poorest and least developed regions of Guatemala.

Among the chief attractions drawing visitors and foreign residents is the gorgeous Río Dulce canyon, connecting Lake Izabal with the Caribbean Sea. Many wealthy Guatemalans and foreign residents own property on the river's shores, particularly at the river's confluence with Lake Izabal in an area known as Fronteras. Lake Izabal harbors some intriguing natural attractions of its own, including a vast, little-explored wetland preserve of astounding biological diversity and a funky Spanish castle built to repel the attacks of 17th-century pirates. From Río Dulce, a number of side streams originate from the main river canyon, harboring a few homes and some small villages. Río Dulce is a popular stop for yachts and sailing vessels plying the western

© AL ARGUETA

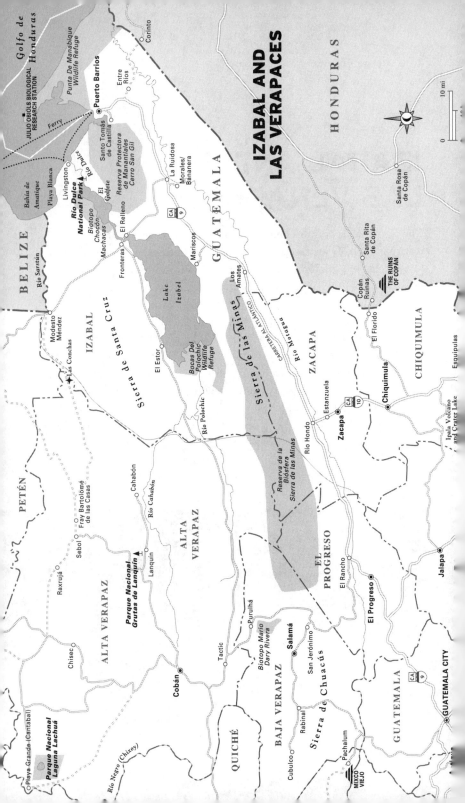

IZABAL AND LAS VERAPACES

Caribbean, as evidenced by the presence of several marinas in and around the town of Fronteras. The coastal town of Lívingston is Guatemala's Garífuna enclave and serves as a gateway to the Caribbean coast northwest toward the Belize border

Southeast of Lívingston lies Puerto Barrios, the country's main shipping port. From Puerto Barrios, it's just a quick hop to remote beaches on the peninsula of Punta de Manabique. The little-explored beaches and wetlands of Punta de Manabique are protected as a wildlife refuge and offer some unique opportunities for ecotourism, wildlife viewing, and beachcombing.

Collectively known as "Las Verapaces," the departments of Alta and Baja Verapaz are mostly mountainous, remote, and clothed largely in verdant forests. Guatemala's national bird, the resplendent quetzal, and its national flower—a rare orchid known as the monja blanca—inhabit the cool cloud forests of this region. The region's main city is the coffee-cultivation hub of Cobán, situated in a lush green valley. Nearby, in the northern reaches of Alta Verapaz, are caves, white-water rivers, limestone pools, lagoons, and even some Mayan ruins. It is easily one of Guatemala's most beautiful regions.

CLIMATE

The Izabal region is warm and humid year-round. During the warmest months of April and May, the temperature and humidity can seem unbearable, though coastal regions get a lightly refreshing sea breeze that helps alleviate some of the tropical swelter. Temperatures can round 38°C (100°F) during this time of year. At other times, it hovers somewhere between 30 and 35°C (85 and 95°F). Izabal is particularly rainy and is sometimes battered by storms or the occasional hurricane.

As elsewhere in Guatemala, the main determinant of climate is the altitude. As both Alta and Baja Verapaz are largely dominated by the presence of mountain chains, you can expect to find some chilly weather at high altitudes. The Sierra de las Minas reaches altitudes of 3,015 meters, while Cobán displays similar temperatures to Guatemala City, which is found at the same altitude. It is considerably damper in these parts, as much of the year sees the *chipi chipi*, a misty drizzle that often dampens the atmosphere for entire days. As such, much of the region is blanketed by cloud forests.

The Baja Verapaz capital of Salamá is in a valley at about 1,100 meters and so is slightly warmer. Its climate is among the most agreeable in the country. Farther north, toward Chisec and the jungle flatlands extending into neighboring Petén, the temperature is substantially warmer and it can be extremely humid. All of these conditions are further influenced by the seasons (rainy and dry) dominating the entire country, though this area tends to see much more rainfall throughout the year with a shorter dry season (December–April) than elsewhere in Guatemala.

Izabal

The Izabal region features a unique kind of Caribbean experience not at all like Cancún or the West Indies but nonetheless beautiful. Tourism promoters have labeled this, "A different Caribbean." Cruise ships regularly dock at Puerto Santo Tomás de Castilla, just across the bay from Puerto Barrios. Its cruise ship terminal is fast becoming a motor for the tourism development of this long-overlooked Caribbean coastal region. Cruise ship day-trippers can explore a rainforest and pristine jungle river with waterfalls and pools in the lush green mountains looming over the port. New real estate projects in the form of luxurious planned communities may soon allow those same visitors to call these gorgeous locales home.

Guatemalans have been living on the shores of Río Dulce for decades despite its official status as a national park. They have more recently been joined by the sailing circuit and other foreigners who have built homes on the shores of this lazy jungle river. Foreign residents have also begun congregating in the town of Lívingston, which sits at the confluence of Río Dulce and the Caribbean Sea. Although its beaches are not particularly impressive, the coastal Caribbean atmosphere has not failed to attract the interest of the sea-faring and backpacking crowd.

THE LAY OF THE LAND

Unlike Guatemala's Pacific coast, which is mostly flat, the Izabal region has some mountains of note. The Montañas del Mico stand as silent sentinels dominating a biological corridor between the emerald waters of Bahía de Amatique and the lazy Río Dulce to the north, which empties into the Caribbean Sea. Inland, Lake Izabal is a huge body of water with some nice beaches of its own and some impressive wetlands.

There are still large expanses of tropical rainforests, which receive ample rainfall when warm, moist air from the Caribbean rises and cools on mountain slopes as it makes its way inland. Guatemala's Caribbean coastline lacks the aquamarine beaches of Cancún and Belize, but the peninsula of Punta de Manabique stands out for its wild and scenic white-sand coastline stretching all the way to the Honduran border. Farther out to sea, heading north, is the tail end of the Belize Barrier Reef and some easily accessible cayes.

WHAT IS A CLOUD FOREST?

Cloud forests are essentially high-altitude rainforests, though the biological characteristics and corresponding classification are much more complicated than a matter of mere altitude. In Guatemala, cloud forests average an annual precipitation between 2,000 and 6,000 millimeters and are found at altitudes between 1,000 and 2,500 meters. The forests essentially serve as a large sponge retaining water that is later distributed to surrounding areas by means of evaporation or the formation of small streams. More than 60 small streams originate in Guatemala's Sierra de las Minas, for example.

A distinct characteristic of these forests is the presence of low-lying cloud banks forming on the mountains, under which the forest is immersed for much of the time. Large amounts of water are deposited directly onto vegetation from the clouds and mist, with the leaves of trees at higher elevations often dripping water. Cloud forests serve as the habitat for many species of plants and animals, including epiphytes, which grow on other plants. You'll see tree branches thick with bromeliads, orchids, and tree ferns. As for wildlife, the forests support an abundance of rare and endangered species including quetzal birds, howler monkeys, jaguars, and wild boars.

The Verapaz highlands still contain many of these forests, including the largest protected cloud forest in Central America, the Sierra de las Minas Biosphere Reserve. The cloud forests that once covered much of the western highlands have been largely lost to subsistence agriculture by indigenous peasants who seek to make a living by clearing the forests to cultivate crops on steep hillsides. Outside of the Verapaces, there are still some patches of cloud forest left in the Sierra de los Cuchumatanes as well as on the slopes of Guatemala's volcanoes.

STAYING SAFE

It should be noted that recently, remote regions of Izabal, and to a lesser extent the Verapaces, have become a hotbed for the activities of drug smugglers. There are at least two major cartels operating in the area, with close ties to Mexican cartels. Izabal's remote and rugged coastal terrain, coupled with a virtual absence of the government, has transformed it into a major drug transshipment point. Drug cartels have found in the local populace willing allies for their covert activities, and they are often aided and abetted by them. The reasons for this are easy to ascertain when taking into account the extreme poverty faced by many of the region's inhabitants and the government's inability to address their material needs. The drug cartels have been only too willing to address locals' needs and fill in where the state has failed them.

The areas near Chocón Machacas Biotope and the Río Lámpara, situated along the Río Dulce, have recently been the scene of intense conflicts over land ownership. Locals, with the aid of drug cartels, have begun invading protected

Río Dulce canyon

areas, among them Chocón Machacas. In February 2008, police authorities in Lívingston captured a peasant leader organizing such invasions. Locals reacted by taking 22 policemen hostage and burning a police station, demanding the release of their leader. In March 2008, the same group took four Belgian tourists hostage as they were taking a sightseeing trip with their local guide and boatman. They were released within 48 hours, unharmed. What does this mean for you? It's probably not a good idea to buy property in the more remote stretches of Río Dulce at this time. It remains to be seen whether the government of Álvaro Colom can get a handle on the local security situation.

DAILY LIVING

Izabal attracts boaters and independent travelers, so as in other remote regions of Guatemala, home schooling would be the best option for families with children. The only one of Izabal's cities with a hospital is Puerto Barrios, though it has a well-documented history of lacking basic infrastructure. Puerto Barrios does have some adequately stocked pharmacies. As for shopping, Puerto Barrios has at least one small shopping mall with a grocery store. There's also an outdoor market.

The region's largest expat presence is found along Río Dulce, where many folks own area lodges and restaurants in the vicinity of Fronteras and Lívingston.

WHERE TO LIVE
Lake Izabal

Guatemala's largest lake lacks the scenic volcanoes of its better-known counterpart, Lake Atitlán, but it nonetheless makes a pleasant place to live. A few expats have set up shop on its shores, which include some pretty lake beaches. Probably the best beach is that at Playa Dorada, where there is an expat-owned lodge at Denny's Beach. Other noteworthy landmarks include the pleasant lakeside town of El Estor, gateway to a jungle river canyon and the Bocas del Polochic Wildlife Refuge, which have become increasingly popular with visitors.

The lake is drained into the Caribbean by Río Dulce and you'll find the greatest expat presence at the lake's confluence with the river. There are a number of good hotels and marinas right on the lake, including Banana Palms Resort and Mansión del Río, in the area adjacent to the San Felipe castle. This makes a good area to look for property if you're looking to settle down here.

Fronteras (Río Dulce Town)

At the confluence of Lake Izabal and Río Dulce is Fronteras, also known simply as Río Dulce. This is the site of Central America's longest bridge, spanning across the wide river. Fronteras is a very busy town these days, with a variety of restaurants, hotels, and marinas springing up in its vicinity catering to an ever-increasing number of visitors. Yachts and sailing vessels seeking refuge from Caribbean storms regularly anchor in these parts. Whether you're arriving by boat or by land, the slow pace of life and warm Caribbean breezes may soon have you dropping anchor here permanently.

This makes a particularly good place for those seeking warmer climates in a jungle environment. The presence of marinas and the sailing set ensure things stay interesting thanks to a steady stream of visitors. Many expats have established lodges and marinas in this area along the river.

It should be noted that sailing vessels should take care to anchor in protected private marinas and not out in the middle of the open water where they may fall prey to local pirates. In June 2008, an American citizen was murdered while attempting to resist armed robbery aboard his yacht anchored in the waters near Río Dulce town.

Río Dulce National Park to Lívingston

Heading east from the Río Dulce bridge and Fronteras, the river continues its lazy trip to the Caribbean, widening at a place known as El Golfete and then narrowing below a tall jungle canyon before arriving in the Garífuna enclave of Lívingston. Lívingston's Garífuna culture was brought to coastal Guatemala from the Caribbean island of St. Vincent by way of Roatán, Honduras. This

LÍVINGSTON'S GARÍFUNA CULTURE

Lívingston is one of Guatemala's most culturally diverse regions, with Garífuna, Hindu, Q'eqchi', and *ladino* cultures peacefully co-existing here. Of these, the Garífuna and Hindu influences are particularly interesting because they are not found elsewhere in Guatemala, giving this region a unique flavor. Guatemalans are often surprised to see Afro-Caribbean people when they visit the Atlantic coast, as they are not readily in evidence elsewhere in the country, and look upon them with a certain sense of wonder simultaneously fueled by a form of racism familiar to the country's Mayan people. There are a number of far-fetched myths, including the belief that seeing an Afro-Caribbean person on the street (outside of Lívingston) means you will soon come in contact with a long-lost acquaintance. Also common is the belief that there is widespread practice of voodoo and cannibalism.

Guatemala's Garífuna population numbers about 4,000 and traces its history back to the island of St. Vincent. Ethnically, they are a mix of Amerindian and African peoples and their language comes from the Brazilian Arawakan language family. These Arawak-speaking peoples migrated from northern Brazil long before the arrival of Europeans in the New World and lived peacefully on the island until they were subdued by Carib-speakers from the South American mainland. The African element of their bloodline came about after intermingling with the survivors from the wreck of a Spanish ship carrying Nigerian slaves just off the coast of St. Vincent. These people eventually became known to the British as black Caribs – in their own language, Garinagu. Garífuna is the Spanish translation of this word. In the 1760s, the British tried to take St. Vincent but were driven off by the Caribs with help from the French. The Caribs would continue to oppose the British on and off for several years until finally being defeated in 1796, when they surrendered. The Garífuna were subsequently captured and imprisoned

black Carib influence provides a fascinating contrast to Guatemala's largely Mayan heritage, with rhythmic dancing and musical customs that complete the Caribbean experience.

Things have been a bit dicey in these parts recently. It's best to check into the updated situation of supposedly landless peasants invading national park lands with the help of local drug traffickers. The activities of river pirates have also made headlines in this region. That being said, the areas in the vicinity of Río Lámpara (a Río Dulce tributary) are absolutely beautiful and make a fine place to establish your very own version of life "Mosquito Coast" style. If things have settled down, it might be worth checking out, but until then I must refrain from recommending this as a place to settle down.

The town of Lívingston itself is slightly less dodgy as it lacks the utter seclusion of isolated stretches of river preferred by river pirates and drug runners.

by the British before being shipped off to the island of Roatán, off the coast of Honduras. One of the ships transporting the prisoners was captured by Spanish forces and sent to the Honduran mainland. Only 2,000 Garífuna made it to Roatán, as many died during their imprisonment on St. Vincent or along the subsequent journey.

Pleas for help from the Garífuna stranded on the tiny island of Roatán were answered by the Spanish forces who arrived some time later to take survivors to Trujillo (Honduras), where they were conscripted to serve in the armed forces or work in agricultural fields.

The Garífuna continued to move along the coast, eventually settling other parts of Honduras as well as Nicaragua. Some were taken to southern Belize to work in logging operations, from where they spread to Guatemala, establishing Lívingston in 1806. Today, the largest population of Garífunas can be found along the coast of Honduras (100,000), but there are also sizable populations in New York (50,000), New Orleans, and Los Angeles. Like other ethnic groups in Central America, they began emigrating to the United States in increasing numbers since the 1970s.

Modern Garífunas speak Spanish, English, and the Garífuna language, which melds French, Arawak, Yuroba, Swahili, and Banti. Central to their culture are music and dance, namely *punta,* a form of musical expression with obvious West African influences incorporating ritual chanting, mesmerizing drum beats, and rhythmic dancing. A traditional Garífuna band consists of three large drums, a turtle shell, a large conch shell, and maracas. You will probably hear live punta music at least once during your visit to Lívingston. Also common is *punta rock,* a more modern version of popular Garífuna music. Another fascinating traditional dance is the *yancunu* New Year's dance, similar to those of indigenous South American rainforest peoples, with distinctly West African musical origins.

There is also a small expat presence here, so at least you're not alone. As mentioned before, Lívingston's beaches are far from spectacular, so it's more the slow pace of life and tropical breezes that have folks settling down here.

Puerto Barrios and Vicinity

Puerto Barrios is a far cry from being a tourist attraction, but you may find yourself needing to pass through here in light of its status as a travel hub for getting to many of the surrounding areas. The port itself lies on the shores of Bahía de Amatique. Its emerald-green waters also harbor Puerto Santo Tomás de Castilla and its cruise ship terminal across the bay from Puerto Barrios. The hills fronting the bay in the vicinity of the cruise ship terminal are clothed in verdant rainforest, and cool jungle rivers and beautiful waterfalls cascade down the slopes. Protected as the 7,700-hectare (19,000-acre) Cerro San Gil reserve, it makes a popular day trip for cruise ship passengers. Pleasant Green

Bay Resort lies nearby, and the mostly undeveloped land all around awaits its time for real estate development.

Just outside Puerto Barrios near its airstrip is the Amatique Bay Resort and timeshares, which includes a marina and several restaurants built in Spanish neocolonial architecture. It somewhat resembles a coastal version of Antigua Guatemala. Future projects in the vicinity call for a Venetian-inspired marina fronted by condos (known as the Mayan Jungle Resort), along with a golf course, hotel, and luxury homes on an adjacent hillside.

In 2008 a group of Polish investors also announced plans for a resort and condos in the vicinity of Punta de Manabique, though details are still sketchy. Plans for the community hinged on the construction of a road from Puerto Barrios to the remote peninsula.

GETTING AROUND

Major roads lead to Puerto Barrios and Río Dulce town (Fronteras). The road to the latter town continues on to Petén department. Along the shores of Lake Izabal, Mariscos and El Estor are serviced by back roads. Lívingston is accessible via scheduled boat service from Río Dulce, Puerto Barrios, and Punta Gorda, Belize. Boats regularly ply the river between Lívingston and Fronteras. The remote beaches of Punta de Manabique are reached only by chartering a boat from Puerto Barrios at a cost of about US$100 each way.

A dirt road connects Puerto Barrios to Santo Tomás de Castilla across the bay, but you can also hire a boat from Puerto Barrios and have it drop you off at the dock of the Green Bay Hotel.

Puerto Barrios enjoys excellent first-class bus service to and from Guatemala City several times a day. The city's airport has been inaugurated more times than I care to remember and even had scheduled service from Guatemala City at one time. Its long runway is meant to accommodate international flights, but it remains to be seen if and when these flights will ever become a reality.

Las Verapaces

The regions of Alta and Baja Verapaz are Guatemala's green heartland, a mountain terrain covered largely by the country's remaining cloud forests This is probably Guatemala's most overlooked area in terms of tourism potential, as it sees surprisingly few visitors. The recreational opportunities and natural attractions are boundless and include spectacular waterfalls, cool mountain forests, mysterious caves, Mayan ruins, turquoise lagoons, and white-water rivers. Perhaps because Guatemala has always had more fame as a cultural destination, its equally splendid natural attractions have been overlooked. Thankfully, this tendency seems to be changing.

Although it might seem the Verapaz highlands are a continuation of the rugged western highlands, they are unique in a number of ways, including their settlement patterns, history, climate, geology, and population. You won't find much traditional attire being worn in these parts, particularly among the men. The women tend to wear traditional skirts with white blouses not nearly as colorful or intriguing as those worn elsewhere in the highlands. Still, Mayan culture is very much alive and well in the mountain towns and villages of the Verapaz highlands. The stunning mountain scenery is on par with that found in the western highlands.

Perhaps most exciting for the visitor or potential resident is the palpable sense of the Verapaces being a well-kept secret just waiting to be told. It's easy to fall in love with all that this wonderful area has to offer. The region has

© AL ARGUETA

Las Verapaces are home to dense cloud forests.

often taken a back seat to better-known expat locales such as Antigua and Lake Atitlán, but its list of attraction is no less impressive. The region's potential for ecotourism is largely untapped and it's my prediction that this region will soon be a major player in the Central American ecotourism circuit.

Infrastructure in these parts can be lacking, and many areas of northern Alta Verapaz have a frontier feel to them. So if you're the explorer/adventurer type, this may just be the place for you.

THE LAY OF THE LAND

Baja (Lower) Verapaz is the name given to the southernmost of the two departments. It is fringed by semi-arid plains at its southern extremes before mountains, most notably the impressive Sierra de las Minas, rise and give way to lush cloud forests. The department is bisected by a number of flat valleys, the most important being the lush river valley that is home to its departmental capital of Salamá. Other interesting towns can be found along this corridor extending west toward the department of Quiché. To the east, the Sierra de las Minas extends into Alta (Upper) Verapaz before descending into the neighboring flatlands of Izabal department. The two regions' unique ecosystems together comprise the bulk of all biodiversity found in Guatemala.

Heading north, Baja Verapaz again collides with the department of Alta Verapaz. Its departmental capital, Cobán, lies north of this boundary in a lush valley flanked by green hills and coffee farms at a comfortable altitude of 1,500 meters. Continuing north, the mountains give way to smaller limestone hills and flatlands pockmarked by a variety of caves and sinkholes. The jungle flatlands extend west into the Ixcán region of Quiché and northward into Petén.

The entry point for most travelers making their way into this region is from the south via Highway CA-14, which branches off from the semiarid plains west of Guatemala City at El Rancho junction and climbs its way northward into the mountains of Baja Verapaz. An excellent paved highway also leads south from Petén into Alta Verapaz, from where you can see the rugged limestone peaks off in the distance. It is one of Guatemala's most wonderfully scenic stretches of highway.

LOCAL DIALECTS

Mayan dialects spoken in the region of Las Verapaces include Achi' (western Baja Verapaz), Poqomchi' (Alta and Baja Verapaz), and Q'eqchi (Alta Verapaz).

DAILY LIVING

Cobán is quite cosmopolitan, with a decent shopping mall (Plaza Magdalena), good restaurants, and even a McDonald's. Other shopping options include the local market for fruits and vegetables. There are Spanish-language private schools for the kids and also at least three local Spanish schools. The town has adequate pharmacies and a decent hospital. Outside of Cobán, services can be quite lacking.

WHERE TO LIVE
Cobán and Vicinity

Cobán has been hosting an expat population since the 19th century when German planters bought up land and sought their fortunes in the coffee trade. Most of the Germans were expelled from Guatemala during World War II, with U.S. pressure, but German names can still be found throughout the region. Today Cobán has a smattering of foreigners, who mostly own restaurants and lodges in Cobán and vicinity.

Following the trend of neo-urbanism which has become quite popular in Guatemala City, real estate developers recently unveiled the new Ciudad Sasay, a planned community east of town on a hill overlooking the city. The project should eventually cover an area roughly one-third the size of Cobán and will encompass schools, hotels, recreational areas, shops, and office-warehouse hybrids. Prices for the various house models built in neocolonial style range US$80,000–160,000.

Many of the surrounding towns and villages lie surrounded by the region's incredible greenery and make great places to buy a plot of land on which to build a home. These include San Juan Chamelco, San Pedro Carchá, and San Cristóbal Verapaz. This is still virgin territory, so get out and explore the countryside. You may just find the property of your dreams at a bargain basement price.

Northern Alta Verapaz

Northern Alta Verapaz is somewhat similar in topography to the

a rustic inn along the road to Cobán

© AL ARGUETA

adjacent Petén department to the north. The mostly flat terrain has a lime-stone bedrock as its base and the land is dotted with turquoise lagoons, caves, rivers, waterfalls, and odd karst hills that look like something straight out of Vietnam. Living in this remote jungle wilderness will require some hard work and gumption, but if you've ever dreamed of owning an ecotourism enterprise in an exotic locale and want to get in early, this may be the place for you.

Among the local attractions are the Lachuá lagoon, the Candelaria caves, the Semuc Champey pools, Las Conchas pools, the Río Cahabón, the ruins of Cancuén, and Lagunas de Sepalau. Many of these lie near the village of Chisec, so it makes a convenient base for exploration despite a relative absence of serviceable accommodations. In many ways, Northern Alta Verapaz resembles inland Belize in the 1980s before adventurous expats turned the area into a hub for ecotourism and established world-class eco-lodges. If you've ever dreamed of following in their footsteps but thought all the good locales were taken long ago, think again. Keep in mind that many of Belize's world-class lodges started out as abandoned farms.

GETTING AROUND

Cobán is easily accessible via a paved highway from Guatemala City. The trip from the capital takes about five hours by car or bus. By plane, Cobán is due north of Guatemala City and the flight takes about 20 minutes. You can sometimes charter a flight to Cobán, and there is an airstrip just outside of town that sees frequent use from local coffee planters.

A newly paved road runs through Alta Verapaz from Cobán all the way to Flores, Petán, providing easy access to the attractions found in northern Alta Verapaz. Likewise, part of the road to Semuc Champey is paved, heading from Cobán. Pickups and minivans run from Cobán to the smaller towns and villages of Alta Verapaz. If you're driving in these parts and are looking to do some off-road exploring, you'll need four-wheel-drive.

PETÉN

Petén is Guatemala's frontier state, much as Amazonas is to Brazil. About a third of this Ohio-sized province is protected as the Maya Biosphere Reserve, harboring the department's remaining rainforest and several Mayan sites. Among the latter is the utterly spectacular Tikal, protected as a 575-square-kilometer national park and easily one of the country's most famous landmarks. Despite the huge potential for ecotourism, Petén has had to deal with ongoing deforestation inside and outside its protected areas at alarming rates. It is Guatemala's poorest department, which soon becomes evident when arriving by road from Belize and continuing the journey down a dirt road surrounded on either side by widespread deforestation.

Petén's struggle to protect its natural heritage has brought in many international conservation organizations and NGOs. These are based in the island city of Flores, on Lake Petén Itzá, right smack in the middle of the department. Along with neighboring Santa Elena, Flores marks the territory's largest urban center.

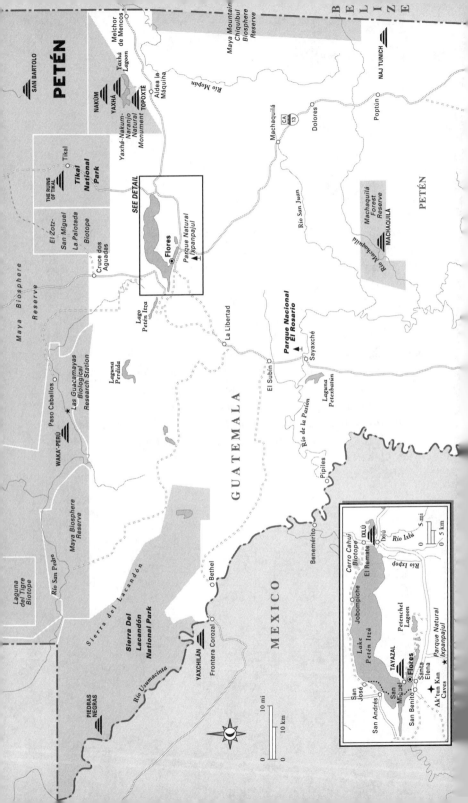

PETÉN

SAN BARTOLO

THE RUINS OF TIKAL
Tikal
Tikal National Park

El Zotz-
San Miguel La Palotada
Biotope

Cruce dos
Aguadas

Melchor de Mencos

Yaxhá Lagoon

NAKÚM
YAXHÁ
TOPOXTÉ
Aldea la Máquina

Yaxhá-Nakúm-Naranjo Natural Monument

Maya Mountain Chiquibul Biosphere Reserve

Río Mopán

NAJ TUNICH

Poptún

Machaquilá
CA 13
Dolores

PETÉN

Río San Juan

Machaquilá Forest Reserve
MACHAQUILÁ

Río Machaquilá

SEE DETAIL

Flores

Parque Natural Ixpanpajul

Lago Petén Itzá

La Libertad

Laguna Perdida

El Subín

Parque Nacional El Rosario

Sayaxché

Laguna Petexbatún

Río de la Pasión

Maya Biosphere Reserve

Las Guacamayas Biological Research Station

Paso Caballos

WAKA'-PERÚ

Pipiles

GUATEMALA

Laguna del Tigre Biotope

Río San Pedro

Maya Biosphere Reserve

Benemérito

Bethel

Sierra del Lacandón

Sierra Del Lacandón National Park

MEXICO

YAXCHILÁN
Frontera Corozal

PIEDRAS NEGRAS

Río Usumacinta

10 mi
10 km

0

10 km
0

Detail inset

San José

Lake Petén Itzá

San Andrés

San Miguel

TAYAZAL

San Benito

Santa Elena

Ak'tun Kan Caves

Flores

Parque Natural Ixpanpajul

Jobompiche

Petenchel

Petenchel Lagoon

Cerro Cahuí Biotope

El Remate

IXLÚ
Ixlú

Río Ixlú

Río Ixpop

5 mi
0   5 km
0

B E L I Z E

It makes sense that the area around Lake Petén Itzá was the first to have been colonized, its waters offering an opportunity to cool off from the stifling midday heat. Still, much land remains on the shores of the lake, which inexplicably remains almost untouched despite the presence of beaches and clear, turquoise waters that resemble a lake version of Cancún.

You'll surely run into many environmentally minded travelers and conservationists working in these parts. Environmental woes aside, Petén's geography is truly enchanting to lovers of tropical forests and Mayan archaeology. The sheer density of cultural sites and natural heritage is astounding, which makes their conservation all the more pressing.

THE LAY OF THE LAND

The jungle plains bordering Guatemala's highlands continue north from Alta Verapaz and extend into Petén department, Guatemala's largest. Almost the entirety of Petén was once rainforest, but about half of it now has fallen to fire, chainsaw, and ax. There are still some remnants of forest left in the department's southern half, though most of what remains is found along the territory's northern border with Mexico and along the eastern border with Belize. The southeastern corner of Petén is a continuation of Belize's mountain pine ridge habitat. With cooler temperatures, abundant pine forests, and at least one expat-owned jungle lodge of note, Poptún is in the vicinity of caves and jungle rivers and makes a rather pleasant place to live.

Lake Petén Itzá, one of Guatemala's largest, sits in the heart of Petén and also harbors its largest population center, the urban area of Flores/Santa Elena. Many smaller towns and villages are also found along the lakeshore. The village of El Remate, along the road heading north from Flores/Santa Elena to Tikal National Park, has become increasingly popular with visitors and expat residents.

The northern third of Petén is protected as the Maya Biosphere Reserve, comprising several national parks, a multiple-use zone, and a buffer zone along its southern fringes. The multiple-use zone has all but disappeared, along with vast areas of some of the national parks. The parks bordering Mexico on the western and northwestern frontiers, Sierra del Lacandón and Laguna del Tigre, have fared far worse than parks bordering Belize to the east. Land invasions by poor peasants, led by loggers, cattle ranchers, and drug traffickers, have taken quite a toll on these two parks. Clandestine airstrips host arriving aircraft with drug payloads while park guards looking to evict settlers are routinely fired upon in these parts. This is an area best avoided for now.

It should be noted that not all of the Maya Biosphere Reserve is tropical

THE MIRADOR BASIN PROJECT

Deep in the untouched forests of northern Petén in what archaeologists call the Mirador Basin, far from the throngs of tourists at other Mayan sites, lie the overgrown remains of the most fascinating cities ever built in pre-Classic times. The Mirador Basin, as defined by its geographical characteristics, is an elevated basin dominated by low-lying swamps known as *bajos* surrounded by karst limestone hills to the south, east, and west, forming a triangular trench covering roughly 2,100 square kilometers. Some of its sites, including El Mirador and Nakbé, are currently being excavated and have yielded many clues concerning the advanced nature of early Mayan civilization. As the excavations continue to yield fascinating new discoveries, archaeologists, conservationists, and local residents remain at odds about how best to preserve the remaining Petén forests and the important monuments they harbor.

At the heart of the controversy is the proposal for a Mirador Basin National Park, spearheaded by UCLA's Dr. Richard Hansen, who heads the excavation project at El Mirador. The park would stretch clear to the Mexican border at its northernmost points, encompassing parts of Mirador-Río Azul National Park. At its southern tip, it would stretch all the way down to El Zotz-San Miguel La Palotada Biotope. The area is home to Petén's last remaining expanses of well-preserved forests.

Hansen envisions a large national park guarded by armed rangers similar to those of the U.S. Parks Service. There would be several luxurious eco-lodges, visitors centers, an airstrip, a narrow-gauge railroad, and hiking trails linking the various restored Mayan sites within the basin. The proposed park would be roughly four times the size of Tikal National Park and would be largely based upon the same management model. Hansen sees the potential to accommodate up to 80,000 visitors per year.

Against the odds, Hansen has made some incredible headway toward achieving his ambitious goals. In 2002, President Alfonso Portillo agreed to create the Regional System for the Special Protection of Cultural Heritage as a means of protecting archaeological sites in Petén and declared 2,400 square kilometers of the Maya Biosphere as a "special archaeological zone." Its official name became the Mirador Basin. The agreement nullified community forestry concessions permitting sustainable logging and forest product extraction in multiple-use zones near the Mirador Basin archaeological sites, much to the dismay of the local communities benefited by the concessions.

More recently, Hansen also found the support of President Oscar Berger and important government officials in the departments of archaeology, forestry, and tourism. He also has representatives lobbying the Inter-American Development Bank for funding and has rallied wealthy investors inside and outside of Guatemala to his cause. All of this is being coordinated through The Foundation for Anthropological Research and Environmental Studies (FARES), established by Hansen in 1996. The Colom administration has provided support for the project under the jurisdiction of a sustainable management plan known as Cuatro Balam.

In 2003, the California-based

Global Heritage Fund and several other organizations donated US$880,000 toward the restoration of four temples at Nakbé. Hansen says he needs US$35 million over the next 13 years to excavate and protect the area while developers build tourist infrastructure. FARES currently provides the funding for year-round protection of the Mirador Basin sites from looters. In the long run, Hansen believes increased tourism could fund the preservation and protection of the sites, making the project self-sufficient while providing new economic opportunities for residents.

Hansen's plans, if a bit grandiose, seem well-intentioned. But they have met substantial opposition from local communities and Petén's powerful environmental groups, who have spent many years and millions of dollars developing relationships with local communities to encourage the sustainable extraction of forest products. The sustainable forestry programs have received support from The Nature Conservancy and the U.S. Agency for International Development, among others.

Some believe the communities could receive greater economic benefit from sustainable forestry than from working as staff in tourist hotels and restaurants. The community of Uaxactún, for example, was awarded a sustainable forestry concession in 2000 by CONAP, and villagers there have made a living from collecting forest products for decades.

Although the park itself will supposedly be without roads, new infrastructure would have to be built to make the region more accessible to visitors, raising the specter of a much-talked-about road connecting Tikal to Mexico's Calakmul. Along these lines, Mexico has been insisting on the construction of a road from Chetumal to Tikal in an attempt to integrate the two countries' archaeological sites as part of the Plan Puebla-Panama, an idea vehemently opposed by local conservationists because it would bisect some of the best-conserved areas of the Maya Biosphere Reserve. Representatives from various NGOs working in Petén cite a recent study predicting the loss of 60 percent of the forest in Mirador-Río Azul National Park within 15 years if the road is constructed. A valuable wildlife corridor would also be severed in half. As demonstrated in other parts of the biosphere reserve, most notably Laguna del Tigre, roads bring in settlers, looters, drug traffickers, and clandestine loggers. Others believe the airstrips and luxurious accommodations would allow high-end tourists to fly in and out of the Mirador Basin without contributing much to the local communities.

Because the forestry concessions are still relatively young, it remains to be seen whether or not they are indeed sustainable. Scientific studies to answer this question have determined it is too early to decide, though it should be noted that the seasonal fires affecting much of the western half of the Maya Biosphere Reserve have been almost absent from the Mirador Basin, Uaxactún, and surrounding areas. Supporters of the concessions believe the vested interest the communities have in protecting the very resources from which they derive their livelihoods will prevent them from destroying the forests.

(CONTINUED ON NEXT PAGE)

THE MIRADOR BASIN PROJECT (continued)

What is certain is that something must be done soon to prevent the Mirador Basin's forests from disappearing and to protect its rich cultural heritage from looting. Time is of the essence, as conservationists, archaeologists, and local communities run the risk of not knowing what they've truly lost until it's gone.

In March 2009, Hansen and Guatemalan authorities unveiled the recent discovery of a frieze at El Mirador depicting a scene from a Maya sacred book, the Popol Vuh, in which the mythi-cal 'Hero Twins' visit the underworld. According to Hansen, the frieze lends further credence to the Popol Vuh's creation myth and its authenticity as a Mayan document, despite its first translation well into the Christian era, in the 1700s. The frieze took three months to excavate and was found while archaeologists were looking for water reservoirs at the site.

For more information on the Mirador Basin project, check out the FARES website at www.miradorbasin.com.

rainforest. Much of it is covered by vast wetlands and seasonal swampland. The dense forests with high trees found near Tikal National Park eventually give way to shorter scrub forests further north, as the ecosystem transitions into the drier forests of the Yucatán Peninsula.

Climate

Petén's climate is very different from that of the rest of (mostly mountainous) Guatemala. If you're arriving by air from Guatemala City, you'll quickly feel the heat and humidity like a blast from a fiery furnace as you walk off the airplane. Welcome to life at sea level on a sweltering jungle plain. The sole exception to the territory's stifling heat is the microclimate found in the vicinity of Poptún, which lies at an elevation of 600 meters. Temperatures here are about 10 degrees cooler than areas of Petén lying directly at sea level. Petén can often get as hot as 100° F in March and April.

DAILY LIVING

The area around Flores/Santa Elena has grown by leaps and bounds in recent years, and it is certainly the region's most cosmopolitan place to live. The presence of an international airport (with flights to Belize, Cancún, and Guatemala City), along with paved roads leading south to Cobán and Río Dulce, has provided the urban center with good communications to the outside world.

El Remate is also well-connected by virtue of its location beside the paved road leading from Flores/Santa Elena to Tikal. Like Flores, it has a small but growing expat community whose members own and run local lodges, restaurants, and tour services.

Health

The nearest hospital is in the town of San Benito, which in some ways is just a continuation of Santa Elena. Medical care, even in the Flores/Santa Elena sprawl, is generally deficient, though you'll at least find some well-stocked pharmacies. Most locals travel to Guatemala City for health care, considering the fact that its modern hospitals are just a 30-minute plane ride away.

Schools

Schools, too, are deficient in terms of what expats would be looking for, namely a bilingual private school. There are, however, Spanish-language private schools in Santa Elena. The area is mostly the haunt of independent travelers, so don't expect this to change anytime soon. If you're living in Petén with school-aged children, I'd strongly recommend home schooling.

Petén does have a number of Spanish schools catering to foreigners. These are found mostly in the twin lakeside towns of San José and San Andrés. All of them have an ecological and community service bent.

Shopping

Flores proper has a small grocery store that carries a number of imported items, including a good assortment of liquors. Locally owned corner stores can be found in all the territory's cities and towns. There are also several grocery stores attached to gas stations found along the road to Tikal from Flores/Santa Elena.

Flores and Santa Elena have recently been abuzz with news surrounding the construction of Mundo Maya International Mall, located along the waterfront adjacent to the causeway, on the Santa Elena side of the lake. Expected to cost US$40 million when completed in three phases, it will encompass a grocery store, 115 retail shops, movie theaters, and fast food outlets, all built in an architectural style reminiscent of ancient Mayan cities. The mall's first phase is nearing completion.

PRIME LIVING LOCATIONS

Flores and Santa Elena

Collectively known simply as "Flores," the towns of Flores and Santa Elena sit across from each other separated by the waters of Lake Petén Itzá and connected by a causeway. Flores proper and its pretty pastel-colored houses float atop the turquoise waters of Lake Petén Itzá. Santa Elena, meanwhile, sprawls on the lake's shore and is a rather ugly, chaotic collection of dilapidated houses, businesses, and transportation infrastructure. Mundo Maya International Airport lies just outside Santa Elena along the road leading to Tikal.

Flores is where you'll find the best restaurants, several nice hotels, reputable travel agencies, and the offices of NGOs operating in Petén. Given its small size, the availability of real estate for rent or purchase on the island is certainly limited, and you may find yourself setting up shop across the causeway in Santa Elena or its environs.

HOUSING

Flores and Santa Elena have nothing in the way of modern condos, so you'll find yourself renting or buying one of the older homes on the island or a slightly more modern home on the mainland in Santa Elena. Both towns lag far behind the rest of Guatemala in terms of infrastructure, so living in

these parts will be a far cry from the more modern amenities you'll find in Guatemala City, Antigua, and even Lake Atitlán. Most expats living here tend to buy a plot along the lakeshore and build a home to their specifications.

A bright spot on the horizon is the newly unveiled gated community of Residenciales El Roble Casa & Campo, located on the lakeshore at kilometer 9.5 on the road to Tikal. Its 117 lots start at 2,500 square *varas* (18,900 square feet), with prices between US$30 and US$40 per square *vara*. Home prices start at US$175,000. The project is the brainchild of the same development group that is building Mundo Maya

Flores has many funky storefronts.

© AL ARGUETA

PRIME LIVING LOCATIONS

International Mall. Its developers are also planning a golf resort in the vicinity of the community.

WHERE TO LIVE

As the local real estate market is still very much in diapers, word of mouth is your best bet for finding available property in and around Flores. People to ask include the front desk staff at your hotel, taxi drivers, boat people, and wait staff. Local expats run many of the area's hotels and restaurants and are usually quite happy to tell you how they did it.

Of the two towns, Flores is certainly the more pleasant. Its main disadvantage is that it's not growing because it's confined to its speck of land in the surrounding body of water. Santa Elena has more available land and property but is a somewhat chaotic agglomeration of houses, businesses, and services. If you're looking for the slower pace of life and have a bit of gumption or enough money to afford prices in a gated community, your best bet might be to settle along the shores of Lake Petén Itzá and build something to suit your tastes and needs.

GETTING AROUND

Getting around Flores and Santa Elena is relatively easy, as the distances are rarely more than a few kilometers. The airport, on the outskirts of Santa Elena, is a three-kilometer walk from Flores. Likewise, crossing the causeway between both towns can be done on foot in a matter of five minutes. *Tuk tuks* and taxis are fairly abundant. The Mundo Maya Airport has a variety of rental car agencies should you need your own wheels. There is frequent bus service to El Remate and Tikal.

Lake Petén Itzá

The waters of lowland Lake Petén Itzá lie smack in the middle of Petén. Much longer than wide, its shoreline resembles that of northern Yucatán thanks in part to white sandy beaches and the karst nature of Petén's bedrock. Much of the shoreline is still covered in forest, and there is even a nature preserve, Cerro Cahuí, on its northern shore. Formal real estate is still in its infancy here, but a good command of Spanish and a pioneering spirit can get you in on some prime lakefront property before the rest of the world gets wind of this undiscovered gem. I'm almost hesitant to write this, as I'm actively searching for land on the lake's shores.

© AL ARGUETA

Lake Petén Itzá is just 30 minutes from Tikal National Park via a paved road.

THE LAY OF THE LAND

Most of the land surrounding the lake is flat, save for a hill known as Cerro Cahuí, protected as a wildlife refuge and located on the northeastern shore near El Remate. The lake has some wonderful beaches, especially around the towns of San Andrés, San José, and El Remate. The latter enjoys the easiest access thanks to its location beside the paved road leading from Flores to the Mayan ruins at Tikal National Park.

Local Dialect

Petén is inhabited by people from all parts of Guatemala lured to the area by the promise of available land for slash-and-burn agriculture. San Andrés and San José are bastions of the Itzá people, who hold strong to their age-old customs and speak the namesake dialect.

WHERE TO LIVE
El Remate

El Remate's strategic location halfway between Flores and Tikal has meant its inevitable growth from a sleepy lakeside village into a new tourism alternative for visitors wanting (or needing) to stay outside the national park. El Remate has a number of good hotels, restaurants, and lakeside swimming holes and has seen an increase in foreign real estate speculation in recent years. Some of the town's hotels are located right on the lakeshore, while others lie separated from the lake by the road, sprawled on surrounding hillsides with wonderful panoramic views of the lake.

You will probably see hand-written signs announcing property for sale. Another way to get wind of deals is to inquire locally through the usual channels. Keep in mind that OCRET laws apply to all lakeside properties.

Jobompiche

From El Remate, the dirt road leads west along the lakeshore past the luxurious Camino Real Tikal hotel, the Cerro Cahuí preserve, and on to the quaint village of Jobompiche. Jobompiche was placed on the map by Francis Ford Coppola, who added a Guatemalan property to his portfolio of luxury jungle accommodations in 2005. La Lancha lies very much secluded but may serve as inspiration for other luxury accommodations or private homes in the vicinity of Jobompiche in the near future.

San José and San Andrés

San José and San Andrés enjoy quiet locations beside the lake, good road access, and a fitting dose of cultural diversity thanks to ancestral pride in the local Itzá culture. There are a number of Spanish schools in the area, started with the help of environmental organizations and now fully taken over by local community ownership. As such, the towns are accustomed to foreign visitors, and a number of small lakeside lodges have sprung up here in recent years. There are some excellent swimming holes in the area.

GETTING AROUND

A road circles all around Lake Petán Itza but is mostly unpaved save for the area along the road to Tikal. There is frequent bus service from Flores/Santa Elena to El Remate, San Andrés, and San José. Jobompiche is also served by bus. Boats for cruising around the lake can be hired from Flores, though there is little in the way of scheduled service to outlying areas due to the high price of fuel to power motorboats and the relative accessibility of these areas by road.

Several lodges in and around El Remate can arrange bike, kayak, and horse rentals.

PRIME LIVING LOCATIONS

FRANCIS FORD COPPOLA ON HIS GUATEMALAN HIDEAWAY

A few years ago, movie director-cum-hotelier Francis Ford Coppola added a Guatemalan property to his two existing resorts in Belize. Its proximity to Tikal and fabulous lakeside setting made La Lancha a natural addition to his portfolio of properties.

I understand La Lancha was an existing property prior to becoming part of the Coppola resorts. When and how did you discover it?
A very sophisticated traveler and friend, John Heaton, told us about La Lancha and described it to us. He thought that it might become available, as the French couple who had created it might be interested in relocating now that their children were getting bigger. I was enchanted by the location and simplicity of the place, and awed by the site at Tikal, which I think is one of the wonders of the world. Also I thought the lake itself was beautiful, and so I was eager to add La Lancha to our group of small resorts – Blancaneaux Lodge and Turtle Inn.

Can you tell me a bit about the process of actually buying the property?
At first the couple was nostalgic about leaving the place they had created, and so finally it was agreed that they'd stay on to manage it. But after a while this proved to be impractical. They moved to Antigua to create a new "Hotel de Charme." This is the website if you don't already know it: www.unpaseoporlaantigua.com.

What do you like most about La Lancha?
I love the unspoiled area with a troop of howler monkeys living just outside the deck of my room and the huge, beautiful lake below.

Poptún

Petén's southeastern flanks feature higher elevations and pine-forest-studded hillsides in addition to cooler temperatures. While hardly an expat colony, Poptún has the climate, scenery, and road access that would make it a very good option for settling down. There is little in the way of infrastructure or civilization, but then again that may be just what you're looking for.

Owned by an American expatriate who moved here with her late husband in 1971, Finca Ixobel is a local landmark and veritable ecotourism institution that has grown from its humble beginnings as a working farm. It is a favorite with travelers. Another well-known local lodge is that of Guatemalan-owned Villa de los Castellanos.

Poptún was once the site of a Guatemalan military base which served as a training area for elite counterinsurgency soldiers, known as *kaibiles*. The base was closed after the 1996 pace accords and the controversial 1990 murder of U.S. citizen and local resident Michael Devine by soldiers stationed at the base.

Have you traveled to other parts of Guatemala? If so, what are some of your favorite spots?

I've spent many years of travel in Guatemala: in Antigua, Guatemala City, Panajachel, and the Petén, where our resort is located. My wife Eleanor and I often visit small markets to purchase carvings, antiques, and other furnishings for La Lancha. We enjoy the country, and particularly the people, who have always been very friendly. Eleanor, who is an authority on textiles, makes buying trips to the mountains to purchase gorgeous hand-woven textiles directly from the weavers. These become bedspreads, pillows, and wall hangings at the resort, plus they are available in our gift shop.

What do you think about the country's untapped tourism potential and specifically that of Petén?

Tikal is certainly the magnet for Petén, with the other attraction being the lake itself and the abundant birds, monkeys, and other animals that make this glorious area their home. The town of Flores is completely charming, and you can spend a delightful day exploring the streets and shops, and dining in the family restaurants.

Are there any future plans to add rooms or additional services to La Lancha?

Yes, I admire and enjoy the lake so much that eventually we plan to add some sort of funicular to connect new and perhaps more luxurious villas on the lake with the existing La Lancha resort.

Are there any plans for new properties in Guatemala?

No, not at this time.

Interview conducted with Mr. Coppola via e-mail in January 2009

THE LAY OF THE LAND

Poptún is accessed via a paved road running north from Izabal's Río Dulce and continuing up to the departmental capital of Flores. It lies at a pleasantly cool altitude of 600 meters. Poptún town proper is located a few kilometers from Finca Ixobel.

Poptún's wonderful setting amidst a pine-studded, karst landscape makes for some phenomenal outdoor recreation opportunities. Among the options are treks to remote Mayan sites, jungle hikes, caving, horseback riding, and inner tubing down lazy stretches of jungle river. All of these can be arranged through the local lodges.

WHERE TO LIVE

You can certainly live in town, though there is nothing really quite yet in the way of rentals or local real estate brokers. A better option might be to buy a plot of land in the surrounding countryside and build a home to suit your tastes and needs. In many ways, this area is reminiscent of inland Belize in

THE MURDER OF MIKE DEVINE

While it's a well-known fact that the CIA provided logistical support to the Guatemalan military in its counterinsurgency campaign, it's a lesser-known fact that it unwittingly contributed to the murder of at least one U.S. citizen in Guatemala during the country's civil war.

Mike and Carol Devine moved to Poptún in 1971 after falling in love with Petén's jungles. They lived a quiet life, adopting two local Mayan children, running a farm, and building a few cabins for guests to sleep in. Despite the civil war raging in the highlands, the Devines felt a world away from the violence. That all changed one day in June 1990, when Mike went out and was never again seen alive.

For Carol Devine, the nightmare leading to uncovering the tangled web involving her husband's murder began with a visit to the local military base. Hoping to find help in locating her missing husband, Devine pleaded with soldiers to speak with base commander Julio Roberto Alpirez. Like so many other family members of Guatemalan citizens "disappeared" during the civil war, Devine was turned away at the gates of the military barracks with no one to speak to her. The next day, her husband's body was found along the road leading to their farm, hands tied and nearly decapitated.

In the ensuing months, Devine would enlist the help of the U.S. Embassy in Guatemala and local eye-witnesses to uncover the truth behind her husband's grisly murder. Locals provided information point-ing to the fact that Colonel Alpirez had knowingly sheltered in his barracks a death squad on a mission to murder Mike Devine. They also gathered evidence of Alpirez's involvement in a subsequent cover-up.

The real shocker came five years after the murder when Congressman Robert G. Torricelli revealed Alpirez had been on the CIA payroll when Devine was murdered. He had in fact remained on the CIA payroll until about two years later, shortly after ordering the murder of captured Guatemalan insurgent Efraín Bámaca, who was the husband of U.S. citizen and lawyer Jennifer Harbury. The United States suspended military aid to Guatemala for a time, following these findings.

The mastermind behind the murder of Mike Devine was eventually found to be Captain Hugo Contreras, who sent five foot soldiers to kill Mr. Devine from his base in Flores. The soldiers were tried and convicted for the murder, as was Captain Contreras. He later escaped from a Guatemala City military barracks where he was being held prisoner and is still at large.

Theories behind the reasons for the murder abound, though it's generally believed Mike Devine stumbled upon narcotics or timber smuggling operations by the Guatemalan army. Carol Devine also points to an incident involving a drunk and belligerent Captain Contreras getting kicked out of their restaurant by Mike some years earlier, and some vague threats issued at the time.

the early 1980s. Mick and Lucy Fleming purchased an overgrown farm in Belize's Cayo district, which, some 20 years later, is one of the world's finest eco-lodges. Similarly, Poptún's Finca Ixobel started out as a working farm when purchased by Carol and her late husband Mike Devine in 1971 but has grown to become one of Guatemala's most famous backpacker lodgings.

If you're interested in buying land in these parts, your best bet is to ask around town. If you're staying at Finca Ixobel, you may have the unique opportunity to pick Carol's brain on the rewards and challenges of living in Poptún over a cup of coffee.

GETTING AROUND

Tuk tuks and taxis regularly circulate through Poptún's streets and can take you out to the nearby jungle lodges. If you're arriving Poptún by bus, the driver can let you off at the turnoff to Finca Ixobel from the main road. From there, it's a 15-minute walk to the lodge.

RESOURCES

Consulates and Embassies

For general information, visit the Guatemala Embassy home page (www.guatemala-embassy.org).

UNITED STATES
CHICAGO
200 N. Michigan Ave., Ste. 610
Chicago, IL 60601
tel. 312/332-1587
fax 312/322-4256

HOUSTON
3013 Fountain View, Ste. 230
Houston, TX 77057
tel. 713/953-9531

LOS ANGELES
1605 W. Olympic Blvd., Ste. 422
Los Angeles, CA 90015
tel. 213/365-9251

MIAMI
300 Sevilla Ave.
Coral Gables, FL 33134
tel. 305/443-4828

NEW YORK
57 Park Ave.
New York, NY 10016
tel. 212/686-3837

SAN FRANCISCO
870 Market St., Ste. 667
San Francisco, CA 94102
tel. 415/788-5651

WASHINGTON, D.C.
2220 R St. NW #210
Washington, D.C. 20008
tel. 202/745-4952
fax 202/745-1908

CANADA
OTTAWA
130 Albert St., Ste. 1010
Ottawa, ON K1P 5G4
tel. 613/233-7188
fax 613/233-0135

UNITED KINGDOM
LONDON
13 Fawcett St.
London, U.K. SW10 9HN
tel. 020/7351-3042
fax 020/7376-5708

FOREIGN EMBASSIES IN GUATEMALA
Most embassies and consulates are open only during weekday mornings. All are in Guatemala City.

AUSTRIA
6a Avenida 20-25
Edificio Plaza, Zona 10
tel. 2364-3460

BELIZE
Avenida La Reforma 8-50
Edificio El Reformador, Suite 803, Zona 9
tel. 2334-5531

CANADA
13 Calle 8-44, Nivel 6
Edificio Edyma Plaza, Zona 10
tel. 2333-6102

COLOMBIA
5a Avenida 5-55
Edificio Europlaza, Torre I, Zona 14
tel. 2385-3432

COSTA RICA
1a Avenida 15-52, Zona 10
tel. 2363-1345

CUBA
13 Calle 5-72, Zona 10
tel. 2333-7627

EL SALVADOR
5a Avenida 8-15, Zona 9
tel. 2360-7660

FRANCE
16 Calle 4-53, Zona 10
Edificio Marbella, Nivel 11
tel. 2337-3639

GERMANY
20 Calle 6-20, Zona 10
Edificio Plaza Marítima
tel. 2364-6700

HONDURAS
19 Avenida A 20-19, Zona 10
tel. 2366-5640

ISRAEL
13 Avenida 14-07, Zona 10
Colonia Oakland
tel. 2363-5665

ITALY
5a Avenida 8-59, Zona 14
tel. 2337-4851

MEXICO
15 Calle 3-20, Zona 10
tel. 2333-7254

NETHERLANDS
16 Calle 0-55, Zona 10
Torre Internacional, Nivel 13
tel. 2367-4761

NICARAGUA
10a Avenida 14-72, Zona 10
tel. 2368-0785

PANAMA
10a Avenida 18-53, Zona 14
tel. 2368-2805

SPAIN
6a Calle 6-48, Zona 9
tel. 2379-3530

SWEDEN
8a Avenida 15-07, Zona 10
tel. 2333-6536

SWITZERLAND
16 Calle 0-65
Torre Internacional, Zona 10
tel. 2367-5520

UNITED KINGDOM
16 Calle 0-65, Zona 10
Torre Internacional, Nivel 11
tel. 2367-5520

UNITED STATES
Avenida La Reforma 7-01, Zona 10
tel. 2331-1541
http://guatemala.usembassy.gov/
contact.html

Government Organizations

**CÁMARA DE COMERCIO
GUATEMALTECO-AMERICANA
(AMERICAN CHAMBER OF
COMMERCE IN GUATEMALA,
OR AMCHAM)**
5a Avenida 5-55, Zona 14
Edificio Europlaza, Torre 1, Nivel 5
Guatemala City
tel. 2336-4766 and 2417-0800
www.amchamguate.com

BANCO DE GUATEMALA
7a Avenida 22-01, Zona 4
Guatemala City
tel. 2429-6000

**CÁMARA DE INDUSTRIA
DE GUATEMALA**
Ruta 6 9-21, Zona 4, Nivel 12
Guatemala City
tel. 2331-9000

CÁMARA DE TURISMO (CAMTUR)
7a Avenida 1-17, Zona 4
Edificio Inguat, Nivel 8
Guatemala City
tel. 2360-0892
www.camtur.org

**CÁMARA GUATEMALTECA
DE LA CONSTRUCCIÓN**
Ruta 4 3-56, Zona 4
Edificio C. Const.
Guatemala City
tel. 2334-2756

RESOURCES

CONSEJO NACIONAL DE ÁREAS PROTEGIDAS (CONAP)
5a Avenida 6-06, Zona 1
Edificio IPM, Plantas 5, 6, y 7
Guatemala City
tel. 2422-6700
www.conap.gob.gt

DEPARTAMENTO DE TRÁNSITO (TRANSIT DEPARTMENT)
Calzada Aguilar Batres 34-70, Zona 11
Galerías del Sur
Guatemala City
tel. 2442-0719

DIRECCIÓN GENERAL DE MIGRACIÓN
6a Avenida 3-11, Zona 4
Guatemala City
tel. 2411-2411
www.migracion.gob.gt

INSTITUTO GUATEMALTECO DE SEGURIDAD SOCIAL (IGSS)
7a Avenida 22-72, Zona 1
Guatemala City
tel. 2412-1224

INSTITUTO GUATEMALTECO DE TURISMO (INGUAT)
7a Ave. 1-17, Zona 4
Centro Civico
Guatemala City
tel. 2421-2800
www.visitguatemala.com

INSTITUTO NACIONAL DE ELECTRIFICACIÓN (INDE)
Guatemala City
tel. 2422-1800

INVEST IN GUATEMALA
10a Calle 3-17, Zona 10
Edificio Aseguradora General, Nivel 4
Guatemala City
tel. 2421-2484
www.investinguatemala.org

MINISTERIO DE AMBIENTE Y RECURSOS NATURALES (MARN)
20 Calle 28-58, Zona 10
Guatemala City
tel. 2423-0500

MINISTERIO DE AGRICULTURA, GANADERÍA Y ALIMENTACIÓN (MAGA)
7a Avenida 12-90, Zona 13
Edificio Monja Blanca
Guatemala City
tel. 2471-3247

MINISTERIO DE COMUNICACIONES, INFRAESTRUCTURA Y VIVIENDA (MICIVI)
8a Avenida 7 15 Calle, Zona 13
Guatemala City
tel. 2423-0500

MINISTERIO DE CULTURA Y DEPORTES
12 Avenida 11-11, Zona 1
Guatemala City
tel. 2253-0543/8

MINISTERIO DE EDUCACIÓN (MINEDUC)
Guatemala City
tel. 2411-9595

MINISTERIO DE TRABAJO, MIGRACIONES LABORALES (MINISTRY OF LABOR)
14 Calle 5-49, Zona 1
Edifico Nasa, Nivel 4 y 6
Guatemala City
tel. 2230-1364 or 2230-1368

OFICINA DE CONTROL DE ÁREAS DE RESERVA DEL ESTADO (OCRET)
7a Avenida 12-23, Zona 9
Edificio Etisa, 6to Nivel ala Norte
Guatemala City

SUPERINTENDENCIA DE ADMINISTRACIÓN TRIBUTARIA (SAT)
7a Avenida 3-73, Zona 9
Guatemala City
tel. 2329-7070
www.sat.gob.gt

Environmental Organizations

ALIANZA VERDE
Parque Central
Flores, Petén
www.alianzaverde.org

This group has done an excellent job of promoting low-impact tourism in Petén as part of its mandate to aid in the protection and conservation of the region's precious natural resources. In addition to marketing efforts, Alianza Verde certifies ecotourism operations and aids in the training of tourism staff to improve Petén's tourism product and visitor experience. It functions as an association of businesses, organizations, and individuals who make their livelihood from Petén's tourism industry.

ASOCIACION AK' TENAMIT
11 Avenida A 9-39, Zona 2
Guatemala City
tel. 2254-1560 Guatemala City
tel. 7908-3392 Lívingston
www.aktenamit.org

A grass-roots, Mayan-run development organization focusing its efforts on education, health care, the creation of alternative income sources, and sustainable agriculture.

ASOCIACION DE RESCATE Y CONSERVACIÓN DE VIDA SILVESTRE (ARCAS)
4a Avenida 2-47, Sector B5, Zona 8
Mixco, San Cristóbal
tel. 2476-6001
www.arcasguatemala.com

ARCAS works to protect and rehabilitate wildlife, including sea turtles on the Pacific coast and animals falling prey to poaching for the lucrative pet trade in Petén, such as cats, monkeys, and birds.

FUNDACIÓN DEFENSORES DE LA NATURALEZA
7a Avenida 7-09, Zona 13
Guatemala City
tel. 2440-8138, 2471-7942
www.defensores.org.gt

Defensores de la Naturaleza administers Sierra del Lacandón National Park, Sierra de las Minas Biosphere Reserve, Bocas del Polochic Wildlife Refuge, and the United Nations National Park (just outside of Guatemala City). Through private land purchases, it has been able to acquire large tracts of land in Sierra de las Minas and Sierra del Lacandón with help from The Nature Conservancy.

FUNDACIÓN PARA EL DESARROLLO Y LA CONSERVACIÓN (FUNDAECO)
7a Calle A 20-53, Zona 11
Colonia Mirador
Guatemala City
tel. 2474-3645
www.fundaeco.org.gt

Together with The Nature Conservancy, FUNDAECO has purchased over 3,600 hectares (9,000 acres) of tropical rainforest in the Caribbean coastal mountain chain of Cerro San Gil.

FUNDARY
Diagonal 6, 17-19, Zona 10
Guatemala City
tel. 2333-4957, 2366-7539, or 2367-0171
www.guate.net/fundarymanabique/
index.htm

Named after the late Mario Dary Rivera, creator of the CECON biotopes, FUNDARY has centered its efforts on the protection of coastal ecosystems, particularly the Punta de Manabique peninsula, on Guatemala's Caribbean coast.

PROPETÉN
Calle Central
Flores, Petén
tel. 7926-1370
www.propeten.org

An off-shoot of Conservation International, ProPetén began operating shortly after the creation of the Maya Biosphere Reserve and is credited with implementing innovative approaches to bridge the gap between the need for environmental conservation and the needs of communities living in or near the biosphere reserve. Among its successful programs are the establishment of a research station for the protection of scarlet macaws, forestry concessions with local communities in the Maya Biosphere Reserve's buffer zone, and two Spanish-language schools owned and operated by local villagers.

PROYECTO ECO-QUETZAL
2a Calle 14-36, Zona 1
Cobán, Alta Verapaz
tel. 7952-1047
www.ecoquetzal.org
Eco-Quetzal works with local communities to provide alternative income sources such as ecotourism and promote sustainable agriculture in the remaining cloud forests of northern Alta Verapaz.

TROPICO VERDE
Vía 6, 4-25, Zona 4
Edificio Castañeda, Oficina 41
Guatemala City
tel. 2339-4225
www.tropicoverde.org
Tropico Verde is a watchdog organization monitoring the state of Guatemala's parks via field studies. In addition to local monitoring, it helps bring awareness of local repercussions of international environmental issues, such as Guatemala's participation in international conventions on whaling, to name just one example.

WILDLIFE CONSERVATION SOCIETY
WCS-Guatemala
Casa #3, Av 15 de Marzo
Flores, Petén
tel. 502/926-0569
www.wcs.org/globalconservation/
latinamerica/mesoamerica/guatemala

Planning Your Fact-Finding Trip

GUATEMALA POST
http://guatemalapost.com
An English-language wrap-up of news on Guatemala from various sources.

GUATEMALA TOURISM COMMISSION
www.visitguatemala.com
The Instituto Guatemalteco de Turismo (INGUAT, Guatemala Tourist Commission) website has a variety of information on Guatemala.

LATIN AMERICAN NETWORK INFORMATION CENTER
http://lanic.utexas.edu/la/ca/guatemala/
The University of Texas has compounded a comprehensive list of links on everything pertaining to Guatemala.

REVUE
www.revuemag.com
The highly recommended *Revue* magazine (in English) can be downloaded online in PDF format.

PLANETA
www.planeta.com
An excellent website with plenty of information on ecotravel in Guatemala and elsewhere in Latin America.

Making the Move

LAWYERS

A list of English-speaking lawyers can be found on the U.S. Embassy in Guatemala's home page at http://guatemala.usembassy.gov/acs_legal_information.html.

EUGENIA MÉNDEZ CÁCERES
Avenida La Reforma 8-60, Zona 9
Edificio Galerías Reforma, Nivel 5, Oficina 513
tel. 5202-7487 or 2360-6203

I can personally vouch for the services of this Guatemala City lawyer, who knows her way through Guatemala's often complicated legal system and has a good list of local contacts in various businesses.

VISAS

DIRECCIÓN GENERAL DE MIGRACIÓN (GUATEMALAN IMMIGRATION)
6a Avenida 3-11, Zona 4
Guatemala City
tel. 2411-2411
www.migracion.gob.gt

MINISTERIO DE RELACIONES EXTERIORES (MINISTRY OF FOREIGN RELATIONS)
2a Avenida 4-17, Zona 10
tel. 2410-0000
www.minex.gob.gt

REGISTRO NACIONAL DE PERSONAS (RENAP)
http://registronacional.com/guatemala/guatemala.htm

U.S. STATE DEPARTMENT
http://travel.state.gov/travel/cis_pa_tw/cis/cis_1129.html

The U.S. State Department's Consular Information sheet on Guatemala documents entry and exit requirements, background information, and safety alerts for U.S. citizens and residents.

BRINGING PETS

IPATA
745 Winding Trail
Holly Lake Ranch, TX 75755
tel. 903/769-2267
fax 903/769-2867
www.ipata.com

Based in Texas, IPATA is an international trade association of kennel operators, pet-moving providers, animal handlers, and veterinarians.

PET CHAUFFEUR
tel. 212/696-9744 or 866/738-7433
www.petride.com

This is a New York-based pet transportation and pet relocation specialist.

INTERNATIONAL SHIPPERS

CROWLEY MARITIME CORPORATION
tel. 800-276-9539
www.crowley.com

This company provides ocean-liner shipping to Guatemala from Gulfport, Mississippi, and Miami, Florida.

PAXTON INTERNATIONAL MOVER
U.S. toll-free tel. 800/336-4536
www.paxton.com/international

RESOURCES

Housing Considerations

CÁMARA DE CORREDORES DE BIENES RAÍCES DE GUATEMALA (CCBRG)
www.bienesraices.com.gt
Guatemala's Chamber of Real Estate Agents.

INMOBILIA.COM
www.inmobilia.com
Publishes a monthly magazine useful for locating property and contracting housing-related services.

MINISTERIO DE FINANZAS, DIRECCIÓN DE CATASTRO Y AVALUÓ DE BIENES INMUEBLES (DICABI)
8a Avenida 20-65, Zona 1
Centro Cívico
Guatemala City
tel. 2248-5144, 2248-5145, 2248-5146 (numbers for DICABI)
www.minfin.gob.gt

OFICINA DE CONTROL DE ÁREAS DE RESERVA DEL ESTADO (OCRET)
7a Avenida 12-23, Zona 9
Edificio Etisa, 6to Nivel ala Norte
Guatemala City
http://ocret.blogspot.com

REGISTRO GENERAL DE LA PROPIEDAD
http://registronacional.com/guatemala/propiedades.htm
Guatemala's property registry page requires you to register and pay a small fee but offers access to public records and information on property titles.

REAL ESTATE AGENTS

Guatemala City
HOMES GUATEMALA
12 Calle 4-50, Zona 14
tel. 2366-4992
www.homesguatemala.com

INMOGUATEMALA
http://www.inmoguatemala.com

RE/MAX GUATEMALA
18 Calle 23-30, Plaza Decorisima
2do. Nivel local 20
Boulevard Los Próceres, Zona 10
Guatemala City
tel. 2389-0800 and 5293-3330
www.guatemalaproperty.com

SOUCIONES FÁCILES
tel. 5525-5811
www.solucionesfaciles.com

La Antigua Guatemala
THE BAMBOO GROUP
Antigua Guatemala
tel. 7832-9530
www.bamboogroupsa.com

CARSTENS REAL ESTATE
6a Calle Poniente #28A
tel. 7832-4068
www.teamantigua.com

CENTURY 21 CASA NOVA
3a Calle Oriente #29
tel. 7832-8729
www.century21casanova.com

SINOS INMOBILIARIA
4a Avenida Norte #16
tel. 5502-4962
www.sinosrealestate.com

Lake Atitlán
ATITLÁN DREAMS
www.atitlandreams.com

ATITLÁN SOLUTIONS
tel. 5493-6161
www.realestateatitlan.com/default.asp
Featured in *The Washington Post* in a story about buying property in Guatemala.

ATITLÁN VISION REAL ESTATE
tel. 5093-6386
www.atitlanvision.com/index.html
Cited by *The New York Times* in a piece on Lake Atitlán real estate.

TERRA X REAL ESTATE
Rincon Sai
Calle Santander 1-30
Panajachel
tel. 7762-1229
www.terraxatitlan.com
A recommended real estate company run by German expat Ralph Krause, who has over 25 years of experience in Guatemala. Featured in *Outside's Go* magazine.

UTILITIES
EMPRESA ELÉCTRICA DE GUATEMALA (EEGSA)
6a Avenida 8-14, Zona 1
Guatemala City
tel. 2277-7000
www.eegsa.com

EMPRESA MUNICIPAL DE AGUA (EMPAGUA)
21 Calle 6-77, Zona 1
Centro Cívico
Guatemala City
tel. 2285-8755

Language and Education

SPANISH-LANGUAGE SCHOOLS
Useful websites for general information and checking out schools include www.123teachme.com and www.guatemala365.com.

Guatemala City
INSTITUTO GUATEMALTECO AMERICANO (IGA)
Ruta 1, 4-05, Zona 4
tel. 2331-0022 or 2334-7218
fax 2334-4392
www.iga.edu
A highly respected institution promoting cross-cultural understanding between the United States and Guatemala.

La Antigua Guatemala
ACADEMIA DE ESPAÑOL ANTIGUEÑA
1a Calle Poniente #10
tel. 7832-7241
www.spanishacademyantiguena.com
A small, well-run school with space for 10 students at a time.

ACADEMIA DE ESPAÑOL PROBIGUA
6a Avenida Norte #41B
tel. 7832-2998
www.probigua.conexion.com
Run by a nonprofit group working to establish and maintain libraries in rural villages.

CENTRO LINGÜISTICO INTERNACIONAL
1a Calle Oriente #11
tel. 7832-0391
www.spanishcontact.com

CHRISTIAN SPANISH ACADEMY
6a Avenida Norte #15
tel. 7832-3922
www.learncsa.com
A very well-run school set in a pleasant colonial courtyard.

ESCUELA DE ESPAÑOL SAN JOSÉ EL VIEJO
5a Avenida Sur #34
tel. 7832-3028
www.sanjoseelviejo.com
This school has its own very attractive campus, where you can stay in comfortable accommodations with facilities that include a tennis court and swimming pool amidst lovely gardens and coffee trees.

PROYECTO LINGÜISTICO FRANCISCO MARROQUÍN
7a Calle Poniente #31
tel. 7832-2886
www.plfm-antigua.org
Antigua's oldest Spanish school is run by a nonprofit foundation working toward

RESOURCES

the study and preservation of Mayan languages and comes highly recommended.

Quetzaltenango

CELAS MAYA
6a Calle 14-55, Zona 1
Quetzaltenango
tel. 7761-4342
www.celasmaya.edu.gt
A fairly popular school; it's set around a pleasant garden courtyard. There's an adjacent Internet café.

CENTRO DE ESTUDIOS DE ESPAÑOL POP WUJ
1a Calle 17-72, Zona 1
tel. 7761-8286
www.pop-wuj.org
A highly recommended school run by a cooperative of experienced teachers who are very active in social projects.

ESCUELA DE ESPAÑOL SAKRIBAL
6a Calle 7-42, Zona 1
tel. 7763-0717
www.sakribal.com
This school was founded and is run by women who also run a project benefiting civil war widows and orphans.

ESCUELA DE ESPAÑOL ICA
19 Avenida 1-47, Zona 1
tel. 7763-1871
www.guatemalaspanish.com
In business for over 30 years; runs social welfare projects that include a medical clinic, adult literacy education and reforestation.

INEPAS
15 Avenida 4-59, Zona 1
tel. 7765-1308
www.inepas.org
Combines quality language instruction with a widely recognized service-learning program.

JUAN SISAY SPANISH SCHOOL
15 Avenida 8-38, Zona 1
tel. 7765-1318, 7761-1586
www.juansisay.com
This school is named after a self-taught indigenous *primitivista* painter who was massacred in his home village on the shores of Lake Atitlán in 1989. It's run by a teachers' collective involved in numerous social projects.

PROYECTO LINGÜISTICO QUETZALTECO DE ESPAÑOL
5a Calle 2-40, Zona 1
tel. 7763-1061
www.hermandad.com
This is an extremely popular school often booked months in advance. Students have the opportunity to volunteer with the school's Luis Cardoza y Aragon Popular Culture Center, next door, providing art, music, and computer skill instruction to underprivileged local children. There are also opportunities to work in reforestation projects and meet with human rights workers, former guerrilla combatants, and union leaders.

ULEW TINIMIT
7a Avenida 3-18, Zona 1
tel. 7761-6242
www.spanishguatemala.org
A good set-up allowing plenty of one-on-one instruction time with your individual teacher.

Lake Atitlán

CASA ROSARIO
San Pedro La Laguna
tel. 7613-6401
www.casarosario.com

ESCUELA DE ESPAÑOL CASA AMERICA
San Pedro La Laguna
tel. 7767-7718
casaamerica@hotmail.com

JABEL TINAMIT
Calle Santander
Panajachel
tel. 7762-0238
www.jabeltinamit.com

JARDÍN DE AMÉRICA
Calle 15 de Febrero, 3a Avenida Peatonal 4-44
Panajachel
tel. 7762-2637
www.jardindeamerica.com

MAYAB' SPANISH SCHOOL
San Pedro La Laguna
7 Avenida, Zona 2
Cantón Chuacante, San Pedro La Laguna
tel. 7815-7722 and 4124-6163
www.mayabschool.com

SAN PEDRO SPANISH SCHOOL
San Pedro La Laguna
7a Avenida 2-20, Zona 2
tel. 7721-8176
www.sanpedrospanishschool.org

SOL DE ORO SPANISH SCHOOL
San Pedro La Laguna
tel. 7614-9618

Monterrico
PROYECTO LINGÜISTICO MONTERRICO
Calle Principal
tel. 5619-8200
www.monterrico-guatemala.com/spanish-school.htm

Cobán and Vicinity
ACTIVE SPANISH SCHOOL
3a Calle 6-12, Zona 1
Cobán
tel. 7952-1432

ECO CABAÑA SPANISH SCHOOL
Km 6 Carretera a Chamil
San Juan Chamelco
tel. 7951-5898
ecocabana@yahoo.com

SCHOOL OF ARTS AND LANGUAGE
16 Avenida 2-50, Zona 1
Cobán
tel. 7953-9062
alftujab@intelnett.com

Lake Petén Itzá
ECO-ESCUELA DE ESPAÑOL
San Andrés
tel. 5498-4539 or 5490-1235
www.ecoescuelaespanol.org
The town's original Spanish school is still going strong and is the area's largest.

ESCUELA BIO ITZÁ
San José
tel. 7926-1363
www.ecobioitza.org/escuela/home.html

MUNDO MAYA ECOLOGICAL SPANISH SCHOOL
San Andrés
tel. 7928-8321
www.mundomayaguatemala.com

NUEVA JUVENTUD SPANISH SCHOOL
San Andrés
tel. 5711-0040
www.volunteerpeten.com
This school is set on a medicinal plant reserve where the focus is largely on volunteer opportunities. Various projects benefiting the local community include construction of a local library and schools.

PRIMARY AND SECONDARY SCHOOLS

Guatemala City
AMERICAN SCHOOL OF GUATEMALA
11 Calle 15-79, Zona 15
Vista Hermosa III
tel. 2369-0791
www.cag.edu.gt

COLEGIO ALEMAN DE GUATEMALA
Diagonal 21, 19-20, Zona 11
tel. 2473-0836
www.dsguatemala.edu.gt

COLEGIO CAPOUILLIEZ
30 Avenida 7-77, Zona 11
tel. 2429-1919 or 2434-7501

COLEGIO INGLÉS AMERICANO
10 Calle 19-70, Zona 15
Colonia Vista Hermosa II
tel. 2369-0829

COLEGIO MAYA
Km 12.5 Carretera a El Salvador
Santa Catarina Pinula, Guatemala
tel. 2365-4868
www.cm.edu.gt

RESOURCES

COLEGIO MONTESSORI
1a Avenida 3-55, Zona 10
tel. 2331-7384

COLEGIO VON HUMBOLDT
27 Avenida 15-00, Zona 16
Colonia San Isidro
tel. 2364-1415

VILLAGE SCHOOL
Km 25.5 Carretera a El Salvador
Boulevard Village
tel. 6634-4369
www.village.edu.gt

Antigua Guatemala
COLEGIO BOSTON BILINGÜE
Carretera Nueva a Ciudad Vieja, Aldea San Lorenzo el Cubo
Sacatepéquez
tel. 7888-6526, 7888-6527, or 7888-6528
www.colegiobostonguatemala.com

COLEGIO COLONIAL BILINGÜE
Manzana G-Lote F-6 Colonia San Pedro El Panorama
Antigua
tel. 7832-8644, 7934-6199, or 7935-6373

COLEGIO EL VALLE
Legión Santiago Los Caballeros No. 6
tel. 7832-3127 or 7832-8573

Western Highlands
ROBERT MULLER LIFE SCHOOL
0 Avenida 5-39 Zona 2
Panajachel
tel. 7762-2615
www.lifeschoolweb.com

PUBLIC UNIVERSITY
UNIVERSIDAD DE SAN CARLOS DE GUATEMALA (USAC)
Ciudad Universitaria, Zona 12
Guatemala City
tel. 2443-9500
www.usac.edu.gt

PRIVATE UNIVERSITIES

Guatemala City
UNIVERSIDAD DEL ISTMO
7 Avenida 3-67, Zona 13
tel. 2429-1400
www.unis.edu.gt

UNIVERSIDAD DEL VALLE DE GUATEMALA
18 Avenida 11-95, Zona 15
tel. 2364-04 92
www.uvg.edu.gt

UNIVERSIDAD FRANCISCO MARROQUÍN
6a Calle Final, Zona 10
tel. 2338-7700
www.ufm.edu.gt

UNIVERSIDAD RAFAEL LANDÍVAR
Vista Hermosa III, Zona 16
Guatemala City
tel. 2279-7979
www.url.edu.gt

STUDY ABROAD
CENTRO DE INVESTIGACIONES REGIONALES DE MESOAMERICA
(CIRMA, Center for Mesoamerican Research)
www.cirma.org.gt

Health

GENERAL HEALTH INFORMATION
THE CENTERS FOR DISEASE CONTROL
www.cdc.gov/travel

TRAVEL HEALTH ONLINE
www.tripprep.com

WORLD HEALTH ORGANIZATION
www.who.int/ith

Insurance
ASISTENCIA AL TURISMO (ASISTUR)
tel. 2421-2810 and 5578-9836 (24 hours)

EMERGENCIES AND REPORTING CRIME

In the event of an emergency, or to report a crime, dial 110 from any phone.

RISK ASSESSMENT AND SECURITY

YANTARNI S.A.
www.yantarni.com.gt

SAFETY

U.S. EMBASSY'S AMERICAN CITIZEN SERVICES
tel. 2326-4405
tel. 2331-2354 and 2331-2354
(after-hours emergency)
http://guatemala.usembassy.gov/
acs_information_residents.html

HOSPITALS AND CLINICS

Public Hospitals

HOSPITAL GENERAL SAN JUAN DE DIOS
1a Avenida 10-50, Zona 1
Guatemala City
tel. 2253-0443

HOSPITAL ROOSEVELT
Calzada Roosevelt, Zona 11
Guatemala City
tel. 2471-1441

Private Hospitals

HOSPITAL BELLA AURORA
10a Calle 2-31, Zona 14
Guatemala City
tel. 2368-1955

HOSPITAL CENTRO MÉDICO
6a Avenida 3-47, Zona 10
Guatemala City
tel. 2279-4949

HOSPITAL DE LAS AMÉRICAS
10a Calle 2-31, Zona 14
Guatemala City
tel. 2384-3535

HOSPITAL HERRERA LLERANDI
6a Avenida 8-71, Zona 10
Guatemala City
tel. 2384-5959

DENTIST

DR. OSCAR RUBÉN CUELLAR
5a Avenida 5-55, Zona 14
Europlaza Torre I, Oficina 503
Guatemala City
tel. 2368-3836
www.doctorcuellar.com

Western Highlands

CENTRO CLÍNICO PANAJACHEL
Avenida Rancho Grande, Callejón Bambi,
1-47 zona 2
Panajachel
tel. 7762.2085

CENTRO MÉDICO HEBRÓN
Diagonal 2 36B-51 Zona 8
Quetzaltenango
tel. 5700-5388

HOSPITAL CENTRO ENDOSCÓPICO CENTRO UROLÓGICO ESPECIALIZADO
6a Calle 13-52 Zona 3
Quetzaltenango
tel. 7767-4646

HOSPITAL EL ROBLE
7a Calle 14A-35 Zona 3
Quetzaltenango
tel. 7767.4912

HOSPITAL PRIVADO LAS ROSAS
7a Avenida 17-98 Zona 5
Las Rosas
Frente a gasolinera Texaco
tel. 7763.0615

HOSPITAL PRIVADO LOS OLIVOS
9a Calle 10-55 Zona 1
Quetzaltenango
tel. 7765-0211

HOSPITAL PRIVADO QUETZALTENANGO
Calle Rodolfo Robles 23-51 Zona 1
Quetzaltenango
tel. 7761-4381

HOSPITAL Y CLÍNICA DE ESPECIALIDADES DE OCCIDENTE
6a Calle 12-28 Zona 3
Quetzaltenango
tel. 7763-5225

Employment and Volunteering

THE JOB HUNT

General Resources
ONLINE CLASSIFIEDS
http://www.gt.computrabajo.com/
http://gt.acciontrabajo.com/

TRANSITIONS ABROAD
www.transitionsabroad.com/listings/work

Work Permits
MINISTERIO DE TRABAJO, MIGRACIONES LABORALES
14 Calle 5-49, Zona 1
Edifico Nasa, Nivel 4 y 6
Guatemala City
tel. 2230-1364 or 2230-1368

STARTING A BUSINESS
CÁMARA DE COMERCIO GUATEMALTECO-AMERICANA (AMERICAN CHAMBER OF COMMERCE IN GUATEMALA, OR AMCHAM)
5a Avenida 5-55, Zona 14
Edificio Europlaza Torre I, Nivel 5
tel. 2417-0800
www.amchamguate.com
A good place to go for networking, business facilitation, job banks, and assistance with government relations.

VOLUNTEER OPPORTUNITIES
ENTREMUNDOS
www.entremundos.org
Quetzaltenango-based organization with tons of information on volunteer opportunities in the western highlands.

IDEALIST.ORG
www.idealist.org
International volunteer website listing several opportunities in Guatemala.

VOLUNTEER ADVENTURES
www.volunteeradventures.com
Features a few Guatemala projects looking for international volunteers, mainly in the areas of wildlife conservation and opportunities to teach English.

NONPROFIT ORGANIZATIONS
CONSERVATION INTERNATIONAL
www.conservation.org

THE NATURE CONSERVANCY
www.nature.org/wherewework/centralamerica/guatemala

WORLD WILDLIFE FUND
www.worldwildlife.org

Finance

BANKING AND CURRENCY

Banks
BAC
7a Avenida 6-26, Zona 9
Edificio Plaza El Roble
Guatemala City
tel. 2361-0909
www.bac.net

BANCO AGROMERCANTIL
7a Avenida 7-30, Zona 9
Guatemala City
tel. 2338-6565
www.agromercantil.com.gt

BANCO CUSCATLÁN
15 Calle 1-04, Zona 10
Edificio Centrica Plaza, Torre 2
tel. 1774
www.bancocuscatlan.com

BANCO G&T CONTINENTAL
6a Avenida 9-08, Zona 9
Plaza G&T Continental
Guatemala City
tel. 2338-6801
www.gytcontinental.com.gt

BANCO INDUSTRIAL
7a Avenida 5-10, Zona 4
Centro Financiero
Guatemala City
tel. 2420-3000
www.bi.com.gt

BANCO INTERNACIONAL
Avenida La Reforma 15-85, Zona 10
Torre Internacional
Guatemala City
tel. 2366-6666
www.bancointernacional.com.gt

BANRURAL
Avenida La Reforma 2-56, Zona 9
Guatemala City
tel. 2426-1100
www.banrural.com

CITIGROUP
3a Avenida 13-78, Zona 10
Citigroup Building
Guatemala City
tel. 2336-8000

SUPERINTENDENCIA DE BANCOS
9a Avenida 22-00, Zona 1
Guatemala City
www.sib.gob.gt

American Express Representative
CLARK TOURS
7a Avenida 14-76, Zona 9
Plaza Clark
Guatemala City
tel. 2412-4700
www.clarktours.com.gt

Federal Benefits
FEDERAL BENEFITS UNIT (FBU)
American Citizen Services Unit,
U.S. Embassy in Guatemala City
tel. 2326-4405
AmCitsGuatemala@State.Gov
http://guatemala.usembassy.gov/
federal_benefits.html

Communications

PHONE COMPANIES
TELEFÓNICA
Boulevard Los Próceres 20-09, Zona 10
Torre Telefónica
Guatemala City
tel. 2379-1301
www.telefonica.com.gt

TELGUA
7a Avenida 12-39, Zona 1
Guatemala City
tel. 147-100
www.telgua.com

WIRELESS SERVICE
CLARO
7a Avenida 12-39, Zona 1
Guatemala City
tel. 147-100
www.claro.com.gt

MOVISTAR
Torre Telefónica
Boulevard Los Próceres 20-09, Zona 10
Guatemala City
tel. 2379-1301
www.telefonica.com.gt

TIGO
Edificio Plaza Tigo
Km 9.5 Carretera a El Salvador
Guatemala City
tel. 2428-0000
www.tigo.com.gt

INTERNET SERVICE PROVIDERS

TURBONETT
7a Avenida 12-39, Zona 1
Guatemala City
tel. 147100
www.telgua.com

TELEVISION

Cable

CLARO TV
7a Avenida 12-39, Zona 1
Guatemala City
tel. 147100
www.telgua.com

National Television

GUATEVISIÓN
www.guatevision.com

POSTAL AND COURIER SERVICES

EL CORREO
7a Avenida 11-67, Zona 1
and
Avenida La Reforma and 14 Calle, Zona 9
Guatemala City
tel. 2413-0202
www.elcorreo.com.gt

DHL
12 Calle 5-12, Zona 10
Guatemala City
tel. 2332-7547

Avenida Hincapie 25-10, Zona 13
Guatemala City
tel. 2379-1111

6a Avenida Sur #12
Antigua
tel. 2379-1111
www.dhl.com.gt/publish/gt/en.high.html

FEDEX
Diagonal 6, 12-20, Zona 10
Plaza Diagonal 6, Local 10
Guatemala City
tel. 1-801/003-3339
www.fedex.com/gt_english

UPS
12 Calle 5-53, Zona 10
Guatemala City
tel. 2423-6000
www.ups.com

PRIVATE MAIL SERVICES

FAST MAIL CENTER
Avenida Las Americas 24-42, Zona 13
Edificio Villa Vista, Local 4
tel. 2333-3559
www.fastmailcenter.com

MAIL BOXES, ETC.
Avenida Las Americas 6-19, Zona 14
Guatemala City
tel. 2485-6262
www.mbe.com

MEDIA

Newspapers and Magazines

If you can read Spanish (or want to use them to practice reading Spanish), Guatemala's main newspapers all have decent web pages.

ELPERIÓDICO
www.elperiodico.com.gt

LA CUADRA
1a Avenida Sur #11C, Antigua

PRENSA LIBRE
www.prensalibre.com.gt

REVUE
www.revuemag.com
The highly recommended *Revue* magazine (in English) can be downloaded online in PDF format.

SIGLO XXI
www.sigloxxi.com

Travel and Transportation

LA AURORA INTERNATIONAL AIRPORT (GUA)
Guatemala City
tel. 2260-6276
http://dgacguate.com

AIRLINES SERVING GUATEMALA CITY
AMERICAN AIRLINES
Hotel Barceló
7a Avenida 15-45, Zona 9
and
Edificio Columbus Center
Avenida Las Americas 18-81, Nivel 2, Zona 14
tel. 2422-0000
U.S. toll-free tel. 800/433-7300
www.aa.com

CONTINENTAL AIRLINES
18 Calle 5-56, Edificio Unicentro,
Local 704, Zona 10
toll-free tel. 801/812-6684 or tel. 2385-9610
U.S. toll-free tel. 800/231-0856
www.continental.com

DELTA
15 Calle 3-20, Zona 10
Centro Ejecutivo, Primer Nivel
tel. 2337-0642
U.S. toll-free tel. 800/221-1212
www.delta.com

IBERIA
Avenida La Reforma 8-60, Zona 9
tel. 2332-0911
www.iberia.com

SPIRIT AIRLINES
U.S. toll-free tel. 800/772-7117
www.spiritair.com

TACA
Avenida Hincapié 12-22, Zona 13
tel. 2470-8222
U.S. toll-free tel. 800/400-8222
www.taca.com

AIRLINES SERVING FLORES/TIKAL
MAYA ISLAND AIR
U.S. toll-free tel. 888/535-8832
www.mayaislandair.com

TAG
Avenida Hinapie y 18 Calle, Zona 13
Guatemala City
tel. 2332-1897 and 2380-9494
U.S. toll-free tel. 800/528-8216
www.tag.com.gt

FERRIES
EXOTIC TRAVEL
Calle Principal
Inside Bahía Azul Restaurant
Lívingston
tel. 7947-0449, 7497-0133, or 7497-0151

TRANSPORTES EL CHATO
1a Avenida between 10a and 11a Calles
Puerto Barrios
tel. 7948-5525 and 7948-8787
www.transporteselchato.com

INTERNATIONAL BUS LINES
AUTOTRANSPORTES RIO CHANCALA
5 de Mayo 120
Palenque, Mexico

HEDMAN ALAS
www.hedmanalas.com
Bus service to Honduras.

LÍNEA DORADA
16 Calle 10-03 Zona 1
Guatemala City
tel. 5232-5506
Flores
tel. 7926-1788
http://tikalmayanworld.com

MOON-RAY TOURS
Antigua
tel. 7832-0198
www.moonraytours.com/index3.html

RESOURCES

PULLMANTUR
inside Holiday Inn, Zona 10
Guatemala City
tel. 2363-6240 and 2363-6241
www.pullmantur.com
Bus service to San Salvador.

SAN JUAN TRAVEL
2a Calle
Santa Elena
Flores
tel. 7926-0041

TICABUS
Calzada Aguilar Batres 22-55, Zona 12
Guatemala City
tel. 2459-2848
www.ticabus.com
Bus service to Costa Rica, stopping in San
Salvador and Managua along the way.

TRANSPORTES MONTEBELLO
Calle Velasco Suárez
two blocks west of the market
Palenque, Mexico

SHUTTLE BUSES
ATITRANS
Antigua
tel. 7832-3371
www.atitrans.com

GRAYLINE TOURS
tel. 5511-9052
www.graylineguatemala.com

TURANSA
Gutemala City
tel. 2437-8182
tel. 5651-2284 after business hours
www.turansa.com

TAXICAB COMPANIES IN GUATEMALA CITY
TAXIS AMARILLO EXPRESS
tel. 2332-1515

TAXIS BLANCO Y AZUL
tel. 2360-0903

CAR RENTAL AGENCIES
These U.S. car rental agencies are repre-
sented in Guatemala and have kiosks at
La Aurora International Airport.

ADVANTAGE
Guatemala City tel. 2332-7525
toll-free U.S. tel. 800/777-5500
www.advantagerentacar.com

ALAMO
Guatemala City tel. 5219-7469
toll-free U.S. tel. 800/462-5266
www.alamo.com

AVIS
Guatemala City tel. 2331-0017
toll-free U.S. tel. 800/331-1212
www.avis.com

BUDGET
Guatemala City tel. 2332-7744
toll-free U.S. tel. 800/472-3325
www.budget.com
www.budgetguatemala.com.gt

DOLLAR
Guatemala City tel. 2331-7185
toll-free U.S. tel. 800/800-4000
www.dollar.com

HERTZ
Guatemala City tel. 2470-3800
toll-free U.S. tel. 800/654-3001
www.hertz.com

THRIFTY
Guatemala City tel. 2379-8747
toll-free U.S. tel. 800/847-4389
www.thrifty.com

ROADSIDE ASSISTANCE
PROVIAL
tel. 2422-7878

Prime Living Locations

GUATEMALA CITY

General Resources
**GUATEMALA CITY
MUNICIPAL GOVERNMENT**
www.muniguate.com
The home page of Guatemala City's municipal government.

LA ANTIGUA GUATEMALA
AROUND ANTIGUA
www.aroundantigua.com
An award-winning website chock-full of information on hotels, restaurants, Spanish schools, and local businesses.

**LA ANTIGUA GUATEMALA
DAILY PHOTO**
http://antiguadailyphoto.com
A great blog with wonderful images and good information on aspects of daily life in Antigua.

THE TRAVEL EXPERT(A)
www.travelexperta.com
A helpful website and relocation guide written by expat Marina Villatoro, who recently relocated to La Antigua Guatemala from Costa Rica.

THE WESTERN HIGHLANDS

Quetzaltenango
XELA PAGES
www.xelapages.com
A guide to Quetzaltenango's Spanish schools, hotels, restaurants, and more.

XELA WHO
www.xelawho.com
A guide to nightlife and entertainment in Quetzaltenango.

Lake Atitlán
ATITLAN.COM
www.atitlan.com
A hotel guide and online magazine covering aspects of travel and daily life on the shores of the world's most beautiful lake.

PANAJACHEL.COM
www.panajachel.com
Contains information on hotels, dining, real estate, and recreational activities centered around the lake's largest town.

THE PACIFIC COAST
MONTERRICO.COM
www.monterrico-guatemala.com
This site provides the lowdown on transportation options and hotels for Guatemala's most popular beach town.

IZABAL AND LAS VERAPACES
LA PUERTA AL MUNDA MAYA
www.infomipyme.com/Docs/GT/sidel/mundomaya.htm
A website developed by local community tourism organizations with help from USAID covering the region of the Verapaces and southern Petén.

Cobán
WWW.COBANAV.NET
www.cobanav.net
A very useful website for exploring Cobán and Alta Verapaz in general; administered by a U.S. expat and local innkeeper.

Lívingston
LÍVINGSTON, IZABAL
www.livingston.com.gt
A good website with resources for exploring this coastal town and Garífuna enclave.

Semuc Champey
SEMUCCHAMPEY.COM
www.semucchampey.com
Good information on this Alta Verapaz natural attraction and the nearby Lanquín caves with links to area hotels, restaurants, and services.

PETÉN
MAYAN-TRAVELER.COM
www.mayan-traveler.com
This site contains good information on archaeological sites in addition to a decent listing of hotels.

TIKAL NATIONAL PARK
www.tikalpark.com
This helpful site contains tons of information on Tikal National Park as well as many of the neighboring Maya sites.

Glossary

acta notarial a legal document produced by a lawyer

aduana customs

agua literally "water" but also used in reference to soda pop

agua pura bottled water

aguardiente cane alcohol or moonshine

aguas! watch out! (slang)

aguas termales hot springs

aguinaldo a yearly bonus given to workers in December

alcalde mayor

alfombra a colorful carpet made of sawdust and flowers central to Holy Week celebrations in Antigua and elsewhere in Guatemala

altense a resident of Quetzaltenango

al tiempo referring to drinks at room temperature

altiplano the highlands

artesanías handicrafts

a todo mecate full speed ahead (slang)

autopista freeway

avenida avenue

ayudante in cheap public buses, the man who helps the driver in collecting fares and helping passengers with baggage

baño compartido/general shared bath (in reference to accommodations)

baño privado private bathroom

babosadas lies or nonsense (slang)

bajo lowland swampy areas of the Petén lowlands

balam Mayan word for jaguar

balneario a bathing or swimming hole

barba amarilla a highly venomous fer-de-lance snake

barranco a ravine

barrio neighborhood

baule a leatherback turtle

bichos bugs

billares pool or billiards

billete a banknote or bill

bistec beef steak

bocadillos appetizers; also *boquitas*

bolo drunk; also *borracho*

bono 14 a yearly bonus given to workers in July

brujo a male witch or sorcerer

caballería a unit of measurement equal to 42.5 hectares or 111.68 acres

cachito a little bit (slang)

cada uno(a) each

cajero automático automated teller machine (ATM)

calle street

camioneta a second-class bus

campesino peasant farmer

canche blond or fair-skinned; also was a term used of guerrilla fighters during the civil war (slang)

canícula a brief one- or two-week dry spell during the rainy summer months of July/August

cantina a seedy bar

caoba mahogany

capearse to play hooky (slang)

caquero arrogant or stuck-up; usually someone of wealth (slang)

casaca tall tales or embellishments (slang)

casa de huéspedes a guest house

catastro the ongoing process of land registration throughout Guatemala in order to determine historical ownership

caudillo a political-military leader exercising authoritarian power

cayuco canoe

cédula a card establishing identity; soon to be replaced by the *documento de identificación personal* (DPI)

cerveza beer

champa thatch-roofed, wall-less structure

chapín/chapina what Guatemalans call themselves

chapinismo Guatemalan slang

chapparro person of short stature (slang)

chichicaste a stinging plant somewhat like poison ivy

chiclero a chewing gum resin tapper of the jungle Petén region

chipi chipi a mist or light drizzle that often blankets higher elevations or cloud-forested regions of the Verapaces

RESOURCES

chuchitos a traditional Guatemalan dish using corn meal, tomato paste, and turkey cooked in a corn husk

chuchos slang word for dogs

chupar to drink alcoholic beverages (slang)

clavos problems (slang)

coche a pig; not a car as in other parts of Latin America

cofradía traditional political-religious organization present in some highland Mayan communities

colectivo public transportation

comedor a simple eatery

compromiso de compraventa a buyer-seller agreement

con with

condones condoms

conectes (tener) to have influence because of important or powerful friends (slang)

confianza confidence and trust in a person and their motives

constancia de carencia de antecedentes penales a police document attesting to the bearer's lack of prior criminal record

corte traditional wraparound skirt worn by Mayan women

costumbre traditional Mayan religious practices that include offerings of flowers, candles, and sometimes animal sacrifices

coyote a smuggler of undocumented immigrants across Mexico and into the United States

criollo Guatemalan of Spanish heritage

cuates buddies (slang)

cucurucho costumed carriers of procession parade floats during Semana Santa celebrations

cuota patronal an employer's contribution to an employee social security fund

curandero traditional healer or shaman

departamento a Guatemalan department; like a state or province

documento personal de identificación new identity document which will replace the *cédula* in 2010

dormitorios bedrooms

edificio a building; used in street addresses in urban areas

encomienda a colonial system enabling landholders to exact tribute and labor from the local indigenous population

escritura a legal document drawn up by a lawyer

farmacia de turno a pharmacy that remains open all night on a rotating basis

finca a farm of any type but usually referring to a coffee farm

fin de semana weekend rental

flete a freight charge

fondo de prestaciones a fund for unemployment, health, and other employee benefits

frente al mar ocean-front

goma (estar de) to be hungover (slang)

güiro a child (slang)

hospedaje inexpensive family-run accommodations

hostales hostels

huipil a colorful traditional woven blouse made and worn by Maya women

impuesto sobre la renta income tax

impuesto único sobre inmuebles property tax

incluye includes

ingenio a sugar mill

Interamericana Interamerican; usually in reference to Highway CA-1 through the highlands and short for *Carretera Interamericana*

invierno literally "winter" but used to describe the May–October rainy season

IVA short for *impuesto al valor agregado* (value-added tax) or VAT; in Guatemala it's 12 percent

jalón a lift or ride in a vehicle (slang)

jocón a spicy traditional sauce usually used to cook chicken in

ladino a person of indigenous descent who has adopted European ways

lancha small motorboat

latifundia large landholding in the form of a plantation or hacienda

lavandería laundry

Licenciado an official term of address for an attorney or anyone holding a bachelor's degree

línea blanca kitchen appliances

línea telefónica phone line

machista a male chauvinist

maestro de obras construction foreman

mango a handsome man (slang)

maquiladora an industrial plant where clothes are assembled for re-export by cheap local labor; more commonly known in the United States as a "sweat shop"

mara a gang but also used to describe a "gang" in the manner referring to an agglomeration of people or a crowd

maras gangs

mestizo person of mixed Spanish-Indian descent

metros cuadrados square meters

milpa a maize or corn plant; also sometimes used in reference to a cornfield

minifundia small landholdings, usually in the hands of Mayan peasantry

mochileros backpackers

mordida bribe (slang)

morería small crafts shop producing costumes and masks for traditional dancing

muchacha a maid or housekeeper

muco a person of low social class; usually used disdainfully by upper-class Guatemalans in reference to lower classes (slang)

organización no gubernamental (ONG) nongovernmental organization (NGO)

palapa a high-ceilinged thatch-roof structure commonly used in restaurant or hotel architecture

para estrenar brand-new

parlama green sea turtle

parque nacional national park

pena shame or embarrassment; related to face-saving

pensión inexpensive accommodations

pensionado a pensioner or retiree living on retirement income from abroad

pepián a spicy Guatemalan dish

permiso a permit

petate a reed mat

picop pickup truck

pila a concrete wash basin with a spicket and adjacent area for washing clothes or dishes found in most Guatemalan homes

pisto money (slang)

planilla a spreadsheet accounting for expenses used to determine income tax

por per

preservativos condoms

primitivista Primitivist painting style

Pullman a first-class bus, though to varying degrees of newness and quality

quetzales local currency

quetzalteco resident of or someone from Quetzaltenango

rancho a simple thatched structure; also sometimes referred to in its diminutive – *ranchito*

recargo a surcharge; usually associated with credit card transactions

refacción snack time between lunch and dinner; also on menus as *refacciones*, consisting of pastries and sandwiches

rentista immigration status granted to a foreigner living in Guatemala on income earned abroad

repatriado returned civil war refugee, usually from Mexico

reserva natural privada a privately owned nature preserve

reserva protectora de manantiales a watershed protection preserve

retablo an altarpiece in a colonial church

revueltos scrambled (eggs)

ron rum

sacbe once-paved Mayan causeways present in the modern-day lowlands of Petén and still used as footpaths

salsa to (mistakenly) think oneself cool and hip (slang)

sho (hacer) to be quiet/shut up (slang)

shuco dirty (slang)

shute nosy (slang)

sin without

stela (stelae) pre-Columbian stone monuments; usually carved

tábanos biting flies inhabiting coastal areas of Central America; somewhat like horseflies but light-colored in appearance

tienda corner store; literally store

timbre a type of stamp sold in banks and used in paying fees such as visa renewals

túmulo a speed bump

todas las comodidades fully furnished

total renta neta total net income for filing taxes

traje traditional Mayan costume worn by inhabitants of individual highland villages

tramitador someone who makes their living standing in line and getting necessary paperwork stamped and approved on behalf of someone else; used for getting driver's licenses or other such permits

tuk tuks a motorized rickshaw like those used in Southeast Asia, consisting of a motorcycle attached to a two-person passenger compartment

varas unit for measuring land; also *varas cuadradas* (square *varas*)

verano literally "summer," but usually in reference to the height of the dry season between March and the beginning of the rainy season in May

virgo cool, hip (slang)

vista a los volcanes volcano view

vonós "let's go"; a shortened version of *vámonos* (slang)

zafra sugarcane harvest in the Pacific lowlands

zancudo mosquito

zona a city zone into which Guatemala's principal urban areas are divided

zona de adyacencia an imaginary border area between Belize and Guatemala's northern Petén province; frequently the scene of land conflicts between Guatemalan peasants and Belizean military forces

zonas francas free trade zones

Spanish Phrasebook

Your Guatemalan adventure will go much more smoothly if you learn some Spanish. Though Guatemalans may smile at your funny accent, they will certainly appreciate your halting efforts to break the ice and transform yourself from a foreigner into a potential friend.

Spanish commonly uses 30 letters—the familiar English 26, plus four straightforward additions: ch, ll, ñ, and rr.

PRONUNCIATION

Once you learn them, Spanish pronunciation rules—in contrast to English ones—don't change. Spanish vowels generally sound softer than in English. (Note: The capitalized syllables below receive stronger accents.)

Vowels

a like ah, as in "hah": *agua* AH-gooah (water), *pan* PAHN (bread), and *casa* CAH-sah (house)

e like ay, as in "may": *mesa* MAY-sah (table), *tela* TAY-lah (cloth), and *de* DAY (of, from)

i like ee, as in "need": *diez* dee-AYZ (ten), *comida* ko-MEE-dah (meal), and *fin* FEEN (end)

o like oh, as in "go": *peso* PAY-soh (weight), *ocho* OH-choh (eight), and *poco* POH-koh (a bit)

u like oo, as in "cool": *uno* OO-noh (one), *cuarto* KOOAHR-toh (room), and *usted* oos-TAYD (you); when it follows a "q" the u is silent; when it follows an "h" or has an umlaut (ü), it's pronounced like "w"

Consonants
b, d, f, k, l, m, n, p, q, s, t, v, w, x, y, z, and ch

pronounced almost as in English; h occurs but is silent – not pronounced at all

c like k as in "keep": *cuarto* KOOAR-toh (room), Tepic tay-PEEK (capital of Nayarit state, Mexico); when it precedes

"e" or "i," pronounce c like s, as in "sit": *cerveza* sayr-VAY-sah (beer), *encima* ayn-SEE-mah (atop)

g like g as in "gift" when it precedes "a," "o," "u," or a consonant: *gato* GAH-toh (cat), *hago* AH-goh (I do, make); otherwise, pronounce g like h as in "hat": *giro* HEE-roh (money order), *gente* HAYN-tay (people)

j like h, as in "has": *jueves* HOOAY-vays (Thursday), *mejor* may-HOR (better)

ll like y, as in "yes": *toalla* toh-AH-yah (towel), *ellos* AY-yohs (they, them)

ñ like ny, as in "canyon": *año* AH-nyo (year), *señor* SAY-nyor (Mr., sir)

r lightly trilled, with tongue at the roof of your mouth like a very light English r, as in "ready": *pero* PAY-roh (but), *tres* TRAYS (three), *cuatro* KOOAH-troh (four)

rr like a Spanish r, but with much more emphasis and trill. Let your tongue flap. Practice with *burro* (donkey), *carretera* (highway), and Carrillo (proper name), then really let go with *ferrocarril* (railroad).

Note: The single small but common exception to all of the above is the pronunciation of Spanish **y** when it's being used as the Spanish word for "and," as in "Ron y Kathy." In such case, pronounce it like the English ee, as in "keep": Ron "ee" Kathy (Ron and Kathy).

Accent

Native English speakers often make errors of pronunciation by ignoring accented, or stressed, syllables. All Spanish vowels—a, e, i, o, and u—may carry accents determining which syllable of a word is emphasized.

The rule for accent, the relative stress given to syllables within a given word, is straightforward. If a word ends in a vowel, an n, or an s, accent the next-to-last syllable; if not, accent the last syllable.

Pronounce *gracias* GRAH-seeahs (thank you), *orden* OHR-dayn (order), and *carretera* kah-ray-TAY-rah (highway) with stress on the next-to-last syllable.

Otherwise, accent the last syllable: *venir* vay-NEER (to come), *ferrocarril* fay-roh-cah-REEL (railroad), and *edad* ay-DAHD (age).

Exceptions to the accent rule are always marked with an accent sign: (á, é, í, ó, or ú), such as *teléfono* tay-LAY-foh-noh (telephone), *jabón* hah-BON (soap), and *rápido* RAH-pee-doh (rapid).

NUMBERS
zero *cero*
one *uno*
two *dos*
three *tres*
four *cuatro*
five *cinco*
six *seis*
seven *siete*
eight *ocho*
nine *nueve*
10 *diez*
11 *once*
12 *doce*
13 *trece*
14 *catorce*
15 *quince*
16 *dieciseis*
17 *diecisiete*
18 *dieciocho*
19 *diecinueve*
20 *veinte*
21 *veinte y uno or veintiuno*
30 *treinta*
40 *cuarenta*
50 *cincuenta*
60 *sesenta*
70 *setenta*
80 *ochenta*
90 *noventa*
100 *cien*
101 *ciento y uno*
200 *doscientos*
500 *quinientos*
1,000 *mil*
10,000 *diez mil*
100,000 *cien mil*
1,000,000 *millón*

one-half *medio*
one-third *un tercio*
one-fourth *un cuarto*

TIME
What time is it? *¿Qué hora es?*
It's one o'clock. *Es la una.*
It's three in the afternoon. *Son las tres de la tarde.*
It's 4 A.M. *Son las cuatro de la mañana.*
six-thirty *seis y media*
a quarter till eleven *un cuarto para las once*
a quarter past five *las cinco y cuarto*
an hour *una hora*
today *hoy*
tomorrow *mañana*
yesterday *ayer*
a week *una semana*
a month *un mes*
a year *un año*
after *después*
before *antes*
last night *anoche*
the next day *el día siguiente*

DAYS OF THE WEEK
Monday *lunes*
Tuesday *martes*
Wednesday *miércoles*
Thursday *jueves*
Friday *viernes*
Saturday *sábado*
Sunday *domingo*

MONTHS
January *enero*
February *febrero*
March *marzo*
April *abril*
May *mayo*
June *junio*
July *julio*
August *agosto*
September *septiembre*
October *octubre*
November *noviembre*
December *diciembre*

USEFUL WORDS AND PHRASES

Most Spanish-speaking people consider formalities important. Whenever approaching anyone for information or some other reason, do not forget the appropriate salutation—good morning, good evening, etc. Standing alone, the greeting *hola* (hello) can sound brusque.

Hello. *Hola.*
Good morning. *Buenos días.*
Good afternoon. *Buenas tardes.*
Good evening. *Buenas noches.*
How are you? *¿Cómo está usted?*
Very well, thank you. *Muy bien, gracias.*
Okay; good. *Bien.*
Not okay; bad. *Mal or feo.*
So-so. *Más o menos.*
And you? *¿Y usted?*
Thank you. *Gracias.*
Thank you very much. *Muchas gracias.*
You're very kind. *Muy amable.*
You're welcome. *De nada.*
Goodbye. *Adios.*
See you later. *Hasta luego.*
please *por favor*
yes *sí*
no *no*
I don't know. *No sé.*
Just a moment, please. *Momentito, por favor.*
Excuse me, please (when you're trying to get attention). *Disculpe or Con permiso.*
Excuse me (when you've made a boo-boo). *Lo siento.*
Pleased to meet you. *Mucho gusto.*
How do you say...in Spanish? *¿Cómo se dice...en español?*
Do you speak English? *¿Habla usted inglés?*
Is English spoken here? (Does anyone here speak English?) *¿Se habla inglés?*
I don't speak Spanish well. *No hablo bien el español.*
I don't understand. *No entiendo.*

What is your name? *¿Cómo se llama usted?*
My name is . . . *Me llamo...*
Would you like . . . *¿Quisiera usted...*
Let's go to . . . *Vamos a...*

TERMS OF ADDRESS

When in doubt, use the formal *usted* (you) as a form of address.

I *yo*
you (formal) *usted*
you (familiar) *tu*
he/him *él*
she/her *ella*
we/us *nosotros*
you (plural) *ustedes*
they/them *ellos (all males or mixed gender); ellas (all females)*
Mr., sir *señor*
Mrs., madam *señora*
miss, young lady *señorita*
wife *esposa*
husband *esposo*
friend *amigo (male); amiga (female)*
sweetheart *novio (male); novia (female)*
son; daughter *hijo; hija*
brother; sister *hermano; hermana*
father; mother *padre; madre*
grandfather; grandmother *abuelo; abuela*

TRANSPORTATION

Where is . . . ? *¿Dónde está... ?*
How far is it to . . . ? *¿A cuánto está... ?*
from . . . to . . . *de...a...*
How many blocks? *¿Cuántas cuadras?*
Where (Which) is the way to . . . ? *¿Dónde está el camino a... ?*
the bus station *la terminal de autobuses*
the bus stop *la parada de autobuses*
Where is this bus going? *¿Adónde va este autobús?*
the taxi stand *la parada de taxis*
the train station *la estación de ferrocarril*
the boat *el barco*

the airport *el aeropuerto*
I'd like a ticket to . . . *Quisiera un boleto a . . .*
first (second) class *primera (segunda) clase*
roundtrip *ida y vuelta*
reservation *reservación*
baggage *equipaje*
Stop here, please. *Pare aquí, por favor.*
the entrance *la entrada*
the exit *la salida*
the ticket office *la oficina de boletos*
(very) near; far *(muy) cerca; lejos*
to; toward *a*
by; through *por*
from *de*
the right *la derecha*
the left *la izquierda*
straight ahead *recto*
in front *en frente*
beside *al lado*
behind *atrás*
the corner *la esquina*
the stoplight *el semáforo*
a turn *una vuelta*
right here *aquí*
somewhere around here *por acá*
right there *allí*
somewhere around there *por allá*
street; boulevard *calle; bulevar*
highway *carretera*
bridge; toll *puente; peaje*
address *dirección*
north; south *norte; sur*
east; west *oriente (este); poniente (oeste)*

ACCOMMODATIONS

hotel *hotel*
Is there a room? *¿Hay cuarto?*
May I (may we) see it? *¿Puedo (podemos) verlo?*
What is the rate? *¿Cuál es el precio?*
Is that your best rate? *¿Es su mejor precio?*
Is there something cheaper? *¿Hay algo más económico?*
a single room *un cuarto sencillo*
a double room *un cuarto doble*
double bed *cama matrimonial*

twin beds *camas gemelas*
with private bath *con baño*
hot water *agua caliente*
shower *ducha*
towels *toallas*
soap *jabón*
toilet paper *papel higiénico*
blanket *frazada; chamarra*
sheets *sábanas*
air-conditioned *aire acondicionado*
fan *ventilador*
key *llave*
manager *gerente*

FOOD

I'm hungry *Tengo hambre.*
I'm thirsty. *Tengo sed.*
menu *lista; menú*
order *orden*
glass *vaso*
fork *tenedor*
knife *cuchillo*
spoon *cuchara*
napkin *servilleta*
soft drink *refresco*
coffee *café*
tea *té*
drinking water *agua pura; agua potable*
bottled carbonated water *agua mineral*
bottled uncarbonated water *agua sin gas*
beer *cerveza*
wine *vino*
milk *leche*
juice *jugo*
cream *crema*
sugar *azúcar*
cheese *queso*
snack *refacción*
breakfast *desayuno*
lunch *almuerzo*
daily lunch special *el menú del día*
dinner *cena*
the check *la cuenta*
eggs *huevos*
bread *pan*
salad *ensalada*
fruit *fruta*

mango *mango*
watermelon *sandía*
papaya *papaya*
banana *banano*
apple *manzana*
orange *naranja*
plantain *plátano*
lime *limón*
fish *pescado*
shellfish *mariscos*
shrimp *camarones*
meat (without) *(sin) carne*
chicken *pollo*
pork *puerco*
beef; steak *res; bistec*
bacon; ham *tocino; jamón*
fried *frito*
roasted *asada*
barbecue; barbecued *barbacoa; al carbón*

SHOPPING
money *dinero*
money-exchange bureau *casa de cambio*
I would like to exchange travelers checks. *Quisiera cambiar cheques de viajero.*
What is the exchange rate? *¿Cuál es el tipo de cambio?*
How much is the commission? *¿Cuánto cuesta la comisión?*
Do you accept credit cards? *¿Aceptan tarjetas de crédito?*
money order *giro*
How much does it cost? *¿Cuánto cuesta?*
What is your final price? *¿Cuál es su último precio?*
expensive *caro*
cheap *barato; económico*
more *más*
less *menos*
a little *un poco*
too much *demasiado*

HEALTH
Help me please. *Ayúdeme por favor.*
I am ill. *Estoy enfermo.*

Call a doctor. *Llame un doctor.*
Take me to . . . *Lléveme a . . .*
hospital *hospital; sanatorio*
drugstore *farmacia*
pain *dolor*
fever *fiebre*
headache *dolor de cabeza*
stomachache *dolor de estómago*
burn *quemadura*
cramp *calambre*
nausea *náusea*
vomiting *vomitar*
medicine *medicina*
antibiotic *antibiótico*
pill; tablet *pastilla*
aspirin *aspirina*
ointment; cream *pomada; crema*
bandage *venda*
cotton *algodón*
sanitary napkins *use brand name; e.g., Kotex*
birth control pills *pastillas anticonceptivas*
contraceptive foam *espuma anticonceptiva*
condoms *preservativos; condones*
toothbrush *cepillo dental*
dental floss *hilo dental*
toothpaste *crema dental*
dentist *dentista*
toothache *dolor de muelas*

POST OFFICE AND COMMUNICATIONS
long-distance telephone *teléfono de larga distancia*
I would like to call . . . *Quisiera llamar a . . .*
collect *a cobrar*
station to station *a quien contesta*
person to person *persona a persona*
credit card *tarjeta de crédito*
post office *correo*
general delivery *lista de correo*
letter *carta*
stamp *estampilla, timbre*
postcard *postal*
air mail *correo aéreo*
registered *registrado*
money order *giro*

package; box *paquete; caja*
string; tape *cuerda; cinta*

AT THE BORDER

border *frontera*
customs *aduana*
immigration *migración*
tourist card *tarjeta de turista*
inspection *inspección; revisión*
passport *pasaporte*
profession *profesión*
marital status *estado civil*
single *soltero*
married; divorced *casado; divorciado*
widowed *enviudado*
insurance *seguros*
title *título*
driver's license *licencia de conducir*

AT THE GAS STATION

gas station *gasolinera*
car *carro*
gasoline *gasolina*
unleaded *sin plomo*
full, please *lleno, por favor*
tire *llanta*
tire repair shop *vulcanizadoraor pinchazo*
air *aire*
water *agua*
oil (change) *aceite (cambio de)*
grease *grasa*
My . . . doesn't work. *Mi . . . no sirve.*
battery *batería*
radiator *radiador*
alternator *alternador*
generator *generador*
tow truck *grúa*
repair shop *taller mecánico*
tune-up *afinación or tune-up*

VERBS

Verbs are the key to getting along in Spanish. They employ mostly predictable forms and come in three classes, which end in *ar*, *er*, and *ir*, respectively:

to buy *comprar*
I buy, you (he, she, it) buys *compro, compra*
we buy, you (they) buy *compramos, compran*
to eat *comer*
I eat, you (he, she, it) eats *como, come*
we eat, you (they) eat *comemos, comen*
to climb *subir*
I climb, you (he, she, it) climbs *subo, sube*
we climb, you (they) climb *subimos, suben*

Got the idea? Here are more (with irregularities marked in **bold**).

to do or make *hacer*
I do or make, you (he, she, it) does or makes *hago, hace*
we do or make, you (they) do or make *hacemos, hacen*
to go *ir*
I go, you (he, she, it) goes *voy, va*
we go, you (they) go *vamos, van*
to go (walk) *andar*
to love *amar*
to work *trabajar*
to want *desear, querer*
to need *necesitar*
to read *leer*
to write *escribir*
to repair *reparar*
to stop *parar*
to get off (the bus) *bajar*
to arrive *llegar*
to stay (remain) *quedar*
to stay (lodge) *hospedar*
to leave *salir (regular except for **salgo**, I leave)*
to look at *mirar*
to look for *buscar*
to give *dar (regular except for **doy**, I give)*
to carry *llevar*
to have *tener (irregular but important: **tengo, tiene**, tenemos, **tienen**)*
to come *venir (similarly irregular: **vengo, viene**, venimos, **vienen**)*

Spanish has two forms of "to be." Use *estar* when speaking of location or a temporary state of being: "I am at home." *"**Estoy** en casa."* "I'm sick." *"**Estoy** enfermo."* Use *ser* for a permanent state of being: "I am a doctor." *"**Soy** doctora."*

Estar is regular except for *estoy,* I am. *Ser* is very irregular:

to be *ser*
I am, you (he, she, it) is *soy, es*
we are, you (they) are *somos, son*

(Courtesy of Bruce Whipperman, author of *Moon Pacific Mexico.*)

Suggested Reading

HISTORY AND POLITICS

Pre-Columbian History

Coe, Michael D. *Breaking the Maya Code.* New York: Thames & Hudson, 1999. Chronicles the work of several scholars involved in the eventual decipherment of the meaning behind the Mayan glyphs.

Coe, Michael D. *The Maya.* 7th edition. New York: Thames & Hudson, 2005. A classic reference manual on the Maya and essential guide for the traveler that includes useful color plates.

Demarest, Arthur. *Ancient Maya: The Rise and Fall of a Rainforest Civilization.* Cambridge: Cambridge University Press, 2005. Written by a prominent archaeologist who has worked on numerous projects in Guatemala, this book explores the ecological aspects of the rise of Mayan civilization and the role of internecine warfare in its demise.

Harrison, Peter. *The Lords of Tikal: Rulers of an Ancient Maya City.* New York: Thames & Hudson, 2000. Traces the history of Tikal from its humble beginning to its apogee in the late 9th century A.D.

Montgomery, John. *Tikal: An Illustrated History of the Ancient Maya Capital.* New York: Hippocrene Books, 2000. Wonderfully illustrated with photos, maps, and drawings, this is a good introduction to Tikal for the visitor and casual Mayanist.

Colonial Era

Lovell, W. George. *Conquest and Survival in Colonial Guatemala: A Historical Geography of the Cuchumatán Highlands.* 3rd ed. Kingston, Ontario: McGill-Queen's University Press, 2004. Quickly becoming a classic, this landmark work covers the Spanish conquest and the survival of the local indigenous culture despite the ravages of colonial legacies while linking the roots of the past in more recent sociopolitical conditions.

Civil War

Arnson, Cynthia J., ed. *Comparative Peace Processes in Latin America.* Washington, D.C.: Woodrow Wilson Center Press, 1999. Provides a good analysis of the peace process that led to a negotiated settlement of the civil war in Guatemala and other countries as well as issues concerning the roles of truth-telling reports, the search for justice, and reconciliation.

Burgos-Debray, Elizabeth, ed. *I, Rigoberta Menchú: An Indian Woman in Guatemala.* London: Verso, 1984. The classic autobiography of Nobel Peace Prize winner Rigoberta Menchú.

Goldman, Francisco. *The Art of Political Murder: Who Killed The Bishop?* New York: Grove Press, 2007. A real page-turner, this book delves into the murder of Archbishop Juan Gerardi following his delivery of a church-led investigation into civil war atrocities. The treatment of the subsequent investigation provides a glimpse into the mayhem that is the Guatemalan judicial system.

Grandin, Greg. *The Last Colonial Massacre: Latin America in the Cold War.* Chicago: The University of Chicago Press, 2004. This thought-provoking book argues that the Latin American Cold War was actually a struggle between two differing notions of democracy, with its main achievement being the elimination of grass-roots attempts at building social democracy. It uses Guatemala as a case study and concludes, somewhat convincingly, that the version of democracy now being extolled as the best option in the war against terror is itself a product of the same.

Handy, Jim. *Revolution in the Country-side: Rural Conflict and Agrarian Reform in Guatemala, 1944–1954.* Chapel Hill: The University of North Carolina Press, 1994. A good in-depth look at the Agrarian Reform Law and the Guatemalan political scene during the Arévalo and Arbenz years.

Manz, Beatriz. *Paradise in Ashes: A Guatemalan Journey of Courage, Terror, and Hope.* Berkeley: University of California Press, 2004. Written by an anthropologist, this book centers around the Ixcán village of Santa María Tzejá, whose inhabitants were caught in the violence between the guerrillas and military during the civil war.

Perera, Víctor. *Unfinished Conquest: The Guatemalan Tragedy.* Berkeley: University of California Press, 1993. A must-read for travelers to Guatemala, covering sociopolitical aspects of the Guatemalan civil war as well as environmental issues in a well-written travel narrative style.

Sanford, Victoria. *Buried Secrets: Truth and Human Rights in Guatemala.* New York: Palgrave Macmillan, 2004. A highly recommended read with well-researched information from a number of different sources, including eye-witness testimonies from massacre survivors, interviews with members of forensic teams, human rights workers, high-ranking military officers, guerrillas, and government officials. It is an instrumental book for understanding the full scale of the genocidal civil war and the attempt to rebuild society in its aftermath.

Schlesinger, Stephen C., and Stephen Kinzer. *Bitter Fruit: The Story of the American Coup in Guatemala.* Cambridge: Harvard University Press, 2005. This is a classic book on Guatemala and its historical relationship with the United States. First published in 1982, it covers in much detail the 1954 CIA-orchestrated coup ousting Jacobo Arbenz.

Simon, Jean-Marie. *Guatemala: Eternal Spring—Eternal Tyranny.* New York: W.W. Norton & Co., 1988. Although currently out of print, this valuable photographic study of victims of civil war atrocities is a must-have for anyone interested in this painful era of Guatemala's history and its effect on its mostly indigenous inhabitants.

Stoll, David. *Between Two Armies in the Ixil Towns of Guatemala.* New York: Columbia University Press, 1993. A controversial book postulating the theory that the Ixil Maya of Nebaj, Chajul, and Cotzal were not so much enamored with revolutionary possibilities for social change as much as simply caught between the opposing fires of the military and guerrilla forces with widely differing sociopolitical agendas.

Stoll, David. *Rigoberta Menchú and the Story of All Poor Guatemalans.* Boulder: Westview Press, 1999. Also quite controversial, this work directly challenges much of the testimony presented by Rigoberta Menchú in her autobiography as embellishments or fabrications while granting that the atrocities described therein were accurate depictions of hypothetical events during the civil war.

Wilkinson, Daniel. *Silence on the Mountain: Stories of Terror, Betrayal, and Forgetting in Guatemala.* New York: Houghton Mifflin, 2002. Part travelogue and part history book, this is a fascinating, well-written account of the American author's experience in Guatemala, which manages to uncover many of the issues relating to the origins and unfolding of Guatemala's civil war as told by those who survived the violence.

Central America

LaFeber, Walter. *Inevitable Revolutions: The United States in Central America.* New York: W.W. Norton, 1993. Traces

RESOURCES

the historical roots of Central America's armed conflicts along with the role of U.S. hegemony in perpetuating them.

TRAVELOGUES AND LITERATURE

Travelogues

Benz, Stephen Connely. *Guatemalan Journey*. Austin: University of Texas Press, 1996. A humorous, insightful, and well-written account of an American traveler's experiences living in Guatemala during the late 1980s.

Huxley, Aldous. *Beyond the Mexique Bay*. New York: Harper and Brothers Publishers, 1934. A classic take on early 20th century travel in Guatemala by a well-known author.

Shaw, Christopher. *Sacred Monkey River: A Canoe Trip with the Gods*. New York: W.W. Norton & Co., 2000. A superbly written adventure travel narrative packed with historical and natural history anecdotes about the mighty Usumacinta River, along the Mexico-Guatemala border.

Stephens, John Lloyd. *Incidents of Travel in Central America, Chiapas, and Yucatán*. New York: Dover Publications, 1969. A classic book and a must-read for the traveler to Guatemala, also featuring the fantastic illustrations of Stephens' friend and traveling companion Frederick Catherwood. It created quite an interest in the region, particularly its Mayan sites, when it was first published in 1841.

Wright, Ronald. *Time Among the Maya: Travels in Belize, Guatemala and Mexico*. New York: Grove/Atlantic, 2000. Another good read with insights on culture, history, adventure, and anthropology by a writer with an evident love for the modern-day Maya people.

Fiction

Goldman, Francisco. *The Long Night of White Chickens*. New York: Grove/Atlantic, Inc., 1998. This well-written novel is a tale of intrigue set in a 1980s Guatemala governed by military dictatorships. It's an entertaining read and does a nice job of bridging the gap between the seemingly parallel worlds of the United States and Guatemala.

ART

Bourda, Ange. *Casa Guatemalteca*. Bogotá: Villegas Editores, 2002. Together with Guatemalan interior designer Katia Niesiolowska and historian Jorge Luján Muñoz, photographer Ange Bourda documents some of Guatemala's most beautiful homes.

Gieseman, Peter, and Ange Bourda. *Six Architects*. Bogotá: Villegas Editores, 2003. An art photography book documenting the architecture of the Guatemala City *Seis Arquitectos* firm.

Moller, Jonathan. *Our Culture is Our Resistance: Repression, Refuge, and Healing in Guatemala*. New York: PowerHouse Books, 2004. A beautiful photographic collection of highland Mayan culture in the aftermath of the civil war with wonderful guest commentaries from Rigoberta Menchú, Francisco Goldman, and various other authors of books on Guatemala.

NATURAL HISTORY

Beletsky, Les. *Travellers' Wildlife Guides: Belize and Northern Guatemala*. Northampton: Interlink Books, 2005.

Lee, Julian C. *Field Guide to the Amphibians and Reptiles of the Maya World: The Lowlands of Mexico, Northern Guatemala, and Belize*. Ithaca: Cornell University Press, 2000.

Peterson, Roger Tory, and Edward L. Chalif. *A Field Guide to Mexican Birds:*

Mexico, Guatemala, Belize, El Salvador. New York: Houghton Mifflin, 1999. Describes and illustrates 1,038 species.

Primack, Richard B., et. al, eds. *Timber, Tourists, and Temples: Conservation and Development in the Maya Forest of Belize, Guatemala, and Mexico.* Washington, D.C.: Island Press, 1998. Covers the delicate political and social issues implicated in conserving the region's remaining rainforests as told from the perspective of social scientists, conservationists, and biologists working in the field.

EDUCATION

Rupp, Rebecca. *Home Learning Year by Year: How to Design a Homeschool Curriculum from Preschool through High School.* Three Rivers Press, 2000. A comprehensive guide for designing a home school curriculum from a well-known home schooling expert.

National Holidays

Following is a list of official holidays in Guatemala. Keep in mind that cities of all different sizes also celebrate their annual *fiesta*. In Guatemala City, the annual festivities take place on August 15.

- **January 1:** New Year's Day
- **Easter Sunday:** Holy Thursday, Good Friday, and Holy Saturday as well
- **May 1:** Labor Day
- **June 30:** Armed Forces Day
- **September 15:** Independence Day
- **October 20:** Day of the Revolution of 1944
- **November 1:** All Saints' Day
- **December 24:** Christmas Eve (as of noon)
- **December 25:** Christmas Day
- **December 31:** New Year's Eve (as of noon)

Index

A

Acatenango: 13
Accesorios Textiles: 218
accidents, car: 268-269
accommodations: see hotels; housing
Accord on Identity and Rights of Indigenous Peoples: 51
Accord on Socio-Economic and Agrarian Issues: 50
Accord on Strengthening of Civilian Power and the Role of the Army in a Democratic Society: 51
address, forms of: 78
agents, rental: 172
agoutis: 24
Agrarian Reform Law (1952): 41
agriculture: 39, 68
Agua: 13
aid organizations: 217
AIDS: 205
airports: 210, 213, 251-253
air quality: 206
air travel: 250-255; baggage and cargo 161-164; domestic 103, 260-261; with pets 160
Aldea El Pumpo: 351
Alpirez, Julio Roberto: 382
Alta Verapaz: 12, 279, 355, 366, 367; see also Las Verapaces
Alvarado, Pedro de: 34
Amatique Bay Resort: 364
American Citizens Services Unit: 230
amphibians: 25
amusement parks: 352
animals: 20-26
Anonymous Societies (S.A.): 218
Antigua: 303-317; climate 306; costs 314; fact-finding trip 105, 115-120; food 116-118; geography 305; history 35, 304-305; housing 311-314; language schools 189; maps 302; neighborhoods 314-317; overview 276; resources 403; transportation 317; visitor accommodations 115-116
Antigua Tours: 118
ants, leaf-cutter: 26
apartments: 314
appearance: 77
Arana Osorio, Carlos: 44
Arbenz Guzmán, Jacobo: 41-42
archaeological sites: 144, 369, 372-374
architecture: 88, 335

Arco de Santa Catalina: 119
Arévalo, Juan José: 40
armed robbery: 212-213
arts, the: 86-90
Arzú Irigoyen, Alvaro: 49, 53, 239
ASISTUR Cards: 197
ATMs: 233
Atrium: 291
ATV rentals: 145
August, Robert: 348
authors: 86-87
Auto Safari Chapin: 131
Avestruces Maya: 131

B

backpacking: 78, 136, 214
Baja Verapaz: 12, 279, 355, 366; see also Las Verapaces
balam (jaguars): 22-23
banking: 232-234
Barrios, Justio Rufino: 37
baseball (béisbol): 96
bats: 24
beaches: 92, 348, 351
beachfront property: 175
Belize, travel from: 259
benefits, U.S. federal: 230
Benz, Stephen Connely: 75-76
Berger, Óscar: 56, 372
biking: 91, 145
Biotopo Mario Dary Rivera: 137
Biotopo Monterrico-Hawaii: 130
birds: 20-22
bird-watching: Laguna Lachuá National Park 138; Lake Atitlán 327; quetzals 137; Río Las Escobas 136; Río Polochic Delta 16
bites, insect: 204
boat, shipments by: 163
boat travel: 94, 255-256, 264
bodyguards: 212
books: 86-87
border dispute, Belize-Guatemala: 62-63
bribes: 208
building permits: 184-185
bureaucracy: 66-68
business guidelines: 220-221
business opportunities: 218-219
bus travel: 102-103, 261

C

cable TV: 245, 246

Cabrera, Manuel Estrada: 38-39
Café No Sé: 308, 309
Cahabón River: 94
Calle Principal: 330
camping: 141
Canal de Chiquimulilla: 340
Candelaria caves: 138, 368
capital, historic: 35
capitalism: 181, 320-321
cargo: 163
carjacking: 213
Carretera a El Salvador: 295
cars: purchasing 265; renting 263, 265-
    266; see also driving
cartels, drug: 211
Carter, President Jimmy: 45
Casa Palopó: 331
Castillo Armas, Colonel Carlos: 42
Catholic church: 36, 84
cats, moving with: 157
caves: 136, 138
ceiba trees: 19
cell phones: 241
Central Antigua: 314-315
Centro Cultural Casa Santo Domingo:
    120
Cerezo Arévalo, Vinicio: 47
Cerro Cahuí: 378
Cerro de la Cruz: 119
Cerro San Gil: 14, 136, 363
Chagas' disease: 204
Chajul: 320
Champerico: 341, 353
chewing gum: 19
chicken, fried: 112
"chicken buses": 249, 261
children, moving with: 156-157, 158-159,
    191-192
children's activities: 131, 145, 352
Chisec: 368
Chocón Machacas: 359
cholera: 202
Chulamar: 345
CIA overthrow: 39, 42
CINCAP (Center for Information on the
    Environment, Culture, and Arts of
    Petén): 144
citizenship: 155-156, 157
Ciudad Vieja: 316
civil defense patrols (PACs): 46
Civil War (1960-1996): 11, 42-54, 337-338,
    382
Claro: 241
class, social: 75-77, 284
classified ads: 170
climate: 16-18; Antigua 306; as based on

elevation 13; Guatemala City 285; Lake
    Atitlán 327
climbing: 91
Clinton, President Bill: 53
clothing: and appearance 77; for a fact-
    finding trip 100; local shopping 161; Nau
    travel wear 99
cloud forests: 14, 19, 357, 359, 365
coastal property: 175
coastal regions: 16
coatis: 24
Cobán: climate 357; fact-finding trip107;
    language schools 191; overview 279,
    367
cocaine: 211
Cocales: 339
coffee trade: 367
colleges: 193
Colom, Álvaro: 58, 59-63
colonization, European: 34-36
communications: 238-247, 399-400
Communist party: 42
con artists: 213
condoms: 205
condos: 174, 290
conservative society: 77
construction, home: 166-167, 183-185
consulates: 386-387
contractors: 185
Contreras, Captain: 382
conversation: 80
Coppola, Francis Ford: 380-381
"Corporate Mafia State": 54
corporation tax (ISR): 220
corruption: and drug trafficking 211;
    historic 31; International Commission
    Against Impunity in Guatemala (CICIG)
    28, 57; police 208; under Ríos Montt
    55
costs: car import 267; high-rise condo
    290-291; homebuilding 185; home
    rental 169; household 186; living 223,
    228-232; phone call 240, 241; private
    school 287; real estate 175-176, 180-
    181; rental car 265; see also specific
    place
country divisions: 12-13
crafts: 89, 331
credit cards: 233
crime: 209-213; historic 53; in Izabal 359,
    362; robbery 127, 212-213; on rural
    buses 103; safety from 103-104; as
    threat to stability 27
crocodiles: 25
cruises: 255
CTL: 218

culture: Accord on complexity of 51; in Antigua 307; the arts 86-90; expats as fitting into 11; Garífuna 362-363; gay and lesbian 82; indigenous 32-35, 87; Las Verapaces 365; wealth/poverty contradictions 73; *see also* Maya culture; society
currency: 232
customs: immigration and 101-102; modernizing 148; social 77-80

D

death squads: Civil War era 44, 48; modern 57-58, 64
debit cards: 233
debt peonage: 38, 39
deforestation: 369, 371
de León Carpio, Ramiro: 48
demographics: 74-75
dengue: 203
dentists: 198, 397
departmentos (departments, geographic): 12
department stores: 229
Devine, Carol: 382
Devine, Mike: 382
DHL: 218, 244
diarrhea, traveler's: 200
disabilities, access for people with: 200
"disappearances," political: 53
disease: 200-205
displaced persons: 47
distance-learning programs: 193
diversity, ethnic: 74-75
diving: 93
Docter, Catherine: 321
doctors: 198
documents, travel: 101-102, 104, 258
dogs, moving with: 157, 160
dolphins: 24
domestic employees: 231
DR-CAFTA: 28, 69, 70, 218-219, 236
dress: 77, 81, 100, 158-159
driver's licenses: 267
driving: 265-271; to Guatemala 164, 257-260; highway holdups 212
drug trafficking: 27, 28, 211, 359, 362, 371
Dulles brothers: 41
dysentery: 201

E

earthquakes: 14, 45, 206, 324
economy: 68-71; historic 38, 41; living standards 26; stability in the 27-29; of the wealthy few 217
ecosystems: 13
ecotourism: 366, 380

education: 191-194; resources 392; Spanish language learning 187-191, 307, 392; *see also* schools
El Correo: 243
elections: 65
electrical wiring: 179
electronics: 229
elevation: 12, 13
elite class: 75-76
El Mirador: 372
elPeriódico: 245
El Remate: 371, 378
El Salvador, Carretera a: 295
El Salvador, travel from: 259
email: 242-243
embassies: 386-387
emergencies: 214, 397
employees: domestic 231; for home construction 185; labor guidelines 220-221
employment: 216-226, 398
encomienda system: 36
en confianza (in confidence): 79
English, teaching: 223
entertainment: 230
entrepreneurial opportunities: 217-223, 398
environmental issues: conservation organizations 389-390; deforestation 369; lake pollution 16; manatee preservation 25; scarlet macaw preservation 21; sea turtle endangerment 24; Tortugario Monterrico 131
Espada, Vice President Rafael: 59, 80
Esquipulas II: 47
ethnicity: 74-75
etiquette: 78
evangelical Christianity: 85
exchange rates: 232
expatriates, foreign: locales preferred by 104, 275; motivations of 29-30; networking with 224; profiles of 308-309; types of 10-11
expenses: 229-232
expressions, linguistic: 190

F

fact-finding trip 97-145; Antigua 115-120; Guatemala City 109-115; itineraries, sample 104-108; Izabal and Las Verapaces 132-138; Pacific Coast 127-132; packing for 99-101; Petén 138-145; planning resources 390; Western Highlands 120-127
family: host families 191; importance of 82; moving with 156-157
fault lines: 14

fauna: 20-26
fax services: 242
federal benefits: 230
FedEx: 244
fees, real estate: 180
Fernandez, Maripaz: 348
ferries: 256
finances: 227-237; banking 232-234; expenses 229-232; remittance money 320-321; resources 398-399; see also costs
financial district, Guatemala City: 289-292
Finca Ixobel: 380
fish: 24
fishing: 92, 348, 350
fleas, sand: 204
flies, sand: 204
flora: 18-20
Flores: 191, 371, 376-377
Flores/Tikal airport: 254, 255
folk saints: 84
food: Antigua 116-118; -borne illness 196, 200-203; cost of 229-230; fried chicken 112; Guatemala City 110-113; Izabal and Las Verapaces 134-135; Lake Atitlán 124; Pacific Coast 130
footwear: 100
forests: 18-20, 144, 358
foxes: 24
fried chicken: 112
frogs: 25
Fronteras (Río Dulce town): 361
fuel: 231
Fuerzas Armadas Rebeldes (FAR): 43
FUNDAECO: 136
fútbol (soccer): 95

G

gang violence: 211
garbage disposal: 208
Garífuna culture: 361, 362-363
gasoline: 231
gastrointestinal disorders: 196
gay culture: 82
gender issues: 81-83
geography: 12-16
Gerardi Conedera, Bishop Juan: 52
German community: 367
golf: 95, 315
government: 31, 64-68, 387
government work: 216-217
gratuities: 103
grebes: 21
greetings: 78
"Guategate": 55

Guatel: 239
Guatemala-Belize border dispute: 62-64
Guatemala City: 281-301; accommodations 109-115, 288; air pollution 206; air travel to 254-255; architecture 88; climate 285; cost of living 228, 290-291; crime 210, 298-299; fact-finding trip 105; food 110-113; geography 283; language schools 188; maps 282; neighborhoods 170, 289-297; overview 276; resources 403; transportation: 297-301
Guatemalan Journey (Benz): 75-76
Guatemalan National Revolutionary Unity (URNG): 46, 49
Guatemalan tax: 234-235
Guatevisión: 245, 246
Guayacán (Macal): 15
guerilla movement: 43-44, 45-46, 337
Guerrilla Army of the Poor (EGP): 44
gum, chewing: 19
Guzmán, Jacobo Arbenz: 39

H

Hacienda San Jerónimo: 316
handicrafts: 89, 331, 337
hand washing: 196
Hansen, Dr. Richard: 372
Hawaii village: 348
health: 195-208; Antigua 310; Guatemala City 287; hazards 200-205; insurance 197-198; Lake Atitlán 329; medical services 198-200; Petén 375; resources 396-397; Xela 325
hepatitis vaccine: 196
heroine: 211
Hettich, Martha: 118
highway holdups: 212
highways: 262-263
hiking: 90-91; Mirador Basin 372; packing for 100; Río Las Escobas 136; robberies during 214; Volcán San Pedro 127
Historical Clarification Commission (CEH): 49, 50
history: 31, 32-64
hitchhiking: 264
HIV/AIDS: 205
holdups, highway: 212
home schooling: 193
Honduras, travel from: 259
horseback riding: 145
hospitals: 198, 397
host families: 191
hotels: Antigua 115-116; Guatemala City 109-110; Izabal and Las Verapaces 132-134; Lake Atitlán 120-123; Pacific Coast 128-130; Quetzaltenango 123-124

houses: 173
housing: 165-186; Antigua 311-314; con-
    struction 166-167; costs 231; Guate-
    mala City 288; homebuilding 183-185;
    purchasing 173-183; resources 392;
    types 173-174; see also specific place
huipiles (embroidered blouses): 89
Human Rights Accord (1994): 50
Hurricane Stan: 57, 338
Huxley, Aldous: 15, 327
hygiene: 195

I
ice: 196, 202
Iglesia Catedral del Espíritu Santo: 323
Iglesias, Enrique V.: 320
Iglesia y Convento de las Capuchinas: 119
illness: 200-205
immigration: 101-102, 149-156
Immobilia.com: 168, 174
importing cars: 267
income distribution: 70
income tax: 221, 234-236
independence, Guatemalan: 36
industry: 68
infrastructure: 28
insect-borne disease: 203-205
insects: 25
insurance: health 197-198; home 186
International Commission Against
    Impunity in Guatemala (CICIG): 28,
    57, 58
international health insurance: 198
international mail services: 244
Internet phone calls: 242
Internet services: 242-243
investments: 236-237; Antiguan real
    estate 312; Juan Gaviota 346; oppor-
    tunity for 217; in the Pacific Coast 342;
    real estate purchases 173-183
iPhones: 241
itineraries, sample: 104-108
Iturbide, Agustín: 36
Izabal: 355, 358-364; climate 357; fact-
    finding trip 132-138; overview 278;
    resources 403
Iztapa: 278, 351

J
jade jewelry: 90
jaguars (balam): 22-23
jaguarundi: 23
Jaibalito: 122, 333
jewelry, jade: 90
job hunting: 223-225, 398
Jobompiche: 379

Jocotenango: 316
Juan Gaviota: 345, 346
judicial branch: 65
justice, for war crimes: 50
justice system: 51, 57, 67

KL
Kaqchikel people: 35
karst formations: 368
kayaking: 93
K'iche' people: 34, 324
kidnapping: 53, 211
kinkajous: 24
La Antigua Guatemala: see Antigua
La Aurora International Airport (GUA):
    251-253, 281
labor: 216-226; business guidelines 220-
    221; laws 222; reform 39, 40
La Cuadra: 245, 309
La Cueva de la Vaca: 136
lagoons: 15
Laguna del Tigre: 371
Laguna Lachuá National Park: 138
Lake Amatitlán: 16
Lake Atitlán: 327-339; expat community
    319; fact-finding trip 105; food 124; ge-
    ography 13, 15, 328; language schools
    189; sights 125-127; visitor accommo-
    dations 120-123
lake fishing: 93
Lake Izabal: 16, 278, 358, 360-361
Lake Petén Itzá: 16, 191, 371, 377-379
lakes: 15
lakeside property: 175
La Lancha: 380-381
land conflicts: 359
land reforms: 41
language: 187-191; English, in Antigua
    307; Las Verapaces dialects 366; Petén
    dialects 378; resources 392; Western
    Highlands dialects 328
Las Pilas: 290
Las Verapaces: 365-368; climate 357;
    fact-finding trip 132-138; resources 403
La Trinidad: 353
lawyers: 180, 391
leases, home: 172
legal issues: 182, 221-222
legends: 22
lesbian culture: 82
limestone: 12-13, 16, 137, 368
limited liability corporations (LLCs): 218
literature: 86
living conditions: changing village
    320-321; and cost 228; in rental homes
    169-172; standards of 26-27

Lívingston: 357, 361, 362-363
lower class: 77
Lucas García, Romeo: 45
luxury shopping: 228

M

Macal, Virgilio Rodríguez: 15
macaws, scarlet: 21, 22
machismo: 81, 205
mafia organizations: 28, 57
magazines: 245
mail services: 243-244
malaria: 196, 203
malls, shopping: 229
mammals: 23-24
manatees: 25
Manchón Guamuchal preserve: 354
mangroves: 130, 346, 349
maps: 99
margay: 23
marijuana: 211
marimba: 88
markets: 338
marriage: 81
Maya Biosphere Reserve: 144, 369, 371
Maya culture: history of: 32-33; Lake
   Atitlán 327; legends 22; Maximón deity
   338; Mirador Basin project 372-374;
   spirituality 83-84
Maya people: civil war violence against
   49, 50; demographics 75; flee the civil
   war 47; photographing 78
media: 245-247
medical services: 198-200, 287
medication: 200, 287
Mérida, Carlos: 87
metro system: 301
Mexico, travel from: 259
Mezcal: 308
middle class: 76-77
military violence: 49, 50, 52-53
mistresses: 81
Mixco: 297
mobile phones: 241
mold: 207
money: 227-237
monkeys: 24
Montañas del Mico: 14, 358
Montenegro, Julio Cesar: 43
Monterrico: 189, 341, 347-354
Monterrico-Iztapa Road: 349
mortgages: 175-176
mountainous regions: 13
Movistar: 241
mudslides: 338
multinational corporations: 217

Mundo Maya International Airport: 254
murder: 64, 209, 382
Museo Ixchel: 114
Museo Lacustre Atitlán: 126
Museo Miraflores: 113
Museo Vigua de Arte Precolombino y Vid-
   rio Moderno: 120
music: 88

NO

Nakbé: 372, 373
Nau clothing: 99
networking: 224
New Age groups: 333
newspapers: 245
NGOs: 217, 226, 369
nonprofit work: 225-226, 398
Nuestra Diario: 245
OCRET: 175, 328, 343
October Revolution (1944): 40
oligarchy: 75
organized crime: 28, 57
Orleans: 290
ostriches: 131

P

Pacaya mountain: 13
Pacific Coast: 340-354; accommodations
   128-130; fact-finding trip 106-107; food
   130; maps 342-343; overview 277;
   Puerto San José 344-348; resources
   403; sights 130-132
packing: 99, 161-164
painting: 87, 337
Palacio Nacional de la Cultura: 113
Panabaj: 338
Panajachel: 330
parasites: 196-197, 202
parks: 90
Parque Acuático Xocomil: 131
Parque Central: 118
Parque Centroamérica: 127, 323
Parque de Diversiones Xetulul: 132, 352
Parque Natural Ixpanpajul: 145
Parque Zoológico Minerva: 324
Partido Guatemalteco de los Trabajadores (PGT): 42
Pasión River: 15
passports: 101-102
pay phones: 242
peace accords, 1996: 49, 50-52
peccaries: 24
pena (feel badly): 79
pensionado (pensioner) visa: 150, 153
permanent residency: 152, 153
personal space: 80

Petalhuleu: 278
Petén: 369-383; climate 374; fact-finding trip 107; Flores/Santa Elena 376-377; food 142-143; geography 13, 14, 16, 371; Lake Petén Itzá 377-379; living conditions 374-375; maps 370; overview 279; Poptún 380-383; sights 143-145; visitor accommodations 138-142
pets, moving with: 157-161, 391
pharmacies: 200
philanthropy: 222-223
phone calls: 239
photography: 78, 99, 100
phrases, common: 190
pickup trucks: 262
Piedras Negras: 15
plantations: 41
plant life: 18-20
Plenum 14: 291
plumbing: 178-179
P.O. boxes: 243-244
police services: 208-209
politics: corruption 57; government organization 64-68; home ownership and 181-182; political parties 66; stability in 27-29; 2007 elections 58-59; U.S. involvement in 44
Politur: 209
Pollo Campero: 112
pollution: 16
Poptún: 380-383
population: 73, 74-75
Portillo, Alfonso: 54, 372
postal services: 243-244
poverty: in the class structure 77; drug cartels as capitalizing on 359; peace accord on 50-51; statistics 70; vs. wealth 26, 73
Pradera Xela: 326
Prensa Libre: 245
prescriptions: 200
preservation: see environmental issues
preventive health: 196-198
print media: 245
privacy: 80
private schools: 192
propane: 231
prostitution: 205
Protestantism: 85
Puerto Barrios: 357, 363
Puerto San José: 344-347
pumas: 23

QR
quetzal, resplendent: 20, 357
Quetzaltenango: 322-326; fact-finding trip 106; food 125; language schools 189; sights 127; visitor accommodations 123-124
radio: 247
rafting: 93, 138, 365
rainforests: 358
ramón (breadnut tree): 19
rape: 213
real estate: in Antigua 312-313; assessing 177-179; beachfront 175; building 183-185; Lake Atitlán restrictions 328; lot buying 184; Pacific Coast restrictions 343; purchases 173-183; renting vs. buying 167; risks 181-183; trends 165
records, medical: 199
recreation: 90-96, 365
registering property: 179-180
religion: 36, 83-86, 338
remittance money: 320-321
rental agents: 172
rental cars: 263, 265-266
rental homes: 167, 169-172, 314
rentista (small investor) visas: 151, 153
reptiles: 25
Reserva Natural Atitlán: 126
residency: application process 153-155; benefits of legal 148; types of 149-152
resplendent quetzal: 20, 357
Retalhuleu: 352
retiree visas: 150
Revolutionary Organization of the People in Arms (ORPA): 44
Revue: 245
Rexer, John: 308-309
Río Cahabón: 94, 138
Río Dulce: 278, 355, 361
Río Dulce National Park: 136, 361
Río Dulce town: 361
Río Las Escobas: 136
Río Motagua: 15
Ríos Montt, Efraín: 46, 55, 85
river, travel by: 256
river pirates: 362
rivers: 15
road rules: 269-271
road signs: 271
robbery: 103, 127, 212-213
rock climbing: 91
Rosenberg, Rodrigo: 64
Rother, Stanley: 337

S
safety: 208-215; from crime 103-104; increased traveler 71; in Izabal 359; resources 397

safety deposit boxes: 214
sailfishing: 92, 348, 350
saints, folk: 84
San Andrés Semetabaj: 331, 379
San Antonio Palopó: 332
sand fleas: 204
sanitation: 196-197, 202, 207
San José: 379
San Juan La Laguna: 336
San Lucas Tolimán: 338
San Marcos La Laguna: 123, 333
San Pablo: 336
San Pedro La Laguna: 123, 336
Santa Ana: 316
Santa Catarina Palopó: 331
Santa Cruz La Laguna: 122, 332
Santa Elena: 376-377
Santa María volcano: 127, 322
Santiago Atitlán: 337
saving face: 79
scams: 213, 237
scarlet macaws: 21, 22
schools: 191-194; Antigua 310; Guatemala
    City 287; Lake Atitlán 329; language
    188, 225, 336; Petén 375; resources
    392-396; Xela 325
screens: 179
scuba diving: 93
sea, travel by: 255-256
sea life: 24
seasons: 16-18, 97
self-employment: 217-223
Semuc Champey Natural Monument: 137,
    368
Serrano Elías, Jorge: 48, 85
sewage runoff: 207
shipping options: 161-164, 243-244, 391
shopping: 228-229; Antigua 310; Guate-
    mala City 287; Lake Atitlán 330; Petén
    375; Xela 325
Sierra de las Minas: 14, 279, 359
Sierra del Lacandón National Park: 15, 371
Sierra de los Cuchumatanes: 14
Siglo XXI: 245
Sipacate: 346
Skype calls: 242
slang: 190
smoking: 207
snakes: 25, 205
snorkeling: 93
soccer *(fútbol):* 95
socialism: 181, 182
social justice reforms: 40-41
Social Security benefits: 230
society: 26-30; class issues 75-77; cus-
    toms 77-80; demilitarization of 51;
foreigners in 29-30; gender issues
    81-83; Guatemalan mentality 11; politi-
    cal/economic factors 27-29; rural vs.
    urban 72; *see also* culture
socioeconomic disparities: 26
Sololá: 320
Spanish conquest: 34-35
Spanish Embassy occupation: 45
Spanish language learning: 188-191, 307,
    392
sports: 93-96
squatters: 182-183
stings, insect: 204
stomach disorders: 196-197
storage, of valuables: 214
stores: 228
strangler fig *(mata palo):* 19
study abroad programs: 194
subway system: 301
sun exposure: 208
surfing: 93, 341, 348
Survivor: 71

T
Tallon, Mike: 308-309
tapirs: 24
taxes: 234-236; corporation (ISR) 220;
    property 186; real estate 180; sales 103
taxis: 102, 103, 256, 263-264, 299
Telefónica: 240
telephone services: 240-242
television: 245
Telgua: 240
temperatures: 13, 16-18
Templo Minerva: 127, 323
temporary residency: 149-150
theft: 103, 212-213
Tigo: 241
Tikal National Park: 107, 143, 369
tipping: 103
title transfers: 179-180, 182
Toltec-Maya: 33-34
Torres de Colom, First Lady Sandra:
    60-61
Tortugario Monterrico: 131, 189
toucan: 22
tourism: coastal 340-341; economic im-
    pact 29, 71; medical 199, 287; Politur
    209; tourist season 98; tourist visas
    148
tours: 118
trade: 68, 236
traffic: 297
traffic citations: 268-269
Transactel: 218
transferring money: 233

Transmetro: 300
transportation: 401-402; air travel 160, 162-164, 250-255; boat travel 94, 255-256, 264; bus travel 102-103, 261; driving 164, 212, 257-260, 265-271; maps 248; for visitors 102
travel clothing: 99
travelers' checks: 233
tropical ecosystem: 13
turkeys, ocellated: 21
turtles, sea: 24, 130
Tzununa: 333
Tz'utujil Maya: 337

U
Ubico, Jorge: 39
UNESCO sites: 144, 311
United Fruit Company (UFCo): 39, 41
United States: agribusiness 39, 41; influence 75-76; military involvement 43, 44; overland travel from 257; taxes 235
Universidad de San Carlos de Guatemala (USAC): 193
Universidad Francisco Marroquín (UFM): 194
universities: 193
upper class: 76-77
UPS: 245
USAID: 75-76
Usumacinta River: 15, 256
utilities: 184, 186

V
vaccinations: 196
valuables: hiding 298; storing 214
vegetation: 18-20
Vergara, Pedro Pablo: 348
village life: 320-321, 327
Villa Los Cabos: 351
violence: gang 211; political 44, 45, 73
visas: 149-156, 391
visitor accommodations: see hotels
Volcán Atitlán: 337
volcanic activity: 14, 321, 328
Volcán San Pedro: 126

Volcán Santa María: 127, 322
Volcán Santiaguito: 127
Volcán Tacaná: 13
Volcán Tajumulco: 13
Volcán Tolimán: 337
volunteering: 225-226, 338, 398

W
waste disposal: 208
watchdog organizations: 28
waterparks: 131
water quality: 196, 207
water sports: 93-95
water taxis: 256
wealthy class: 75-76, 284
wealth distribution: 70
weather: 16-18, 97
Western Highlands: 319-339; climate 321; fact-finding trip 120-127; maps 318; overview 277; Quetzaltenango 322-326; resources 403
whales: 24
wheelchair access: 200
Whitbeck, Harris: 331, 334-335
white-water rafting: 93, 94, 138, 365
wildlife: 20-26, 131
Wilson, Brian: 312-313
windows: 179
wire transfers: 233
women travelers: 81
work: 216-226

XYZ
Xela: 322-326
Xetulul: 131, 352
Xocomil: 131, 352
ziplines: 145
Zona 10 (Guatemala City): 289-292
Zona 14 (Guatemala City): 292
Zona 15 (Guatemala City): 292
Zona 16 (Guatemala City): 292
Zona 3 (Xela): 323
Zona Militar: 324
Zona Viva: 114
zoos: 131

Acknowledgments

This book is quite simply dedicated to my mother and father, who instilled in me a love for Guatemala and helped equip me with everything I needed to write this book. I know someday you'll return to the land you love.

To everyone else who aided me in any way with the research for this book, my sincere gratitude. As always, I'd like to acknowledge the Higher Power, always Good and always acting to inspire, comfort, and heal. "God is working through me."

www.moon.com

DESTINATIONS | ACTIVITIES | BLOGS | MAPS | BOOKS

MOON.COM is all new, and ready to help plan your next trip! Filled with fresh trip ideas and strategies, author interviews, informative blogs, a detailed map library, and descriptions of all the Moon guidebooks, Moon.com is all you need to get out and explore the world—or even places in your own backyard. As always, when you travel with Moon, expect an experience that is uncommon and truly unique.

MAP SYMBOLS

▦ Expressway		○ City/Town		✕ Airfield		⬟ Archaeological Site
▬ Primary Road		◉ State Capital		✈ Airport		♦ Church
▬ Secondary Road		✻ National Capital		▲ Mountain		⬛ Gas Station
⋯ Unpaved Road				⬥ Park		▦ Mangrove
⋯ Ferry		★ Point of Interest				▦ Reef
⋯ Railroad		■ Other Location		✦ Unique Natural Feature		▦ Swamp

CONVERSION TABLES

°C = (°F - 32) / 1.8
°F = (°C x 1.8) + 32
1 inch = 2.54 centimeters (cm)
1 foot = 0.304 meters (m)
1 yard = 0.914 meters
1 mile = 1.6093 kilometers (km)
1 km = 0.6214 miles
1 fathom = 1.8288 m
1 chain = 20.1168 m
1 furlong = 201.168 m
1 acre = 0.4047 hectares
1 sq km = 100 hectares
1 sq mile = 2.59 square km
1 ounce = 28.35 grams
1 pound = 0.4536 kilograms
1 short ton = 0.90718 metric ton
1 short ton = 2,000 pounds
1 long ton = 1.016 metric tons
1 long ton = 2,240 pounds
1 metric ton = 1,000 kilograms
1 quart = 0.94635 liters
1 US gallon = 3.7854 liters
1 Imperial gallon = 4.5459 liters
1 nautical mile = 1.852 km

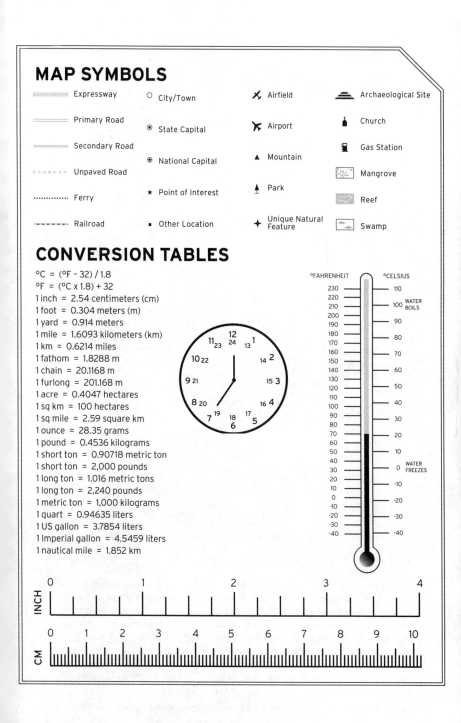

MOON LIVING ABROAD
IN GUATEMALA

Avalon Travel
a member of the Perseus Books Group
1700 Fourth Street
Berkeley, CA 94710, USA
www.moon.com

Editor and Series Manager: Elizabeth Hansen
Copy Editor: Deana Shields
Graphics Coordinator: Kathryn Osgood
Production Coordinator: Darren Alessi
Cover Designer: Kathryn Osgood
Map Editor: Albert Angulo
Cartographer: Chris Markiewicz, Kat Bennett
Indexer: Rachel Kuhn

ISBN-13: 978-1-59880-207-8
ISSN: 1948-8211

Printing History
1st Edition – October 2009
5 4 3 2 1

Text © 2009 by Al Argueta.
Maps © 2009 by Avalon Travel.
All rights reserved.

Some photos and illustrations are used by
permission and are the property of the original
copyright owners.
Front cover photo: Guatemalan Blanket
  © Al Argueta
Title page photo: © Al Argueta
Interior color photos: © Al Argueta

Printed in Canada by Friesens Corp.

KEEPING CURRENT

Although we strive to produce the most up-to-date guidebook that we possibly can, change
is unavoidable. Between the time this book goes to print and the time you read it, the
cost of goods and services may have increased, and a handful of the businesses noted
in these pages will undoubtedly move, alter their prices, or close their doors forever.
Exchange rates fluctuate – sometimes dramatically – on a daily basis. Federal and local
legal requirements and restrictions are also subject to change, so be sure to check with
the appropriate authorities before making the move. If you see anything in this book that
needs updating, clarification, or correction, please drop us a line. Send your comments via
email to feedback@moon.com, or use the address above.